Essential Readings On Political Terrorism

Analyses of Problems and Prospects for the 21st Century

Essential Readings On Political Terrorism

Analyses of Problems and Prospects for the 21st Century

Edited, with a Foreword, by
Harvey W. Kushner

Gordian Knot Books

A Division of Richard Altschuler & Associates, Inc.

Distributed by The University of Nebraska Press, Lincoln, Nebraska

Library of Congress Control Number: 2002105025

ISBN 1-884092-58-6

Distributed by University of Nebraska Press,
Lincoln, Nebraska

Cover Design: Josh Garfield

Printed in the United States of America

Contents

Part I: Defining Terrorism

Part II: The "Mind of the Terrorist:" Psychosocial Aspects of Terrorism

Part III: State, Culture and Terrorism

Part IV: Media, Communications and Terrorism

Part V: The Victims of Terrorism

Part VI: Chemical and Biological Warfare Agents and Terrorism

About the Authors

Sean K. Anderson is Associate Professor of Political Science at Idaho State University, Pocatello, Idaho.

William J. Apfeldorf is Associate Professor of Clinical Psychiatry, Weill Medical College of Cornell University, New York, New York.

Thomas Arvanites is Associate Professor of Sociology and Chair of the Department of Sociology at Villanova University, Villanova, Pennsylvania.

Richard G. Braungart is Professor of Sociology, Political Science, and International Relations in the Maxwell School of Citizenship and Public Affairs at Syracuse University, Syracuse, New York.

Margaret M. Braungart is Professor of Psychology in the Center for Bioethics and Humanities at SUNY Upstate Medical University, Syracuse, New York.

Marylene Cloitre is Associate Professor of Psychology in Psychiatry, Weill Medical College of Cornell University, New York, New York.

H.H.A. Cooper is a Professor in the School of General Studies, University of Texas, Dallas, Texas.

Martha Crenshaw is John E. Andrus Professor of Government at Wesleyan University, Middletown, Connecticut.

Kelly R. Damphousse is Associate Professor in the Department of Sociology and the Director of the Center for Crime and Justice Studies at the University of Oklahoma, Norman, Oklahoma.

JoAnn Difede is Associate Professor of Psychology in Psychiatry, Weill Medical College of Cornell University, New York, New York.

Charles Engel is Associate Professor of Psychiatry and Director of the Deployment Health Clinical Center at Uniformed Services University of the Health Sciences in Bethesda, Maryland.

David E. Fosnocht is Assistant Professor in the Division of Emergency Medicine and Medical Director of Summit County EMS at the University of Utah Health Sciences Center, Salt Lake City, Utah.

Danny Goldstick is Professor of Philosophy at the University of Toronto, Toronto, Canada.

Jerome M. Hauer prepares governments to respond to terrorism, and was the first commissioner of the Mayor's Office of Emergency Management of the City of New York.

Bruce Hoffman is Vice President, External Affairs, and Director of the Washington, DC office of the RAND corporation.

Alfred Jin, an industrial hygienist and certified microbiologist, is the biosafety officer for the Hazards Control Department at Lawrence Livermore National Laboratory in Livermore, California.

Robert Kirvel is a senior technical writer for the Technical Information Department and Environmental Protection Department at Lawrence Livermore National Laboratory, Livermore, California.

Cheryl Koopman is Associate Professor (Research) of Psychiatry and Behavioral Sciences at Stanford University, Stanford, California.

Steven Kuhr is an international consultant on security and emergency management who served as Deputy Director of the New York City Mayor's Office of Emergency Management.

Harvey W. Kushner is a Professor and Chair of the Department of Criminal Justice and Security Administration at Long Island University, Brookville, New York.

Lauren Langman is Professor of Sociology at Loyola University of Chicago, Chicago, Illinois.

Xian Liu is Assistant Professor of Psychiatry at Uniformed Services University of the Health Sciences and Senior Research Scientist at Deployment Health Clinical Center in Bethesda, Maryland.

Ray McGuire is retired from the Lawrence Livermore National Laboratory and consults with the Department of Defense on projects concerning chemical and biological terrorism.

Douglas Morris has a Master's degree in Applied Social Research and is completing a Ph.D. in Sociology at Loyola University Chicago, Chicago, Illinois.

Brigitte L. Nacos is Associate Professor of Political Science, Columbia University, New York, New York.

Kathleen Noonan is the Deputy Department Head for Health Services at the Lawrence Livermore National Laboratory in Livermore, California.

Satya R. Pattnayak is Associate Professor of Sociology and Director of Latin American Studies at Villanova University, Villanova, Pennsylvania.

Samuel W. Perry, deceased, was Professor of Psychiatry, Weill Medical College of Cornell University, New York, New York.

Jerrold M. Post is Professor of Psychiatry, Political Psychology and International Affairs and Director of the Political Psychology Program at The George Washington University, Washington, DC.

Ellen Raber is the Department Head for Environmental Protection at the Lawrence Livermore National Laboratory, in Livermore, California.

T.P. Schwartz is Director of Social Research Services in East Greenwich, Rhode Island.

Brent L. Smith is a Professor and Chair of the Department of Justice Sciences at the University of Alabama at Birmingham, Birmingham, Alabama.

Jordan Steiker is the Cooper K. Ragan Regents Professor of Law at the University of Texas School of Law, Austin, Texas.

Jessica Stern is a faculty affiliate of the Belfer Center for Science and International Affairs and a Lecturer in Public Policy at the Kennedy School, Harvard University, Cambridge, Massachusetts.

Eric R. Swanson is Assistant Professor in the Division of Emergency Medicine and Medical Director of AirMed at the University of Utah Health Sciences Center, Salt Lake City, Utah.

Robert Ursano is Professor and Chairman of the Department of Psychiatry, Uniformed Services University of the Health Sciences in Bethesda, Maryland.

Carol Winkler is Associate Professor and Chair of the Communication Department at Georgia State University, Atlanta, Georgia.

Gerald H. Zuk, a psychologist, and **Carmen Veiga Zuk**, a psychiatrist, are a husband and wife team who are principals in Zuk Consultants, based in Santa Clarita, California.

Editor's Foreword

Harvey W. Kushner

The egregious acts of September 11, 2001 precipitated a newfound interest in all that is "terrorism." I offer the latter term in quotes both to emphasize the much-debated concept and flag the neophyte reader of this foreword to how difficult it is to define terrorism. I will return to the problem of definition later. For now, however, I turn to the aftermath of the destruction of the World Trade Center and the considerable rush to publish everything and anything that supposedly relates to the concept of terrorism.

A visit to the neighborhood bookstore reveals prominently displayed shelves overflowing with new offerings meant to explore any conceivable event and circumstance that might impact our understanding of September 11. Books on the history of Islam, Middle Eastern politics, and Osama bin Laden and his Al Qaeda all abound. There are also a variety of monographs, manuals and pocket guides devoted to the possibility of the unmentionable terrorist atrocities to come—such as nuclear, biological and chemical terrorism, or as these horrors are categorized, "NBC terrorism." The interested can even find titles as absurd as those that could be labeled "Terrorism for Dummies" and "Terrorism 101."

Some of this new literature on terrorism is well planned and articulated. In other words, the authors researched, ruminated and wrote before putting pen to paper. There was no urgency to get the work to market to placate a need to sell books, which is not necessarily a disingenuous goal. This said, however, there is no paucity of literature whose content is replete with conjecture concerning September 11, and its causes and solutions. Interestingly enough, the same people who bring us the evening news on terrorism are responsible for many of these new works. What happened to the separation between reporting and speculation? To be sure, the line has blurred and is dangerously close to impacting the understanding of the type of terrorism aimed at the United States in the 21st century.

There were certainly other watershed-type events in history that have precipitated a rush for publication profits. A scandal surrounding a presidency, a particularly hideous crime and the sexual escapades of a revered movie star all saw authorized, as well as unauthorized, biographies come to market. Today, the veritable explosion (no pun intended) of information available to the public through their local bookstores, on the evening news, or on the Internet is unprecedented—and so the public is saturated with information concerning the events surrounding the aftermath of September 11.

September 11, or the ensuing so-called "declared war against terrorism," is not your usual "important" event. For all alive today, it might well turn out to be the main event of the new millennium. At this time, it impacts almost every aspect of our daily lives.

As a consequence, all the literature surrounding this catastrophic event takes on added meaning, in that it is meant to inform and educate the public about September 11 *vis-à-vis* terrorism. It forms public opinion and public policy. It provides the building blocks of knowledge that in no small way become the wherewithal for action, good or bad.

As certain as the events of September 11 are still fresh in our memories, it is also certain that the full story of the attack and the ensuing U.S. response is still unwritten, albeit unknown. It will take years to fully contemplate these events and come to grips with a thorough understanding. As for defining the concept of terrorism, however, a totally acceptable definition may never be reached. The same might be said of all concepts that straddle the fence of ethnocentrism, and spout the assertion "One man's terrorist is another man's freedom fighter." The latter part of the assertion is even regrettably echoed when revisiting the unforgivable and evil acts of September 11.

In this anthology, authors who understood the importance of explaining different aspects of the terrorist puzzle penned the offerings. They were there—involved with terrorism—when others saw fit to devote their efforts to things other than terrorist-related issues. One author in this book tried to come to grips with the problem of defining terrorism by revisiting his classic treatise on the issue. Other writers addressed a number of topics concerned with the psychological aspects of terrorism. From the mindset of the suicide bomber to the inner workings of a serial bomber to the worldview of a terrorist cell, they tried to unravel the psychology behind terrorist actions. Leaving no stone unturned, they also considered the victims of terrorism. From the trauma visited on the survivors of the 1993 bombing of the World Trade Center to posttraumatic stress disorder among veterans of the Persian Gulf War they asked, studied, and offered their conclusions about victims of terrorist events.

Other contributors to this volume examined specific events in order to come to grips with a slice of history. From the SDS and the Weatherman to the Iranian state-run media to a 1985 TWA hostage crisis, our contributors pushed the envelope of historical explanation. Another contributor involved with a specific case study asked whether the Oklahoma bombers succeeded, while yet another prodded the context of a political crime by investigating a terrorist on trial. Still other contributors ventured into the governmental aspect of terrorism by questioning the role of the state in international terrorism as well as counterterrorism policy and the political process related to countering terrorism.

Venturing into the unthinkable, our contributors were on the cutting edge of what might befall us in the new millennium. In a most timely piece, the threat of biological terrorism in the new millennium was widely and cleverly discussed. Others asked, "How clean is clean" when it comes to decontamination issues surrounding biological and chemical warfare agents? And in a most prophetic article, our authors investigated past anthrax threats that became all-too-real after the destruction of the World Trade Center twin towers on September 11.

In short, our contributors were describing and explaining events related to terrorism well before the nineteen suicide terrorists set off to attack America. They all had reason to believe in their research and develop it without a pressing need to meet a commercial interest. To be sure, much of the post-9/11 public and academic interest in all that was terrorism was fleeting. Interest waned as soon as the population was able to get back to "business as usual," which for many was surprisingly fast.

It is for this reason that our contributors should be commended, not only for their vision but also for their focus. Many were categorized as either alarmists or misinformed. At one time or another they were most likely admonished for involving themselves in unpopular research. Today, however, their celebrity is on the rise considering the amount of attention given to the topic of terrorism by both the lay public and academic community.

I welcome all readers of this volume to digest the information within the context of the totality of current events pertaining to terrorism. The information contained in these articles will no doubt provide the framework from which future explanations of the events of September 11 and the war on terrorism will be built. Our authors have made a commitment to understanding terrorism. I invite you to make a similar commitment and attempt to cut the Gordian knot that binds our understanding of terrorism.

Harvey W. Kushner, Ph.D.
New York, April 2002

Terrorism: The Problem of Definition Revisited

H. H. A. Cooper

Abstract: *How can terrorism be defined when the process of defining is wholly frustrated by the presence of irreconcilable antagonisms? It is certainly not easy to define, much less comprehend. With respect to terrorism, there is among the many participants to the discussion no agreement on the basic nature of the fruit under consideration. In any case, the definition of terrorism has undergone a number of small refinements as experience has suggested. This article considers how to define terrorism or at least know it when it is seen in the coming decades.*

> A living language has no existence independent of culture. It is not the loom of culture but its data bank. As such, it serves the needs, past and present, of a given community. As those needs change, language evolves to accommodate them. — Raymond Cohen (1990, pp. 41-42)[1]

With the advent of the new millennium, whatever one's preference for the mathematics of the event, a certain nostalgia for the past is inevitable. Although it is still difficult for many of us to adjust to no longer living in the 20th century, it seems even harder for others to let go of even the most recent of bygone memories. As the century raced to its anticlimactic close, a wave of recall swept through the media worldwide, made possible by new technologies that have given potent meaning to the yet ill-defined term *globalization.* Amid this feverish search for the most memorable this and the most renowned that, the sensitive observer might discern a hankering for earlier times, a kind of golden age in which everything was simpler, much easier to understand and, to use appropriate *fin de siècle* terminology, less stressful. No examination of these impressions in general is essayed here. Yet, it is of some importance to notice them in relation to the present topic if for no other reason than to offer a pertinent rejoinder.

It can be stated with absolute certainty that there has never been, since the topic began to command serious attention, some golden age in which terrorism was easy to define or, for that matter, to comprehend. And, as we plunge gaily into the brave new world of the 21st century, there is not the slightest reason to suppose that the problem of definition, or as it was once described, the problem of the problem of definition (Cooper, 1978), will come any closer to sensible resolution. With that solemn caveat in place, let us proceed to consider how, variously, we may come to define terrorism or at least know it when we see it in the coming decades.

Definition Is Truly an Art

Parenthetically, we must deal here with what is implied in the process of definition itself. Definition is truly an art. The artist seeks to represent, in concrete or abstract terms, something he or she has conceptualized or observed so as to give it some meaning of a distinctive character. The resultant work is a vehicle of communication for the thought or revelation that the artist seeks to convey to others. The central problem in the process is that no two human beings ever see the same thing, however simple, in exactly the same light or from the same standpoint. There is rarely, if ever, an exact correspondence of interpretation, and the introduction of but the slightest complexity can alter the meaning intended by the artist. Most ordinary, social communication is imprecise by nature. It simply is not necessary that we define our terms with exactitude; it suffices that we are generally understood. Of course, misunderstandings abound, especially between the genders[2] and persons of differing status, culture, occupation, education, and the like. This is sometimes a source of irritation and occasionally cause for amusement, but it is not often of great consequence. Yet, in serious discourse, especially on matters involving a potential for substantial disagreement or those bearing controversial or emotional overtones, the closest correspondence of understanding as to the meaning of the language employed is imperative. If we are discussing fruit, and I believe you are talking about apples when in fact you are trying to convey to me that you are referring to oranges, we are not going to get very far without timely clarification. With respect to terrorism, there is among the many participants to the discussion no agreement on the basic nature of the fruit under consideration. For some, it will always, unalterably be apples; for others, with equal rigor, it will remain oranges. No amount of sophistry or the introduction of other varietals will be helpful in resolving the issue of meaning. One person's terrorist will ever remain another's freedom fighter. The process of definition is wholly frustrated by the presence of irreconcilable antagonisms.

A Definition of Terrorism

Hope springs eternal in the human breast, and perhaps for this reason alone, so many conferences and writings on the subject of terrorism begin with the obligatory, almost ritualistic recitation by the presenter of some preferred definition of terrorism.[3] This is not wholly an exercise in futility; whatever the discrepancies detected by others, the definitions at least provide starting points for debate. The search has always been for one all-embracing statement that could stand at least a chance of gaining a high degree of acceptance by others as well as covering a majority of the bases. It can be reasonably confidently asserted that this procedure will continue unaltered as we transit the 21st century. In a similar spirit, then, the following definition of terrorism is offered here so that we may have a basis for reflection on the problems of terrorism and how it is likely to present itself in the new millennium.

> Terrorism is the intentional generation of massive fear by human beings for the purpose of securing or maintaining control over other human beings.

This definition evolved over some 25 years of teaching about the topic of terrorism in a university setting, and during that time, it has undergone a number of small refinements as experience has suggested. Other definitions have similarly been subject to modification as those who propounded them sought to meet criticisms extended by others and to perfect the concepts enshrined in the words employed. In a very real sense, all the earlier definitions had to be subject to this process of refinement if they were to survive at all. Even the most assiduous wordsmiths were humbled by the task of encapsulating such powerful, at their simplest, contradictory ideas in one all-embracing sentence. It is no surprise, then, to encounter definitions that run for paragraphs, even pages, in frantic attempts to capture the elusive meaning embodied in the word terrorism. This is dialectic rather than definition, but it is an inescapable part of the process whether it is reduced to writing or articulated only in discussion. The above definition, in the form it is presented here, owes much to classroom discussion and the acuity of the students to whom it was offered as a starting point for an exploration of the subject. Before examining its components in detail, it seems helpful to explain the underlying philosophy orienting its construction. Although it is always dangerous to generalize, it may be observed that university students tend to be an unforgiving bunch. They are quick to seize on any errors or inconsistencies they detect in the formula. And, if they have cause to doubt as a result, their overall confidence in the instruction and the instructor is shaken. In particular, in the matter of defining terrorism, the product offered had necessarily to address succinctly the thorny issue of "one person's terrorist is another's freedom fighter"; hence the formulation offered here.

Again, a further thought has to be inserted at this juncture. However much you may buy into the freedom fighter argument, you are forced, if you are intellectually honest, to the conclusion that whatever label it might bear, terrorism is a bad thing. All you can sensibly say in its defense is that sometimes it may be necessary to do bad things to other people, most usually with the apologetic justification that it is done to prevent or deter them from doing bad or worse things to you. If it is conceded that there is no "good" terrorism, that such an import would be a contradiction in terms, any definition must unambiguously take this into account, for it goes to the fundamental nature of the concept. In practice, the definition of terrorism has been consistently plagued by an ever increasing need to justify the reprehensible. This has proved the biggest obstacle to the production of anything approaching a widely acceptable definition, especially in the international arena. It must be stressed that there is a basic antinomy here: What I do, however unpleasant, is not terrorism; what you do is terrorism. From the point of view of definition, this is not a question of degrees such as dogs, for example, the term *high crimes and misdemeanors* in the impeachment realm (see Posner, 1999, pp. 98-105). What is asserted is a difference in kind; I don't commit terrorism, you do. You can no more have a little bit of terrorism than you can be a little bit pregnant. From a definitional perspective, it ought not to matter who does what to whom. Terrorism should be defined solely by the nature and quality of what is done. Difficult as this is, definition should strive for impartiality in this field, or the exercise must fail in its purposes.

Is Terrorism a Freestanding Concept?

Is terrorism, then, a freestanding concept? In terms of penal policy or normative configuration, is it something autonomous or simply a constituent element of certain kinds of criminal behavior that are already defined? What is offered above certainly has to be carefully considered in that light. An examination of any coherent legal system will reveal many crimes where the creation of great fear in the victim (e.g., rape) is a central, defining feature. Many would agree that rape is a terroristic act, especially when it is employed in warfare as an instrument of subjugation or humiliation. In any unbiased analysis, it might reasonably be put forward as terrorism par excellence. Yet, it is not the crime of rape that comes readily or immediately to mind in any discussion of the meaning of terrorism. This is not to deny the terroristic content within what is understood about the crime of rape, at least in its violent manifestation, but rather an unexpressed preference for seeing terrorism as something separate, distinct, and having an existence all its own. For those taking such a position, and no objection is taken to it here, terrorism seems to inhabit a different universe from the ordinary, from even the most heinous of otherwise criminal behavior. That it can or should do so comes as no surprise to the legal positivist.

Although norms cannot be simply conjured up out of thin air, the power to create new crimes in response to altered circumstances is an inherent faculty of any legal system. At this point, it must be made clear that what has been offered above as a conceptualization of terrorism is in no way to be regarded as an inchoate norm awaiting the interposition of the legal system's authority to give it independent being. And, herein lies the central dilemma, which cannot be readily overcome by recourse to any legal artifice. It is only possible to construct a freestanding penal figure denominated *terrorism* out of elements borrowed from preexisting crimes already defined as such in their own right. Thus, rape can in this view be seen as a constituent element of an autonomous crime of terrorism, just as terrorism can be seen as a necessary ingredient in a violent rape. Although this does little to advance the process of definition per se, it does serve to expose a critical problem that cannot be evaded.

Even the most cursory examination of the many definitions of terrorism on offer should quickly persuade the critic how many of these rely for any sort of precision on the adjectives employed in their elaboration. These definitions tend to focus on purpose, and that, in each of them, is primarily political. Reduced to its simplest terms, terrorism is seen as extreme political coercion. This, truth to tell, is the *raison d'etre* of virtually all these definitional exercises. For it is only in the realm of the political that these definitions have any useful employment; hence their adversarial nature. Yet, assuredly, the abused child knows exactly what terrorism is, even though he or she might be quite unable to enunciate the word. More is revealed in this of the purposes of the definers, or refiners, than of the nature of terrorism itself. All who seek to find a meaning in the term *terrorism* would have to agree on the centrality of the massive fear, or terror,[4] it inspires in those on whom it is inflicted, as well as its coercive nature. What is in dispute is whether there is anything in the nature of a right to inflict such misery on others and, if so, in whom it inheres. Here, we come to another dilemma that cannot escape the notice of anyone seeking to define terrorism. In its nature, terrorism, by reason of its coercive aspects, has a marked similarity to the corrective and deterrent functions vested by common understanding and political theory in the state—and the responsible parent. The distinction is in degree rather than anything else. Consider, for example, the ultimate sanction permitted the nation-state seeking to exercise its authority internally to control crime, namely the death penalty. Those who subscribe to a belief in its efficacy, whether by way of deterrence or social hygiene, can only rely on its intimidatory effect; if it does not frighten others by way of example, its value is very limited. The state's power to wage war to maintain its integrity against external foes can be viewed in much the same way. Clearly, effectiveness turns on the ability to secure the desired result through intimidation. Here lies the road to Dresden, Hiroshima, and Nagasaki, but we accord the nation-state considerable latitude in these matters. But there comes a point when the line is crossed and we would say that the state has begun to rule by terror. There are issues of proportionality involved of a most delicate kind, but they are the ones that perturb the definitional process in most awkward ways. Terrorism becomes, for those in power, an affront to established authority. Power, when stretched to its limits is, to many, no more than a reign of terror. Any definition that ignores this is open to attack as pure cant. The point here is that the way in which these things are done has always assumed lesser importance from the point of view of their characterization as terrorism than who does them and to whom.[5]

It should be observed that there is a kind of parallel in this regard with what have come to be known in recent times as "hate crimes." Those who oppose the promulgation, altogether, of such a category argue simply that it is otiose; murder is murder is murder. What can be done to increase the gravity with which certain matters seem to clamor for attention? Is any greater protection afforded potential victims by this increment? Nothing is added, for example, to the crime of murder that might serve as a special deterrent to those who would commit it against some class supposedly in need of particular protection. Many behaviorists and mental health professionals would argue, with considerable force on their side, that an individual who kills any victim in a singularly vicious way is exhibiting a hatred of that person regardless of the class to which that person belongs; in fact, so personalized may be the hatred that no issue of a class character enters into the matter (see Gourevich, 2000). None of this would satisfy those who argue for special hate crime legislation. Once more, the focus is plainly on who does what to whom and why. Hatred is an emotion and one that in civilized society is regarded as reprehensible, unhealthy, and socially harmful. It is the "why" of the matter that is troubling to those who see themselves as likely to be victimized by those who bear and exhibit these ugly emotions. The problem resides herein: The feelings we characterize as hatred cannot be punished unless they are exhibited in a way that is criminal in itself or in association with conduct that is already criminalized. If the device of making the element of hate is a way of making this latter punishable in a more severe fashion than would otherwise be the case, the position has something to commend it, but in the case of the most serious crimes, such as murder, they are already punishable to the limit; the rest is merely posturing. As with terrorism, we should define by reference to what is done rather than by shifting our focus to those who are victimized and the reasons they are targeted.

Good News / Bad News

Viewed in the formulation set down here, terrorism is a game of fixed quantities. It is cold comfort, but comfort nevertheless, that as we enter the new millennium, no new terrorism is possible. How can this be? Creating massive fear in human beings is based on the same principles that have always informed the process: You can kill them, you can mutilate them or otherwise damage their physical or mental integrity, you can deprive them of their liberty, you can damage or destroy their relationships with people and things, you can adversely alter the quality of their lives by affecting their environment or their economic prospects or by imposing onerous burdens on them, or you can achieve your ends by credibly threatening to do all or any of these things. It is not possible to conceive of anything else that might accomplish the goal of creating the massive fear, or terror, that is at the heart of terrorism. That is the good news. The bad news—and it is very, very bad—is that with each passing moment ever newer and more horrible ways of undertaking these things are being imagined and made possible by the implacable, onward sweep of technology. That is the awful prospect that looms before us as we proceed into the new millennium. The 19th-century terrorist, if he or she were lucky, might have anticipated a body count in the hundreds, although none attained that target. It was probably easier for the terrorist, especially the anarchist, to concentrate on trying to effect change through coercion against selected individual targets, for example, the assassination of key members of the ruling classes. The 20th-century terrorist never truly reached his or her potential, for which we should be devoutly grateful. The ingredients were there, but somehow, the deadly brew was never administered to its deadliest effect. With regard to the concept and the resources available to it, the attack by Aum Shinrikyu on the Tokyo subway, judged on its results, was puny in the extreme; a 19th-century anarchist operating alone with black powder might have accomplished much more. The [1993] World Trade Center bombing in New York, similarly from the terrorists' point of view, produced a pathetically small death toll and nothing like the property damage that was possible. Although the horrific attack on the Murrah Building in Oklahoma City stands above them all in terms of execution, magnitude, and a lasting impression on the psyche of the American people, it is not difficult to imagine how much worse it might have been. This is the frightening face of the future, but in the matter of definition, it is no different from what we have struggled with in the past. This is the fact that is urged here on those who will have to cope with the practical implications of terrorism in the new millennium.

Comprehending Terrorism

We seek to define terrorism so as to be better able to cope with it. We cannot begin to counter effectively that which we are unable to fully comprehend or agree on as to its nature. Some 50-odd years have been wasted in trying to disentangle the topic of terrorism from the much grander subject of wars of national liberation.[6] A great deal of time and effort has been expended in trying to make the truly reprehensible politically respectable. As the awesome possibilities of the new millennium are translated into ever more frightening realities, we can no longer afford the fiction that one person's terrorist may yet be another's freedom fighter. Fighting for freedom may well be his or her purpose, but if the mission is undertaken through the employment of terroristic means, a terrorist he or she must remain; we ought not to confuse the sophistry of refinement for the process of definition. This assumes considerable importance as the older forms of terrorism give way, as they must, before the newer and more horrible ways of going about this grim business. For the advances of technology have not all aided the terrorist's purposes. As in so many other departments of modern life, the audience has become increasingly difficult to shock. Indeed, the terrorist nowadays has to struggle mightily against a kind of ennui affecting those he or she would seek to impress. The audience, with the ever present assistance of television reporting of the contemporaneous, has become sated on a diet of death and destruction. The misery of others is fast losing its ability to horrify or, at least, to horrify for very long. Terroristic violence on the screen, whether fact or fiction, has become commonplace; much of the mystery has faded. This has made the terrorist's task increasingly difficult: How do you recapture and refocus the jaded attention of such an audience? The possibilities are really quite limited. You can strive to increase the toll in terms of the body count; compared to conventional warfare, deaths resulting from acts of terrorism have been numerically insignificant. To measure the true potential of terrorism, one would have to look to, say, Rwanda. Alternatively, the terrorist has to imagine novel, strikingly horrible means for doing the traditional things; and, significantly, the execution must match the imaginings. Clearly, whichever course is chosen, some of the mystery has to be reintroduced. Fear feeds off the unknown. We must be careful not to allow this development to warp the process of definition.

From Weapons of Mass Destruction To Cyberterrorism

The expression "weapons of mass destruction" has now entered firmly into common currency. The expression conjures up visions of lots and lots of casualties and people dying in horrid ways as a result of the employment of such weapons. Because of its awesome, proved potential, nuclear weaponry is perhaps the first type to come to mind when the expression is used. Credible fears of the terrorist nuclear bomb go back at least to the 1970s; much fiction has been written around the theme of the "basement nuclear bomb." The concept has dominated futuristic theorizing about the direction terroristic escalation might take. Nuclear terrorism has, thankfully, remained in the realm of fiction. But, as we stand on the threshold of the new millennium, we would be most unwise to conclude that it will be ever thus. Indeed, it is little short of a miracle that we have not had to face the realities of nuclear terrorism to date. The knowledge and the materials have long been available to those who might have been tempted to engage in some feat of superterrorism (see Schweitzer, 1998). The point here is that if and when this awful eventuality materializes, it will not require any redefinition of terrorism; it will simply sharpen the terms with which it is drawn. We might remind ourselves at this juncture that it matters little to the instant victims whether they are done to death with a hatpin or consigned to perish in a nuclear conflagration. But, viewed in prospect, which is the more fearful, which the more likely to produce social nightmares? Even serially, you cannot account for a great many victims with hatpins. A simple nuclear device in the possession of a competent terrorist would demolish much property, alter the landscape, and kill and horribly maim a great many human beings. Its employment would alter forever the face of terrorism, and the way we have come to think about it. It would not, however, require us to alter the way we define it.

Until the late 1980s, many tended to think of terrorism in almost climatological terms, as though it were blown by a cold wind out of the East. It was, for the most part, an indelibly Cold War phenomenon; terrorism was often referred to as a form of surrogate warfare. Unpleasant it undoubtedly was, especially for the instant victims, but there did exist a useful measure of control applied by the patron states. The euphoria of the early 1990s blinded us to the dangers inherent in the collapse of the control factor. Whether or not one subscribed to the mutually assured destruction theory, it was very unlikely that the principal antagonists would encourage their surrogates to use weapons of mass destruction that they would be unwilling themselves to employ. The disintegration of the "evil empire" had another unpleasant consequence for terrorism: It unleashed deadly material and put a lot of disengaged experts on the "free" market. Now, we have to face the real possibility of a revitalized Cold War with old Cold Warriors such as Vladimir Putin in the driver's seat. What is uncertain is whether the old controls will be reimposed, or even whether they can. Although none of this is likely to unleash fresh fears of small-group nuclear terrorism in the West, it is likely to have an impact in other areas of perhaps greater concern. The fearful instruments of chemical and biological warfare, largely eschewed by a majority of civilized nations, have acquired the soubriquet of "the poor man's nuclear bomb." Certainly, as death-dealing implements, the term is well applied. There is a kind of inevitability about the employment of these weapons by terrorists. The amount of publicity they have received over the past decade or so alone would have assured that outcome. It is worthy of note, yet again, that these possibilities encouraged by technological advances and political shifts have no definitional significance. The alterations have been simply adjectival. But they will change the way we think about terrorism as well as about those whose job it is to undertake countermeasures. Sooner maybe than later, one of those packets or envelopes is going to contain anthrax spores, the real thing, rather than the miscellaneous hoax powders that have turned up so far. There is a kind of fearfulness about handling this stuff that, as much as anything else, has probably protected society until now. The fears are not misplaced. Considering the number of terrorists who have blown themselves up with their own bombs, the very unfamiliarity with the handling of some of these substances, especially the nerve gases, suggests perils of an entirely different order from those previously experienced. The first successful employment of chemical and biological agents by terrorists will doubtlessly overcome any lingering inhibitions.

Now, yet another term has to be employed by those seeking to give precision to their particular definitions of terrorism. Not long after heaving a sigh of relief and congratulating ourselves at having avoided the catastrophes of Y2K predicted by the doomsayers, we have been hit with a wave of what is being called "cyberterrorism." Modern society is becoming more and more computer dependent. Everything from electronic commerce to the supply of energy is vulnerable, and although this may not be the immediate objective of the perpetrators, the potential for the associated loss of human life is not inconsiderable.[7] This cyberterrorism is still very much in its infancy; the methods are primitive and unsophisticated but effective. This is not "virtual" terrorism or Game Boy stuff. Cyberspace is a real place; real operations and real functions take place there, and real interests are at risk. The methods are new, but the principles behind their application are as old as terrorism itself. The technology employed has enabled the terrorists to reintroduce a useful, from their point of view, element of mystery into the process. They can, for a little while at least, operate from a considerable distance, concealing their identities and their purposes. The authorities, for the moment, can only confess to a sense of bafflement and try to reassure the affected public that everything possible is being done to protect the systems at risk and to apprehend the culprits. All this is going to generate a new lexicon, and already familiar terms such as *hackers, computer viruses, trap doors,* and the like will gain greater currency. Yet, we could as easily say these cybersystems were being "kidnapped," "hijacked," or "taken hostage," and when demands are presented to desist, the term *extortion* will come into play. Of greatest interest, perhaps, for the present purposes, a participant in an online discussion opined, "Hackers are freedom fighters for cyberspace" (Weise, 2000, p. 2A). Those who do not learn the lexical lessons of history are obliged to repeat the semester!

Terrorism, by its nature, seeks out and exploits its opponents' weaknesses. Again, a well-known aphorism has it that "terrorism is the weapon of the weak." This was a definitional device intended to characterize those tarnished with the terrorist label as being those who challenged rightful authority rather than those who abused it through practices that smacked of vicious cruelty. The nation-state has always been ultrasensitive to accusations that it is guilty of terrorism, whether against its own lawful residents or others (see, e.g., Herman & O'Sullivan, 1989). Where these cruelties are egregious, as in the case of Nazi Germany, few would cavil at defining what is done as terrorism. Yet, even that awful regime would claim its actions were in the nature of self-defense, a deterrent to behavior that threatened its cohesiveness and purposes.[8] Unhappily, such state terrorism is very far from being a thing of the past. As we proceed into the new millennium, we shall be confronted more and more with terrorism that proceeds from the mighty rather than the weak. A practical consequence of this delicacy in the matter of labeling can be seen by studying in any particular year the nations that find themselves on the U.S. State Department's list of "terrorist states," and those that do not. There is a kind of hypocrisy about this process that no definitional sophistry can hide; it simply highlights the perennial difficulty of describing forthrightly what terrorism is, for fear of upsetting those we might find it inconvenient to criticize. This is unfortunate on much more than a linguistic level. Definition is dictated under such circumstances by the harsh realities of power: None dare call it by its rightful name. This is surely the road to Tiananmen Square, and the consequences of ignoring the route are much more than merely academic.

Terrorism is a naked struggle for power, who shall wield it, and to what ends. The coercive character of what is done is plain enough to require little beyond description. Where the process does not produce the requisite submission, escalation is inevitable; action begets reaction. This is the real challenge to the high-minded. It is here that the state finds it especially needful to characterize what its opponents do as terrorism while seeking to distinguish its own counteraction as something quite different, lacking in reprehensible qualities. While looking at the conduct of those whose political philosophies we do not share, we ought not to disregard too cavalierly the mote in our own eye. No nation-state can relinquish its sovereign authority to an adversary, attempting to seize it by force, and retain its own integrity. Retaliation is an imperative in such cases, but one of the objectives of the adversary is to produce an overreaction. Brutal repression serves the adversary's purposes, so as to give rise to the charge, "See, you are as bad, or worse, than we are. Who is the terrorist now?" The audience is the community of nation-states, which has become increasingly censorious in judging the responses of others, especially when the judges are not directly confronted, for the moment, with terrorism problems of their own. In an ideal world, responses would be measured by much the same criteria as those against which an individual's rights of self-defense at law are evaluated, namely that the response should be necessary, reasonable, and proportionate to the harm suffered or apprehended (Cooper, 1998). We are forced to recognize that the real world in which modern-day terrorism takes place is very far from ideal. It is, rather, a Hobbesian universe in which all life is to be regarded as "nastie, brutish and shorte"—and cheap in the bargain. Terrorism thus becomes a battle for the moral high ground, with those in legitimate power trying to preserve their positions against opponents bent on dragging them into the gutter. The outcome is yet another phenomenological element in the process of defining terrorism that is likely to be of increasing importance in coming decades.

The Problem of Definition Remains Unaltered Throughout

Thus, at the start of the new millennium, we can say with a high degree of certainty that the definition of terrorism is as needful and as illusory as ever. The fine minds that have engaged in the task over the past three decades or so have provided much fuel for the crucible and a great deal of raw material for the process, but a truly pure ingot has eluded all. Once again, the focus here has been on the problem of definition, which remains unaltered throughout. It is realism rather than pessimism that prompts the observation that this is really a problem without a solution, for none can voluntarily yield the high ground to the others. Terrorism is not a struggle for the hearts and minds of the victims nor for their immortal souls. Rather, it is, as Humpty Dumpty would have said, about who is to be master, that is all. Yet, withal, no one who has experienced terrorism in the flesh has the slightest doubt about what it is or the sensations that it engenders.[9] Ask any concentration camp survivor. Ask those fortunate enough to have returned from the gulag. Ask those who have experienced the more recent examples of ethnic cleansing in the former Yugoslavia or in East Timor. They may not be able to encapsulate the horrors of their respective experiences in a finely turned phrase or two, but what they have undergone is to them and countless others not in the slightest doubt, for it is indelibly engraved on their psyches. Although this cannot suffice for the purposes of the polemic, it does help to focus the debate. As with obscenity, we know terrorism well enough when we see it. For the minds and bodies affected by it, this suffices; definition for these is otiose. This will not and cannot change in the years to come, strive as we may to give precision to the concept. It is diffidently opined here that we would be better employed in refocusing our efforts on what is done, the terrible acts themselves, whether by way of original initiative or retaliation. It might be more admirable to call a spade a spade, in the hands of whoever might be wielding it. These pathetic attempts at making the contemptible respectable will seem as ridiculous to those approaching the end of the present millennium as efforts to rehabilitate Attila the Hun or Genghis Khan would appear in our own times. So we are left, as we began, with our own imperfect formulas and the ever insistent need to explain and expound. As the incomparable Ludwig Wittgenstein (1921/1961) instructed us, "There are, indeed, things that cannot be put into words. *They make themselves manifest.* They are what is mystical" (p. 151). Terrorism is one of those things.

Notes

1. Cohen's (1990) *Culture and Conflict in Egyptian-Israeli Relations: A Dialogue of the Deaf* is an excellent scholarly work that deserves to be more widely known.

2. See, for example, the excellent scholarly works of Deborah Tannen, especially *You Just Don't Understand: Women and Men in Conversation* (1990).

3. Representative of these worthy efforts is *International Terrorism: National, Regional, and Global Perspectives* (1976), edited by Yonah Alexander.

4. Terror and terrorism tend to be confused, somewhat awkwardly, in Frederick J. Hacker's (1976) well-known work *Crusaders, Criminals, Crazies: Terror and Terrorism in Our Time.*

5. See, generally, the thoughtful arguments of Noam Chomsky, especially his chapter "International Terrorism: Image and Reality" in *Western State Terrorism* (1991), edited by Alexander George.

6. One of the more thoughtful and eclectic symposia on this subject was held in 1976 at Glassboro State College. The splendidly edited proceedings volume, *International Terrorism in the Contemporary World* (Livingston, 1978), contains the following, written by the author, on its first page: "Many nations have recognized the great potential of terrorism; the terrorist is now the spearhead of a developing theory and practice of surrogate warfare."

7. Such an attack on the air traffic control system, for example, has long been feared.

8. "Terrorism was the chief instrument of securing the cohesion of the German people in war purposes" (Office of the Chief Counsel for the Prosecution of Axis Criminality, 1946, p. 144).

9. There is something faintly paradoxical about this that is reminiscent of the renowned cat of Schrodinger, seemingly capable of being alive and dead at the same time.

References

Alexander, Y. (Ed.). (1976). *International terrorism: National, regional, and global perspectives.* New York: Praeger.

Cohen, R. (1990). *Culture and conflict in Egyptian-Israeli relations: A dialogue of the deaf.* Bloomington: Indiana University Press.

Cooper, H.H.A. (1978). Terrorism: The problem of the problem of definition. *Chitty's Law Journal,* 26(3),105-108.

Cooper, H.H.A. (1998). Self-defense. In *Encyclopedia Americana* (Vol. 25, pp. 532). Danbury, CT: Grolier.

Chomsky, N. (1991). International terrorism: Image and reality. In A. George (Ed.), *Western state terrorism* (pp. 12-38). New York: Routledge.

Gourevich, P. (2000, February 14). A cold case. *The New Yorker,* 42-60.

Hacker, F. J. (1976). *Crusaders, criminals, crazies: Terror and terrorism in our time.* New York: Norton.

Herman, E., & O'Sullivan, G. (1989). The Western model and semantics of terrorism. In *The "terrorism industry": The experts and institutions that shape our view of terror.* New York: Pantheon.

Livingston, M. H. (with Kress, L. B., & Wanek, M. G.). (Eds.). (1978). *International terrorism in the contemporary world.* Westport, CT: Greenwood.

Office of the Chief Counsel for the Prosecution of Axis Criminality. (1946). *Nazi conspiracy and aggression.* Washington, DC: Government Printing Office.

Posner, R. A. (1999). *An affair of state: The investigation, impeachment, and trial of President Clinton.* Cambridge, MA: Harvard University Press.

Schweitzer, G. E. (with Dorsch, C. C.). (1998). *Superterrorism: Assassins, mobsters, and weapons of mass destruction.* New York: Plenum.

Tannen, D. (1990). *You just don't understand: Women and men in conversation.* New York: Ballantine.

Weise, E. (2000, February 10). Online talk is of conspiracy, crime and punishment. *USA Today,* p. 2A.

Wittgenstein, L. (1961). *Tracratus logico-philosophicus.* London: Routledge Kegan Paul. (Original work published 1921)

Defining "Terrorism"

Danny Goldstick

Abstract: *Analyzing the concept of "terrorism" under the general heading of "acts of war," the author considers the motivational, legal, military and political dimensions of terrorism to arrive at a definition. In the analysis, distinctions are also drawn between "wholesale" and "retail" terrorism and "freedom fighters" and "terrorists."*

In his time Bertrand Russell invented what he used to call "emotive conjugations," for example, "I am firm. You are stubborn. He is pig-headed." This suggests an emotive conjugation relevant to contemporary geopolitics: "I am a freedom-fighter. You are a guerrilla. She is a terrorist." Certainly all of us who are not pacifists are apt to join in taking our hats off to any freedom-fighters. And practically all of us join in reprehending terrorists. According to the cynical, freedom-fighters and terrorists really amount to the same thing, only with a value judgement shift from plus to minus.

Is it possible to avoid such hypocrisy without adopting the stance either of pacifism or of "anything goes" amoralism here? Can we somehow define "terrorism"—that is, what the ethical non-cognitivists used to call the "descriptive meaning" of the concept— in such a way as to make clear the reprehensibility of terrorism, in contrast to some other acts of war?

I am simply assuming here, as against amoralism and pacifism, that some but not all acts of organized violence really do merit the sort of near-universal condemnation evoked by the word "terrorism." This is not to suggest that all evil acts of organized violence should be called "terrorist," still less that nothing could ever be morally worse than any act of terrorism.

"Acts of war," I think, is indeed the proper heading to pursue this inquiry under. Like all who wage wars, whether offensive or defensive, terrorists use violence so as to compel the acceptance of certain political results. Sheer senseless slaughter, motivated by psychopathology or by revenge, say, without any political goal in view, is hardly terrorism.

Motivations of psychopathology and revenge are certainly prominent enough among terrorists, and the political goal may. to an outsider, be patently unrealistic or even rationalized, but in the absence of any political goal whatever, it seems a misnomer to speak seriously of any such "-ism" as "terrorism." Should we add that, besides being politically motivated, "terrorist" acts are always, from a legal point of view, crimes? Laws, of course, are made by winners, as the old epigram reminds us:

> Treason doth never prosper: what's the reason? For if it prosper, none dare call it treason.

Unless we are willing to concede to the cynics that might makes right from a moral as well as a legal point of view, we ought to be wary of any definitions of "terrorism" which confine it simply by stipulation to acts of violence against an existing state. There is apt to be more than a little manipulative "persuasive" definition involved in such stipulations. In Washington today there is no small interest in directing public condemnation specifically onto those who use violence against existing governments—at any rate, such existing governments as are currently friendly to the government of the United States.

Here, for instance, is a 1983 definition of "terrorism" from the Department of Defense:

> The unlawful use or threatened use of force or violence by a revolutionary organization against individuals or property with the intention of coercing or intimidating governments or societies, often for political or ideological purposes.[1]

Of course, almost any offensive military action whatsoever is meant to attack certain "immediate victims" in order to intimidate the leaders on the enemy side into surrendering or making concessions: for instance, counterattacks against armed aggression are apt to be intended, if possible, to intimidate the government of the aggressor state into calling its invasion off. Note the specification of "a revolutionary organization" here. On the one hand, that rules any "counter-revolutionary terrorism" out by definition. On the other hand, this definition makes George Washington a "terrorist." He certainly did lead a revolutionary organization in the unlawful use of force or violence with the object of coercing the British government for a political purpose (independence). This definition is rather an extreme example.

But, more generally, in the verbal output of so many self-appointed "anti-terrorism experts" today, the smug double standard is all too transparently obvious. Why, we ask, is it "terroristic" to place a bomb on a plane, but not "terroristic" to drop a bomb from a plane? Of course, the people riding on a plane are usually going to be more affluent individuals, by and large, then those residing under a bomb-dropping plane. The cynical view exists that "terrorism" is nothing but the term of moral censure which the world's haves employ to cover all acts of war against them by the world's have-nots.

But such a view is over-simple. What is called terrorism offends the conscience of practically all—not just haves and their supporters. To be sure, from different quarters quite different things do get called terrorism. But it doesn't follow that nothing *really* is terrorism. The key to delineating the proper concept of terrorism will be to follow the thread of the near-universal moral condemnation, insofar as it is justified. The object will be to identify a subclass of acts of war which really are morally objectionable for a distinct reason.

At that rate, the overall justification, or lack of it, of the war or war-aims in furtherance of which the objected-to acts are performed will not be the issue. Arguably all acts in furtherance of an unjust war are morally unacceptable. Terroristic acts will have to be unacceptable for some further reason having to do with the specific sorts of acts that they are. In that case, acts having the specific character in question, even in furtherance of a just war, might be unacceptable because they are terroristic. And other acts of war, whether engaged in while fighting a just war or an unjust one, might have a specific character making them morally abhorrent even if they didn't have the specific character of being terrorist acts.

Terrorism has something to do with terror, I suppose. I take it that mass terror is its express aim. Any side in a war, of course, will seek as far as possible to paralyze the other side with fear. The specific reprehensibility of terrorism consists in the deliberate attack on civilian targets not directly involved in the war effort in order to spread wholesale terror among the ordinary population for the sake of securing whatever political end is in view. "Terrorism" is a species of crimes against humanity, morally speaking if not legally, and the nub of the offence is the deliberate aiming at civilians not directly involved in the opposing war effort. We are in the general area called that of war crimes by international lawyers, who are accustomed to cite laws of war prohibiting or severely limiting attacks upon civilians.

We are also in that general area called by traditional Roman Catholic moral theory the realm of "double effect." Roman Catholic moral theory sharply distinguishes between aiming at an evil, for whatever desirable or undesirable end, and merely bringing such an evil about as a foreseeable or even foreseen byproduct of action taken in furtherance of an otherwise acceptable end. If the end being sought is not actually meant to be caused by the evil in question, even though that evil can be expected to result from the means selected, as a distinct byproduct, the action taken may be morally innocent (according to traditional Catholic moral thought) where it would not be innocent action were the evil in question instead being specifically aimed at, even if only as a means to an otherwise acceptable end. According to a more consequentialist view, the only duty is to do, as far as possible, whatever will secure the net maximization of good results. From such a consequentialist viewpoint, the distinction between bad results actually aimed at and bad results merely foreseen as the indirect byproduct of activities aimed at other results, is a distinction which makes no real moral difference. From that point of view, "double effect" is simply double-talk. If it is immoral specifically to aim bombs at a hospital, is it not immoral likewise to aim bombs at an adjacent military target knowing full well that their successful detonation will destroy the hospital also? Doubtless this often is the case, but I am not convinced that there is never something specifically reprehensible about aiming at a definite evil result, whether for its own sake or as a means to something else, in contrast to merely accepting such a result, while actually aiming elsewhere.

In any case, the reprehensibility of terrorism consists in aiming specifically at civilian targets not directly involved in the opposing side's war effort in order to spread massive terror among the general population in furtherance of whatever political result is being pursued.

With this understanding of "terrorism," the distinction still exists between what has been called retail terrorism and wholesale terrorism, the latter practised primarily by governments waging a certain kind of war. We could call it Blitzkrieg war, in memory of Guernica and Rotterdam, which certainly do fit the definition of "terrorism" just given. But so do the cases of Dresden, Tokyo and Hiroshima. There too you had the definite targeting of ordinary civilians in order to further their enemy's war-aims by producing massive terror among them. The same thing obviously applies to the wholesale antipersonnel terror-bombing of Vietnam, South and North, with which the United States attempted to make the Vietnamese surrender in the late sixties and early seventies.

Let me close with some remarks on military strategy. Blitzkrieg warfare did work most impressively in Rotterdam and perhaps in Hiroshima, but not in London, Berlin, or Tokyo, where it only stiffened the other side's resistance. It appears that (as the very name "lightning war" implies) it probably has to be part of a sudden short-sharp-shock to succeed. In a protracted war it is self-defeating. The opposing population is aroused, not terrorized. Its morale is strengthened, not weakened, the longer the process goes on. That is why small-scale, retail terrorism is so glaringly ineffective around the world. And even larger-scale foreign-financed terrorist banditry has failed to bring down the governments targeted.

Let us now contrast this phenomenon with that of people's war. This is war fought not merely on behalf of an entire people but by that people itself, or at least its majority. Such was the war of national liberation led by General Washington. Such was the long-drawn-out war of liberation fought by the Vietnamese people against Japanese, French, and finally U.S. imperialism. To quote Mao Zedong's famous words, in a people's war guerrilla partisans are like fish and the people like the sea. For the guerrillas depend on the people for recruits, for food, for information on the movement of government forces, and for keeping their own movements secret from those government forces. The government forces are for a long time much stronger than their opponents—more numerous, better armed, with much better transport and communications—and thus in a much better position to terrorize the local population. The main thing the freedom-fighters have going for them on the other side is popular support. Otherwise their cause is lost, they are like fish out of the sea. In these circumstances what kind of military sense does terrorism make? On the other hand, to cow a subject population, will not massive terror tend to serve the interests of a military occupation or a military dictatorship? These strategic reflections ought to qualify our recognition that the reprehensibility of terroristic military means is in principle independent of the justice or injustice of the war being waged.

Terror and Terrorism In the Koran*

T. P. Schwartz

Abstract: *Are there statements in the Koran that could be used literally and selectively by violence-prone people to engage in and to justify political terrorism? If so, which statements, and how could they be used? A careful reading and an objective analysis of every chapter and verse in an esteemed English translation of the Koran reveals no words, images or metaphors closely akin to "terrorism," "terrorize," or "terrorist." The Koran does not portray or defend the kinds of behaviors that have come to characterize isolated, terrorist attacks by a small group of non-military personnel who operate independently from established authority. However, the Koran has at least ten verses that profess that Muslim armies under Muhammad engaged in raids, battles and other operations that inflicted so much terror on armies, cities, and civilian populations that entire communities, generations and tribes were annihilated. There is plenty of terror, if not terrorism, in the Koran. Given the terror-laden statements in the Koran, it is not difficult to understand how literalists could ignore historical and literary contexts in such ways as to use these statements to plan, incite, execute, and justify inflicting terror on their enemies, including large numbers of civilians.*

> (Ali, 8: 13) "When thy Lord revealed to the angels, saying, 'I am with you; so give firmness to those who believe. I will cast terror into the hearts of those who disbelieve. Smite, then, the upper parts of their necks, and smite off all finger-tips'."[1]

It is widely reported in the mass media that some contemporary terrorists, including Osama bin Laden, and some regimes that harbor terrorists, including the Taliban and al-Qaeda, often make operational decisions based on very literal readings of certain verses of the Koran, the holiest book of Islam, that assembles the sacred revelations of Allah to Muhammad. We see captioned photographs that purportedly show al-Qaeda fighters in victory circles, thrusting their Korans and Kalashnikovs towards the heavens. A captured videotape of a sit-down dinner in November 2002, between bin Laden and a Muslim friend who was visiting from outside Afghanistan is edited and televised throughout the world. In it, a printed translation of their conversation has them discussing a verse of the Koran that supposedly prescribes terrorizing the opponents of Islam. Osama then describes how he had calculated the probable number of deaths from the attacks on the World Trade Center twin towers days before they occurred.

At the same time, however, the mass media often present interviews and editorials in which scholars of Islam and Muslim leaders assert that the Koran and Islam prohibit terrorism and would never allow Muslims to participate in the violent attacks of September 11, 2001. For example, an article by Teresa Watanabe of the *Los Angeles Times* quotes Professor Hamid Dabashi, Chair of the Middle Eastern Languages and Culture Department at Columbia University as saying, "Nothing in the Koran, Islamic theology or Islamic law in any way, shape or form justifies ramming two airliners into civilian buildings." According to another article, by Associated Press reporter Ed Garsten, Mohamed E.M. El-Sayed, a university instructor and a Muslim spiritual leader in Dearborn, Michigan, gave a lecture to sixty employees of Ford Motor Company that rejected any relationship between the Koran and killing in any form. El-Sayed said that the terrorists who attacked the World Trade Center might have confused the Koran's definition of "fight" with "kill." "The Koran forbids killing anything, even a tree, he said." On the other hand, a few critics, such as the Reverend Franklin Graham, son of the famous religious leader, Reverend Billy Graham, have stated publicly that the Koran clearly advocates violence and killing in a number of ways. His statements have been vehemently opposed in public, in turn, by various religious and political leaders and by spokespersons for the Bush administration.

Who is correct, or, more importantly, what is the truth regarding terror and terrorism in the Koran? Given the immediacy and gravity of this controversy, it is time to examine the Koran as objectively as possible in order to determine what, if anything, in the Koran could possibly motivate and direct anyone to use terror or terrorism, especially someone who is prone to violence and to accepting certain verses in the Koran as literally as possible, and with little regard for other verses of the Koran or for what is often referred to as the "context" of the Koran. For convenience, henceforth in this paper I will refer to people who are inclined to behave in this way as "literalists."[2]

With this purpose in mind, I read all of Pickthall's highly regarded and long-established translation and commentary on the Koran, *The Meaning of the Glorious Koran*, and noted any and all verses that used the words "terror," "terrorism," "terrorist," or their synonyms, or mentioned behaviors that inflicted terror, extreme fear, or panic upon other people. I then compared these verses with the verses in two other well-known translations of the Koran, by Ali and by Arberry. To reduce the likelihood that I had missed any relevant verses from the more than 1,400 verses in the Koran, I also used *A Concordance of the Qur'an*, by Kassis, and I read additional commentaries and interpretations by Ali and Haleem, among others.

Some Working Definitions

Terror is generally defined as "intense, sharp, overmastering fear," "any period of frightful violence or bloodshed likened to the Reign of Terror in France," and "violence or threats of violence used for intimidation or coercion." *Terrorism* is generally defined as "the use of violence and threats to intimidate or coerce, especially for political purposes," and "a terroristic method of governing or of resisting a government." A *terrorist* is "a person, usually a member of a group, who uses or advocates terrorism" (*Webster's*, 1996: 1960).

As might be expected, definitions by scholars and by government leaders and agencies are much more varied and controversial. Thackrah reviewed more than one hundred definitions of terrorism in his *Encyclopedia of Terrorism and Political Violence* and concluded that, "In spite of the spread of terrorist incidents throughout the world, terrorism has neither a precise definition nor one which is widely acceptable" (1987: 54). Many of the definitions differ as to whether the sources and the targets of terrorism can include governments and military forces as well as civilians, and as to whether the inflicting of terror is ever an end in itself, rather than just a means to some other goal, political change in particular. And yet, it seems to me that the essence of terrorism is the willful, planned inflicting of terror into a number of people, including a large number of people beyond the immediate targets and victims. Vladimir Lenin, the architect of the Russian Revolution and the mastermind of the "Red Terror," 1917-22, is quoted as saying "The purpose of terrorism is to produce terror." The basic logic behind it is conveyed in the old Chinese proverb: "Kill one, frighten ten thousand" (*Encyclopedia of World Terrorism,* 1997: 12). Therefore, for our purpose here, *terrorism* is defined as *intentional actions (usually violent in word and deed) that are executed by individuals, groups, organizations and/or governments in order to produce a sense of extreme fear (i.e. terror) in a large number of other people, including people in the general "civilian" population beyond the immediate targets and victims. Political terrorism*, a sub-category, is *terrorism that is intended to do these things in such a ways as to coerce political leaders to accede to the political demands of the perpetrators.*[3] It is intended to be an instrument of dramatic political change, not just an expression of outrage, frustration, loathing, hatred, prejudice, or other emotions.

Some Findings

In the Koran I did not find the words "terrorist," "terrorize," "terrorism," or synonyms and metaphors for these words. Nor did I find verses in the Koran that encourage or instruct individual Muslims, acting alone, to engage in terrorism as individuals or in small, informal groups. However, I did find at least ten verses that readily could be used by literalists to engage in and to justify terrorist actions *collectively*, if not individually, if they believe that Allah has commanded them to do so. These verses use the word "terror" or its close synonyms (fear, panic) in such ways as to allow or encourage Muslim literalists to collectively inflict extreme terror on non-Muslims ("disbelievers") under at least some circumstances. For example, the verse (8:13) in the epigraph at the head of this paper is Ali's translation of a verse in a well-respected Arabic edition of the Koran. It quotes Allah revealing to Muhammad that He "will cast terror" into the hearts of disbelievers. Then Allah seems to command the smiting of the necks and fingers of disbelievers. Pickthall gives the verse a slightly different number (8:12) and translates the verb as "fear" rather than as "terror."

> (8:12) "When thy Lord inspired the angels, (saying): I am with you. So make those who believe stand firm. I will throw fear into the hearts of those who disbelieve. Then smite the necks and smite of them each finger."

I believe that the verses and their meanings are interchangeable, even if they are not completely identical. Notice that both translations have Allah claiming that he is the source of the terror or fear and that the targets are "those who disbelieve." The form of the terror includes "smiting" of fingers and necks, in both translations. By the way, it might be noted that Pickthall comments that this verse relates to the

Battle of Badr, in which Muhammad's army of about three-hundred Muslim cavalry from Medina repulsed an attack of an army of more than six hundred non-Muslim cavalry from the Qureysh tribe from Mecca and won a surprising victory (Pickthall, 1051: 138). So, in the case of this verse, the terrorism is military-to-military terrorism rather than political terrorism per se, as defined for the purposes of this paper, in that a civilian population was not the direct target, and the goal was not primarily to influence political leaders in Mecca so much as it was to simply repulse or defeat the opposing military force. However, literalists who are frustrated and inclined towards violence might easily ignore these contextual considerations, and might use this verse, and the others that follow, to motivate, plan and justify terrorist actions against civilian populations for any purpose.

In each of the following verses, particular attention should be given to the *nature* of the verse (exhortation, description, explanation, justification, warning, or a combination of these), the *sources* of the terror (Allah, Muhammad, Muslim armies, and others), the *targets* and *victims* of the terror (all disbelievers, specific categories of disbelievers such as the ungrateful ones, the treaty breakers, the "People of the Scripture" [i.e. Jews and Christians], houses, lands, cities, communities, and entire tribes), the *means and forms* of terror (frontal assaults by armies in ranks, night raids, noontime raids, burning by fire, smiting backs and fingers, tormenting, taking captives, torturing, pillaging, taking other spoils, and slaying), and the apparent *goals and consequences* of the terror (to carry out a threat, to end religious persecution, punishment for idolatry, expulsion of the enemy combatants and their supporting civilians from their lands, towns, and strongholds, "shattering" entire enemy townships, tribes, and ethnic groups, making those who are behind the enemy army remember the punishment inflicted upon them by Muslim forces, laying waste to enemy lands, the complete annihilation of many generations of enemies, extinction of certain tribes of people, and raising-up other tribes in their place).

Other Verses Related to Inflicting Terror

> (3: 151) "We shall cast terror into the hearts of those who disbelieve because they ascribe unto Allah partners, for which no warrant hath been revealed. Their habitation is the Fire, and hapless the abode of the wrong-doers."

Notice that this verse does not restrict the casting of terror into the hearts of disbelievers who are in the enemy forces or those who are in the attack. Rather, the targets of terror are those disbelievers who commit some other type of offense against Allah. Terror is not an end in itself.

> (8:13-14) "That is because they opposed Allah and His messenger. Whoso opposeth Allah and His messenger, (for him) lo! Allah is severe in punishment. That (is the award), so taste it, and (know) that for disbelievers is the torment of the Fire."

> (8: 55-57) "Lo! The worst of beasts in Allah's sight are the ungrateful who will not believe; Those of them with whom thou madest a treaty and then at every opportunity they break their treaty, and they keep no duty (to Allah). If thou comest on them in war, deal with them so as to strike fear in those who are behind them, that haply they may remember."

Is it possible that literalists could understand the preceding verses as Allah or Muhammad instructing them to strike fear during "war" (not just during one battle), not only against the disbelievers who are fighting them, but also to "those who are behind them," the ungrateful, and the treaty-breakers? And should this be done in such a way that the enemies will remember the fearful actions, possibly forever? Perhaps we should consider whether literalists could understand verses like these as their inspiration and their directive to conduct terrorist actions like those of September 11, 2001. Could verses like these, taken literally and in isolation, constitute a terrorist's manifesto?

> (59: 1-2) "In the name of Allah, the Beneficent, the Merciful. All that is in the heavens and all that is in the earth glorifieth Allah, and He is the Mighty, the Wise. He it is Who caused those of the People of the Scripture who disbelieved to go forth from their homes unto the first-exile. Ye deemed not that they would go forth, while they deemed that their strongholds would protect them from Allah. But Allah reached them from a place whereof they recked (sic) not, and cast terror in their hearts so that they ruined their houses with their own hands and the hands of the believers. So learn a lesson, O ye who have eyes!"

The two preceding verses might suggest to literalists not only that Allah is beneficent, wise, mighty, and merciful (statements that are frequent throughout the Koran), but that Allah is the ultimate source of terror, when he wills it. At times He has done this against Jews and Christians by destroying their houses so that they may learn a lesson.

> (33: 26) "And He brought those of the People of the Scripture who supported them down from their strongholds, and cast panic into their hearts. Some ye slew, and ye made captive some."

Pickthall (1951: 299-300) comments that the preceding verse relates to the "War of the Trench" outside Medina, where Muhammad had his Muslim army dig a long trench in front of the approach route of the much larger enemy army of Arab and Jewish tribes from Mecca. The trench, brutally hot and destructive windstorms, Muslim sympathizers in the enemy camp, and other forces confused and frustrated the Meccan army for more than a month and kept it from completing the attack. After the enemy forces abandoned the attack and retreated towards Mecca, the Muslim forces went on the offensive and destroyed a number of enemy strongholds. However, considerations like this regarding historical context might be ignored by literalists, who might understand this verse to say that Allah brought Jewish people out of their protected places, terrified them, and had Muslims slay some of them and capture others.

> (7: 4-5) "How many a township have we destroyed! As a raid by night, or while they slept at noon, Our terror came unto them. No plea had they, when our terror came unto them, save that they said: Lo! We were wrong-doers."

Literalists might understand this verse to mean that Muslims imposed terror on others through raids at night and while the victims slept during the day, destroying many townships in the process. The next three verses might be understood by literalists to extend the claims of the previous verses about inflicting terror, even without using the word "terror," by describing, possibly even boasting about, how Muslims have often threatened, expelled, ravaged, wasted, annihilated, and replaced many communities, generations, and tribes of "wrongdoers." Is it possible to perform such destructive and massive actions without inflicting terror, even if terror is not an end in itself? Could literalists assume inflicting terror is a necessary means to these other ends?

(17: 5-8) "So when the time for the first of the two came, We roused against you slaves of Ours of great might who ravaged (your) country, and it was a threat performed. Then we gave you once again your turn against them, and We aided you with wealth and children and made you more in soldiery, (Saying) If ye do good, ye do good for your own souls, and if ye do evil, it is for them (in like manner). So, when the time for the second (of the judgments) came (We roused against you other of Our slaves) to ravage you, and to enter the Temple even as they entered it the first time, and to lay waste all that they conquered with an utter wasting."

(17: 16-17) "And when We would destroy a township We send commandment to its folk who live at ease, and afterward they commit abomination therein, and so the Word (of doom) hath effect for it, and We annihilate it with complete annihilation. How many generations have we destroyed since Noah. And Allah sufficeth as Knower and Beholder of the sins of His slaves."

(21: 11-15) "How many a community that dealt unjustly have We shattered, and raised up after them another folk! And, when they felt Our might, behold them fleeing from it! (But it was said unto them): Flee not, but return to that (existence) which emasculated you and to your dwellings, that ye may be questioned. They cried: Alas for us! Lo! We were wrongdoers. And this their crying ceased not till We made them as reaped corn, extinct."

Analysis and Some Considerations About Context

As just shown, there are at least ten verses in the Koran that could suggest to literalists that inflicting terror can have a variety of goals and consequences, means and forms, targets and victims. Some of the verses are descriptions and explanations of past events while others might be taken as directives for now and the future. Terror is not suggested as an end in itself so much as it is a means to realizing other goals and consequences, including carrying out threats, punishing wrongdoers and idolaters, ending religious persecution, taking captives, expelling adversaries, laying waste to enemy lands and communities through the point of annihilation of generations and tribes, and replacing them with other people. So, too, there are many means and forms of terror, including frontal assaults by armies, night raids, burning by fire, smiting backs and fingers, tormenting, torturing, taking captives and other spoils, and slaying. There are also many types of targets and victims, not all of whom (e.g. "wrongdoers") are necessarily and explicitly enemy combatants, members of the enemy government, or even non-Muslims. Victims certainly included enemy civilians, according to some of the verses just presented — and there were plenty of them.

Regarding sources of terror in the Koran, the operative sources apparently included Muhammad and members of his armies, raiding parties, and whatever other forces he directed to engage in terror. There is also at least one verse in the Koran that might be understood by literalists as establishing that Allah is the originative source of all violence, including terror, and that he revealed to Muhammad that true believers are only the vehicles of his will whenever they engage in terror.

> (8: 17) "Ye (Muslims) slew them not, but Allah slew them. And thou (Muhammad) threwest not when thou didst throw, but Allah threw, that he might test the believers by a fair test from Him. Lo! Allah is Hearer, Knower."

Of course, the verses just presented are only a few of the more than 1,400 verses in the Koran, many of which have little obvious relationship to violence. Then again, there are dozens of other verses in the Koran, not presented here, that might be used by literalists to practice additional forms of violence besides terror, such as murder and mass warfare, albeit only under certain conditions (See Schwartz, 2002a, 2002b). For example, several verses in the Koran make conditional statements like the following regarding slaying:

> (12: 152) ". . . And that ye slay not a life which Allah hath made sacred, save in the course of justice. This He hath commanded you, in order that Ye may discern."

Could it be that some literalists might understand this verse to allow them to slay non-sacred lives, and possibly even sacred lives, including their own, if doing so is "in the course of justice"?

Although it might not be "politically correct" to admit it, at times it seems as though the Koran's historical and rhetorical contexts are infused with violence and threats of violence. Three of Muhammad's twenty-seven military campaigns (Badr, Uhud [where he was wounded and, for a few hours, was thought to have been killed], and The War of the Trench) are justified repeatedly in many places in the Koran. A number of the chapters (Surahs) in the Koran have titles that suggest warfare and violence: "Spoils of War," "Those Who Set the Ranks," "The Troops," "Victory," "The Ranks," "The Overthrowing," and "The Overwhelming," although these chapters deal with many subjects besides war and violence (Pickthall, 1951: 456-458). Dozens of verses throughout the Koran have Allah threatening eternal damnation and burning in hell to anyone who does not worship him alone, let alone to anyone who violates his sacred prescriptions regarding righteous behaviors on Earth. The phrases "severe in punishment" and "awful doom" abound. Taken literally, at least one verse might even threaten doom on Muslims who are timid about the subject of war.

> (47: 362) "And those who believe say; If only a Surah were revealed! But when a decisive Surah is revealed and war is mentioned therein, thou seest those in whose heart is a disease looking at thee with the look of men fainting unto death. Therefore woe unto them!"

Could it be possible for some literalists to use a verse like this to recruit warriors, or even terrorists, by calling their courage into question and mentioning to them that they can expect a terrible afterlife—if they refuse?

Some Concluding Thoughts and Encouragements

Based on the evidence presented here, it seems to me that both sides are partially right and partially wrong in the debate about terrorism in the Koran. The defenders of the Koran are right about the Koran not explicitly advocating terrorism in the form of events like the attacks on the World Trade Center. They are wrong about the Koran not defending or justifying the use of terror against a variety of non-military targets including civilian populations. On the other hand, critics of the Koran are wrong if they contend that the Koran explicitly allows or encourages individuals and small, informal groups to take it upon themselves to inflict terror upon others. It might be acknowledged, however, that none of the verses in the Koran admonish Muhammad or his believers for any terror that they inflicted upon any of their enemies.

Confusion and controversy swirl about these issues in part because, somewhat ironically, the Koran might not be definite, to literalists at least, in prohibiting anyone other than "Allah through Muhammad" to authorize terror. For literalists it might also not be definite enough in prohibiting them from individually and collectively engaging in terror.

Encouragements

Given the current threats of terrorism in so many places in the world, it seems to me that everyone who is deeply concerned about trying to reduce terrorism, particularly leaders in civic, government, and military affairs, should keep in mind several key points about terrorism. It did not originate with Islam, but much earlier in herding societies and in the Greek and Roman empires (*Encyclopedia of World Terrorism*, 1997: 27). There should be more acknowledgment that other "holy books," including the Bible and the Torah (Tanakh), especially the verses of Ezekiel, have more than a dozen verses with references to some tribes inflicting terror on other tribes. Also worth acknowledging is that contemporary terrorism is by no means restricted to Muslim perpetrators and non-Muslim targets (*The State of War and Peace Atlas*, 1997: 22-23) and that only a small percentage of the more than one billion Muslims have engaged in terrorism.

Regarding the Koran as a possible source of inspiration, direction, and justification for terrorism, especially for literalists, we should emphasize that it bears no words closely akin to "terrorism," "terrorize," or "terrorist." It does not portray the kinds of terrible behaviors that have come to characterize contemporary terrorists, let alone defend or advocate these kinds of behaviors. Yet we should also honestly acknowledge that the Koran has a small number of verses that describe how Muslim armies under the direction of Muhammad during the last ten years of his life, 622-632, engaged in raids and battles and, at times, were allowed to inflict terror on enemy lands, armies, communities, and civilian populations. Admittedly, these acts are not prohibited or condemned in the Koran, and some of the attacks are described as being so destructive they annihilated entire communities, generations, and tribes—what might be called genocide in contemporary parlance. Nonetheless, there is no claim in the Koran that inflicting terror ever was an end in itself. Rather, it was a means to other ends that either were military, religious, economic, or political, or a combination of these. Also worth emphasizing is that none of the verses in the Koran explicitly allows individual Muslims or small, informal groups of Muslims to act independently to inflict terror without the authority of Allah as revealed to Muhammad over thirteen hundred years ago.

Regarding literalists who might be inclined to misuse isolated verses in the Koran for inflicting terror, we should enable and induce them to associate with a broader range of people who read and understand the Koran more expansively. This should also be done for a second type of literalist—those who might be inclined to react to a few isolated verses of the Koran by stereotyping, persecuting or even terrorizing Muslims. It is worth remembering that there are many other verses in the Koran that might be more hopeful and reassuring to literalists and non-literalists alike than the verses that have been the subject of this analysis, one of which is quoted now to serve as a helpful encouragement for peace and honesty in these troubled times:

> (224: 53) "And make not Allah, by your oaths, a hindrance to your being righteous and observing your duty unto Him and making peace among mankind. Allah is Hearer, Knower."

Acknowledgments

* While any and all errors in this paper are mine alone, I want to thank the following people for various comments related to the content or the preparation of this paper: Professor Donna Schwartz-Barcott and Professor Mohammed Sharif of the University of Rhode Island, Professor Muhammad Qasim Zaman of Brown University, and Pat Chaney of OneonOnePC, East Greenwich, Rhode Island.

Notes

1. This quotation is from Ali's translation of the Koran in Arabic, chapter 8, verse 13. All other quotations from the Koran in this paper are from Pickthall's translation and commentary, for reasons explained in the body of the paper.

2. Although the term "literalist" is my own, there is a growing body of knowledge that distinguishes literalists from fundamentalists and other categories of people who have often been said, probably mistakenly, to be highly inclined towards terrorism. Behavioral and attitudinal characteristics that distinguish literalists from fundamentalists are identified in recent publications by Sprinzak (2000), Finkel (2001), and by Appleby and Marty (2002).

3. This definition is informed by Grant Wardlaw's definition in his book on political terrorism as quoted in *The Directory of International Terrorism* (1987: 18):

"The threat or use of violence by an individual or a group, whether acting for or in opposition to established authority, when such action is designed to create extreme anxiety and/or fear-inducing effects in a target group larger than the immediate victims with the purpose of coercing that group into acceding to the political demands of the perpetrators."

References

Ali, Maulawi Sher. *The Holy Quran. Arabic Text and English Translation.* Rabwah, West Pakistan. The Oriental and Religious Publishing Corporation Ltd. 1955.

Arberry Arthur J. *The Koran Interpreted.* New York: Macmillan. 1955.

Appleby, R. Scott and Martin E. Marty. "Fundamentalism." *Foreign Policy,* January/February 2002. Pages 16-22.

Encyclopedia of World Terrorism. Volume 1. Armonk, NY: M.E. Sharpe, Inc. 1997.

Finkel, Michael. "Naji's Taliban Phase." *The New York Times Magazine.* December 16, 1991. Pages 78-81.

Garsten, Ed. "The Drive for Diversity." Associated Press story published in *The Providence Journal,* September 30, 2001. Page E1.

Haleem, Muhammad Abdel. *Understanding The Qur'an: Themes and Style.* I.B. Tauris. 1999.

Kassis, Hanna. *A Concordance of the Qur'an.* Berkeley: University of California Press. 1983.

Pickthall, Mohammed Marmaduke. *The Meaning of the Glorious Koran.* New American Library. 1951.

Rosie, George. *The Directory of International Terrorism.* New York: Paragon House. 1987

Schwartz, T.P. "The Qur'an as a Guide to Conduct of and in War, Including Treatment of Prisoners of War." *Marine Corps Gazette.* February, 2002.

__________ "Waging War Against Combat Units That Fight According to Al Qur'an (The Koran)." *Marine Corps Gazette.* Forthcoming.

Sprinzak, Ehud. "Rational Fanatics." *Foreign Policy.* September/October, 2000. Pages 66-73.

Thackrah, John Richard. *Encyclopedia of Terrorism and Political Violence.* London: Routledge & Keegan Paul. 1987.

Smith, Dan. *The State of War and Peace Atlas, New Edition.* New York: Penguin Reference. 1997.

Wardlaw, Grant. *Political Terrorism.* New York: Cambridge University Press. 1985.

Watanabe, Teresa. "Understanding Islam." *Los Angeles Times,* as quoted in *The Providence Sunday Journal,* September 30, 2001, pp. B1 and B4.

Webster's New Universal Unabridged Dictionary. New York: Barnes & Noble. 1996.

Suicide Bombers: Business as Usual

Harvey W. Kushner

Abstract: *Muslims have been using religion sanctioned suicide as an effective tool against the West for several centuries. In keeping with this practice, Islamic suicide bombers attack a superior Israeli military and government. Suicidal terrorism is actually an act of martyrdom that can trace its origins back 13 centuries to the Battle of Karbala. Appealing to tradition, recruiters enlist potential bombers from schools and mosques in the West Bank and Gaza Strip. Bombers study religion, politics, and explosives. Students willingly become martyrs to secure a future for their families. Understanding that suicidal terrorism is not anathema to a significant proportion of the Muslim population is the first step in countering the problem.*

On April 18, 1983, a terrorist driving a van carrying approximately 400 pounds of explosives rammed into the US Embassy in Beirut, killing 63 and injuring many more. Among the dead were several prominent US officials. The radical Shiite terrorist group Islamic Jihad claimed responsibility for the attack.[1] Six months later, a suicide bomber representing the same terrorist group drove a truck loaded with explosives into the US Marine Headquarters at the Beirut Airport, killing 241 marines.

Perhaps to quell their own fears, scholars and policymakers concerned with terrorism delude themselves into thinking that these intimidating suicidal attacks are rare events even for the Middle East[2]; but, as Stephen Frederic Dale[3] notes, religiously sanctioned suicidal attacks are not unique to the modern period or confined to the Middle Eastern region. Similar types of assaults are known to have occurred over a span of several centuries in three little known Muslim communities in the Indian Ocean region: those on the Malabar coast of southwestern India, Atjeh in northern Sumatra, and Mindanao and Sulu in the southern Philippines. Although these earlier suicide attacks in Asia were not undertaken with the same political awareness that characterizes the organizers of the incidents in Beirut, they represent essentially the same phenomenon—protests against Western authority or colonial rule.

Recent events in the Middle East indicate that there is no shortage of suicidal terrorists willing to die for a cause,[4] even though Palestinian approval of a *jihad* (holy war) against Israel seems to be waning. In only a short nine-day span, four separate suicide bombers in Israel killed 59 people, including two Americans.[5] Almost 200 Israelis have died as a result of suicide attacks since the Oslo accords of 1993. This is the largest number of Israelis killed by terrorists in any 30-month period since the establishment of the state of Israel. Clearly, a spate of suicide attacks that exposes Israel's vulnerability makes Israelis and their American supporters anxious.

The Path to Martyrdom

It would be naïve to think of suicidal terrorists as merely fanatics.[6] Fanatic, like terrorist, is a pejorative term that "is applied to the state of mind of those who are wholeheartedly committed to a set of beliefs and condemned for it."[7] In this way, the term fanatic becomes a descriptive label, rather than an explanation. Attributing the actions of suicidal terrorists to the influence of incendiary Islamic clerics is equally foolish. No one should dismiss the impact of Sheik Omar Abdel Rahman, the blind cleric, in the assassination of President Anwar Sadat of Egypt and in the World Trade Center bombing. Still, categorizing these suicide bombers' actions as just acts of *taqlid,* that is, the blind following of a spiritual leader, underestimates the choices these suicidal terrorists make independently. Fathi Shikaki, the spiritual leader of Islamic Jihad before he was assassinated in Malta in 1995, told a reporter that he didn't personally choose suicide bombers: "Some of the youths insist that they want to lead a suicide operation—perhaps because they are influenced by the teachings of Islamic Jihad. My orders are to persuade them not to go, to test them. If they still insist they are chosen."[8]

The suicide bombers live an explosive faith—no pun intended—that requires outlets for the passions it encourages[9]; these outlets may be devotional, as in doing *taqlid,* or political, as in the earlier suicide missions in Beirut or those in Israel today.

Today's suicide bombers perform an act of martyrdom that was first documented 13 centuries ago, following the death of Muhammad. The Prophet's death in 632 A.D. left the Muslim community without a leader to watch over the faith. Several followers met to rectify this by selecting a Caliph, a temporal authority to guide the Muslim community, but religion soon gave way to politics. Within 40 years after the Prophet's demise, various Caliphs had managed to assassinate their way to power, and Islam had divided into two sects. The orthodox Sunnis accepted the reign of temporal leaders, whereas the Shiites believed their imams (or leaders) were the divinely inspired and infallible descendants of Muhammad.

In 680, Hussein (or Husayn), the son of Ali (cousin of Muhammad) and his wife Fatima (daughter of Muhammad), marched on the Sunnis in what Hussein hoped would be a gesture of reconciliation. Hussein, however, dreamt that no reconciliation was possible, and that he and his followers would die in a battle with the Sunnis. A badly outnumbered Hussein disregarded the premonition and knowingly marched to his death near the village of Karbala, which today is located in Iraq. To this day, especially in Iraq and Iran, passion plays and mass processionals are performed each year in commemoration of Karbala. These events are sometimes marked by rites of self flagellation; young men scrape their backs with hooks to draw blood, especially on Ashura, the tenth day of the month of Muharram, the anniversary of Hussein's martyrdom.

Karbala is not an act of suicide—Islam forbids the taking of one's own life. Rather, it symbolizes the supreme willingness to submit to the will of Allah with the understanding that rewards will come after death. Islam emphasizes that life on earth is merely a transition to a better life. A suicide bomber is making a transition that will put him alongside the other heroes of Islam and next to Allah.

Members of groups such as the *Arous Ad-Damm* (the Brides of Blood), who are sworn to avenge the death of Hussein through their martyrdom, indicate their own willingness to become martyrs; but the choice is not theirs, just as it wasn't Hussein's. Actually, Allah selected Hussein for martyrdom because of his special merit. In the same way, Allah's representatives here on earth, the mullahs, select whom to honor with martyrdom.[10] This is the intimate link between the practice of martyrdom in Islam, expressed in the act of suicide, and the official structure of Islam as a political entity. Given that there is no distinction between church and state in Islam, an act of religious devotion—such as suicide—becomes an instrument of state policy for the militant Muslim.

The perfector of this instrument was a Shiite sect known as the Ismalis-Nizari (or simply the Assassins), which survived two centuries (1090-1275). The leaders were reputed to have endowed the members with courage in the form of hashish, thus the name *hashishiyun* (or assassin). Controversy aside, the Assassins, according to Rapoport, prepared the assailant for political assassination "by preventing him from entertaining the idea that he might survive. His weapon, which 'was always a dagger, never poison, never a missile,' seems designed to make certain that he would be captured or killed. He 'usually made no attempt to escape; there is even a suggestion that to survive a mission was shameful'."[11]

Viewing suicide as a form of religious devotion allows the uninformed to make sense of the bizarre features of the actions of suicide bombers. Consider, for example, the affable smile worn on the face of the bomber as he made his way into the compound to blow up the US Embassy in Beirut in 1983. This smile, known as the *bassamat al-Farah* (smile of joy) symbolizes the joy of martyrdom.[12] The notion of joy in the act of suicide is also evident in the videotape left behind by a 17-year-old girl. On April 9, 1985, San'ah Muheidli drove her yellow Mercedes Benz, which was loaded with explosives, into an Israeli military convoy in southern Lebanon, killing two soldiers and herself. On the tape, San'ah instructs her mother not to mourn her untimely death but, "be merry, to let your joy explode as if it were my wedding day." A suicide bomber's death is described by Muslim militants as "the martyr's wedding," an occasion of joy and celebration.

The Chosen Ones

The refugee camps in the West Bank and Gaza Strip provide an endless flow of Islamic recruits raised under Israeli occupation,[13] as their questionable futures can fuel feelings of hopelessness and anger. Evidence exists that suicide bombers are not necessarily recruited from a life of poverty, however. There are reports that a number of recruits were members of affluent families, students or graduates of the West Bank's Bir Zeit University.[14] Their involvement in Islamic terrorism tends to belie the notion that such activity is bred solely by desperate poverty, and that the introduction of economic improvements will eliminate Islamic fervor. Nevertheless, years of controlled checkpoints, work permits and curfews certainly reinforce their frustration.

The selection of recruits is made by Hamas. Hamas is a militant mass movement with solid support among approximately 20 percent of the two million Palestinians in the West Bank and Gaza Strip. Leadership is divided between those inside the territories and those operating outside, mainly from Damascus, Syria. Hamas traces its roots to the Muslim Brotherhood founded in Egypt during the 1920s by Hassan al-Banna. The Brotherhood's strategy is to fight what it sees as the Westernization and corruption of Arab governments by running its own educational system, hospitals, and other social services.

Sheik Ahmed Yassin and the other founders of Hamas were involved with supplying social services through their mosques when the Palestinian uprising, *Intifada,* against Israeli occupation of the West Bank and Gaza Strip broke out in 1987. The uprising saw Palestinian youths turn away from the Muslim Brotherhood and toward the Palestine Liberation Organization (PLO). To counter this flight, Sheik Yassin formed Hamas, an Arabic acronym for Islamic Resistance Movement that means "zeal." Its military wing is called the Izzadin el-Kassam brigade, named after a Muslim cleric in Haifa who led an Arab revolt against both British rule and Zionist settlement in the 1930s and died in the battle.

The selection process begins with members of the Izzadin el-Kassam or even the Palestinian Islamic Jihad[15] circulating among the organizations' schools and mosques during religious instruction. The recruiters broach the subject of dying for Allah with a group of students and watch the students' reactions. Students that seem particularly interested in the discussion are immediately singled out for possible special merit.

These potential bombers, who range in age from 12 to 17 years, almost invariably have a relative or close friend who was killed, wounded, or jailed during Israeli occupation. Bombers are also likely to have some long standing personal frustration, such as the shame they suffered at the hands of friends who chastised them for not throwing stones at the Israeli troops during the *Intifada.* Theirs is a strong hatred of the enemy that can only be satisfied through a religious act that gives them the courage to take revenge. Martyrdom, for them, is what throwing stones or going to prison is for others.

The potential bombers attend classes in which trained Islamic instructors focus on the verses of the Qur'an and the Hadith, the sayings of the Prophet Muhammad that form the basis of Islamic law and idealize the glory of dying for Allah. Students are promised an afterlife replete with gold palaces, sumptuous feasts, and virgin brides. Students are also told that their martyrdom guarantees that 70 of their relatives and friends will gain entry to heaven.[16]

Aside from religion, the indoctrination also includes wild farragoes of anti-Israeli propaganda. Students entering the program quickly learn that the Jews have no right to exist on land that belongs to the Muslims. Students are assigned various tasks to test their commitment: Delivering weapons for use in clandestine activities is a popular way to judge the student's ability to follow orders and keep a secret. Some students are even buried together in mock graves inside a Palestinian cemetery to see if the idea of death scares them.[17] Students who survive this test are placed in graves by themselves and asked to recite passages from the Qur'an that explain how the angels come back and ask what one has done in one's life. It is at this stage that the recruits, organized in small groups of three to five, start resembling cult members, i.e., they are mentally isolated from their families and friends.

Graduates of these suicide schools know that their supreme sacrifice will see their families protected for life. This is no small reward for someone used to a life of poverty; Hamas awards monthly stipends in the range of $1,000 to the families of bombers. Scholarships for siblings are also made available. The monies to support the families of suicide bombers come from Hamas' estimated $70 million annual budget. It is reported that half of their budget comes from the oil rich Gulf states and another 35 percent from Europe, mainly England, and the United States.

Hamas pays for the resettlement of all families of suicide bombers who lose their homes as a result of Israeli retribution. A young Palestinian man was overheard to say: "It's no big deal. They'll [Hamas] build another home"[18] after Israeli troops blew up the two-story cinderblock house inhabited by the widow and two children of Yahya Ayyash, who was known as Mehandess or "the Engineer" for his bomb making expertise[19] and killed by an explosion from the ear piece of a telephone he was holding. The Hamas promise should not be underestimated.

The Mission

The suicide bombers leave for their missions directly from their mosques, after having completed many days of chanting the relevant scriptures aloud with their spiritual handlers. A favorite verse reads: "Think not of those who are slain in Allah's way as dead. No, they live on and find their sustenance in the presence of their Lord." The bombers' frenzied mantras are said to create a strong, albeit pleasurable, belief that they will sit with Allah. So strong is this belief that the bomber is able to walk among his enemy without exhibiting the slightest anxiety. On February 25, 1996, Israel television "reported that the suicide bomber was dressed in an Israeli army uniform and mingled with soldiers at the bus stop [and hitchhiking post in coastal Ashkelon] before setting off the explosion, killing two Israeli soldiers and himself."[20] Witnesses to other bombings have told the authorities that they never suspected the bomber on the bus was a suicidal terrorist on a mission.

To ensure the utmost secrecy, a bomber only learns how to handle explosives immediately before the mission. The use of explosives over time might give the bomber second thoughts about his martyrdom. In the past, it was common for the bomber to leave a written will or videotape. This custom is no longer practiced, since the General Security Service, the secret service known as Shin Bet by its Hebrew initials, was able to arrest other suicide bombers from the information left by these records. Now, the name or the picture of the bomber sometimes is not even released after the suicide attack. Hamas has also stopped publicly celebrating successful suicide attacks. A spokesman connected to Hamas' military wing in the Gaza Strip said, "We don't want Israeli security to know the circles from which we are operating."[21]

Still, pictures of past suicide bombers hang on the walls of barbershops inside the refugee camps. Small children collect and trade baseball-card-like pictures of suicide bombers.[22] There is even a teenage rock group, with requisite greased hair and black leather jackets, known as the Martyrs that sings the praises of the latest bomber that entered heaven.

Material for the bombs comes from Egypt either by sea or through secret tunnels under the border. The bombs themselves are rather simple: One of the most popular is made of old Egyptian issue land mines dug up from the Sinai desert. Carried in duffel bags along with bags of nails and ball bearings, they weigh about 50 pounds. Wires extend up from the mines through a series of nine volt batteries to a switching device; the wiring passes through a hole in the bag and up into the bomber's trouser leg, so the bomb can be detonated by a hand in the pocket. Some suicide bombers are known to have dressed up either as religious Jews or Israeli army officers when boarding a targeted bus.

Another popular device consists of a belt with pouches for six to eight sticks of dynamite; shoulder straps help support the weight of the belt. This device requires a detonator with a control switch placed inside the trouser leg. Here, too, the bomber sets the bomb off from inside the pocket.

No one is sure from where the general orders about timing for the bombings come. Intelligence reports from the region indicate that they are most likely given by Hamas leaders based in Jordan, Syria, Sudan, and the United States. Authorities are sure, however, that local Hamas leaders control the details of the specific attacks. The different actors within the suicide support team have no knowledge of each other. Each does a specific job, and they know that they have accomplished the act when the bomb goes off.

Beyond their mission to martyrdom and salvation, suicide bombers also intend to derail the peace process between Israel and the Palestinians. Their ultimate goal is the destruction of the state of Israel. In its place they would have an Islamic state that makes no distinction between religious and secular law; in Islam, religion and the state are one. It is often said that the distinction between what is Caesar's and what is God's is alien to Islam.

Conclusion

The use of suicidal terrorism in Israel today corroborates the widely appreciated need to make fundamental changes in prevailing social and economic relationships or political structures if terrorism is to be brought to an end. This is true in Israel as it is in Northern Ireland, and as it was in the three Muslim communities on the Indian Ocean. Neither British, Dutch, French, nor Spanish authorities succeeded in preventing suicidal attacks by implementing stringent police techniques or undertaking punitive military actions.

Military retribution will not change the beliefs of Abdel-Latif

Ayyash, the 58-year-old farmer and father of "the Engineer" who said, upon hearing of his son's assassination, "If he is dead, then God bless his soul. If he has acquired martyrdom, then congratulations."[23] Too many parents of suicide bombers react like Mrs. Abu Wanda, the mother of the 18-year-old suicide bomber Majdi Abu Warda, who ignited a satchel packed with TNT on a Jerusalem bus killing himself and 25 others. Upon hearing of her son's deed, she said, "He seemed normal. There was just nothing, and we never sensed he had such feelings. But from a religious point of view we have to accept he is a martyr and thank God ."[24]

It is difficult for Israelis and their supporters, who are the targets of suicide attacks, to convince themselves that they should understand why Mrs. Warda supports suicidal terrorism. Equally difficult for Israelis to understand is why Sayed Abu Musamah, the editor of the Hamas newspaper *Al-Wantan,* writes that "the highest form of courage" is suicide bombings against Israeli targets.[25] Probably the most difficult of all to comprehend is that no cleric in the West Bank and Gaza Strip has issued a *fatwa,* a religious decree, denouncing suicidal terrorism. "It would be suicidal in itself," admits a senior official of Jerusalem's Waqf, the Holy City's Islamic religious authority.[26]

"The life of this world is just a game and accumulation of possessions and children," wrote Hisham Hamad, a suicide bomber from the Palestinian Islamic Jihad who killed three Israeli soldiers in the Gaza Strip in November 1994. "What God has is better for me than all this."[27] These are the beliefs and actions that will not be changed by force; understanding why this is so is the first step in solving the problem of suicidal terrorism.

Notes

1. Islamic Jihad is another name for Hizbollah (Party of God). Formed in Lebanon, Islamic Jihad is dedicated to the creation of an Iranian style Islamic republic in Lebanon and the removal of all non-Islamic influences from the area. This Shiia group is not to be confused with the Palestinian based Islamic Jihad that grew out of the 1970s fundamentalist Muslim Brotherhood. Palestinian Islamic Jihad, numbering under a few hundred, devotes much of its energy to suicide missions inside Israel.

2. The US Department of State reports that less than nine percent of terrorist bombing victims from 1977 to 1983 were terrorist bombers. Those terrorist deaths that did occur were largely thought to be the result of accidental explosions, rather than

deliberate suicidal missions. See US Department of State, *Terrorist Bombings* (Washington, DC: Office for Combating Terrorism, 1983). For a view that the notion of Islamic terrorism, especially suicidal terrorists, is largely an invention of various Western experts, see M. Jansen, "At War with Islam," *Toward Freedom* (April/May 1993).

3. S. F. Dale, "Religious Suicide in Islamic Asia: Anticolonial Terrorism in India, Indonesia, and the Philippines," *Journal of Conflict Resolution* 3 (March 1988):38-39.

4. Suicidal terrorism may be more common than believed. See M. Hazani, "Sacrificial Immortality: Toward a Theory of Suicidal Terrorism and Related Phenomena," in L. B. Boyer, R. M. Boyer, and S. M. Sonnenberg (eds.), *The Psychoanalytic Study of Society: Volume 18* (Hillsdale, NJ: The Analytic Press, 1993), pp. 415-442.

5. On February 25, 1996 (6:42 AM), a suicide bomber destroyed an Egged bus in Jerusalem (24 dead); on February 25, 1996 (7:40 AM), a suicide bomber targets a hitchhiking post outside coastal Ashkelon (2 dead); on March 3, 1996 (6:25 AM), a suicide bomber again strikes the Jerusalem bus route targeted eight days earlier (19 dead); and on March 4, 1996 (4:00 PM), a suicide bomber blows himself up if front of an Automatic Teller Machine in Tel Aviv's Dizengoff Center (14 dead).

6. For an analysis of the practice of religious suicide, see Dale, pp. 37-59, and A. H. Sobley, "Religious Terrorists: What They Aren't Going to Tell Us," *Terrorism* 12 (1990):240-260.

7. M. Taylor and H. Ryan, "Fanaticism, Political Suicide and Terrorism," *Terrorism* 11(1989):92.

8. L. Beyer, "Can Peace Survive," *Time* (6 February 1995), p. 32.

9. The centrality of the passion motive in Islam is the central thesis in the work of Fazlur Rahman. See *Islam,* 2nd ed. (Chicago, IL: University of Chicago Press, 1979).

10. In Iran, this was the Ayatollah Khomeini, who was also the head of state. Those to be honored by martyrdom were chosen through his representatives, the mullahs. Given that there was no distinction between religion and state in the Iran of Khomeini, what amounts to a form of religious devotion becomes an instrument of state policy.

11. D. C. Rapoport, "Fear and Trembling: Terrorism in Three Religious Traditions," *American Political Science Review* 78 (September 1984):665. Muslims are not alone in the systematic use of suicide to further political ends, although for the moment, they might have captured the public's attention. The Japanese have a long tradition of employing suicide in a range of different situations, including warfare. Of more current vintage are the Tamil Tiger rebels (Hindus), whose fight for an independent homeland in Sri Lanka has claimed nearly 40,000 people since 1984. The Tamil Tigers have effectively used suicidal terrorists to further their cause. On February 1, 1996, a terrorist drove his truck, which was loaded with between 110 and 220 pounds of explosives, into the 10-story Central Bank in Columbo, Sri Lanka, killing himself and 52 others, and injuring 1,400 people.

12. A. Taheri, *Holy Terror: The Inside Story of Islamic Terrorism* (London: Century Hutchinson, 1987).

13. The Al Fawwar refugee camp in the West Bank (pop. 6,000) is the home base for many suicide bombers. Palestinian students are recruited outside of the territories as well. The Beirut daily *Al-Diyar* reports that a group of 60 Palestinian

youths between the ages of 12 and 17 are completing suicide training in the Ein al-Hilweh refugee camp in Lebanon. *The Jerusalem Report* (18 May 1995), p. 11.

14. Editorial, "The Hamas New Era," *The Jerusalem Post (*30 December 1995), p. 10.

15. The Palestinian Islamic Jihad, like Hamas, grew out of the Muslim Brotherhood. After its founder Fathi Shikaki was assassinated in 1995, Ramadan Abdullah Shallah, an adjunct professor in Florida, was named its leader. Numbering only a few hundred, Palestinian Jihad devotes much of its energy to suicide attacks against Israelis.

16. For the story of a 15-year-old Gaza boy who turned down martyrdom, see "Heaven Can Wait," *The Jerusalem Report* (6 April 1995), pp. 24-125.

17. J. Bartholet, "A Guaranteed Trip to Heaven," *Newsweek* (24 April 1995), p. 42.

18. Ayyash was behind 77 deaths and the wounding of more than 300. Israeli authorities believe Ayyash personally built the bombs that killed 35 people and also trained another bomb-maker, whose work claimed 10 more victims. Israeli officials say Ayyash oversaw much of the logistics of the attacks, including deciding their time and location.

19. N. MacFarquhar, "Blow for Blow: Israelis Demolish Bomb Maker's Family Home," *New York Times* (15 March 1996), p. A9.

20. "Suicide Bombers Kill 24, Wound 80," *The Jerusalem Post* (2 March 1996), p. l.

21. L. Beyer, "Death Ends Its Holiday," *Time* (4 September 1995), p. 40.

22. There is scientific evidence that suggests that props similar to baseball cards may generate imitative behavior in other teenagers. See M. S. Gould and D. Shaffer, "The Impact of Suicide in Television Movies," *The New England Journal of Medicine* 315 (11 September 1986): 690-694, and D. P. Phillips, "The Impact of Fictional Television Stories on U.S. Adult Fatalities: New Evidence on the Effect of the Mass Media on Violence," *American Journal of Sociology* 87(1982): 1340-1359.

23. N. Goldberg, "Foe of Israel Killed," *Newsday* (6 January 1996), p. A10.

24. N. MacFarquhar, "Portrait of a Suicide Bomber: Devout, Apolitical and Angry," *New York Times* (18 March 1996), p. A8.

25. Bartholet, p. 42.

26. "And Which Face Now?" *U.S. News & World Report* (18 March 1996), p. 47.

27. MacFarquhar, p. A8.

Terrorist on Trial: The Context of Political Crime

Jerrold M. Post

Abstract: *Could a Palestinian who committed a terrorist act in which more than 50 innocent men, women, and children died be judged sane? Making sense to a jury how such a terrorist could be a sane individual was the task of the author, who served as expert for the U.S. Department of Justice. When political terrorists stand trial for their violent acts, the political context inevitably plays a major role. The subject was socialized to violence in the refugee camps, where he was inspired to be a soldier in the revolution in order to reclaim his family lands. This article describes his trial in federal court for skyjacking an Egyptian airliner. The defense portrayed the traumas of the Palestinian people and of the defendant at the hands of the Israelis, offering a not guilty by reason of insanity defense on the basis of posttraumatic stress disorder. Nationalist-separatist terrorism, represented by the defendant, is particularly intractable because of the generational transmission of hatred and revenge. The generational transmission of hatred exemplified by this terrorist's life argues for the continuation of Palestinian/Israeli hatred and perpetuation of the violent struggle.*

In the turbulent Middle East, the psychopolitics of hatred flourishes, as violence begets counterviolence. The landscape is pockmarked with the craters of terrorist bombs. There is a widespread assumption in the lay community that groups and individuals who kill innocent victims to accomplish their political goals must be crazed fanatics. Surely no psychologically "normal" individual could perpetrate wanton violence against women and children.

In fact, those of us who have studied terrorist psychology have concluded that most terrorists are normal in the sense of not suffering from Axis I disorders. Indeed, terrorist groups exclude mentally unstable individuals, for they pose a severe security risk. However, conclusions concerning terrorist psychology generally are drawn from secondary and tertiary sources. Belonging to closed clandestine groups, fleeing from the law, terrorists are not readily available for interview.

When the rare occasion to interview a terrorist in depth presents itself, it offers a unique opportunity to gain insights on the mind of a terrorist. I had such an opportunity in the spring of 1996 in connection with the trial in federal district court of Omar Rezaq for the federal crime of skyjacking. It was Rezaq, a member of the Abu Nidal group, who played a central role in seizing the EgyptAir plane that was forced down in Malta in 1985. Rezaq shot five hostages, two Israeli women and three Americans, before the botched special weapons attack team (SWAT) offensive by Egyptian forces, which led to 50 plus casualties. Convicted of murder in a Maltese court, after seven years Rezaq was given amnesty and released. Subsequently, however, he was arrested by FBI agents for the crime of skyjacking.

The defense, with the assistance of a forensic psychologist who had testified in the Menendez brothers' case, developed a creative theory. They acknowledged Rezaq's direct and indirect role in the carnage that resulted but claimed that, as a consequence of the multiple traumas the Palestinian people had incurred at the hands of the Israelis, the defendant was suffering from posttraumatic stress disorder and accordingly did not appreciate the wrongfulness of his act. I was asked by the Department of Justice to participate in the case as a psychiatrist expert in the psychology of terrorism. The other prosecution experts would demonstrate that Rezaq was legally sane, but it was my task to provide a sense-making explanation for the jury of how an individual who was sane could commit such a bloody atrocity.

Terrorist Psychologies

Individual Psychology

Initial efforts to comprehend terrorist psychology were concentrated on elucidating the psychology of individual terrorists. These research efforts were seriously compromised by the lack of a research population available for systematic study, including clinical interviewing and psychological testing. As a result, the study of individual terrorist psychology has tended to be inductive rather than deductive, generalizing from individual anecdotes, memoirs, or biographical accounts. An interesting effort to get at terrorist psychology through their own words was that of Cordes,[1] who systematically content-analyzed terrorist statements and writings. Her work does not illuminate individual psychology, however, but rather the degree to which individuals became captive to group rhetoric and group psychology.

Indeed, the most striking aspect of these collective efforts to decode "the mind of the terrorist" was that they did not in fact identify a unique terrorist psychology. A wide range of psychologies—from entirely normal to severe personality disorders—has been found in individual terrorists. For the most part, extremely psychiatrically disturbed individuals were not involved in carrying out terrorist acts. Just as mentally unstable individuals pose a security threat to military units, so too do such individuals pose a security threat to terrorist groups and organizations and therefore tend to be excluded from their ranks. In the words of the noted terrorist scholar Martha Crenshaw, commenting on terrorist psychology, it is critical to combat the "stereotypes of 'terrorists' as irrational fanatics. . . .The outstanding characteristic of terrorists is their normality."[2]

While no one personality type, psychological pattern, or trait emerged from these studies, an impression emerged that two personality types were disproportionately represented among terrorists, especially among terrorist group leaders: Individuals with narcissistic/sociopathic features and angry paranoids.[3] Narcissistic/sociopathic individuals tend to be restless and action oriented, with low frustration tolerance. These self-oriented individuals suffer from both impaired consciences and an impaired capacity to empathize with the pain and suffering of others. Angry paranoids tend to externalize their problems, idealizing the "in group" and demonizing the "out group." Such individuals, who often suffer from a lack of personal, educational, and professional success, seek an outside enemy to blame for their problems. The externalizing rhetoric of the terrorist group—"It's not us, it's them; they are responsible for our problems"—provides a psychologically satisfying explanation for what has gone wrong in their lives. It is therefore not only not immoral, it becomes a moral imperative to strike out at "them," to remove the source of the problems.

These psychological defense mechanisms contribute to the striking uniformity of terrorists' rhetorical style and psycho-logic. Polarizing and absolutist, it is a rhetoric of freedom fighters against an evil establishment, of the "brothers of light" against the "brothers of darkness." Psychologically vulnerable personalities find such rhetoric extremely attractive. This analysis suggests that individuals become terrorists not to achieve instrumental (e.g., political, economic) goals but rather to rationalize violent acts that they are compelled to commit. The groups to which these emotionally susceptible individuals belong accordingly are characterized by especially powerful group dynamics. For these individuals, the act of joining a terrorist group represents an attempt to consolidate a fragmented psychological identify, and most importantly, to belong.

Group Dynamics

The author has observed elsewhere that group and organizational psychology rather than individual psychopathology powerfully explains terrorist behavior and the extremities to which otherwise normal individuals can go in pursuit of their group causes.[4,5] As demonstrated in Fig. 1, there is a broad spectrum of terrorisms, and each of these types has its own characteristic psychology. As demonstrated in Fig. 2, generational issues are particularly prominent for two types of terrorism, social-revolutionary terrorism and nationalist-separatist terrorism.[6]

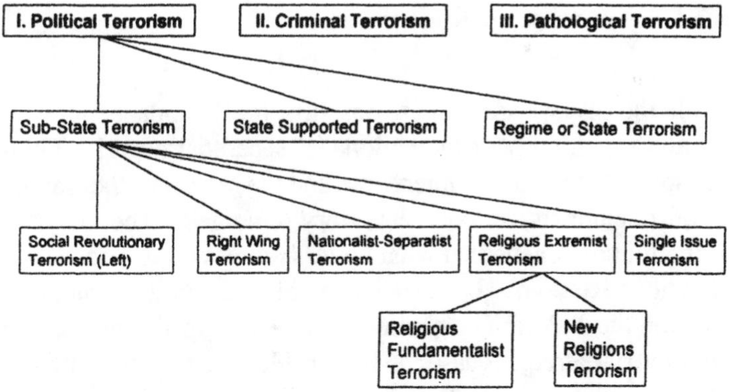

Figure 1. New typology of terrorism.

In many ways, these psychologies are polar opposites. The social-revolutionary terrorist is striking out against the generation of his parents who are loyal to the regime. His acts of terrorism are acts of revenge for hurts, real and imagined. A member of the German terrorist group, Red Army Faction, declared, "These are the corrupt old men who gave us Auschwitz and Hiroshima."[7] In contrast, the nationalist-separatist terrorist is loyal to parents who are disloyal to the regime. He is carrying on the mission of his parents and grandparents who were damaged by the regime and are dissident to the regime.

	Parents' Relationship to Regime	
Youths' Relationship to Parents	Loyal	Disloyal Damaged Dissident
Loyal	—	*National Separatist Terrorism*
Disloyal	*Social Revolutionary Terrorism*	—

Figure 2. Generational pathways to terrorism

In the case we are about to describe, the defendant epitomized the life and psychology of the nationalist-separatist terrorist. On the basis of some eight hours of interviews and the review of thousands of pages of documents, a coherent story emerged. The defendant assuredly did not believe that what he was doing was wrong, because from boyhood Rezaq had been socialized to be a heroic revolutionary fighting for the Palestinian nation. Demonstrating the generational transmission of hatred, his case can be considered emblematic of many from the ranks of ethnic/nationalist terrorist groups, from Northern Ireland to Palestine, from Armenia to the Basque region of Spain.

The Omar Rezaq Case

Social History

The third child of a family of six, Omar Rezaq was born in 1958 in Jordan but as a young boy moved to a village on the West Bank. His father worked as a nurse for the Jordanian military. His mother was from Jaffa originally, but after the 1948 Arab-Israeli war she left for the West Bank where she and her family lived in refugee camps. The mother's displacement from her ancestral home by Israel was an event of crucial importance, which became a key element in the family legend.

Rezaq spent his childhood in the West Bank village where his grandfather was a farmer. As a career military nurse, his father was often away from home. Rezaq described his boyhood in the village as pleasant; they lived in their own home, with no economic problems, no worries about food or money.

This relatively pleasant existence changed abruptly in the aftermath of the 1967 Arab-Israeli war (the subject was 8 years old). His father, serving with the Jordanian military, had already left in anticipation of the arrival of the Israeli army. After two months, his mother decided to follow his father. According to Rezaq, "From this time, everything changed."

Jordan was crowded with refugees. They moved into crowded circumstances, initially with their cousin, then into a small home of their own. The father was a strict, harsh man, who when he was at home, on leave from the military, would punish his son with a belt or stick for minor infractions. The subject felt closer to his mother, a quiet and gentle woman, who took responsibility for the family. She would often discuss her life and how it had changed in 1948 when her family had to leave Jaffa, so this was the second time the Israelis had forced her from her home.

After staying in Amman, Jordan for one year, the family moved to the refugee camp Talibiya, some 25 to 35 kilometers outside of Amman. The living circumstances there were very difficult, with the whole family crowded into two rooms, with no bathroom or kitchen and little privacy. Food was supplied by the United Nations (UN). There was little money.

Indoctrination in Palestinian Nationalism And Recruitment into the Movement

In 1968, the battle of Karameh occurred, in which Yasir Arafat led a group of Palestinian guerrillas who fought a 12-hour battle against a superior Israeli force, galvanizing the previously dispirited Palestinian population. The spirit of the revolution was everywhere, especially in the camps, and the Palestine Liberation Organization (PLO) became a rallying point. In Rezaq's words, "The revolution was the only hope."

With his sister and brother now gone, Rezaq was the man of the family. In the UN school, where Rezaq was an average student, he was rewarded for learning Palestinian songs. He had Palestinian teachers who would propagandize the students, focusing their resentment for the difficult living circumstances on Israel and instilling Palestinian nationalism. Feelings of hatred were aimed at Israel. As young teenagers, Rezaq (now 12) and his friends went to the youth camp two to three hours a day, where they received some political indoctrination and began military training (learning how to clean and handle guns, jump barriers, etc.). Rezaq's father did not join the revolution and was opposed to Rezaq's becoming involved. If he saw his son go to the camp, the father beat him.

The subject was the only one in his family to join the revolution. His Palestinian teacher, who was in the Palestinian Liberation Organization (PLO) and was a member of Al Fatah, the mainline Palestinian revolutionary group founded by Yasir Arafat, was a model for him. This juxtaposition of the harsh father who was opposed to the revolution with the positive model of the Palestinian teacher who was a member of Fatah intensified young Rezaq's attraction to joining the revolution, and he began to develop an identity as a soldier for the Palestinian cause.

After finishing intermediate school, he went on to technical school under UN auspices. There were branches of the revolution in this school; each group tried to recruit the new students. Rezaq became more deeply involved in politics. He was taught that the only way to get back his country was if the PLO would fight against Israel, and he was increasingly determined to join that fight. Two years of obligatory service in the Jordanian army were required. In 1977, at age 19, he was sent to a camp near Iraq for military training. There, the Palestinians were treated as second-class citizens.

Joins the Revolution and Becomes Indoctrinated in Anti-Zionist, Anti-U.S. Views

After only three months in the Jordanian army, Rezaq deserted and joined Fatah. He went to a military camp where he was given a military uniform and was trained in the use of machine guns, pistols, and hand grenades. He also received intense political indoctrination. This was the first time he heard of Zionism.

Now he was energized, fully committed, at last in a fighting revolutionary organization. He wanted "to work, wanted to fight. There was only one way to regain Palestine and that was to fight Israel to regain all of Palestine, from the sea to the river."

In 1978, fighting in Lebanon broke out between the PLO and Israel. The camp in which Rezaq was training sent 100 people to join the fight in south Lebanon against Israel. Rezaq was there for two months, close to the action. There was fighting every day, and he felt part of the revolution. After returning to base camp and being away from the scene of action, Rezaq became restless and resigned from the Fatah branch. Interrogated as to why he was leaving, he replied that he was bored and had nothing to do, that he had joined Fatah to fight and was not fighting.

He moved from terrorist group to terrorist group, initially enthused, then disillusioned, with each group he joined more militant than the preceding. When he was next involved in guerrilla action, he had pride in what he was doing as a soldier for the revolution. "I started dreaming that one day we will have a country, have an identity, [be] our own citizens." After attacking an Israeli patrol, his morale took a major boost. "This was for my country." He felt this was the right way, the path for him to follow. He felt a sense of excitement in the danger.

Rezaq was still with the PLO in Lebanon in 1980, the year the "explosive war" occurred, with the Phalangists and Israel against the Palestinians and other Lebanese. There were bombs and explosions everywhere, every day, bombs in cars and in supermarkets. In a close call, Rezaq almost lost his life in a car bomb explosion that destroyed a cafeteria he had just left. Had he remained, he realized, he would have died. He had never thought of his own death before. He began to have dreams about his death, started getting suspicious, feeling on guard, while before he had not cared.

The 1982 Israel Invasion of Lebanon and Disillusionment with the PLO

When Israel invaded Lebanon in 1982 and penetrated deeply into Lebanon, there was very little resistance by the PLO. Rezaq found himself wondering about the revolution, which had lost to the Israelis so easily. He had been ready to fight for two years, and when the opportunity came, the movement to which he had committed himself had not fought in any meaningful way. It was a disillusioning experience.

As a result of U.S.-brokered negotiations, Arafat and the PLO were to leave Lebanon. Disillusioned with Arafat and the mainstream PLO, Rezaq decided to stay on in Lebanon to fight. He first joined the militant Fatah Intifada group, but finding it insufficiently militant, he ultimately made his way to the most violent of the Palestinian terrorist groups, the Abu Nidal group.

After intense training, he was given an important mission. He was told the mission was to hijack an airliner to obtain the release of anti-government Egyptians in prison in Egypt. He felt good about the mission. He now had a purpose. This is what he had been preparing for since boyhood. On the night before the mission, he did not sleep well. He described himself as being on edge, keyed up. It was the feeling of the soldier on the eve of battle.

The Operation

In describing the operation, Rezaq related the entire episode in a cool, matter of fact manner—logical, detailed, calm, not emotionally overwrought—the professional military man reporting on a military action.

After the terrorists took over the plane in accordance with the plan, they forced it down in Malta to refuel before the final leg of its journey. Control tower personnel said they would not provide petrol until the hostages were released. Rezaq informed the control tower that they (the terrorists) would not release the hostages until the plane was refueled. Malta control refused, insisting that the hijackers release all of the hostages or there would be no petrol.

He remembered the mission instructions concerning the Israelis and Americans. If there were Israelis in the plane, he was told he must kill them directly, for they were enemies of Palestine. Since America supported Israel, Americans should then be used as leverage and should be killed if no petrol was provided. Rezaq now went through the passports, and found the passports of two Israelis and three Americans. Having given an ultimatum to the control tower that he would begin killing hostages unless they refueled the plane, when they did not provide petrol, Rezaq told the stewardess to bring him an Israeli. It was a woman. He had her taken to the staircase where he shot her in the head.

When I asked him about his emotional state at the time of the killings, and how he reacted to killing a person at close range, he looked at me with perplexity and responded as if it should be self-evident that it was what he had been instructed to do, it was the plan for the mission. As to the impact of killing a woman, he responded that there was no difference. He had been told that both Israeli men and women served in the army, so both were the enemy.

Having demonstrated that they should take him seriously, Rezaq gave a second ultimatum. By now he was hungry, so he had some lunch. The calm, matter of fact manner in which he described being hungry and eating his lunch was indistinguishable from the manner in which he described shooting the Israeli woman in the head. In the same matter of fact way, he then told of shooting the second Israeli woman in the head. The Maltese authorities still had not provided petrol, so Rezaq then ordered the air crew to bring him the Americans. The first American was shot. Because there was still no petrol, he had them bring the second American whom he then shot. The storming of the plane followed.

Formulation

Like many of his generation, the developmental experiences of Omar Rezaq shaped his attraction to the path of terrorism, defined in his mind as "joining the revolution." The psychological soil had already been prepared by his mother's recounting of their family's expulsion and uprooting from Jaffa in 1948; at age 9, Rezaq and his family moved into the refugee camp.

The father's harsh discipline (not unusual in the cultural setting, according to the subject) did leave Rezaq, in early adolescence, ripe to idolize an alternative model, which he found in his Palestinian teacher. Like many young men of his generation in the camps, Rezaq was psychologically lost, with no clear path before him. His teachers both focused his hatred against Israel as the cause of his people's problems and charted a valued identity, fighting for the revolution.

Throughout his life, Rezaq demonstrated a restless, action-oriented temperament. Zealous to fight and impatient for action, on occasion after occasion Rezaq became disillusioned with the leadership, leaving one organization to join another, seeking to find a group in which he could carry out his role as a fighter for the Palestinian cause. He moved progressively from the Jordanian army to the main-line Fatah, to the rejectionist front group Fatah Intifada, to the extremely violent Abu Nidal group.

The near miss when the cafeteria was destroyed by a car bomb during the "explosive war" in Lebanon (1980-1981) apparently was extremely traumatic for Rezaq, and in the aftermath he experienced symptoms of posttraumatic stress disorder—insomnia, recurrent dreams about his death, depression, feelings of suspiciousness and being on guard, avoidance of public places, and a feeling that his life would be foreshortened by violence. These symptoms subsided over the subsequent years.

When Rezaq was selected for the special mission, it was an opportunity to carry out an action as a soldier for the revolution. The keyed up feeling on the eve of the action was that of the soldier on the eve of battle. Rezaq was professional in the manner in which he carried out the instructions, deliberate and under control. In his own words, he was "normal" and his "true self was under control." He knew exactly what he was doing when he shot the Israeli women and the Americans. He was executing the operational plan according to instructions, a soldier carrying out orders, killing the enemy.

Like his fellow terrorists, he believed that his actions were justified, were not wrongful but were righteous acts in the service of the Palestinian revolution. He had been socialized to blame all of his and his people's difficulties on the enemy and that violent actions against the enemy were justified. He rationalized that the Israeli injustices against the Palestinian people justified his violent acts.

When one has been nursed on the mother's milk of hatred and bitterness, the need for vengeance is bred in the bone. In ethnic/nationalist conflicts, hatred has been transmitted generationally, and the psychopolitics of hatred are deeply rooted.

The Trial

Any trial is a contest of dueling frames of reference, of alternate explanations. The defense in effect put Israel on trial. They were aided in their endeavor by a remarkably one-sided portrayal of the Arab-Israeli struggle by a Middle East scholar, who depicted the Palestinian people as victims of Israeli aggression, neglecting to mention the bloody history of aggression visited upon Israel by Palestinian terrorists and in the three Arab-Israeli wars. From the collective trauma of the Palestinian people, it was but a small further step to the specific traumatization of the defendant. Rezaq was, they contended, suffering from posttraumatic stress disorder, and accordingly did not appreciate the wrongfulness of his act. The jury, however, had not been provided with a sensemaking alternative frame of reference, an alternate explanation. How could a sane man wreak such carnage?

The following was the alternate sense-making explanation provided to the jury. Like thousands of his generation, Rezaq did indeed experience many traumas. In 1968 he experienced the hardships of life in the refugee camps, having been forced out of the family home on the West Bank. At that time he was told by his mother of her having lost her home in 1948. This was in many ways a classic case of generational nationalist-separatist terrorism, carrying on the family cause, seeking revenge for damage done to parents and grandparents. When Rezaq was a preadolescent in the refugee camp schools, the camps were aflame with revolutionary enthusiasm after Arafat's success in 1968 at Karamah. Rezaq was inspired by his Palestinian teacher, who was a member of the PLO. Like thousands of his generation, Palestinian radicals identified for him the heroic career path of joining the revolution, fighting for Palestine. As Rezaq moved along this path, his identity was consolidated—his role was that of a soldier for the cause. His besieged society had rewarded violence against the identified Israeli enemy, making it a permanent part of personality.

This description of Rezaq's pathway into terrorism was the alternate explanation that was provided. He did indeed believe what he was doing was right, but this belief was not as a consequence of severe mental disease or defect but a consequence of his education, socialization, training, inspiration by his Palestinian teachers and role models. They provided him with a sense-making explanation of what was wrong and who was responsible, and therefore to take violent action against those whom he had been taught were responsible—

Israelis and their supporters, the Americans—was justified and redemptive. The issue of rebutting Rezaq's alleged mental illness was important. The government and its forensic psychiatrists had been quite effective in countering the defense assertions in support of not guilty by reason of insanity, demonstrating that the defendant was fully aware of the legal consequences of his act. The findings in my own examination augmented their findings. His demeanor in the cockpit was consistent with that of a soldier on a mission: well-trained, cool, and professional. When he related the incidents to me, it was in the manner of a military after-action report or briefing. He was quite matter of fact when he described shooting the Israeli women, explaining with no fluctuation of emotion that because Israeli women served in the military, they too were the enemy and should be killed. In describing events, he told of having lunch in the same manner in which he described declaring the ultimatums and killing the hostages. Rezaq clearly knew that this action was a crime. The discussion of why the terrorists wore ski masks was quite revealing. He indicated to me that the purpose of the mask was so that if he were successful he would not be recognized and pursued for his role in hijacking. If he were recognized, people would go the police and he would be caught and sent to jail. Similar reasons were given for all of the security precautions. The defense psychiatrist asserted that when Rezaq was in the cockpit, he was less carrying out a hijacking than reconstructing the boundaries of his mind. But he had made clear that he was acutely aware when he was in the cockpit that he was carrying out a hijacking. He knew this fact clearly. He was cool, collected, professional, a soldier carrying out a mission, which was confirmed by analysis of the cockpit tapes and by witness reports.

It was important to augment technical forensic testimony by conveying the understanding that serious psychiatric illness is incompatible with the role of the terrorist. Political terrorists are not seriously psychiatrically ill. A psychiatrically disturbed, mentally unstable terrorist is a major security risk, just as a military unit cannot tolerate an emotionally unstable soldier because he would pose a danger to the unit. Rezaq was in the Abu Nidal Organization (ANO) for two years, in training and being observed. ANO more than other groups was especially careful about their members and monitored their performance closely in training. In analyzing a 1994 terrorist attack in the United States, which was attributed to the ANO, terrorist experts doubted that it was an ANO operation because it was executed so unprofessionally. On the basis of Rezaq's extensive period in camp and in training, he was selected for this important mission and was named number two, indicating the ANO leadership's belief in his stability and professionalism. He confirmed their judgment. His demeanor in the cockpit was that of a cool professional carrying out a mission.

Moreover, during a period of depression, prior to the mission, Rezaq saw a psychiatrist who was a member of the PLO. He was told that his reactions were normal and was encouraged to pursue his role as a fighter for the revolution. Had he been seriously disturbed, this would have been immediately evident to the psychiatrist, who would have diagnosed his psychotic condition and told the organization that he should not go on a mission.

It was important to convey to the jury that the ANO is the bloodiest and most professional of terrorist organizations, with operations in more than 20 countries and having killed or injured more than 900 people. Abu Nidal was the architect of the massacres at the Rome and Vienna airports and was responsible for shooting the Israeli ambassador to Great Britain, which was the final trigger in the Israeli invasion of Lebanon, after a long campaign of terrorism against Israel by terrorist groups operating out of Lebanon. Although Rezaq may not have known who the Abu Nidal group or the Fatah Revolutionary Council were when he first joined the organization, by the time he rejoined the ANO he surely knew their reputation. He moved progressively from violent group to ever more violent group. When Arafat left Lebanon, this was a crucial turning point for young Rezaq and the Palestinian movement. Rezaq was not abandoned. He chose to stay behind to fight, joining Abu Musa—who saw Arafat as a traitor to the cause—and his 12,000 fighters. When Rezaq subsequently became disappointed in Abu Musa, he chose to join the bloodiest terrorist of them all, Abu Nidal.

Individuals with posttraumatic stress disorder (PTSD) tend to avoid circumstances resembling that which occasioned the original trauma. Not only did Rezaq not seek to avoid violent circumstances, such as the bombing identified by the defense as precipitating his PTSD, but he sought out ever more violent circumstances. Indeed, when a group was insufficiently violent, he left them for a more violent group, finally reaching the very acme of violence in the Abu Nidal organization. As he proudly declaimed, "I live to fight, and only feel alive when I am fighting," not the utterance of an individual suffering from PTSD. Rezaq by history may well have had some of the symptoms of PTSD, but he assuredly was not in a dissociated flashback state when he carried out the hijacking.

Did Rezaq believe that what he did was wrong? Assuredly not. He had rationalized, justified that what he was doing was in the service of Palestine. He believed it was the right thing to do; but this belief was not a consequence of mental illness. It was the consequence of his entire life experience, of being inspired and trained to be a soldier for the cause. His beliefs and activism were common to thousands of his peers; but thousands of his countrymen who had suffered similar traumas did not choose to participate in killing innocent victims for the cause, choosing the path of political activism instead. A defense psychologist asserted Rezaq would not have carried out the hijacking if he had not been suffering from PTSD. Psychologically Rezaq was of the same mindset as the radical Palestinian terrorists, who were also socialized to the path of violent terrorism. His decision to carry out the hijacking was not a consequence of PTSD.

When Rezaq was selected for the hijacking mission, it was the culmination of a dream. Rezaq had been taught to hate all Israelis and their American sponsors. He was taught to blame all of the difficulties in his life on the Israelis, whom he saw as enemies in the war in which he was a heroic soldier. When he carried out the hijacking, it was the very pinnacle of his life, a dream come true. But the dream turned into a nightmare, with tragic consequences. More than 50 people lost their lives in the hijacking and SWAT team attack. Rezaq is now serving a life sentence in federal prison.

The generational transmission of hatred exemplified by this terrorist's life argues for the continuation of Palestinian/Israeli hatred and perpetuation of the violent struggle. While there is guarded optimism concerning the Middle East peace process, the signatures of Yasir Arafat and Ehud Barak to a comprehensive peace agreement will not signal the end of the fear and hatred that has been passed from generation to generation.

References

1. Cordes B: Terrorists in their own words, in Contemporary Research on Terrorism. Edited by Wilkinson P, Stewart AM. Aberdeen: Aberdeen University Press, 1987, pp 318-36

2. Crenshaw M: The logic of terrorism: terrorist behavior as a product of strategic choice, in Origins of Terrorism: Psychologies, Ideologies, Theologies, States of Mind. Edited by Reich W. Cambridge: Cambridge University Press, 1990, pp 7-24

3. Post JM: Terrorist psycho-logic: terrorist behavior as a product of psychological forces, in Origins of Terrorism: Psychologies, Ideologies, Theologies, States of Mind. Edited by Reich W. Cambridge: Cambridge University Press, 1990, pp 25-40

4. Post JM: Hostilité, conformité, fraternité: the group dynamics of terrorist behavior. Int J Group Psychother 36:211-24, 1986

5. Post JM: "It's us against them": the group dynamics of political terrorism. Terrorism 10:22-36, 1987

6. Post JM: Notes on a psychodynamic theory of terrorism. Terrorism 7:241-56, 1984

7. Baeyer-Kaette W, personal communication, 1982

The Mind of the Terrorist: Perspectives From Social Psychology

Bruce Hoffman

Abstract: *This article explores the psychosocial aspects of terrorism, including ideological and operational imperatives, future orientation, and resiliency within terrorist groups. The author also emphasizes the unswerving belief held by all terrorists in the efficacy of violence.*

Like Victorian-era cartographers who mapped from vast distances lands that they knew existed but had never seen, the study of terrorism is mostly conducted far removed from the actual human subjects of the analyst's scholarly attentions. In this respect, the terrorist mindset and the geographic interior of 19th-century Africa bear remarkable similarities: both equally diverse and seemingly impenetrable to their distant observers. The terrorists themselves, unfortunately, do little to facilitate this search to divine the nature, functions, and phenomena of their thinking and thought processes. Although they are loquacious and prolific as the authors of often lengthy, turgid, and overwrought communiques and ideologic manifestoes, most terrorists are notoriously reticent to talk or to write about themselves and especially their innermost thoughts and emotions.

What few terrorist memoirs have been published (e.g., Menachem Begin's *The Revolt*[1] and Bommi Baumann's *Terror or Love?*[2] or Abu Iyad's *My Home, My Land*[3] and Leila Khaled's *My People Shall Live*[4]) are considerably less informative about the authors themselves than about recounting, in excruciatingly detailed, self-serving or self-congratulatory prose, either the inequities or the injustices that originally drove them to terrorism, or the adversities over which they triumphed to champion themselves and their respective causes. Instead, the analyst must frequently draw inferences from observation and empirical evidence, from the study of terrorist trends and patterns, and from other research techniques such as psycholinguistic analysis of terrorist treatises to attempt to begin to understand why terrorists do what they do.

The Nexus of Ideologic and Operational Imperatives

Contrary to both popular belief and media depiction, most terrorism is neither crazed nor capricious. Terrorists use violence (or the threat of violence) because they believe that only through violence can their cause triumph and their longterm political aims be attained. Terrorists therefore plan their operations in a manner that will shock, impress, and intimidate, ensuring that their acts are sufficiently daring and violent to capture the attention of the media and, in turn, the attention of the public and the government. Thus, rather than being seen as indiscriminate or senseless, terrorism is actually a deliberate and planned application of violence.[5]

Terrorism is also a means to communicate a message. Although the aims and motivations of different types of terrorists—left-wing and right-wing, ethno-nationalist and religious, single issue and broadly utopian—may differ, they all want maximum publicity to be generated by their actions and therefore aim at intimidation and subjection to attain their objectives. Equally important, the terrorist act is conceived and executed in a manner that simultaneously reflects the terrorist group's particular aims and motivations, fits its resources and capabilities, and takes into account the "target audience" at whom the act is directed. The tactics and targets of various terrorist movements, as well as the weapons they favor, are therefore ineluctably shaped by a group's ideology, its internal organizational dynamics, the personalities of its key members, and a variety of internal and external stimuli.

In this respect, all terrorist groups seek targets that are lucrative from their point of view. As such, they employ tactics that are consonant with their overriding political aims. Whereas left-wing terrorists such as Germany's Red Army Faction (RAF) and Italy's Red Brigades (RB) have selectively kidnaped and assassinated persons whom they blamed for economic exploitation or political repression to attract publicity and promote a Marxist-Leninist revolution, terrorists motivated by a religious imperative have engaged in more indiscriminate acts of violence, waged against a far wider category of targets: encompassing not merely their declared enemies, but anyone who does not share their religious faith. Ethno-nationalists arguably fall somewhere in between. On the one hand, the violent campaigns waged by groups such as the Palestine Liberation Organization (PLO), the Irish Republican Army, (IRA), and the Basque separatist group, ETA (Freedom for the Basque Homeland), have frequently been more destructive and have caused far greater casualties than those of their left-wing counterparts. But, on the other hand, their violence has largely been restricted to a specifically defined "target set" (i.e., the members of a specific rival or dominant ethno-nationalist group).[6]

Perhaps the least consequential of all these terrorist group categories (in terms of both frequency of incidents and impact on public and governmental attitudes) has been the disparate collection of recycled Nazis, racist "political punk rockers," and other extreme right-wing elements who have emerged through the years in various Western countries. But even their sporadic and uncoordinated, seemingly mindless violence is neither completely random nor unthinkingly indiscriminate. Indeed, for all these categories, the point is less their innate differences than the fact that their tactical and targeting choices correspond to, and are determined by, their respective ideologies, attendant mechanisms of legitimization and justification, and, perhaps most critically, their relationship with the intended audience of their violent acts.

Living for the Future

All terrorists have one other trait in common: they live in the future, that distant—yet imperceptibly close—point in time when they will assuredly triumph over their enemies and attain the ultimate realization of their political destiny. For the religious groups, this future is divinely decreed and the terrorists themselves specifically anointed to achieve it. For secular terrorists, their eventual victory is as inexorable as it is predetermined. Indeed, the innate righteousness of their cause itself ensures success. "Our struggle will be long and arduous because the enemy is powerful, well organised, and well sustained from abroad," Leila Khaled wrote in her autobiography published 26 years ago. "We shall win because we represent the wave of the future . . . because mankind is on our side, and above all because we are determined to achieve victory."[4]

Comparatively small in number, limited in capabilities, isolated from society, and dwarfed by both the vast resources of their enemy and the enormity of their task, secular terrorists, accordingly, necessarily function in an inverted reality where the sought-after, ardently pursued future defines their existence, rather than the oppressive, angst-driven, and incomplete present. "You convince yourself that to reach this utopia," the Red Brigades' Adriana Faranda later recalled of the group's collective mindset, "it is necessary to pass through the destruction of society which prevents your ideas from being realized."[7] By ignoring the present and literally soldiering on despite hardship and adversity, terrorists are able to compensate for their abject weakness and thereby overcome the temporal apathy or hostility of a constituency whom they claim to represent. "We made calculations," Faranda's comrade-in-arms, Patrizio Peci, explained in his memoirs. "The most pessimistic thought that within twenty years the war would be won, some said within five, ten. All, however, thought that we were living through the most difficult moment, that gradually things would become easier. . . ."[8] The left-wing terrorists thus console themselves that the travails and isolation of life underground are but a mere transitory stage on the path to final victory.

The longevity of most modern terrorist groups, however, would suggest otherwise. Noted terrorism scholar David Rapoport, for example, estimates that the life expectancy of at least 90% of terrorist organizations is less than 1 year and that nearly half of those that make it that far cease to exist within a decade.[9] Thus, the optimistic clarion calls to battle issued by terrorist groups the world over in communiques, treatises, and other propaganda have a distinctly hollow ring given the grim, empirical reality of their organizational life cycles.

Hopes and Dreams

Some categories of terrorist groups admittedly have better chances of survival—and perhaps success—than others. Although religious movements such as the Assassins persisted for nearly two centuries and the Thugs remained active for more than 600 years, in modern times ethnonationalist terrorist groups typically have lasted the longest and have been the most successful. Al-Fatah, the Palestinian terrorist organization led by Yasir Arafat, for example, was founded in 1957. The PLO itself is now 34 years old. The Basque group ETA was established in 1959. The current iteration of the IRA, formally known as the Provisional Irish Republican Army, is nearly 30 years old and is itself the success of the older Official IRA that was founded nearly a century ago and that can, in turn, be traced back to the various Fenian revolutionary brotherhoods that had periodically surfaced since Wolfe Tone's rebellion in 1789.

However, except the immediate postwar era of massive decolonialization, success for ethnonationalist terrorist organizations has rarely involved the actual realization of their stated, long-term goals of either self-determination or nationhood. Rather, it has more often amounted to a string of key tactical victories that have sustained prolonged struggles and breathed new life into faltering, and, in some instances, geriatric, terrorist movements.

The resiliency of these groups is doubtless a product of the relative ease with which they are able to draw sustenance and support from an already existent constituency (e.g., their fellow ethno-nationalist brethren). By contrast, both left-wing and right-wing terrorist organizations must actively proselytize among the politically aware and radical, although often uncommitted, for recruits and support. Thus, they render themselves vulnerable to penetration and compromise.

The ethno-nationalists derive a further advantage from their historical longevity by being able to appeal to a collective revolutionary tradition and even at times a predisposition to rebellion. This ensures successive terrorist generations both a steady stream of recruits from their respective community's youth and a ready pool of sympathizers and supporters among their more nostalgic elders. Hence, these groups' unique ability to replenish their ranks from within already close, tightly knit communities means that even when an ongoing campaign shows signs of flagging, the mantle can be smoothly passed to a new generation. Abu Iyad, Arafat's intelligence chief, can therefore dismiss as mere ephemeral impediments the cul-de-sacs and roundabouts that have long plagued the Palestinian liberation movement. "[O]ur people will bring forth a new revolution," he wrote some 20 years ago. "They will engender a movement much more powerful than ours, better armed and thus more dangerous to the Zionists. . . . And one day, we will have a country."[3]

The ethno-nationalists' comparative success, however, may have as much to do with the clarity and tangibility of their envisioned future—the establishment (or reestablishment) of a national homeland from within some existing country—as with these other characteristics. The articulation of so concrete and comprehensible a goal is by far the most potent and persuasive rallying cry. It also makes victory appear both palpable and readily attainable, if, of course, prolonged and protracted. Few, therefore, would have doubted Martin McGuinness's 1977 pledge that the IRA would keep "blathering on until Brits leave"[10] or Danny Morrison's declaration 12 years later that only "when it is politically costly for the British to remain in Ireland, they'll go . . . it won't be triggered until a large number of British soldiers are killed and that's what's going to happen."[11]

Left-wing terrorist movements, by comparison, appear doubly disadvantaged. They lack not only the sizeable, existing pool of potential recruits available to most ethno-nationalist groups, but also a clear and well-defined vision of the future. Although their myriad denunciations of the evils of the militarist, capitalist state may be prolific and prodigious, little information is forthcoming about its envisioned successor. "That is the most difficult question for revolutionaries," Kozo Okamoto, the surviving member of the three-man IRA team that staged the 1972 Lod Airport massacre, replied when asked about the postrevolutionary society that his group sought to create. "We really do not know what it will be like."[12]

The RAF's Gudrun Ensslin similarly brushed aside all questions about the group's long-term aims. "As for the state of the future, the time after victory," she once said, "that is not our concern . . . we build the revolution, not the socialist model."[13] This inability to coherently, much less cogently, articulate their future plans possibly explains why the left-wing's terrorist campaigns have historically been the least effectual.

Indeed, all terrorists are driven by this burning impatience coupled with an unswerving belief in the efficacy of violence. The future that they look forward to is neither temporal nor born of the natural progression of mankind. Rather, it is contrived and shaped, forged and molded, and, ultimately, determined and achieved by violence. "What use was there in writing memoranda?," Begin rhetorically inquired to explain the Irgun's decision to resume its revolt in 1944.[1]

> What value in speeches? . . . . No, there was no other way. If we did not fight we should be destroyed. To fight was the only way to salvation.
>
> When Descartes said: "I think, therefore, I am," he uttered a very profound thought. But there are times in the history of peoples when thought alone does not prove their existence. . . .There are times when everything in you cries out: your very self respect as a human being lies in your resistance to evil.
>
> We fight, therefore we are! (p. 46)

Thirty years later, Leila Khaled similarly invoked the primacy of action over talk and bullets instead of words. "We must act, not just talk and memorize the arguments against Zionism," she counseled[4]; this view was echoed by Yoyes, an ETA terrorist who lost faith in the endless promises that "independence can be won by peaceful means. It's all a lie. . . .The only possibility we have of gaining our liberty is through violence."[14] As the neo-Nazi Ingo Hasselbach recalled of his own experience, "The time for legal work and patience was through. The only thing to do was to turn our *Kameradschaft* into a real terrorist organization."[15]

As such, all terrorists exist and function in hope of reaching this ultimate, inevitable, and triumphant end. For them, the future, rather than the present, defines their reality. Indeed, they can console themselves that it was only a decade ago that the then Prime Minister Thatcher said of the African National Congress, "Anyone who thinks it is going to run the government in South Africa is living in cloud-cuckoo land."[16] Exactly 10 years after Mrs. Thatcher's remark, Queen Elizabeth II greeted Nelson Mandela on his first official state visit to London.

References

1. Begin M. *The Revolt: Story of the Irgun.* Jerusalem: Steimatzky's Agency; 1977.

2. Baumann M. *Terror or Love? Bommi* Baumann's *Own Story of His Life* as a *West German Urban Guerrilla.* New York: Grove Press; 1979:19-20.

3. Iyad A. *My Home, My Land: A Narrative. of the Palestinian Struggle.* New York: New York Times Books; 1981.

4. Khaled L. *My People Shall Live: The Autobiography of a Revolutionary.* London: Hodder and Stoughton; 1973.

5. Jenkins BM. International terrorism: a new mode of conflict. In: Carlton D, Schaerf C, eds. *International Terrorism and World Security.* London: Croom Helm; 1975:16.

6. Merkl PH. Prologue. In: Merkl PH, ed. *Political Violence and Terror.* Berkeley CA: University of California Press; 1986:8.

7. Quoted in Jamieson A. *The Heart Attacked: Terrorism and Conflict in the Italian State;* London: Marion Boyars; 1989:271.

8. Peci *P.Io, Infame.* Milan: Arnaldo Mondadori; 1983:46.

9. Rapoport D. Terrorism. In: Hawkesworth M, Kogan M, eds. *Routledge Encyclopedia* of *Government and Politics,* vol. 2. London: Routledge; 1992: 1067.

10. Quoted in Blundy D. Inside the IRA. *Sunday Times* (London). July 3, 1977.

11. Quoted in Smith MLR. *Fighting for Ireland? The Military Strategy of the Irish Republican Movement.* London; Routledge; 1995: 224.

12. Quoted in Steinhoff PG. Portrait of a terrorist: an interview with Kozo Okamota. *Asian Survey.* 1976;16:844-845.

13. Quoted in Fetscher I, Rohrmoser G. *Analysen zum Terrorismus: Ideologien und Strategien, vol. 1.* Bonn: Westdeutscher Verlag; *1981: 327.*

14. Quoted in Taylor P *States of Terror Democracy and Political Violence.* London: Penguin; 1993:159.

15. Quoted in Hasselbach I. *Fuhrer-Ex: Memoirs* of *a Former Neo-Nazi.* London: Chatto & Windus; 1996:272.

16. Quoted in 'Don't spoil the party.' *The Economist* (London). July 13, 1996.

Negation Theory as a Cause Of Delusion: The Case of The Unabomber

Gerald H. Zuk
Carmen Veiga Zuk

Abstract: *The case of the Unabomber is examined as a test of the authors' theory of negation, which is based on four steps: (1) negation, (2) persecutory ideation, (3) attachment to a transcendental source, and (4) evangelism/martyrdom. The Unabomber sent bombs that killed three persons and injured others, and became a cause celebre in the 1990s when he threatened to blow up an airliner in flight if his 36,000 word manifesto was not published in a leading periodical. Eventually captured and tried, he refused an insanity defense but accepted a sentence of life imprisonment without possibility of parole. The authors' theory is a phenomenological model which encourages an intensive analysis of observations of behavior, with the goal of abstracting dimensions that serve to integrate the observations, codify them, and bind them into a unitary system.*

Negation theory is the authors' name for an explanation of a delusional disorder, such as paranoia. It is composed of four steps: (1) negation, (2) persecutory ideation, (3) attachment to a transcendental idea, and (4) evangelism/martyrdom. We believe these steps tend to be sequential, linear steps, one occurring after the other, but this may not always be the case.

In previous articles (Zuk, 1989; Zuk & Zuk, 1992, 1995, 1998) we applied negation theory to cases of prominent individuals no longer living who had been diagnosed as paranoid schizophrenic, or with a closely related disorder. In this article we focus on Ted Kaczynski, still living although confined, who became a cause celebre in the 1990s when he threatened to blow up an airliner in flight if a 36,000 word manifesto he had written, damning industrialization and technology and their agents, was not published in a leading periodical. Over a 17-year period, Ted, by mailing letter bombs, killed three persons and injured numerous others. When captured he refused an insanity defense, having been diagnosed as a paranoid schizophrenic (Graysmith, 1996), tried to serve as his own counsel, but finally accepted a plea bargain in which he was to serve a life term in prison without possibility of parole. Ted's ploy to publish his manifesto worked: a leading newspaper did publish it.

Our effort in this study is to take an entirely different case from those we have previously examined of individuals diagnosed as paranoid schizophrenic, and then attempt to fit their mental disturbance to the 4-point theory we call negation theory. We have focused on the problem of delusional states or ideation over approximately a dozen years because we believe that delusion is a fundamental constituent of several severe mental disorders, as well as one in itself, and that it well may be that at one time or another nearly everyone "suffers" from delusional ideation because it is a derivative of a perfectly normal human activity, that is, belief, which we believe is akin to or a subset of human intelligence, and necessary to human development. We are in perfect agreement with the first sentence of the recent article by Applebaum, Robbins, and Roth (1999, p. 1939) that, "Delusions are the quintessential symptoms of psychotic disorders." That statement perfectly captures our commitment to the problem over the past dozen years.

Negation Theory

Definitions

Previously we have defined negation theory, but have not called it such. Here we will refer to it as a theory, which is a statement of cause and effect presuming that one leads directly to another and with a degree of predictability that exceeds what could be claimed as chance. Negation theory defined here will differ slightly from previous versions, but we do not believe there is a serious divergency in the revision:

Negation: The first and principal element of the theory, negation refers to a wrenching turnabout in the lifestyle of an individual, not necessarily predictable, but where the individual undertakes an activity that may be entirely at odds with what the individual has done before, and which may be of extraordinary surprise to those that know the individual. As regards Kaczynski, we think there was a violent turnabout in his life, probably not starting at about 30 years of age but much before, which caused him to turn his back on all of the reward that had been given to him as a result of his superb intelligence in mathematics.

Negation may be intrapersonal or interpersonal. The intrapersonal type is exemplified by Freud's (1911) concept of projection, restated later by H. S. Sullivan (1953) as "paranoid transformation," in which an unacceptable part of the Self is displaced to another, where the other is tagged as a persecutor and the victim is terrorized and retaliates. The retaliation may be severe, incurring danger to the victim or others. The other form of negation is interpersonal: the victim is the subject of a loss, rejection, disappointment caused by outsiders, particularly parents or family. The belief that one is being persecuted is the same, as is the wish to retaliate for unfairness.

Attachment to a Transcendental Source: In a state of despair, the individual turns to a source that may bring comfort, and we call that the transcendental source—nature, the cosmos, religion, and so on. The individual surrenders personal responsibility to the transcendental source. The source dictates the behavior of the person; the person is the servant, the agent.

Evangelism / Martyrdom: An obligation of the source is that the individual spread, so to speak, the gospel to the world. In Ted's case, it would be the manifesto. The widest public must be reached, and any means to reach the widest public is held to be legitimate because of the importance of the message for mankind. Thus one can threaten life and not be personally responsible, in essence, because the end justifies the means. If the person fails in the mission to convert the world to the message of the transcendental source, then punishment is expected and even desired as a sign of loyalty to the transcendental. If the punishment is death, so much the better: the individual stands a chance of becoming acclaimed as a martyr, one who for a just cause suffered the ultimate penalty.

An odd example of martyrdom is found in what happened to Adolph Eichmann, the Nazi responsible for the massacre of Jews and others in prison camp during World War II. Eichmann, while in captivity in Israel in the early 1960s, maintained a diary, excerpts of which were published in the *Los Angeles Times* newspaper on March

1, 2000, in which he claimed (1) not to have been an anti-Semite, (2) to have been sickened by the sights and smells of death, and (3) to have been a bureaucrat (nothing more) in the extermination of Jews and others; that is, one merely serving the will of others of a higher station or calling. One is required to think hard about Eichmann's mental status during the time he served the Nazi regime and later, and also of the power of any dictatorship to cause its disciples to engage in acts often associated with mental disorder, such as the delusional state including paranoid schizophrenia.

About the Unabomber

Ted's Career: Early Years, Criminal Activity and Manifesto, Capture, and Punishment

Ted Kaczynski was born in Chicago on May 22, 1942, of working-class parents, Polish-Catholic in origin. His early years were uneventful except for the fact that his teachers considered him a bright student, but somewhat withdrawn and shy. Upon graduation from high school in Chicago he was recommended for a scholarship at college, and obtained one that took him to Harvard. At Harvard he completed the Bachelor of Arts (BA) degree, and was awarded an additional scholarship for graduate study. He graduated with a Doctor of Philosophy (PhD) degree from the University of Michigan. His area was mathematics, and he quickly obtained an appointment at the University of California, Berkeley, in the Department of Mathematics. This was in the period of the late 1960s when UC Berkeley, normally politically active, was in a period of intense political turmoil due to the war in Vietnam. His teaching career at Berkeley did not get off to a great start: students graded him poorly. But according to report of his departmental chairman, he was due for reappointment for a second year. Unexpectedly, in the fall of 1969, Ted wrote a letter of resignation to the chairman which offered no explanation and which took the chairman by surprise.

In 1971 Ted moved from Berkeley to a location near Lincoln, Montana which is approximately 60 miles from Helena, probably the state's major city. Temporarily he held odd jobs in the area, but quit each with the explanation that he was being exploited. Ted maintained written communication with his younger brother, David, throughout this period. David shared certain characteristics with Ted: Both were shy and withdrawn, but intellectually capable. David moved to a rural community in the state of Texas, but life there proved unsatisfactory and eventually he returned to his home in Chicago and married a childhood sweetheart. Later on he qualified for a degree as a social worker.

Ted returned home from Montana briefly in the mid-1970s, hoping apparently to heal any wounds he inflicted on those still living, but things did not go very well. He returned to Montana, writing that he was angry with his family, including David, and never wanted to see them again. In Montana he had built a makeshift cabin in the woods near Lincoln, and bicycled into the town for supplies. Generally people there considered him friendly and appealing, but Ted became, as recorded in his later discovered diaries, increasingly bitter and discontent. It was in the late 1970s that Ted began his career as a mailer of bombs to persons he associated with the deterioration of society due to industrialization and technology. He traveled to Sacramento, California, to mail the bombs.

The first death recorded was in 1985, the victim an owner of a computer rental store. From that time over a period of nearly 17 years, Ted mailed bombs, which exploded killing a total of three persons and injuring others. In 1994 and 1995 he killed two persons; that is, he became increasingly skillful at this activity.

While the authorities were alarmed and eagerly sought his capture they were unsuccessful until in the 1990s when the wife of his brother, David, noticed a resemblance between the notice that Ted sent out and material she had read from Ted to David and other family members. She called this to David's attention, but David's immediate reaction was to dismiss the resemblance. David's wife persisted (Douglas & Olshaker, 1996), and he finally made contact with a private investigator, who conducted an intensive investigation of the brother. The investigator concluded that there was a high likelihood that Ted and the Unabomber were the same and that, if David refused to report his brother that he, the investigator, had an obligation to do so. David agonized, but finally decided to inform the authorities.

Ted was arrested and brought to Sacramento to face a grand jury which, in June 1996, handed down a ten-count indictment against him. Trial began in November 1997, after a lengthy period of discovery. Ted was a difficult defendant. He refused an insanity defense, despite the insistence of his attorneys. He became angry with them for their insistence, asking the court if he could defend himself. For a time he was allowed to do so, but then the judge became less sympathetic and demanded that Ted undergo a psychiatric examination that was extensive. The examination resulted in a diagnosis of paranoid schizophrenia with significant delusional ideation. Eventually his lawyers intervened to obtain a plea agreement by which Ted would serve a life sentence in prison without possibility of parole for his crimes. Initially Ted accepted the plea bargain, but sometime in late 1998 or early 1999 he filed a motion to have it dismissed. He wanted another trial to prove that he was not responsible. Of course the alternative, meaning if another trial were granted, would show him at cause for the death of others and could mean the imposition of a death penalty in California.

We believe the case of Kaczynski supports negation theory. At approximately age 30 he turned his back on the world he knew which had rewarded him substantially since young manhood. He fled that world, and we would term that flight a significant negation, even while we cannot identify all of the elements that might have contributed to it. He isolated himself in the wilderness. We assume that in his flight he felt threatened and there was an element of persecution. When he undertook to kill by constructing mail bombs, we understand by that that he had already entered a delusional state. He was certainly a danger to others, and proved it. He also felt he had a "message" he had to share with the world, and composed a 36,000 word statement damning the industrial and technological world, and certain of its agents. It seems reasonable that he assumed the message was one that was legitimate, somewhat messianic, one that would have the support and endorsement of a deity. If it became necessary to threaten the destruction of individuals in pursuit of his messianic mission, he probably felt he had an entitlement. If in the course of his effort to inform the world he would be captured and perhaps put to death for murder, he was prepared because his demise would promote a presumed wish to become a martyr.

Discussion

One of the puzzles presenting the therapist treating the delusional is why normal logic and reasoning have little or no positive effect. We think the reason for this is provided by negation theory: Each argument proposed is opposed by a number of others comprising the theory. The victim is thus shielded from ordinary logic and reason.

We believe that a psychiatric disturbance such as delusional disorder is a derivative of a perfectly normal human function; namely, the capacity of the human to believe what he or she cannot perceive directly, but is told to believe as true by others who are significant to the person. Belief in humans is a function probably akin to intelligence; it is an essential learning mechanism. But that which ordinarily serves the individual so well as a principal basis for learning how to function in daily life, may, under certain circumstances, cause serious dysfunction, and one of these we consider to be delusional disorder.

Although the standard psychiatric nomenclature—the Diagnostic and Statistical Manual of Mental Disorders, DSM-IV—(American Psychiatric Association, 1994), cites a small incidence for delusional disorder—that is, the state where psychiatric treatment is needed—it seems to us that delusional ideation is probably a universal phenomenon affecting at one time or another everyone. Ordinarily the ideation is short-lived, relatively harmless to the individual, family, or co-workers, and recedes from the forefront of consciousness.

We have avoided personal recommendation regarding treatment of delusional disorder because we agree with the treatment proposals offered by Sir Martin Roth (1989): Little or no interpretation or confrontation; support, and sympathy for the person regardless of the specifics of the delusion, without specific endorsement; and the intelligent use of psychotropics to reduce the hypervigilance and high anxiety that tend to characterize these patients.

In closing we wish to bring attention to the interesting definitional changes that have occurred in various editions of the DSM with respect to delusion. In DSM-III (1980), the definition included the term "paranoia" and also "critical false belief." In DSM-III-R (1987), "paranoia" was retained, but "critical false belief" dropped out. In DSM-IV (1994) both "paranoia" and "critical false belief" were removed. The types of delusional disorder were reduced to the bare minimum of description: persecutory, grandiose erotomanic, jealous, and somatic. From a historical point of view, we do not wish to omit the contributions of several—but by no means all—who contributed to the psychodiagnosis of the delusion: Kraepelin (1909-1915), Jaspers (1913), and Strauss (1969), and encourage readers to acquaint themselves with their contributions that focused on the descriptive or reductionistic level.

References

American Psychiatric Association (1994). *Diagnostic and statistical manual of mental disorders (4th ed.)*. Washington, DC: Author.

American Psychiatric Association (1980). *Diagnostic and statistical manual of mental disorders (3rd ed.)*. Washington, DC: Author.

American Psychiatric Association (1987). *Diagnostic and statistical manual of mental disorders (3rd ed., rev.)*. Washington, DC: Author.

Applebaum, P.S., Robbins, P.C., & Roth, L.N. (1999). Dimensional approach to delusions: Comparison across types and diagnoses. *American Journal of Psychiatry*, 156, 1938-1943.

Douglas, J., & Olshaker, M. (1996). *Unabomber: On the trail of America's mostwanted serial killer*. New York: Simon and Schuster.

Freud, S. (1961). Psycho-analytic notes on an autobiographical account of a case of paranoia (dementia paranoides). In J. Strachey (Ed. and Trans.), *The standard edition of the complete psychological works of Sigmund Freud* (Vol. 12, pp. 7-79). London: Hogarth Press. (Original work published 1911)

Graysmith, R. (1996). *Unabomber: A desire to kill*. New York: Berkley Books.

Jaspers, K. (1913). *General psychopathology* (7th ed., trans. by Hoenig Hamilton). London: Manchester University Press.

Kraepelin. E. (1909-1915). *Psychiatrie: ein lehrbuch fur studierende and artzte* (8th ed.). Leipzig, Germany: Aufl. J. A. Barth.

Roth, M. (1989). Delusional (paranoid) disorders. In *Treatment of psychiatric disorders* (Vol. 2., pp. 1609-1652). Washington, DC: American Psychiatric Association.

Strauss, J. (1969). Hallucinations and delusions as points on continua function. *Archives of General Psychiatry, 21*, 581-586.

Sullivan, H. S. (1953) *The interpersonal theory of psychiatry*. New York: Norton.

Zuk, G. H. (1989). Learning to be possessed as a form of pathogenic relating and a cause of certain delusions. *Contemporary Family Therapy, 11*, 89-100.

Zuk, G. H., & Zuk, C. V. (1992). The logic of delusion. *Contemporary Family Therapy, 14*, 273-284.

Zuk, G. H., & Zuk, C. V. (1995) Freud's theory of paranoid delusion based on the Schreber case contrasted with related theories. *Contemporary Family Therapy, 17*, 209-216.

Zuk, G. H. & Zuk, C. V. (1998). When more is better than less: three theories of psychosis-projection, double bind, and possession. *Contemporary Family Therapy, 20*, 3-13.

From Protest to Terrorism: The Case of SDS and The Weathermen

Richard G. Braungart
Margaret M. Braungart

Abstract: *This case study examines the origins, organization, and activities of the Weathermen as it evolved out of the Students for a Democratic Society (SDS) in the late 1960s and early 1970s. Employing a social psychological approach, the SDS and the Weathermen are compared, focusing on the psychological motivations of their members, sociohistorical experiences, and group dynamics. Results indicate that time of entry into the student movement was a significant factor, with the Weathermen more prone to distort reality, to have experienced different cohort and period effects than SDS members, and to have engaged in an all-or-nothing style of politics and totalistic group dynamics. Explanations for these differences are evaluated, and a framework is offered that summarizes the findings.*

> June, 1969. Enter the Weathermen. . . . It swooped from giddy Third Worldism to a call for "antipig self-defense" movements and "cadre organization" on the way to a "Marxist-Leninist party" and "armed struggle.". . . Compared to the general run of SDS members . . . , they came from wealth; they were used to getting what they demanded, stamping their feet if they had to, wriggling away without punishment (Gitlin 1987, pp. 384-385).

> October, 1969. [T]he Weathermen blew up the statue commemorating the police victims of the Haymarket bombings a century before. On October 8 . . . the Weathermen were running through the Gold Coast [in Chicago], smashing expensive cars and shop windows. It was the beginning of three days of steady rampages (Hayden 1988, pp. 360-361).

> Early 1970s. [T]he Weather Underground at the height of its activities . . . claimed responsibility for a number of bombings—including an explosion at the U.S. Capitol (McGrath 1981, p. 32).

> October, 1981. [A] group of armed robbers tried to pull off "the big dance"—the code name they gave to a planned armed robbery of over a million dollars from a Brink's truck in Nyack, New York . . . two police officers and a Brink's guard were killed, and several men and women were captured. The best known was Kathy Boudin . . . who . . . was the most prominent political fugitive still at large (Frankfurt 1983).

These were the Weathermen—a fringe group of the youthful 1960s political generation that mobilized to challenge the status quo and tried to change the course of politics in the United States. The result of a takeover of the Students for a Democratic Society (SDS) in 1969, the Weathermen was spearheaded by bright, energetic youth, mostly from affluent backgrounds, who attended some of the most prestigious colleges and universities in the United States. This was a group that delighted in acrimonious rhetoric, applauded terrorist tactics, and eventually went underground to carry out a revolution against "Amerika," taking credit for over 25 bombings in the United States in a five-year period (Schlagheck 1988). Though small in number, the Weathermen became the focus of considerable government and media attention in the late 1960s and early 1970s.

The young people that joined the Weathermen were not the disadvantaged and downtrodden in America who had plenty of cause for anger, but were youth that appeared to "have it all." Despite their privileged backgrounds, the Weathermen relished in statements such as, "We are the incubation of your mother's nightmare." They talked of "turning New York into Saigon" and "smashing the pig inside ourselves," and they devoted several years to trying to engineer a revolution in America that clearly had little sympathy, support, or following (Jacobs 1970; Sale 1973; Gitlin 1987). The question is why?

Although there have been a number of descriptive accounts of the Weathermen and their activities, not much systematic effort has been devoted to explaining the Weathermen—why the group emerged from SDS in 1969 as part of the 1960s Generation, why it became a clandestine organization involved in acts of terrorism, and why young people from affluent and educated backgrounds decided to participate in the group? In order to address these questions, this study examines the formation of the Weathermen and the motivations of its members.

The term motivation often is taken to mean psychological motivation, but it is argued here that attempts to understand the Weathermen need to go beyond the individual level of analysis.

Especially when trying to understand a group of young people actively involved in politics during a certain era, consideration must be given to the larger sociohistorical context and to the dynamics of the political group to which the young activists belong. What is needed is a social psychological approach that incorporates analysis at the individual, societal, and group levels in order to provide a broad perspective on political activist groups such as the Weathermen.

To accomplish this task, the origins, organization, and activities of the Weathermen are described as background information on the group. Second, psychological, sociohistorical, and group dynamic explanations are examined as each of these approaches provides a perspective on the Weathermen and the motivations for their behavior. Comparisons are made with SDS, the forerunner of the Weathermen, to try to identify why the 1960s generation became increasingly hostile and violent, and why the Weathermen became one of the few clandestine political youth groups to have operated in the United States. The intent is to develop a broad framework for evaluating youthful political groups in order to better understand the dynamics of political generations and the motivations of their participants.

From Protest to Terrorist Politics

The Origins of the Weathermen

The Weathermen evolved out of one of the largest and most visible New Left organizations of the 1960s—the Students for a Democratic Society (SDS). Full of idealism, SDS formed in 1962 at a conference in Michigan and codified its values and purposes in *The Port Huron Statement* (Students for a Democratic Society 1964). Authored largely by Tom Hayden, the document began, "We are people of this generation, bred in at least modest comfort, housed now in universities, looking uncomfortably to the world we inherit" (Students for a Democratic Society 1964, p. 3). Under the banner of "participatory democracy," SDS advocated a "more human capitalism," antidiscrimination, support for third world peoples, and university reform. Referring to themselves as the "beloved community," this group of radical intellectuals, many of whom found socialist ideas appealing, spent their time organizing educational and economic development projects in various cities throughout the United States, headed South to be part of the civil rights struggle, and by mid-decade were staging marches, sit-ins, teach-ins, student strikes, and demonstrations to demand university reform and an end to the war in Vietnam (Sale 1973; Gitlin 1987; Miller 1987; Hayden 1988).

As the Vietnam War continued to escalate in the mid 1960s and racism in the North seemed as intractable as that in the South, "protest" politics appeared to be having little tangible effect, with the result that SDS moved toward a new phase of "resistance" politics. The goal at this stage, according to Todd Gitlin (1987, p. 252), former activist leader of SDS, was to "conduct yourself in a disorderly way, close off the streets, retreat when attacked, make interesting trouble, and protect yourself." The year 1968 was a pivotal one for SDS—described in a 1989 special issue of *Time* magazine as "a knife blade that separated past from future." Political violence spiraled in America: the Tet offensive by the Viet Cong in what was perceived to be the unending Vietnam war; assassinations of Martin Luther King, Jr. and Robert Kennedy; flashfires of rioting in urban areas across the country and heightened black militancy; the burning of hundreds of 1-A draft classification records at a Catonsville, Maryland Selective Service office by the Berrigan brothers and seven other priests; and the notorious student uprising at Columbia University, led by the confrontational Mark Rudd of SDS. Events came to a head in August 1968 at the Democratic Party Convention, as young people from a plethora of New Left groups and Mayor Richard Daley's police declared war on each other in the streets of Chicago. "Shoot to kill," Daley was quoted as saying (Gordon and Gordon 1987, p. 455).

Soon after the Democratic Convention, talk in SDS turned to revolution and "smashing the state," with a new kind of "all-or-nothing politics" taking hold (Braungart 1988). At the same time, problems were increasing within SDS, with a growing decline in tolerance for alternative views, a "frustrating intellectualization" of political problems, a coercive parliamentary manipulation of meetings, and a disaffection among SDS women for the rampant male chauvinism in the group (Gitlin 1987; Young 1977). Factional struggles abounded over ideology and tactics, played out on a grand scale at the June 1969 SDS convention in Chicago. One prominent faction was Progressive Labor (PL) that argued for a working-class perspective necessary to bring about the revolution in America, whereas other factions demanded that SDS be more concerned with racism and the need for armed struggle.

At the 1969 SDS Convention, an 11-member committee was charged by the national SDS office to write a position paper challenging PL. The resulting 16,000-word statement was titled "You Don't Need a Weatherman to Know Which Way the Wind Blows," a line from one of singer Bob Dylan's 1965 songs—a song, commented Sale (1973, p. 559), appealing to the "SDSian soul," with its overtones of "antiauthoritarianism and youthful independence." In contrast to the 1962 *Port Huron Statement*, the 1969 Weatherman manifesto began, " . . . the main struggle going on in the world today is between US imperialism and the national liberation struggles against it . . . . The goal is the destruction of US imperialism and the achievement of a classless world" (Jacobs 1970, pp. 51-52). All-out support was advocated for black liberation and for opening a new front against American foreign policy by establishing urban-based collectives. The diatribe included a quote from Lin Piao, "Long Live the Victory of People's War!"

Calling themselves the "Weathermen," the group quickly gained control at the SDS convention. At center stage was the charismatic Bernardine Dohrn, described as "chorus-line figured, articulate law-school graduate . . ." and "the object of many an SDS male's erotic fantasy . . . who fused the two premium images of the movement: sex queen and streetfighter" (Gitlin 1987, pp. 385-386). After tiresome rounds of factional bickering, Dohrn seized the microphone, demanded that PL be expelled, and stalked off stage, leading a walk-out of about 700 participants chanting, "Power to the people, power to the people; Ho! Ho! Ho Chi Minh!" The major SDS factions caucused at various locations in Chicago. A slate of candidates from the different factions was announced, with the top three leadership positions in SDS won by Weathermen Mark Rudd, Bill Ayers, and Jeffrey Jones. These were the second generation SDS, who came to the organization in 1966 or thereafter, eschewing the tedious radical intellectualizing of the SDS founders in favor of all-or-nothing, action politics. The election results signaled the demise of SDS and a several-year foray into a more vituperative style of youth politics, infused with elements of terrorism and secrecy (Jacobs 1970; Sale 1973; Gitlin 1987).

Organization and Activities

Once formed, the leaders of the Weathermen, known as the Weather Bureau, took over the SDS National Office in Chicago and changed the name of SDS's journal *New Left Notes* to *Prairie Fire*. Gitlin (1987, p. 386) commented that initially the Weathermen made revolution look like fun, with their LSD, sexual orgies, celebration of the presumed guerrilla exploits of five-year-old Marion Delgado who derailed a train in California, and songs like "I'm dreaming of a white riot" (to the tune of "White Christmas") and "When you're a red, you're a red all the way" (to the tune of "All the Way"). In this first phase of its organization, the Weathermen attempted to implement a two-pronged program: (1) urban action projects designed to awaken and recruit working-class youth to revolution; and (2) anti-Vietnam War actions (Sale 1973; Unger 1974). Estimates of the numbers of young people involved in the Weathermen vary, ranging from a high of about 3,000 to a low of 200. Organized into collectives, members of the Weathermen were assigned to various cities such as Chicago, New York, Seattle, Newark, Denver, and Cleveland, among others, to carry out "urban action projects." The collectives were able to function on relatively little money, with funding acquired through personal savings accounts, part-time jobs, stealing credit cards, and some money donated from the central office (Sale 1973; Franks 1981). Women were at the forefront of many of the Weather actions, taking sizable risks in their struggle for feminist recognition (Stern 1975; Alpert 1981; Gitlin 1987).

The Weathermen championed "politics by action," drawing inspiration from the black power movement, especially the Black Panthers. Uncomfortable about their "white-skin privilege," the Weathermen attempted to win the respect of the black movement and to prove themselves as legitimate white revolutionaries by outraging middle-class America. Noted Hornblower and Valentine (1980, p. A2): "They believed that if they proved, through violent acts, that they were not wimpy middle-class intellectuals, but 'guerrillas fighting behind enemy lines,' working-class youths would rise and join them." To that end, the Weathermen planned a series of provocative actions for the late summer and fall of 1969—raiding two Detroit junior colleges to "rap" with students about imperialism, racism, and the excesses of capitalism; staging a "jailbreak" and rally outside a Pittsburgh high school; and spray-painting public buildings and statues with political slogans. As Gitlin (1987, p. 391) described, "They . . . talked about 'kicking ass' and 'getting us a few pigs,' and dared the local kids to fight."

The Weathermen's most ambitious project at this stage was the Days of Rage in Chicago. Under the slogan "Bring the war home," the Weathermen spent four days trashing property, bombing a statue honoring police in Haymarket Square, and skirmishing with Chicago police, doing thousands of dollars worth of property damage in the wealthy Gold Coast section. Weatherwomen were highly instrumental in these "actions," and police responded with force. Injuries, arrests, and indictments followed, with total bail for the Weathermen amounting to 2.3 million dollars (Sale 1973). Though the Weathermen declared victory, Black Panther Fred Hampton called their actions "adventuristic, opportunistic and custeristic" (Unger 1974, p. 174). Membership declined in the Weathermen, as SDS campus chapters closed down or changed their name.

These early actions, which also included passing out leaflets and marching the National Liberation Front (NLF) flag around in various cities, did not have the intended effect of inspiring thousands of young working-class youth, especially blacks, to join the ranks of the revolutionary force—quite the reverse. Although some youth joined in the Weathermen escapades, such events more likely met with open hostility, not only from the public and community but from bands of youth who declared the Weathermen crazy and chased collectives out of their neighborhoods. Weathermen were not easily daunted, however. As an example, at one high school when students started fighting against the Weathermen, a Weatherman remembered yelling in fear to Cathy Wilkerson, "This is terrible," to which she yelled back in surprise, "Oh no, this is terrific. People are communicating" (Hornblower and Valentine 1980).

With the two-pronged Weathermen program largely a failure and SDS in a shambles, the Weatherman organization intensified its strategy and began converting the group into a clandestine organization devoted to guerrilla warfare and bombing (Unger 1974). Bernardine Dohrn announced, "revolutionary violence is the only way. Now we are adopting the classic guerrilla strategy of the [Uruguayan] Tupamaros . . . in the technically most advanced country in the world" (Young 1977, p. 276). In order to forge "instant" revolutionaries, the Weathermen turned inward, focusing the group's energies on reconstructing the personal lives of its members.

Individualism and personal privacy were declared "out" in the collectives; shared drugs and sex were "in," and Weather members were expected to give themselves over totally to the group. Endless self-criticism sessions, labeled "Weatherfries," were initiated in each collective, personal possessions went to the group, and monogamous relations, including marriages, were to be "smashed," since, it was argued, such relationships put women in a dependent position relative to men. Experimentation with sex and drugs was promoted "to establish new connections both personal and political." As a Weatherman pamphlet extolled, "We're . . . knowing our bodies as part of our lives, becoming animals again after centuries of repression and uptightness" (Sale 1973, p. 624). Such behaviors among some members, especially homosexuality, estranged many Weathermen who left the group. This was a time when the organization was under threat both externally and internally: externally from police and FBI surveillance, indictments for offenses, and fear of infiltration; internally by a growing feminist movement and enormous ego battles among the leadership (Jacobs 1970; Sale 1973; Unger 1974; Hayden 1988).

The last public event of the Weathermen before going underground was the National War Council, held in Flint, Michigan, in December 1969. About 400 people attended, some of whom were infiltrators, curiosity or thrill-seekers, or "hangers-on" (Sale 1973; Gitlin 1987). Rhetoric and style escalated to a new level of nastiness at Flint, as politics was transformed into theatrics, partially to help build an illusion of strength (Jacobs 1970). Mass meetings were billed as "wargasms," and much of the time was spent on alcohol, pot, and sex; practicing karate exercises; and singing songs about trashing, bomb throwing, and killing "pigs" (Unger 1974). A kind of Alice-in-Wonderland, Queen of Hearts logic prevailed. One debate at the meeting concerned whether killing white babies was correct, and John Jacobs declared to the audience, "We're against everything that's 'good and decent,' in honky America. We will burn and loot and destroy." It was here that Bernardine Dohrn made her infamous remark about the Charles Manson gang killings, "Dig it. First they killed those pigs, then they ate dinner in the same room with them, then they even shoved a fork into the victim's stomach. Wild" (Unger 1974, p. 181).

Another phase was launched in "Weatherpolitics." War was declared on the state by building a self-styled Red Army, and collectives were broken down further into cells or "focos" to go underground. Observed Gitlin (1987, p. 395), "The world having failed their analysis, they rejected it." In February 1970, the SDS Chicago office was closed and its files sold to the Wisconsin Historical Society. Contacts with family and friends were severed, identities were changed, and the organization was renamed the "Weather Underground" (a name much more palatable to Weatherwomen). Going underground was an honored tradition among some of the Weathermen's most revered political organizations, such as the Tupamaros, who the Weathermen saw as heroes for their Robin Hood style politics. In small groups, members moved to city apartments or to isolated rural areas, often rotated by orders from the Weather Bureau (Sale 1973; Stern 1975; Alpert 1981). Isolation was not complete, however, with informal contacts made with families and friends through post-office boxes and pay phones. A network of support was provided by above-ground activists who would transfer messages and supply quick cash, while an organization in Canada for U.S. military deserters helped with border crossings and false identification papers (Franks 1981).

The need for heightened violence and bombing in America was justified by the Weathermen. As Mike James harangued a crowd in Chicago:

> Non-violent marches have their place, but they won't bring about the changes necessary for freedom. Capitalism won't crumble because of moral protest.... They've got the guns, we've got the people .... The time will come when we'll have to use guns. Don't let that hang you up. Some of you say violence isn't human. Well, taking oppression isn't human; it's stupid. You only live one time, so you'd better make it good and make it liberating .... Violence, when directed at the oppressor, is human as well as necessary (Sale 1973, p. 631).

The most active of the Weather Underground bombing groups was the New York City cell that included Cathy Wilkerson, Kathy Boudin, Diana Oughton, Terry Robbins and Ted Gold—all from wealthy backgrounds (Unger 1974). On February 21, 1970, this group was said to be responsible for setting off three firebombs at Judge John Murtagh's home (Murtagh was the presiding judge for a trial of a group of New York Black Panthers). However, on March 6, a bomb, which was to be planted at Columbia University, was being assembled in the basement of a fashionable Greenwich Village townhouse belonging to Wilkerson's vacationing father. But something went wrong, and the bomb and house exploded, killing Gold, Oughton, and Robbins, while Wilkerson and Boudin escaped to a neighbor's house (Unger 1974; Franks 1981). Several days later, three commercial buildings in New York City were bombed, and at the end of the month police raided a Kenmore Avenue apartment where Dohrn and Jacobs had stayed, which was described as a "bomb factory" (Sale 1973).

In the first part of May 1970, following Nixon's decision to invade Cambodia, waves of student protest erupted throughout the United States, which climaxed with the killing of six students by National Guard and police at Kent State University and Jackson State University. From the underground, Dohrn issued the first Weather communique in late May—a nihilistic statement fusing the youth culture and politics:

> All over the world, people fighting Amerikan imperialism look to Amerika's youth to use our strategic position behind enemy lines to join forces in the destruction of the empire. ...We fight in many ways. Dope is one of our weapons. ... Guns and grass are united in the youth underground. ... If you want to find us, this is where we are. In every tribe, commune, dormitory, farmhouse, barracks and townhouse where kids are making love, smoking dope and loading guns—fugitives from Amerikan justice are free to go ... (Jacobs 1970, pp. 508-510).

She went on to warn that the Weather Underground soon would attack "a symbol or institution of Amerikan injustice," and some 19 days later, a bomb exploded at New York City police headquarters. A second communique followed that blamed the police for murdering blacks and brutalizing "Latin and white youth on the Lower East Side."

> The pigs in this country are our enemies .... Every time the pigs think they've stopped us, we come back a little stronger and a lot smarter .... They build the Bank of America, kids burn it down. They outlaw grass, we build a culture of life and music. The time is now. Political power grows out of a gun, a Molotov, a riot, a commune ... and from the soul of the people (Jacobs 1970, p. 512).

The Weathermen were not the only ones bombing. During the 1969-1970 school year, there were 174 major bombing attempts on campus and more than 70 off campus attributed to the white left—an eight-fold increase from 1968-1969; nationally, estimates of bombings and attempts reached nearly 5,000 from January 1969 to April 1970 (Sale 1973, p. 632).

Concomitant with the bombing episodes were intensive investigations carried out by police, the FBI, and U.S. Attorney's Office. According to Schlagheck (1988), every member of SDS and the Weather Underground was investigated by the FBI, while the CIA's "Operation Chaos" for movement surveillance, that had been established under the Johnson Administration, was expanded under the Nixon Administration. Gitlin (1987, p. 378) recounted:

> The Nixon administration used militants (including agents provocateurs) to taint moderates, on the principle that the more destructive the protest, the easier it was to discredit. It authorized wiretaps, grand jury investigations, felony prosecutions. It tried to intimidate news media . . . . State and local police contributed their own burglaries, stole mailing lists, instigated harassment by landlords and disconnection by phone companies. Eventually, even mild liberals were placed on a White House "enemies list."

During early April a federal grand jury in Chicago indicted 12 key Weathermen leaders for crossing state lines with the intention of inciting riots, and for assorted charges stemming from inflammatory remarks in speeches, in addition to hitting a policeman (Sale 1973, p. 648). In July 1970, a Detroit federal grand jury indicted 13 Weathermen (some of whom were already indicted in previous cases) on conspiracy charges, and Dohrn made the FBI's most-wanted persons list. Then on July 26 in celebration of a Cuban national holiday, a bomb went off in the entrance of a Bank of America branch on Wall Street, with the Weather Underground taking credit. Two Viet Cong flags were left at the scene, and a third communique was issued, ending with the message to Attorney General John Mitchell, "Don't look for us, Dog; Well find you first" (Jacobs 1970, p. 515).

In September 1970, the Weathermen arranged the escape of Dr. Timothy Leary, guru of the drug culture, who had been sentenced to ten years for marijuana possession in California's San Luis Obispo prison. A fourth communique followed that hailed Leary for "creating a new culture on the barren wasteland that had been imposed on this country by Democrats, Republicans, Capitalists, and creeps." The statement ended with "Our organization commits itself to the task of freeing these prisoners of war. We are outlaws, we are free" (Jacobs 1970, p. 517). Leary issued his thanks in the *San Francisco Good Times*:

> There is a time for peace and the time for war . . . . I declare that World War III is being waged by short-haired robots whose deliberate aim is to destroy the complex web of free willed life by the imposition of mechanical order . . . . Total war is upon us. Fight to live or you'll die (Jacobs 1970, pp. 517-519).

Bombings continued in the United States, with the Weather Underground taking credit for some of these, which included the Army Mathematical Research Center at the University of Wisconsin where a graduate student was killed, courthouses in California and Long Island, the Senate men's restroom in the U.S. Capitol, the Pentagon, ITT corporate offices, and the U.S. State Department (Unger 1974; Schlagheck 1988). Nonetheless, clandestine life became increasingly wearing, with no real revolution in sight. As Alpert recounted in a letter to "Sisters in the Weather Underground" published in *Ms.* magazine in 1973 (Alpert 1973, p. 88), "My first year underground was very hard. Expecting to die for the Revolution in a matter of months, I was unprepared to find myself not only alive but living a rather unadventurous and secluded existence less than a year after 'disappearing.'" Infighting persisted underground over issues such as feminism versus chauvinism, staying underground versus surfacing, and whether to direct violence at select targets with no killing or to engage in kidnap and assassination like the Red Brigades in Italy (Hornblower and Valentine 1980).

By 1974, however, the momentum was gone, despite occasional issues of *Prairie Fire*. Some observers date the end of the Weathermen in 1976, although isolated urban guerrilla groups continued activities. By the late 1970s, there were two remaining groups: the Prairie Fire collective, which favored surfacing from underground life; and the May 19th Coalition (May 19 is the birthday of Ho Chi Minh and Malcolm X), which wanted to become part of a black terrorist army (Franks 1981; McGrath 1981). In 1979, a police raid on a Hoboken, New Jersey apartment uncovered another "bomb factory," attributed to Jeff Jones and Eleanor Raskin of the Weather Underground. In 1981, a remnant underground group that included David Gilbert, Judith Clark, and Kathy Boudin robbed a Brinks truck in Nyack, New York, and killed a guard and two police officers (one of whom was the first black policeman in Rockland County). The gang was caught. Gilbert and Clark were convicted of murder and sentenced to 75 years in prison. Boudin, who plead guilty to robbery and murder, was given 25 years to life in prison (Frankfurt 1983; Gitlin 1987).

Throughout the late 1970s, Weathermen members left the underground, and in the early 1980s, some of its more prominent leaders abandoned fugitive life: Rudd surfaced in 1977, was fined $2,000 and given two-years probation; Wilkerson surrendered in 1980 and was given a three-year term in a New York state prison; in 1980 Dohrn surfaced and was fined and put on probation, while Ayers's charges were dropped. Dohrn and Ayers married in 1982 and have two sons (McGrath 1981, pp. 30-34; *Newsweek*, 1985, p.15). As Franks (1981, p. 36) summarized:

> [These] white radicals . . . traveled down a long spiral: from idealistic students to peaceful protestors to rioters trashing the streets to revolutionary cadres bent on shedding their "white-skin privilege" to fugitives planting bombs in empty buildings to women and men accused of assassinating the very "people" they said they were fighting for.

The question why young people decided to join the Weathermen and carry out such actions is explored in the next section of this study on motivation, organized around psychological, sociohistorical, and group dynamic explanations.

Motivations of the Weathermen

Psychological Explanations

There are several possible psychological explanations for the Weathermen and their behavior. First, the Weathermen were part of the 1960s generation, and since generational movements are carried out by youth, then it must be asked whether there is something about the stage of youth that makes young people receptive to political movements and extremist behavior? Second, because some of the Weathermen were involved in terrorist acts, then, in keeping with the terrorist literature, consideration must be given to personality characteristics—including the possibility that their personalities were pathological. And third, since many of the Weathermen were from affluent professional homes, it seems reasonable to ask if their family background and parents' politics could be at the root of some of the Weathermen's attitudes and behavior. Each of these psychological explanations is considered as it pertains to the Weathermen.

It has been argued that youthful political movements are partially rooted in the life-cycle developmental characteristics of youth: high energy levels, improved cognitive skills, heightened political awareness, the need for self independence or "genital primacy," and a socioemotional search for identity, fidelity, and a place in society (Erikson 1968; Keniston 1968; Feuer 1969; Braungart and Braungart 1986). While these are characteristics that help explain why young people in general are prone to create generational movements—whether in politics, literature, science, or other fields—in order to understand the motivations of any specific youthful political group such as the Weathermen, it is necessary to explore the way in which these developmental tasks were approached and carried out.

Typical of the stage of adolescence and youth are important new cognitive developments: the ability to think abstractly, a wider awareness of possibilities and alternatives, and a greater recognition of the world of politics (Erikson 1968; Gallatin 1980; Vander Zanden 1989). And although research has indicated that adolescent political conceptions are often untested and somewhat simplistic, Adelson reported that among some of the highly politicized young, their ideals are not diffuse but are "highly organized, intellectualized, systematic, and a bit blood-thirsty. It's a cold-blooded sort of utopianism: *we* know what to do, and *we* are going to do it" (Adelson 1987, p. 93).

Adelson's remarks describe well the cognitive political thinking of the Weathermen. In comparison to SDS's statements and writings, those of the Weathermen were often more categorical, rigid, over-simplified, and "bloodthirsty." For example, when asked in a *Life* magazine interview, "What do you hope to obtain by bombing?" the anonymous Weatherman responded:

> We are revolutionaries, not reformists. We are not trying to frighten the Establishment, we are trying to destroy it, so that a just society can be built based on human values, not financial or commercial values. . . . Ours is an attempt to attack capitalism, racism, exploitation—directly and militarily. These are not attacks on individuals who work in these offices or happen to be there. It is the use that the buildings are put to that we are attacking (*Life* 1970, p. 30).

The Weathermen, said SDS leader Tom Hayden (1988, p. 358), "had no patience for the complicated moral and political philosophizing of the Port Huron Generation." Another SDS member commented about Weatherwoman Cathy Wilkerson, "She was driven by guilt about being born white and privileged . . . . Any doubts about radical theory were thought to be signs of weakness, so she would draw herself further and further into a fantasy world about the way the world works. You could never have an intellectual discussion with her" (Hornblower and Valentine 1980, p. A2).

The youthful search for identity, fidelity, and a place in society was carried out in a distinct fashion by the Weathermen, which differed from youth in general and from their predecessors in SDS. According to Erikson (1968), an important aspect of adolescent identity development involves experimentation, and this was one of the Weathermen's appeals. As Hayden (1988, p. 359) observed: "there was an attraction about them, a sinister one, for many radicals. The mystery of what was out there, beyond normal experience, was magnetic to some from bourgeois backgrounds." Thus, youth who wanted to indulge in personal exploration and experience high risk were drawn to the Weathermen, who provided, encouraged, and justified going beyond the bounds of convention into a never-never land of forbidden pleasures and acts. Youthful experimentation with drugs, sex, life styles, and violence was endorsed in the Weather collectives and at their meetings. Personal experimentation was then tied to political experimentation. As one radical told a reporter, "No one knows whether terrorism will work . . . . No one has really tried it yet." Another described the Weathermen as "an experiment to see if an underground can be set up in this country" (*Newsweek* 1970, pp. 27, 36).

Besides experimentation, part of youthful identity formation may involve an identity crisis, which occurs when young people lose their way and suffer what Erikson (1968) termed "identity diffusion."

In the process, the young person may embrace a negative identity, which Erikson said is evident in a "scornful and snobbish hostility toward the roles offered as proper and desirable in one's family or immediate community," and which may be due to "the excessive ideals either demanded by morbidly ambitious parents or indeed actualized by superior ones" (Erikson 1968, p. 175). As Franks (1981) described them, the Weathermen were youth who, though nurtured by advantaged backgrounds, thought that if you were not poor, black, and hungry, your conscience should suffer.

> White-skin privilege. Rich bitches. Spoiled kids. Bourgeois liberals. The young radicals of the Vietnam era set out to prove that such phrases did not apply to them (Franks 1981, p. 44).

They had to reject their bourgeois past, and one way to accomplish that task was to take on a negative identity.

The Weathermen offered what many of these youth thought they needed. In fact, much of the basis for the Weathermen's recruitment rested on the group's style rather than on a coherent persuasive argument (Gitlin 1987). Role models for the group were often outlaws, and the experimental nature of their cultivated negative identity has been described by SDS leader and historian Carl Oglesby.

> They knew they were crazy . . . . Terry [Robbins] and Billy [Ayers] had this Butch Cassidy and Sundance attitude—they were blessed, they were hexed, they would die young, they would live forever . . . . I believe they thought they looked cute, and that everybody would know it was basically a joke. The next minute, they were lost in it and couldn't get out (Gitlin 1987, pp. 386-387).

Problems with identity and identity diffusion may also explain the Weathermen's enthusiasm for going underground. As Weatherwoman Susan Stern (1975, p. 244) recounted in her autobiography:

> I was about to jump off, make a clean break, split. Soon there would be no more Susan Stern. She would be dead, and the person she had been would have another face, another color hair, another name, another past. She would invent it, build it, engineer it to be exactly what she wanted

> it to be, what she had never been . . . . Susan Stern Sham would end finally, finally she would end.

Another part of the search for identity involves a quest for meaning in life, which some youth, Erikson (1968) noted, try to find by linking their personal lives to politics. As one Weatherman expressed it, "You give meaning to your life by fighting the system" (*Newsweek* 1970, pp. 26-30). Susan Stern (1975, p. 275) echoed the theme:

> I want to join with the black liberation movement, and struggle with the Vietcong. They are all building a new kind of life in the midst of war and they sing while they work, because their life has meaning. They're not cogs in the wheel any more; they are the wheel and they are rolling onto their own heritage, and those are the people I want to identify with.

For a number of youth, the Weathermen may have provided a way station in their struggle for personal identity. The Weatherman organization was a totalistic group where the self and personal responsibility could be abandoned, and to fill the void, the group offered a kind of patched-together, utopian political thought and prescriptions for behavior. As Kanfer (1981, p. 32) commented, "Dylan furnished the phrases, Che [Guevara] and [Regis] Debray the shibboleths, Timothy Leary the smoke, Marcuse the philosophy." Moreover, according to Crenshaw (1986, p. 394), for those involved in groups that engage in terrorist acts:

> To individuals already suffering from identity confusion, the attention paid them by the government not only confirms a negative identity but makes them feel like "somebody." They are gratified to be sufficiently important to be the object of excessive attention, even if that attention is negative. Harassment or surveillance is preferable to being ignored by society.

At the same time, the decision to leave the Weather Underground may have rested partially on a desire to have one's old identity again. As Jane Alpert (1981, p. 314) recounted, "At the Albuquerque HEW office I had applied for a new Social Security card in the name of Carla Weinstein—Weinstein because, after two years 'passing,' I wanted my

Jewish identity back. . . ." Thus, there is strong evidence that much of the Weathermen's psychological motivation had to do with their youthful cognitive style and their quest for identity through experimentation, negative identity, and trying to finding meaning in life. The evidence for the role of personality factors in distinguishing Weathermen's behavior is less clear.

One dimension of personality that needs to be considered is aggression, since much of the style, rhetoric, and actions of the Weathermen were highly aggressive. To a greater extent than in SDS, the Weathermen had a penchant for what Fromm (1973) termed "malignant aggression": a preoccupation with destruction (self, relationships, society, America)—often evident in their writings, language, humor, style, and actions. However, it has been cautioned in the terrorist literature that while aggression may be part of the psychological make-up of terrorists, it is not clear to what extent such aggression is derived from the inner personality of individual members or has been "assumed" (willed or cultivated) because of group norms and pressure (Crenshaw 1986). In addition, while the Weathermen displayed a fascination for aggression and violence, it is another matter whether this characteristic was a dominant feature of all personalities in the group. For example, Knutson (1981) interviewed West German terrorists and reported there was an ambivalent attitude toward violence; for many, creating fear was less important than demonstrating commitment to a cause through self-sacrifice.

In addition, Crenshaw (1986, p. 387) pointed out that "rather than being attracted to the inherent violence of terrorism, some individuals are seduced by the lures of omnipotence and grandeur to compensate for feelings of inferiority or impotence;" thus, terrorism may be one response to a lack of self-confidence. Feelings of inferiority predominate both the Stern (1975) and Alpert (1981) accounts of life with the Weathermen. Stern's longing for recognition and elitism is evident in one passage where she describes being in jail with Bernardine Dohrn but feels too intimidated to approach Dohrn.

> But she was still the high priestess. Whatever quality she possessed, I wanted it. I wanted to be cherished and respected as Bernardine was. More than that I wanted to know Bernardine. I wanted to be an aristocrat too (Stern 1975, p. 144).

Rather than a single orientation toward aggression, it is likely there was a variety of attitudes represented within the Weathermen, with members engaging in destructive actions (rhetoric, behavior, self, others, political) for a combination of reasons.

Besides aggression, there have been a number of additional personality characteristics attributed to individuals who commit acts of terrorism, some of which include low self-esteem, high aspirations, goal-directed behavior, high stress-seeking and risk-taking, impatience, uncompromising attitudes, a tendency to blame others, and fear of anonymity (Jenkins 1980; Crenshaw 1986). However, Bell (1980, pp. 201-202) noted that there seems to be a lot of faith in but very little evidence for a terrorist personality profile, and Laqueur (1987) commented that while some terrorists may be stress-seeking, hostile, and unstable, others have none of these personality traits.

A related issue is whether those who engage in terrorism have personalities that are pathological, but the consensus in most of the terrorist literature is that only a minority are certifiably "disturbed," partially because groups are not likely to tolerate highly irratic, unpredictable behavior, and they require a certain amount of stability among their members in order to plan and carry out terrorist acts (Storr 1978; Lebow 1980). Accounts of the Weathermen written by Stern (1975) and Alpert (1981) document how the Weather Bureau readily weeded out those who threatened the group in any way. Stern herself was under suspicion by Mark Rudd and other leaders for being emotionally unstable and was dismissed from the Weathermen at one point. Although few terrorists who operate in groups may be truly pathological, Crenshaw (1986) pointed out there may be elements of neuroticism, both for individuals within the group and the group as a whole.

In a general sense, however, personality is not a useful predictor of participation in groups such as the Weathermen, since a variety of different personalities were represented in the group. Second, a number of individuals who possessed these same traits did not join the Weathermen or any terrorist group and could be found in diverse careers (Laqueur 1987). And third, it does not appear that only certain types of personalities were drawn to the Weathermen, since it has been observed that personalities changed as a result of affiliation with the group. For example, Hayden (1988, p. 422) commented:

> I had seen personality changes in the Weathermen and Panthers as they struggled to become "tools of necessity." They became drained of human feelings, in readiness to die or perhaps kill, to accept personal oblivion for an ideology.

Hayden (1988, p. 359) further described his friend Terry Robbins, whose personality changed after becoming a Weatherman from "a shy introvert to a devilish charmer exuding a charisma of violence."

Along with developmental and personality considerations, an examination of individual political motivations requires a discussion of family background characteristics—the kinds of families that produced offspring who joined the Weathermen. One salient feature of the Weathermen was that they came from affluent homes, which differed somewhat from the backgrounds of the early SDS group. As Gitlin (1987, p. 385) contrasted: Whereas the initial SDS organizers—the first generation SDS—were "the children of public-school teachers, professors, accountants, and the like," the Weathermen "came from wealth."

For example, Bill Ayers's father was the chairman of the Board of the Commonwealth of Illinois electrical combine; Kathy Boudin's father was a well-known attorney who defended political leftists; Diana Oughton's father was a banker in a small Midwest town who was also a Republican state legislator; Cathy Wilkerson's father owned radio stations; Mark Rudd's father had been a Lieutenant Colonel in the Army Reserves and sold real-estate; and Bernardine Dohrn's father was a Hungarian immigrant, who moved the family from Chicago to the Milwaukee suburbs (Sale 1973; Gitlin 1987). One of Cathy Wilkerson's associates commented, "It used to be a joke in the movement that you can't get into the Weathermen unless your parents are millionaires" (Hornblower and Valentine 1980, p. A2).

Part of the dynamic for these Weathermen from privileged homes may have been rooted in the youthful developmental need to become independent and in the generational desire to go beyond one's parents (Bettelheim 1963; Erikson 1968). As Franks (1981, p. 44) observed about two Weatherwomen:

> Diana [Oughton] could not become richer than her father, but she could become poorer and purer. Kathy [Boudin] who grew cynical about the law, had to go one step farther than her radical father; she had to find a more powerful—and forbidden—way to fight injustice.

Sheltered, protected, supported, and accustomed to getting their own way at home, these Weathermen felt invincible, knowing little of life's fears or harshness (Franks 1981; Gitlin 1987).

Not all Weathermen came from affluence, of course; some were from middle- and lower-middle-class homes. Yet, it may not have been family income per se that was important. What bound both the affluent and not-so-affluent youth together in the Weathermen was their feeling of guilt: regardless of class background, "all had the illusion of great—and shameful—advantage" (Franks 1981, p. 44). A kind of cognitive dissonance was created between their awareness of poverty, racism, and the exploitation of humanity in society, relative to their own comfortable, secure personal backgrounds. Their attempt to reduce this tension was by linking their individual lives to revolutionary politics.

Besides economic background, the political socialization literature indicates that parents' politics have an important bearing on offspring political views. And in keeping with this literature, parents' politics was found to be a key predictor of the political behavior of SDS leaders—who tended to come from left-wing, liberal, or Democratic homes (Flacks 1967; Braungart 1979; Braungart and Braungart 1988). The leaders of the Weathermen, on the other hand, came from more mixed political backgrounds—Republican, Democrat, liberal, leftist, and pacifist (Sale 1973; Franks 1981).

Like personality, however, family background leaves much to be desired as a predictor of why some young people join extreme political groups. First, the overwhelming majority of youth from privileged homes did not join the Weathermen or any other political or terrorist group. Second, the Black Panthers and Symbionese Liberation Army, which operated around the same time as the Weathermen and employed similar tactics and rhetoric, had very different family backgrounds from the Weathermen (Laqueur 1987). The limitations of many of these psychological explanations indicate the need to go beyond the individual level of analysis and examine additional factors. As social psychologists have pointed out, individual behavior often has less to do with dispositional characteristics than with situational factors and the larger social context (Forsyth 1983).

Sociohistorical Explanations

In attempting to explain the groups that arise within a political generation, besides psychological factors and youthful developmental characteristics, consideration must be given to sociohistorical forces, such as (1) cohort effects—the shared socialization experiences of an age group as its members grow up together in a society during a certain time in history; and (2) period effects—the historical events and trends occurring as a generation takes form and mobilizes around a certain set of sociopolitical issues (Knoke 1984; Braungart and Braungart 1986, 1989b; Delli Carpini 1986). Both of these factors are important to understanding the attitudes and behavior of the Weathermen, particularly why the Weathermen became increasingly extreme and violent.

There are several dimensions of the cohort effect to consider in relation to the Weathermen. One distinguishing characteristic of most political generations in history was that they were part of a large-size birth cohort (Moller 1972; Wallimann and Zito 1984). The 1960s generation was an extraordinarily large birth group—sometimes referred to as the Baby Boom—born during the post-World War II years. As Ryder (1965, p. 845) noted, "Any extraordinary size deviation is likely to leave an imprint on the cohort as well as on the society." And, as teenagers in the 1950s, the first wave of baby-boom youth made a difference, vexing their elders by creating a lively, rebellious youth culture of music, dress, and language, and applauding antiheroes such as Marlon Brando, James Dean, and Elvis Presley. As the cohort reached college age from 1960-1970, the size of the youth population (ages 17-24) increased by 52 percent, and more youth than ever before went off to college, escalating college and university enrollments by 121 percent in a decade (Ryder 1974).

A cohort also shares a particular set of socialization experiences as its members grow up together in a society at a similar stage in life-cycle development. The baby-boom cohort came of age during the postwar years when America was changing rapidly, with increasing suburbanization, new technology, bureaucratization, and corporate consolidation, coupled with a growing GNP, white-collar labor force, and middle class (Current, Williams, Freidel, and Brinkley 1983). Yet, in contrast to the growing affluence and changing technology, the baby-boom cohort also shared fearful images of World War II, Nazi atrocities, the atomic bomb, and the Cold War.

According to generational theorists, it is these cohort experiences that provide the basis for the formation of a generational consciousness (Mannheim 1952; Ortega y Gasset 1961; Esler 1984). Mannheim (1952) made the distinction between a cohort, as an age group "in itself," and a generation, as an age group "for itself." The importance of shared growing-up experiences, generational awareness, and the generation gap is reflected in the writings of the early SDS organizers. The *Port Huron Statement* began with a section called "Agenda for a Generation;" part of Todd Gitlin's (1987) explanation for why he and other members of SDS became active in politics rests heavily on the collective memories of their growing-up years during the 1950s; and Tom Hayden as editor of the campus newspaper in his college days wrote:

> The present student generation was born on the brink of war and has never seen their country at more than wobbling peace.... Theirs is a generation... stultified and frustrated by intense cold war pressures, particularly as those pressures have been illustrated in the unique concept of The Bomb (Miller 1987, p. 51).

Hayden (1988, pp. 178-179) was well aware too of the consequences of differential sociohistorical experiences for his father's versus his own generation:

> What became known as the generation gap stemmed from the very different world views of those of my father's era and my own. My father's generation believed—correctly—that they had defended democracy against foreign despotism; we believed we were defending democracy from its enemies at home....In my generation's world view, the most apparent and unwanted invaders were our own armed forces—"white boots marchin' in a yellow land," as Phil Ochs sang—the very opposite of the dynamics of World War II.

However, the Weathermen—or second generation SDS—were born a few years later than the youth who formed SDS, and although also part of the baby-boom cohort, had a slightly different set of cohort experiences. The teenage years of many Weathermen were not the 1950s but the 1960s (Gitlin 1987; Hayden 1988). As Weatherwomen

Cathy Wilkerson commented, "Our revolutionary consciousness was the result of growing up in the age of the atom bomb, of growing up in the '60s. We are who we are because Malcolm X was around teaching, and Rap Brown . . ." (Hornblower and Valentine 1980).

Yet, such shared cohort experiences are not sufficient to explain the formation of an active political generation. Another important factor is the sociohistorical context or period effect—the events and trends at any given time in history that affect all age groups in society—which has been found to have considerable influence on the formation, activities, and demise of various political generations in history (Braungart and Braungart 1989b). It is significant that SDS formed in the early 1960s and the Weathermen in the late 1960s. The historical influences were qualitatively different for these two groups, which may partially explain why the Weathermen turned to violence.

The significant events that influenced the formation of SDS occurred in the early 1960s, which represented an opening-up era in American history, as the youthful President John F. Kennedy led the country away from the "old," the conservative, and the domination of privatist interests of the 1950s to the "young," the progressive, and public spiritedness of the 1960s (Klapp 1975; Schlesinger 1986). It was a decade that began with the civil rights struggle in the South, full of hope that social inequities could be corrected and a firm conviction that the world could become a better place through human effort. These were the social and political forces that influenced the organization of SDS in 1962, and in keeping with the spirit of the times, much of SDS's early efforts were devoted to implementing its shibboleth of "participatory democracy" through civil rights, community action programs, and university reform efforts.

However, events and trends began to shift with the Kennedy assassination and Johnson presidency. Increasing numbers of U.S. troops were committed to fight in Vietnam, and events worsened on the domestic front. The civil rights movement headed North to become an acerbic black power movement, and as the Vietnam war escalated, so did youthful protests against the war and against the draft. By the mid 1960s, the baby-boom cohort crowded many college campuses and worked to change the *in loco parentis* policies of university administrations. All the while, the ubiquitous youth culture was dividing over a number of issues: activists versus nonactivists; the druggies, hippies, and flower children versus the collegiates; the feminists versus the traditionalists and chauvinists; the gays versus the straights; the black power movement versus the "honkies." America was heating up, as the mix of events and trends spiraled and escalated; actions were met with counteractions.

The events of 1968 set the stage for the entrance of the Weathermen in the United States. The 1968 Democratic Convention in Chicago and ensuing Chicago conspiracy trial along with the Columbia University uprising oriented the New Left in America toward direct action, confrontation, disruption, and violence and provided the meeting ground for many of the Weathermen's leaders (Gitlin 1987; Hayden 1988). Frustrated over the intransigent American elitist system (government, corporate, university), protesting groups often spearheaded by SDS, intensified their tactics, while authorities countered with heightened rigidity, force, and surveillance, which political youth characterized as "repressive" and "fascistic." For example, according to Sale (1973, p. 406), the extent and scope of the 1968 Pentagon protest demonstration caught the Johnson Administration by surprise, despite the government's "elaborate plans and surveillance." After the demonstration, the Administration responded in a number of ways, including escalating surveillance, reclassifying students involved in draft resistance as 1-A and getting them sent to Vietnam, handing down indictments against protestors, and setting up special Congressional committees to investigate left-wing organizations such as SDS. Local FBI and police units deployed student informers and infiltrators as well as undercover agents at the campus level. Exaggeration and overreaction on both sides kept the momentum going—a dynamic that helped assure Nixon's election to the presidency under the banner of "law-and-order" (Hayden 1988; Schlagheck 1988).

The youth culture and political activism in America were part of a larger global trend of heightened youthful activity that was becoming increasingly utopian, violent, and revolutionary. Terrorism was on the increase in the world, and extremist youth groups applauded and copied the style and actions of some of these terrorist groups—most notably Germany's Baader-Meinhof gang, Italy's Red Brigade, and the Japanese Red Army that terrorized and murdered in the 1960s and 1970s (Carroll 1978). Worthy of note was the high female participation in these terrorist-styled youth groups, which one West German criminologist attributed to "deficiencies in their socialization process," characterizing these women as "more out of touch with reality than male terrorists, and as a result some become even more fanatical extremists" (Getler 1977, p. A15). More likely, the aggressive participation of women in these groups, including the Weathermen, was rooted in the larger struggle for feminist identity and recognition that was a dominant issue in the late 1960s and 1970s (Stern 1975; Hayden 1988).

These were some of the historical events and trends that influenced the evolution of the Weatherman organization as distinct from SDS in 1969. Once formed, other specific events were associated with the Weathermen's decision to become a clandestine organization and to engage in acts of bombing. The idea of going underground did not originate with the Weathermen. In the late 1960s and early 1970s, the Black Panthers were going underground, the Berrigan brothers were contemplating going underground, and many American draft evaders were hiding out as fugitives in Canada and Sweden (Hayden 1988). In addition, there was a further hardening of the lines between youth and the government following Nixon's invasion of Cambodia in 1970 when massive student disruptions occurred across the country and protesting students were killed at two universities. Foreshadowing the Watergate affair, the Nixon Administration intensified the pressure on student political groups initiated by President Johnson; not only did the government engage in surveillance and infiltration but in harassment and entrapment. These practices later were cited by a Senate investigating committee as "excessive," involving serious breaches of law that jeopardized democratic values (Schlagheck 1988, pp. 102-103). In addition, Weathermen were incensed over two events related to the Black Panthers—Bobby Seale was bound and gagged at the Conspiracy 8 trial and later hustled off to jail, and two other Black Panther leaders were killed by police in an early morning raid.

Despite these polarizing and increasingly violent events, it was becoming clear in late 1969 that there was not much support for the Weathermen's "white revolution." The Weather Bureau then decided to shift away from the idea of a mass youth revolution in favor of an elitist one and formed a clandestine organization. Stern (1975, pp. 202-203) recounted how the Weather Bureau explained their decision to the group:

> . . . there was no longer any hope for white youth. American defeatism had conquered; they were not willing to struggle for themselves, let alone the peoples of the world. Weatherman, with a clear vision of what had to be done,

> could wait no longer. To hold back now would be to fail the Vietnamese, the blacks, and the revolution.

Going underground meant that the tactics employed by the Weathermen were to be more destructive. Since American society could not be saved, it would have to be destroyed. The dark side of politics held seductive appeal to the Weathermen. "We have to force the disintegration of society, creating strategic armed chaos where there is now pig order," Weathermen wrote before going underground in "Revolution in the 70s" (Jacobs 1970, p. 366). Hayden (1988, p. 360) summarized the difference in perspectives between SDS and the Weathermen:

> Revolutionaries like the Weathermen, having given up on changing American society, thought of themselves as a "fifth column" or, in Malraux's phrase "doomed executioners." There would be no social revolution in America, just wreckage .... While I was still very much a child of Port Huron, they were war orphans. As I said in a bitter argument with Terry [Robbins of the Weathermen], they were not the conscience of a generation, but its id, finally surfacing.

Underground they went in the early 1970s, with several of their cells highly active in bombing. But the event that shook the Weathermen's confidence was the townhouse explosion in March 1970 that killed three members. Stern's (1975, p. 238) response was:

> Those were people who were real .... I was horrified that they had blown themselves up, that they had not known enough, that they had made a mistake when a mistake was deadly. But their deaths were instructive to me .... No mistakes. No more children's crusade. To go up against serpents ... you must be a serpent yourself.

> "The times were driving people toward madness," said Hayden (1988, p. 420).

But several years later, American politics had become less divisive, and life underground had become tedious for many Weatherpeople. As Alpert (1981, pp. 327-328) remembered, "By 1974, the Weathermen were of little interest to prosecutors ... I no longer believed, as I had in 1970, that the country was in any way ready for a revolution, leftist or otherwise." In the latter 1970s and early 1980s, most members of the Weather Underground quit clandestine life to live above ground. Rank-and-file members Stern and Alpert tired of an underground existence, became saddened and lonely as some of their friends abandoned the revolution, and longed for their old contacts. In 1977, it was reported that a split occurred among Weather Underground leaders about whether, how, and when to surface. One faction hatched a plan by Jeff Jones in 1975, which was called "inversion," or the process of emerging from fugitive life in order to enlist above-ground radicals into the cause. According to statements made by the dissenting leadership, which included Bernardine Dohrn, the plan involved having lawyers prepare a defense, and showing the film "Underground" to "sanitize the image of the organization and to raise money for legal defense" (*New York Times* 1977, p. 22).

From the late 1970s through the 1980s well-known Weather leaders, such as Mark Rudd, Bernardine Dohrn, Bill Ayers, and Cathy Wilkerson surfaced from the underground. The Weather Underground did not cease to exist, however. The "last gasp" of the Weather Underground was the 1981 Brinks robbery. The robbery was bungled, a guard and two policemen were shot, and Kathy Boudin, Judith Clark, David Gilbert of the May 19th Coalition faction of the Weathermen, along with several others possibly from the Black Liberation Army, were caught, charged, and sentenced for their crimes (Franks 1981; McGrath 1981; Gitlin 1987).

While it is apparent that historical-period effects influenced both the formation of the Weathermen and their activities, in order to more fully understand the Weatherman organization and decisions, an important consideration is the group itself. Committing acts of terrorism, Crenshaw (1986, p. 385) noted, "is a result of group interaction as much as individual choice." As the terrorist literature has indicated, the group is a major source of radicalization for individual members, providing the rationale, norms, and reinforcement for extreme behavior (Braungart and Braungart 1983; Wasmund 1983). In the next section, attention is given to the group dynamics within the Weathermen that indicate why some youth joined the group and document the pronounced group effect of the Weathermen on individual members.

Group Dynamic Explanations

One question of interest is how young people became involved in the Weathermen organization. Many of the leaders came directly from SDS, but recruitment of rank-and-file members into the Weathermen appears to have been less based on radicalized individuals seeking out extremist groups to join than on friendship and personal-network factors. Studies of terrorist groups, entry into SDS, and accounts of those who joined the Weathermen indicated that individuals, some of whom were not initially radical or political, became involved in the group because of friends and lovers, or they drifted into the group under fortuitous circumstances (Wasmund 1983; Laqueur 1987; Braungart and Braungart 1988). The stage of youth is a time in life where peer associations and the group are especially important, with many of the Weathermen exhibiting a high need for group affiliation. Once a member, these youth found a sense of identification and belonging. As one newcomer to the Weatherman expressed it:

> It struck me, at a meeting I went to, that they were a family. A big, very tight family. I wanted to be part of that. People were touching each other. Women together, men together. They were beautifully free. I felt that they were experiencing a whole new life-style that I really hadn't begun to understand. They were so full of life and energy and determination and love (Sale 1973, p. 625).

The Weathermen was more than just a membership group; it was a highly committed reference group that demanded the total involvement of the individual. New members perceived themselves to be under close scrutiny or "test"—another dynamic that is characteristic of terrorist groups (Wasmund 1983). This kind of reference group quickly gains control over individual members' perceptions, attitudes, and behavior, especially for the highly ego-involved members. Experiments in group psychology have demonstrated the effects of groups on their members. For example, individual group members tend to relinquish their personal norms for those of the group (Sherif 1936), they conform to group pressure (Asch 1955) and roles (Zimbardo 1975), they commit distasteful, abhorrent acts because they are told to do so (Milgram 1974) and are conforming to group norms and practices (Sherif and Sherif 1969; Turner and

Killian 1987). Group effects such as these are predicted to be even more pronounced in self-selected or intact radical political groups (Stephan 1985; Tajfel and Turner 1986).

The Weathermen organization was an important source of political socialization for many of its members. And it was often *after* joining the group that many individuals became more radicalized and extreme in their behavior. For example, Alpert (1981, p. 122) described:

> As Sam and I became closer to each other, I became drawn into the world of radical politics which I had admired from the outside for so many years and to which I'd never quite managed to gain entry on my own . . . . As I adopted the radicals' viewpoint for myself, I came to see all antiestablishment uprisings as aspects of a world revolution . . . . Instead of feeling anxiety that the world order I'd grown up with was breaking down, I came to welcome the prospect, identifying my own discontent with that of rebels around the globe and cheering for our eventual victory.

Totalistic groups such as the Weathermen provide clear, simplistic structure for the members' lives. To some individuals, part of the initial appeal of the Weathermen was the feeling of belonging and giving one's self over to the group. For the drifters, the timing of group affiliation came when they felt their lives to be "in transition," with the Weathermen attracting some individuals who were Vietnam veterans, recently divorced or from a broken relationship, and college drop-outs (Stern 1975; Alpert 1981). Part of the attraction to the Weathermen may also have been the excitement of being in a group environment where conventional values are eschewed, with the group "giving permission" to young people—along with positive reinforcement—for engaging in a variety of taboo behaviors, both personal and political. The Weathermen was a high risk-taking, extremist group, and as social psychological studies have demonstrated, individuals are more apt to support extreme types of behavior sanctioned by the group than they would if acting alone (Myers and Lamm 1976; Forsyth 1983). This kind of strong group support may partially explain why these youth from middle- and upper-middle-class families and prestigious schools could discard conventional norms to engage in the highly experimental and destructive acts promoted by the Weathermen.

It is worthy of comment that some of the most extreme and violent actions in the Weathermen were conducted by women—as was also the case in the Baader-Meinhof gang and Red Brigades. No doubt the charismatic Bernardine Dohrn was a compelling role model for women in the group, but much of the explanation for women's behavior may rest in the feminist movement of that particular time in history, with Weatherwomen feeling that they had to prove their toughness to group members in their fight for recognition and respect. While the male-female struggle within the group was an ongoing battle, Hayden (1988) pointed out that relative to other political activist groups operating during that time, the Weathermen was a group where women had relative freedom and could act out their conflicts and hostilities. Yet, as several Weather Underground members—one a female and the other a male—admitted years later: "We've made many mistakes . . . . Male supremacy undermined us;" and "The Weather Underground has always emphasized that men and women had to struggle together . . . . But macho attitudes were largely responsible for our downfall" (Boeth 1977; Hornblower and Valentine 1980).

What helped to sustain the Weatherman organization was group conflict. The Weathermen were constantly "at war" with some "enemy": at its formative stage it was SDS and the other factions within SDS; during its rampage stage in the summer and fall of 1969, it was bourgeois white America; and in the clandestine stage it was the state (government, FBI-CIA, police) and the corporate sectors. The enemy was given focus by the Weathermen's vitriolic language, evident in its communiques and statements, such as when Mark Rudd told the audience at the National War Council, "It's a wonderful feeling to hit a pig" (Sale 1973, p. 628). As Gitlin (1987, p. 390) observed, "Language became a cudgel in this shadow play." Having an enemy to hate and vilify facilitated group solidarity and provided a target for group energy and efforts to maintain organizational momentum. Escalating the level of intergroup conflict, as the Weather Bureau did, also helped divert attention from the ongoing intragroup conflict to some outside enemy.

Because the Weathermen was a totalistic group and in continual conflict with the authorities, the group was able to exert a powerful influence over individual members' perception, thinking, and behavior—a dynamic that facilitates distorted social judgments and destructive behavior at both the individual and group levels (Sherif and Sherif 1969; Forsyth 1983). Group-based evaluations were exaggerated—termed the assimilation-contrast effect—providing the basis for stereotyping, unrealistic expectations, negative intergroup attitudes, dehumanization of outgroups, and the promotion of conflict that once established becomes difficult to end (Stephan 1985; Tajfel and Turner 1986; Braungart and Braungart 1989a). Similar group dynamics occurred within the Nixon Administration and local police forces. Distortion effects were further heightened within the Weathermen when it became a clandestine organization. As Gitlin (1987, p. 395) observed, "The more insulated . . . from counterarguments and complicated reality, the easier it was to hold onto abstract revolutionary schemes. The Weathermen developed this hermetic tendency to a coarse art."

As with groups engaging in terrorist actions (whether substate, nihilist, issue-oriented, or the government), the individual is socialized into committing destructive acts by the reference group (Braungart and Braungart 1983; Wasmund 1983; Crenshaw 1986). In the Weathermen, individual identities were broken down ("Weatherfries"), along with morality and personal concerns about harming others through violence. Encouraging Weather members to abandon personal misgivings was partially facilitated through extensive sexual and drug experimentation, with the group totally controlling the individual's life, even in the sexual area. The Weathermen readily supplied the rhetoric and rationale as well as the positive reinforcement for unconventional or destructive behavior. As Alpert (1981, p. 194) recounted:

> In the same way I had convinced myself that sexual possessiveness was reactionary, I was now trying to overcome my scruples against bombings, which I was convinced were a residue of the same bourgeois upbringing. I was afraid to seem cowardly: I didn't want Sam or anyone else to accuse me of timidity or conservatism, and I didn't want to be excluded from Sam's plans for the future.

Weathermen absolved the individual of guilt by justifying harmful actions. As one said, "It's not a question of whether to use violence or not. There's no other way" (*Newsweek* 1970, p. 27). Proving oneself and gaining status in the group was achieved through destructive acts, and engaging in behavior against one's better judgment to impress the group is a theme echoed in several personal accounts (see Stern 1975; Alpert 1981). Yet, as with terrorist or criminal organizations, after participating in such instrumental and illegal activity, even if the individual no longer wants to be part of the group, alternatives to the group are increasingly restricted and the path back to conventional society and a positive identity becomes blocked. Susan Stern (1975, pp. 208-209) described the burden of underground life as well as the Weathermen's inability to read reality:

> There was no escape . . . . We were alone and isolated. We constituted a fraction of a fraction of the population at large. Everyone was disgusted with the Weathermen. The dream had turned into a nightmare . . . . We were finished, but we didn't know it yet. The end was coming swiftly, but no one warned us. Ignoring the reality, we filled our minds with visions of the new underground . . . . I was living science fiction. It was the loneliest, most morbid time of my life.

In reviewing Stern's book, *With the Weathermen*, Brownmiller (1975, p. 6) observed, "But the real story here is one of group tyranny over individual lives." In the end, what weakened the Weathermen had far less to do with government harassment than with the faceless existence of underground life, the convoluted "Weatherlogic," and infighting within the group.

Why the Weathermen?

In this study it has been suggested that in order to more fully understand the formation and motivations of a youthful political group such as the Weathermen, a social psychological approach is needed. Toward that end, a framework was developed, organized around psychological, sociohistorical, and group dynamic explanations. Combining macro and micro levels of analysis, each approach suggested certain key concepts and relationships that were applicable to explaining the Weathermen and their behavior. Some of the major results are summarized in Table 1.

A Social Psychological Assessment

From a psychological perspective, focusing on the developmental

Table 1. Social Psychological Framework for Assessing Motivations of the Weathermen

LEVEL OF ANALYSIS		*WEATHERMAN ORGANIZATION*
Psychological		
	Development	•Cognitive style categorical, "blood-thirsty," ideological-utopian •Identity diffuse, experimental, and negative, with a search for meaning of life
	Personality	•Mixture of personality types and traits in the group •Some individuals innately aggressive, while others less aggressive but conformed to group pressure •Some individuals' personalities changed as a result of group membership
	Family Background	•Many from affluent or middle-class backgrounds, who felt guilty about their comfort relative to the poor •Parents' politics mixed: Democrat, liberal, Republican, radical-chic, pacifist
Sociohistorical		
	Cohort Effects	•Grew up as part of the large baby-boom cohort •Came of age as teenagers during turbulent 1960s when black power movement and Vietman war were important issues
	Period Effects	•Violent late 1960s: international terrorism and extremist youth groups active in Europe and Japan; assassinations of Martin Luther King, Jr. and Robert Kennedy; 1968 Democratic Convention; Columbia University uprising •Increasingly unpopular Vietnam war continued •Youth culture highly experimental and cynical •Competing activist movements (feminist, black power, gay rights) vied for attention •Domestic politics polarized, fragmented, and conflict-oriented under Nixon Administration •Intensive government surveillance of youthful political activists in era of widespread student protests
Group Dynamics		
	Affiliation	•Joined through friends, lovers, or by chance
	Structure	•Totalistic reference group: authoritarian and isolated, enhancing group effect on individual
	Dynamics	•Intensive intergroup and intragroup conflict •Distorted perception, judgment, and behavior •Negative role models and destructive behavior reinforced

processes of youth provided more information about the Weathermen's motivations and behavior than did a search for similar personality traits or a terrorist personality profile. The journey into "Weatherpolitics" by individual members appeared to be strongly rooted in resolving the developmental issues of the stage of youth. Young people drawn to the Weathermen tended to engage in a categorical all-or-nothing style of political thinking, struggled with identity formation, and found the personal and political experimentation as well as the negative identity offered by the Weatherman appealing and exciting. Often coming from well-to-do families, a number of youth who became members of the Weathermen were deeply concerned with resolving the dissonance between their own relative comfort and the poverty, exploitation, and misery of those less fortunate in America and the third world. Many of the young people who joined the Weathermen were looking for meaning in their lives and linked their personal lives to politics by affiliating with this highly controlling and contentious political youth group. Consideration of psychological features, while necessary, does not appear sufficient to explain the Weathermen's attitudes and actions.

Much of the behavior of the Weathermen and its members had to do with the larger sociohistorical context, including both cohort and period effects. One important sociohistorical influence involved growing up as members of the large baby-boom cohort, who were teenagers during the tumultuous 1960s when racial conflict and the Vietnam war were divisive issues in American society. These middle- and upper-middle-class youth appeared especially attuned to the violent, unjust, and shrill America in which they came of age, and their political attitudes and style were a partial reflection of their interpretations and responses to the cohort influences of their youth in the 1960s. As college students and young adults in the late 1960s and early 1970s, the Weathermen's rhetoric and style was a partial outcome of their political socialization experiences and psychological needs.

Another type of sociohistorical influence on the Weathermen included the particular mix of events and trends in the late 1960s and early 1970s as the group organized and took political action. The formation of the Weathermen stemmed largely from the escalating political polarization, fragmentation, and violence, coupled with the failure of SDS and other leftist political groups to effectively bring about the changes that had concerned many youth since the early 1960s in the areas of civil rights/racism, the Vietnam War-U.S. imperialism, and university reform. Global trends such as the heightened youthful revolutionary and terrorist political activity helped sustain the momentum of the Weathermen, while on the domestic front the Weathermen were strongly influenced by the black power movement, the feminist struggle, and the Nixon Administration's Vietnam policy, surveillance, and disdain for youthful protest.

These were among the unique period effects that contributed to the escalation of the Weathermen's tactics and strategy as well as the Weather Bureau's decision to become a clandestine organization engaging in acts of violence and terrorism. However, as the political issues shifted in the mid-1970s, the activities of the Weatherman organization subsided, and most Weather leaders and rank-and-file members began to emerge from their underground life. Only a few Weathermen remained fugitives, such as those who attempted the Brinks robbery—an act that Franks (1981, p. 46) described as "a chilling perversion of every purpose they had ever had: the children of the rich killing the less privileged in the name of revolution."

Mediating between the individual members and society was the Weathermen group, which was both strongly affected by social and political events and in turn exerted a dominant influence over the personalities, attitudes, and behavior of its participants. Often joining because of friends or lovers, part of the appeal of the Weathermen was the group's ability to meet the affiliative needs of youth. As a highly controlling reference group, the Weathermen provided a vehicle for many young individuals to abandon their weak identities, give themselves over to the group, and find meaning in life. The self-selected isolation of the group, its intensive inter- and intragroup conflict further enhanced the power of the group over its members. Distorted social judgments and extremist political behavior were the result, as the group interpreted (distorted) reality, romanticized revolution, encouraged the violation of conventional society's taboos, and offered support for engaging in destructive personal and political behavior.

From SDS to the Weathermen

To help put these findings in clearer perspective, comparisons can be made between the Weathermen and SDS, which are of interest in this study, since SDS helped launch the 1960s Generation in the United States, whereas the Weathermen are often credited with bringing the

1960s political generation to an end. Though both groups were part of the New Left movement in the stormy 1960s, the style and tactics of the two groups differed, partially due to the unique interplay among sociohistorical, group, and psychological forces. Especially important to understanding the behavior of SDS and the Weathermen were their somewhat different locations in history. SDS, whose members were slightly older than the Weathermen and had grown up as teens in the late 1950s, organized during the optimistic early 1960s in the United States. Members of the second generation SDS, the Weathermen came of age during the more dramatic and divisive later 1960s, with the organization evolving out of the frustrations of the student left in 1969 in an era of heightened political conflict and rage.

Both SDS and Weathermen participated in and contributed to the momentum of the 1960s generation, but, of critical importance, each had emerged from a different starting point and had acted and reacted to a different set of escalating societal and political conditions. The Weathermen became active during a time when the larger student movement had intensified its activity and expanded to more college and university campuses. The tactics that had been "radical" in the early phases of SDS, by the late 1960s had become "conventional;" therefore, in order to keep the New Left Movement going, more extreme tactics were required, especially since a variety of new groups and causes (feminism, gay rights, Yippies, black power) were vying for public attention.

While the momentum and mix of historical events and trends strongly affected the origins of SDS and Weathermen, a significant factor accounting for differences in their organizations and actions was the group effect. Although those joining either SDS or the Weathermen often entered for similar reasons—friends, lovers, fortuitous circumstances—once involved in their respective groups, individual members were exposed to a specific set of sociohistorical conditions and group dynamics that influenced the identities, attitudes, and behavior of their members. An important difference between SDS and the Weathermen was the totalistic structure of Weathermen, which became more pronounced when the group became a clandestine organization.

Both SDS and the Weathermen attempted to transform politics, but the Weathermen attempted to transform individual members as well. The Weathermen had special appeal to youth struggling with an identity crisis who were drawn to a revolutionary group that espoused an over-simplified, utopian, and violent form of politics. These were some of the same reasons given by SDS leaders Tom Hayden (1988) and Todd Gitlin (1987) for *not* joining the Weathermen, although they, like many of their Weathermen friends, were highly frustrated over the events and issues in the late 1960s.

The impact of a political generation is not curtailed when a particularly active era such as the 1960s has ended. There are "spillover effects," especially on the lives of a political generation's participants. Although both SDS and the Weathermen activists have aged and society has changed markedly since the 1960s and early 1970s, the political loyalty and outlook of these former activists remains partially "frozen" in generational time, continuing to reflect the orientation and style of their respective groups. Now middle-aged, Tom Hayden, founder and former leader of SDS, closed his book *Reunion* (1988, p. 507) with the statement:

> Times filled with tragedy are also times of greatness and wonder, times that really matter, and times truly worth living through. Whatever the future holds, and as satisfying as my life is today, I miss the sixties and always will.

A more caustic analysis came from several Weathermen entering mid-life. Noted Cathy Wilkerson after leaving the underground: "I have the same commitment to struggle . . . . It is 1980, but the conditions still exist which caused colonized peoples to fight for liberation. . ." (Hornblower and Valentine 1980, p. A2). Said Bill Ayers upon surfacing from the underground in 1980: "It's a system built on genocide and slavery and oppression, a system that poisons the earth and cripples future generations for profit . . ." *(Syracuse Herald Journal* 1980, p. A11). SDS and the Weathermen were part of the same 1960s Generation and shared a fervent commitment to radical left-wing politics. But as the 1960s decade wore on and SDS's aspirations to reform and radicalize society were thwarted, the way was paved for the Weathermen's journey into clandestine politics and terrorist tactics. The Weathermen, like the Queen of Hearts in *Alice in Wonderland*, had only one solution for settling difficulties both great or small. "Off with their heads!" the Queen would say, "without even looking round."

References

Adelson, J. 1987. "Children and Other Political Naifs." Pp. 88-102 in *Growing and Changing*, edited by E. Hall. New York: Random House.

Alpert, J. 1973. "Mother Right: A New Feminist Theory." *Ms.*, August, pp. 52-55, 88-94.

_____. 1981. *Growing Up Underground.* New York: Morrow.

Asch, S. E. 1955. "Opinions and Social Pressure." *Scientific American* 193:31-35.

Bell, J. B. 1980. "The International Scientific Conference on Terrorism, Berlin." *Terrorism: An International Journal* 3:201-202.

Bettelheim, B. 1963. "The Problem of Generations." Pp. 64-92 in *Youth: Change and Challenge*, edited by E. H. Erikson. New York: Basic.

Boeth, R. 1977. "The Return of Mark Rudd." *Newsweek* (September 26), p. 34.

Braungart, R. G. 1979. *Family Status, Socialization and Student Politics.* Ann Arbor, MI: University Microfilms International.

_____. 1988. "Journey into All-or-Nothing Politics." *Contemporary Sociology* 17(November):733-737.

Braungart, R. G. and M. M. Braungart. 1983. "Terrorism." Pp. 299-337 in *Prevention and Control of Aggression*, edited by Center for Research on Aggression, Syracuse University. New York: Pergamon.

_____. 1986. "Life Course and Generational Politics." *Annual Review of Sociology* 12:205-231.

_____. 1988. "The Life-Course Development of Left- and Right-Wing Youth Activist Leaders from the 1960s." Paper presented at the Annual Scientific Meeting of the International Society of Political Psychology, Secaucus, New Jersey, July 1-5.

_____. 1989a. "Generational Conflict and Intergroup Relations as the Foundation for Political Generations." Pp. 107-30 in *Advances in Group Processes* (Vol. 6), edited by E. J. Lawler and B. Markovsky. Greenwich, CT: JAI Press.

_____. 1989b. "Political Generations." Pp. 281-319 in *Research in Political Sociology* (Vol. 4), edited by R.G. Braungart and M.M. Braungart. Greenwich, CT: JAI Press.

Brownmiller, S. 1975. "With the Weathermen." *New York Times Book Review* (June 15), p. 6.

Carroll, R. 1978. "Inside the Red Brigades." *Newsweek* (May 15), pp. 43-44, 49.

Crenshaw, M. 1986. "The Psychology of Political Terrorism." Pp. 379-413 in *Political Psychology*, edited by M. G. Hermann. San Francisco: Jossey-Bass.

Current, R. N., T. H. Williams, F. Freidel, and A. Brinkley. 1983. *American History: A Survey*. 6th ed. New York: Knopf.

Delli Carpini, M. X. 1986. *Stability and Change in American Politics: The Coming of Age of the Generations of the 1960s*. New York: New York University Press.

Erikson, E. 1968. *Identity: Youth and Crisis*. New York: Norton.

Esler, A. 1984. "'The Truest Community': Social Generations as Collective Mentalities." *Journal of Political and Military Sociology* 12:99-112.

Feuer, L. 1969. *The Conflict of Generations*. New York: Basic.

Flacks, R. 1967. "The Liberated Generation: An Exploration of the Roots of Student Protest." *Journal of Social Issues* 23:52-75.

Forsyth, D.R. 1983. *An Introduction to Group Dynamics*. Monterey, CA: Brooks/Cole.

Frankfurt, E. 1983. *Kathy Boudin and the Dance of Death*. New York: Stein and Day.

Franks, L. 1981. "The Seeds of Terror." *New York Times Magazine* (November 22, pp. 34-38, 46).

Fromm, E. 1973. *The Anatomy of Human Destructiveness*. New York: Holt, Rinehart and Winston.

Gallatin, J. 1980. "Political Thinking in Adolescence." Pp. 344-382 in *Handbook of Adolescent Psychology*, edited by J. Adelson. New York: Wiley.

Getler, M. 1977. "Women Play Growing Role in Slayings By West Germany's Terrorist Groups." *Washington Post* (August 6), p. A15.

Gitlin, T. 1987. *The Sixties: Years of Hope, Days of Rage*.New York: Bantam.

Gordon, L. and A. Gordon. 1987. *American Chronicle: Six Decades in American Life*. New York: Atheneum.

Hayden. T. 1988. *Reunion: A Memoir*. New York: Random House.

Hornblower, M. and P. Valentine. 1980. "Cathy Wilkerson: The Evolution of a Revolutionary." *Washington Post* (July 15), p. 2.

Jacobs, H., ed. 1970. *Weatherman*. New York: Ramparts.

Jenkins, B. M. 1980. "The International Scientific Conference on Terrorism, Berlin." *Terrorism: An International Journal* 3:246-250.

Kanfer, S. 1981. "The Politics of the Playpen." *New Republic* (December 23), 30-32.

Keniston, K. 1968. *Young Radicals*. New York: Harcourt, Brace and World.

Klapp, O. E. 1975. "Opening and Closing in Open Systems." *Behavioral Science* 20:251-257.

Knoke, David. 1984. "Conceptual and Measurement Aspects in the Study of Political Generations." *Journal of Political and Military Sociology* 12:191-201.

Knutson, J. N. 1981. "Social and Psychodynamic Pressures Toward a Negative Identity: The Case of an American Revolutionary Terrorist." Pp. 105-50 in *Behavioral and Quantitative Perspectives on Terrorism*, edited by Y. Alexander and J. M. Gleason. New York: Pergamon.

Laqueur, W. 1987. *The Age of Terrorism*. Boston: Little Brown.

Lebow, R. N. 1980. "The Origins of Sectarian Assassination: The Case of Belfast." Pp. 41-53 in *International Terrorism: Current Research and Future Directions*, edited by A. D. Buckley and D. D. Olson. Wayne, NJ: Avery.

Life. 1970. March 27, p. 30.

Mannheim, K. 1952. "The Problem of Generations." Pp. 276-320 in *Essays on the Sociology of Knowledge*, edited by Paul Kecskemeti. London: Routledge and Kegan Paul.

McGrath, P. 1981. "Return of the Weathermen." *Newsweek* (November 2), pp. 30-34.

Milgram, S. 1974. *Obedience to Authority*. New York: Harper and Row.

Miller, J. 1987. *Democracy in the Streets*. New York: Simon and Schuster.

Moller, H. 1972. "Youth as a Force in the Modern World." Pp. 215-223 in *Youth and Sociology*, edited by Peter K. Manning and M. Truzzi. Englewood Cliffs, NJ: Prentice-Hall.

Myers, D. G. and H. Lamm. 1976. "The Group Polarization Phenomenon." *Psychological Bulletin* 83:602-627.

Newsweek. 1970. March 23, pp. 27-36.

_____. 1985. November 2, p. 15.

New York Times. 1977. January 16, p. 22.

Ortega y Gasset, Jose. 1961. *The Modern Theme*. New York: Harper and Row.

Ryder, N. B. 1965. "The Cohort as a Concept in the Study of Social Change." *American Sociological Review* 30:843-861.

_____. 1974. "The Demography of Youth." Pp. 45-61 in *Youth: Transition to Adulthood*, edited by the Panel on Youth of the President's Science Advisory Committee. Chicago: University Chicago Press.

Sale, K. 1973. *SDS*. New York: Random House.

Schlagheck, D. M. 1988. *International Terrorism*. Lexington, MA: D.C. Heath.

Schlesinger, A. M., Jr. 1986. *The Cycles of American History*. Boston: Houghton Mifflin.

Sherif, M. 1936. *The Psychology of Social Norms*. New York: Harper Torchbooks.

Sherif, M. and C. Sherif. 1969. *Social Psychology*. New York: Harper and Row.

Stephan, W. G. 1985. "Intergroup Relations." Pp. 599-658 in *Handbook of Social Psychology* (vol. 2), edited by G. Lindzey and E. Aronson. New York: Random House.

Stern, S. 1975. *With the Weathermen*. New York: Doubleday.

Storr, A. 1978. "Sadism and Paranoia." Pp. 231-239 in *International Terrorism in the Contemporary World*, edited by Marius Livingston. Westport, CT: Greenwood.

Students for a Democratic Society. 1964. *The Port Huron Statement*. New York: Students for a Democratic Society.

Syracuse Herald Journal. 1980. December 4, p. A11.

Tajfel, H. and J. C. Turner. 1986. "The Social Identity Theory of Intergroup Behavior." p. 724 in *Psychology of Intergroup Relations*, edited by S. Worchel and W. G. Austin. Chicago: Nelson-Hall.

Turner, R. H. and L. M. Killian. 1987. *Collective Behavior*. 3rd. ed. Englewood Cliffs, NJ: PrenticeHall.

Unger, I. 1974. *The Movement: A History of the American New Left*, 1959-1972. New York: Dodd Mead.

Vander Zanden, J. W. 1989. *Human Development*. 4th ed. New York: Knopf.

Wallimann, I. and G. V. Zito. 1984. "Cohort Size and Youthful Protest." *Youth and Society* 16:67-81.

Wasmund, K. 1983. "The Political Socialization of Terrorist Groups in West Germany." *Journal of Political and Military Sociology* 11:223-240.

Young, N. 1977. *An Infantile Disorder? The Crisis and Decline of the New Left*. Boulder, CO: Westview.

Zimbardo, P. 1975. "Transforming Experimental Research into Advocacy for Social Change." Pp. 33-66 in *Applying Social Psychology*, edited by M. Deutsch and H. A. Hornstein. Hillsdale, NJ: Erlbaum.

Pakistan's Jihad Culture

Jessica Stern

Abstract: *Pakistani militant groups are killing civilians and engaging in terrorism in Indian-held Kashmir under the guise of holy war. The government in Islamabad supports these militants and their religious schools as cheap ways to fight India and educate Pakistan's youth. But this policy is creating a culture of violence that exacerbates internal sectarianism and destabilizes the region. Without change, this monster threatens to devour Pakistani society.*

Free Agents

Although much has been written about religious militants in the Middle East and Afghanistan, little is known in the West about those in Pakistan—perhaps because they operate mainly in Kashmir and, for now at least, do not threaten security outside South Asia. General Pervez Musharraf, Pakistan's military ruler, calls them "freedom fighters" and admonishes the West not to confuse jihad with terrorism. Musharraf is right about the distinction—the jihad doctrine delineates acceptable war behavior and explicitly outlaws terrorism—but he is wrong about the militant groups' activities. Both sides of the war in Kashmir—the Indian army and the Pakistani "mujahideen"—are targeting and killing thousands of civilians, violating both the Islamic "just war" tradition and international law.

Pakistan has two reasons to support the so-called mujahideen. First, the Pakistani military is determined to pay India back for allegedly fomenting separatism in what was once East Pakistan and in 1971 became Bangladesh. Second, India dwarfs Pakistan in population, economic strength, and military might. In 1998 India spent about two percent of its $469 billion GDP on defense, including an active armed force of more than 1.1 million personnel. In the same year, Pakistan spent about five percent of its $61 billion GDP on defense, yielding an active armed force only half the size of India's. The U.S. government estimates that India has 400,000 troops in Indian-held Kashmir—a force more than two-thirds as large as Pakistan's entire active army. The Pakistani government thus supports the irregulars as a relatively cheap way to keep Indian forces tied down.

What does such support entail? It includes, at a minimum, assisting the militants' passage into Indian-held Kashmir. This much Pakistani officials will admit, at least privately. The U.S. government believes that Pakistan also funds, trains, and equips the irregulars. Meanwhile, the Indian government claims that Pakistan uses them as an unofficial guerrilla force to carry out "dirty tricks," murders, and terrorism in India. Pakistan, in turn, accuses India's intelligence service of committing terrorism and killing hundreds of civilians in Pakistan.

Pakistan now faces a typical principal-agent problem: the interests of Pakistan (the principal) and those of the militant groups (the agent) are not fully aligned. Although the irregulars may serve Pakistan's interests in Kashmir when they target the Indian army, they also kill civilians and perform terrorism in violation of international norms and law. These crimes damage Pakistan's already fragile international reputation. Finally, and most important for Pakistanis, the militant groups that Pakistan supports and the Sunni sectarian killers that Pakistan claims it wants to wipe out overlap significantly. By facilitating the activities of the irregulars in Kashmir, the Pakistani government is inadvertently promoting internal sectarianism, supporting international terrorists, weakening the prospect for peace in Kashmir, damaging Pakistan's international image, spreading a narrow and violent version of Islam throughout the region, and increasing tensions with India—all against the interests of Pakistan as a whole.

Pakistan, Taliban-Style?

The war between India and Pakistan over the fate of Kashmir is as old as both states. When Pakistan was formally created in 1947, the rulers of Muslim-majority states that had existed within British India were given the option of joining India or Pakistan. The Hindu monarch of the predominantly Muslim state of Jammu and Kashmir chose India, prompted partly by a tribal rebellion in the state. Pakistan responded by sending in troops. The resultant fighting ended with a 1949 cease-fire, but the Pakistani government continued covertly to support volunteer guerrilla fighters in Kashmir. Islamabad argued then, as it does now, that it could not control the volunteers, who as individuals were not bound by the cease-fire agreement. (On the other hand, Maulana Abul A'la Maududi, the late founder of the Islamist party Jamaat-e-Islami, argued that as individuals, these "mujahideen" could not legitimately declare jihad, either.)

Pakistani officials admit to having tried repeatedly to foment separatism in Kashmir in the decades following the 1948 cease-fire. These attempts were largely unsuccessful; when separatist violence broke out in the late 1980s, the movement was largely indigenous. For their part, Indian officials admit their own culpability in creating an intolerable situation in the region. They ignored Kashmir's significant economic troubles, rampant corruption, and rigged elections, and they intervened in Kashmiri politics in ways that contradicted India's own constitution. As American scholar Sumit Ganguly explains, the rigged 1987 state-assembly elections were the final straw in a series of insults, igniting, by 1989, widespread violent opposition. By 1992, Pakistani nationals and other graduates of the Afghan war were joining the fight in Kashmir.

What began as an indigenous, secular movement for independence has become an increasingly Islamist crusade to bring all of Kashmir under Pakistani control. Pakistan-based Islamist groups (along with Hizb-ul-Mujahideen, a Kashmir-based group created by Jamaat-e-Islami and partly funded by Pakistan) are now significantly more important than the secular Kashmir-based ones. The Indian government estimates that about 40 percent of the militants in Kashmir today are Pakistani or Afghan, and some 80 percent are teenagers. Although the exact size of the movement is unknown, the Indian government estimates that 3,000 to 4,000 "mujahideen" are in Kashmir at any given time.

Whatever their exact numbers, these Pakistani militant groups —among them, Lashkar-i-Taiba and Harkat-ul-Mujahideen—pose a long-term danger to international security, regional stability, and especially Pakistan itself. Although their current agenda is limited to "liberating" Kashmir, which they believe was annexed by India illegally, their next objective is to turn Pakistan into a truly Islamic state. Islamabad supports these volunteers as a cheap way to keep India off balance. In the process, however, it is creating a monster that threatens to devour Pakistani society.

Schools of Hate

In Pakistan, as in many developing countries, education is not mandatory. The World Bank estimates that only 40 percent of Pakistanis are literate, and many rural areas lack public schools. Islamic religious schools— madrasahs—on the other hand, are located all over the country and provide not only free education, but also free food, housing, and clothing. In the poor areas of southern Punjab, madrasahs funded by the Sunni sectarian political party Sipah-e-Sahaba Pakistan (SSP) reportedly even pay parents for sending them their children.

In the 1980s, Pakistani dictator General Mohammad Zia-ul-Haq promoted the madrasahs as a way to garner the religious parties' support for his rule and to recruit troops for the anti-Soviet war in Afghanistan. At the time, many madrasahs were financed by the zakat (the Islamic tithe collected by the state), giving the government at least a modicum of control. But now, more and more religious schools are funded privately—by wealthy Pakistani industrialists at home or abroad, by private and government-funded nongovernmental organizations in the Persian Gulf states and Saudi Arabia, and by Iran. Without state supervision, these madrasahs are free to preach a narrow and violent version of Islam.

Most madrasahs offer only religious instruction, ignoring math, science, and other secular subjects important for functioning in modern society. As Maududi warned in his 1960 book, *First Principles of the Islamic State*, "those who choose the theological branch of learning generally keep themselves utterly ignorant of [secular subjects, thereby remaining] incapable of giving any lead to the people regarding modern political problems."

Even worse, some extremist madrasahs preach jihad without understanding the concept: They equate jihad—which most Islamic scholars interpret as the striving for justice (and principally an inner striving to purify the self)—with guerrilla warfare. These schools encourage their graduates, who often cannot find work because of their lack of practical education, to fulfill their "spiritual obligations" by fighting against Hindus in Kashmir or against Muslims of other sects in Pakistan. Pakistani officials estimate that 10 to 15 percent of the country's tens of thousands of madrasahs espouse such extremist ideologies.

Pakistan's interior minister Moinuddin Haider, for one,

recognizes these problems. "The brand of Islam they are teaching is not good for Pakistan," he says. "Some, in the garb of religious training, are busy fanning sectarian violence, poisoning people's minds." In June, Haider announced a reform plan that would require all madrasahs to register with the government, expand their curricula, disclose their financial resources, seek permission for admitting foreign students, and stop sending students to militant training camps.

This is not the first time the Pakistani government has announced such plans. And Haider's reforms so far seem to have failed, whether because of the regime's negligence or the madrasahs' refusal to be regulated, or both. Only about 4,350 of the estimated 40,000 to 50,000 madrasahs in Pakistan have registered with the government. Some are still sending students to training camps despite parents' instructions not to do so. Moreover, some chancellors are unwilling to expand their curricula, arguing that madrasahs are older than Pakistan itself—having been "designed 1,200 years ago in Iraq," according to the chancellor of the Khudamudeen madrasah. The chancellor of Darul Uloom Haqqania objects to what he calls the government's attempt to "destroy the spirit of the madrasahs under the cover of broadening their curriculum."

Mujibur Rehman Inqalabi, the SSP's second in command, told me that Haider's reform plan is "against Islam" and complains that where states have taken control of madrasahs, such as in Jordan and Egypt, "the engine of jihad is extinguished." America is right, he said: "Madrasahs are the supply line for jihad."

Jihad International, Inc.

If madrasahs supply the labor for "jihad," then wealthy Pakistanis and Arabs around the world supply the capital. On Eid-ul-Azha, the second most important Muslim holiday of the year, anyone who can afford to sacrifices an animal and gives the hide to charity. Pakistani militant groups solicit such hide donations, which they describe as a significant source of funding for their activities in Kashmir.

Most of the militant groups' funding, however, comes in the form of anonymous donations sent directly to their bank accounts. Lashkar-i-Taiba ("Army of the Pure"), a rapidly growing Ahle Hadith (Wahhabi) group, raises funds on the Internet. Lashkar and its parent organization, Markaz ad-Da'wa Wal Irshad (Center for Islamic

Invitation and Guidance), have raised so much money, mostly from sympathetic Wahhabis in Saudi Arabia, that they are reportedly planning to open their own bank.

Individual "mujahideen" also benefit financially from this generous funding. They are in this for the loot, explains Ahmed Rashid, a prominent Pakistani journalist. One mid-level manager of Lashkar told me he earns 15,000 rupees a month—more than seven times what the average Pakistani makes, according to the World Bank. Top leaders of militant groups earn much more; one leader took me to see his mansion, which was staffed by servants and filled with expensive furniture. Operatives receive smaller salaries but win bonuses for successful missions. Such earnings are particularly attractive in a country with a 40 percent official poverty rate, according to Pakistani government statistics.

The United States and Saudi Arabia funneled some $3.5 billion into Afghanistan and Pakistan during the Afghan war, according to Milt Bearden, CIA station chief in Pakistan from 1986 to 1989. "Jihad," along with guns and drugs, became the most important business in the region. The business of "jihad"—what the late scholar Eqbal Ahmad dubbed "Jihad International, Inc."—continues to attract foreign investors, mostly wealthy Arabs in the Persian Gulf region and members of the Pakistani diaspora. (As World Bank economist Paul Collier observes, diaspora populations often prolong ethnic and religious conflicts by contributing not only capital but also extremist rhetoric, since the fervor of the locals is undoubtedly held in check by the prospect of losing their own sons.)

As the so-called jihad movement continues to acquire its own financial momentum, it will become increasingly difficult for Pakistan to shut down, if and when it tries. As long as "Jihad International, Inc." is profitable, those with financial interests in the war will work to prolong it. And the longer the war in Kashmir lasts, the more entrenched these interests will become.

Addicted to Jihad

As some irregulars are financially dependent on what they consider jihad, others are spiritually and psychologically so. Many irregulars who fought in Afghanistan are now fighting in Kashmir and are likely to continue looking for new "jihads" to fight—even against Pakistan itself. Khalil, who has been a "mujahid" for 19 years and can no longer imagine another life, told me, "A person addicted to heroin can get off it if he really tries, but a mujahid cannot leave the jihad. I am spiritually addicted to jihad." Another Harkat operative told me, "We won't stop— even if India gave us Kashmir. . . . We'll [also] bring jihad here. There is already a movement here to make Pakistan a pure Islamic state. Many preach Islam, but most of them don't know what it means. We want to see a Taliban-style regime here." Aspirations like these are common among the irregulars I have interviewed over the last couple of years.

The "jihad" movement is also developing a spiritual momentum linked to its financial one. Madrasahs often teach their students that jihad—or, in the extremist schools, terrorism under the guise of jihad—is a spiritual duty. Whereas wealthy Pakistanis would rather donate their money than their sons to the cause, families in poor, rural areas are likely to send their sons to "jihad" under the belief that doing so is the only way to fulfill this spiritual duty. One mother whose son recently died fighting in Kashmir told me she would be happy if her six remaining sons were martyred. "They will help me in the next life, which is the real life," she said.

When a boy becomes a martyr, thousands of people attend his funeral. Poor families become celebrities. Everyone treats them with more respect after they lose a son, a martyr's father said. "And when there is a martyr in the village, it encourages more children to join the jihad. It raises the spirit of the entire village," he continued. In poor families with large numbers of children, a mother can assume that some of her children will die of disease if not in war. This apparently makes it easier to donate a son to what she feels is a just and holy cause.

Many of these families receive financial assistance from the militant groups. The Shuhda-e-Islam Foundation, founded in 1995 by Jamaat-e-Islami, claims to have dispensed 13 million rupees to the families of martyrs. It also claims to provide financial support to some 364 families by paying off loans, setting them up in businesses, or helping them with housing. Moreover, the foundation provides emotional and spiritual support by constantly reminding the families that they did the right thing by donating their children to assist their Muslim brethren in Kashmir. Both Lashkar-i-Taiba and Harkat have also established charitable organizations that reward the families of martyrs—a practice common to gangs in inner-city Los Angeles and terrorist groups such as al Qaeda and Hamas. Although these foundations provide a service to families in need, they also perpetuate a culture of violence.

Bad Boys

The comparison to gangs and terrorist groups is particularly apt because the irregulars often hire criminals to do their dirty work—and sometimes turn to petty or organized crime themselves. Criminals are typically hired to "drop" weapons and explosives or to carry out extreme acts of violence that a typical irregular is reluctant or unable to perform. For example, members of the Dubai-based crime ring that bombed the Bombay stock exchange in March 1993 later confessed that they had been in Islamabad the previous month, where Pakistani irregulars had allegedly trained them to throw hand grenades and fire Kalashnikov assault rifles. Law-enforcement authorities noted that the operatives' passports contained no Pakistani stamps, suggesting the complicity of the Pakistani government.

Criminals joining supposed jihad movements tend to be less committed to the group's purported goals and more committed to violence for its own sake—or for the money. When criminals join private armies, therefore, the political and moral constraints that often inhibit mass-casualty, random attacks are likely to break down. Criminal involvement in the movement also worsens the principal-agent problem for Pakistan: pure mercenaries are even harder to control than individuals whose goals are at least partly aligned with those of the state.

Exporting Holy War

Exacerbating the principal-agent problem, Pakistani militant groups are now exporting their version of jihad all over the world. The Khudamudeen madrasah, according to its chancellor, is training students from Burma, Nepal, Chechnya, Bangladesh, Afghanistan, Yemen, Mongolia, and Kuwait. Out of the 700 students at the madrasah, 127 are foreigners. Nearly half the student body at Darul Uloom Haqqania, the madrasah that created the Taliban, is from Afghanistan. It also trains students from Uzbekistan, Tajikistan, Russia, and Turkey, and is currently expanding its capacity to house foreign students from 100 to 500, its chancellor said. A Chechen student at the school told me his goal when he returned home was to fight Russians. And according to the U.S. State Department, Pakistani groups and individuals also help finance and train the Islamic Movement of Uzbekistan, a terrorist organization that aims to overthrow secular governments in Central Asia.

Many of the militant groups associated with radical madrasahs regularly proclaim their plans to bring "jihad" to India proper as well as to the West, which they believe is run by Jews. Lashkar-i-Taiba has announced its plans to "plant Islamic flags in Delhi, Tel Aviv, and Washington." One of Lashkar's Web sites includes a list of purported Jews working for the Clinton administration, including director of presidential personnel Robert Nash (an African American from Arkansas) and CIA director George Tenet (a Greek American). The group also accuses Israel of assisting India in Kashmir. Asked for a list of his favorite books, a leader of Harkat recommended the history of Hitler, who he said understood that "Jews and peace are incompatible." Several militant groups boast pictures of burning American flags on their calendars and posters.

Internal Jihad

The "jihad" against the West may be rhetorical (at least for now), but the ten-year-old sectarian war between Pakistan's Shi'a and Sunni is real and deadly. The Tehrik-e-Jafariya-e-Pakistan (TJP) was formed to protect the interests of Pakistan's Shi'a Muslims, who felt discriminated against by Zia's implementation of Sunni laws governing the inheritance and collection of zakat. Iran helped fund the TJP, probably in hopes of using it as a vehicle for an Iranian-style revolution in Pakistan. Five years later, Haq Nawaz Jhangvi, a Jamaat-ul-Ulema-e-Islam (JUI) cleric, established the SSP to offset the TJP and to promote the interests of Sunni Muslims. The SSP was funded by both Saudi Arabia and Iraq. Since then, violent gangs have formed on both sides.

After Lashkar-e-Jhangvi, a Sunni sectarian gang, attempted to assassinate then Prime Minister Muhammad Nawaz Sharif in early 1999, Sharif proposed to expand the special military courts that try terrorist crimes from Karachi to the rest of the country. Pakistan's

Supreme Court later deemed the special courts unconstitutional. Musharraf has continued Sharif's attempt to rein in the terrorist groups by implementing, among other things, a "deweaponization" plan to reduce the availability of guns to sectarian gangs and criminals.

The problem for Musharraf is that it is difficult to promote the "jihad" in Kashmir and the Taliban in Afghanistan without inadvertently promoting sectarianism in Pakistan. The movements share madrasahs, camps, bureaucracies, and operatives. The JUI, the SSP's founding party, also helped create both the Taliban and Harkat. Deobandi madrasahs issue anti-Shi'a fatwas (edicts), and boys trained to fight in Kashmir are also trained to call Shi'a kafirs (infidels). Jaesh-e-Mohammad, an offshoot of Harkat and the newest Pakistani militant group in Kashmir, reportedly used SSP personnel during a fundraising drive in early 2000. And the SSP's Inqalabi, who was recently released after four years in jail for his alleged involvement in sectarian killings, told me that whenever "one of our youngsters wants to do jihad," they join up with the Taliban, Harkat, or Jaesh-e-Mohammad—all Deobandi groups that he claims are "close" to the SSP.

Sectarian clashes have killed or injured thousands of Pakistanis since 1990. As the American scholar Vali Nasr explains, the largely theological differences between Shi'a and Sunni Muslims have been transformed into full-fledged political conflict, with broad ramifications for law and order, social cohesion, and government authority. The impotent Pakistani government has essentially allowed Sunni Saudi Arabia and Shi'a Iran to fight a proxy war on Pakistani soil, with devastating consequences for the Pakistani people.

Whither Pakistan?

Pakistan is a weak state, and government policies are making it weaker still. Its disastrous economy, exacerbated by a series of corrupt leaders, is at the root of many of its problems. Yet despite its poverty, Pakistan is spending hundreds of millions of dollars on weapons instead of schools and public health. Ironically, the government's "cost-saving" measures are even more troubling. In trying to save money in the short run by using irregulars in Kashmir and relying on madrasahs to educate its youth, Pakistan is pursuing a path that is likely to be disastrous in the long run, allowing a culture of violence to take root.

The United States has asked Pakistan to crack down on the militant groups and to close certain madrasahs, but America must do more than just scold. After all, the United States, along with Saudi Arabia, helped create the first international "jihad" to fight the Soviet Union during the Afghan war. "Does America expect us to send in the troops and shut the madrasahs down?" one official asks. "Jihad is a mindset. It developed over many years during the Afghan war. You can't change a mindset in 24 hours."

The most important contribution the United States can make, then, is to help strengthen Pakistan's secular education system. Because so much international aid to Pakistan has been diverted through corruption, both public and private assistance should come in the form of relatively nonfungible goods and services: books, buildings, teachers, and training, rather than money. Urdu-speaking teachers from around the world should be sent to Pakistan to help. And educational exchanges among students, scholars, journalists, and military officials should be encouraged and facilitated. Helping Pakistan educate its youth will not only cut off the culture of violence by reducing ignorance and poverty, it will also promote long-term economic development.

Moreover, assisting Pakistan will make the world a safer place. As observers frequently note, conflict between India and Pakistan over Kashmir is one of the most likely routes to nuclear war in the world today. The Pakistani militants' continued incursions into Indian-held Kashmir escalate the conflict, greatly increasing the risk of nuclear war between the two countries.

Although the United States can help, Pakistan must make its own changes. It must stamp out corruption, strengthen democratic institutions, and make education a much higher priority. But none of this can happen if Pakistan continues to devote an estimated 30 percent of its national budget to defense.

Most important, Pakistan must recognize the militant groups for what they are: dangerous gangs whose resources and reach continue to grow, threatening to destabilize the entire region. Pakistan's continued support of religious militant groups suggests that it does not recognize its own susceptibility to the culture of violence it has helped create. It should think again.

Islamic Terrorism: From Retrenchment To Ressentiment and Beyond

Lauren Langman
Douglas Morris

Abstract: *Using a Weberian perspective informed by Critical Theory, this paper investigates the interaction of economic, cultural and political causes and potential outcomes of Islamic terrorism. Islam's decline vis-à-vis Christendom was constrained through three major internal moments: 1) limits to modernity, 2) religious conservativism, and 3) ressentiment of the West. Islamic societies responded proactively to the rise of the West through two strategies: 1) Westernization and 2) Islamic modernism, which have both been strongly resisted. In the 20th century, due to the internal suppression of secular political movements among other factors, puritanical fundamentalisms such as Wahhabism arose. Fundamentalisms in various religions explain reality by blaming social problems on the departure from religious morality and promise redemption via a return to an idealized community. In the face of decline, colonization, and economic stagnation, ressentiment of the West became widespread in Islam. Fundamentalisms interacting with ressentiment may turn militant, as in the case of Al Qaeda. A war on terrorism is not likely to end terrorism. To solve the problem of terrorism requires addressing its roots: internal constraints, dictatorships sponsored by the West and the underdevelopment that results form neo-liberal globalization. We suggest terrorism will wane in the face of the evolution of modern Islamic public spheres that might challenge religious conservatism. In the wake of 9/11, both moderate and radical religious movements are likely to remain a basis for mobilizing alternative identities to globalization.*

Introduction

At the end of the 15th Century, Islamic societies stood at an economic, political and cultural apex. They were affluent and philosophically, scientifically, technologically, and administratively advanced. Mighty armies and trade networks had spread the hegemony of Islamic culture from the Atlantic coast through the southern Mediterranean and North Africa to the Middle East, Southeast Asia and parts of China. Challenges were repelled. The Crusades affected a small part of the

Islamic world. After the sacking of Baghdad by the Mongols (who were converted to Islam within one hundred years), politically and economically, Islam more than recovered. However, religious conservatism had become a major influence in Islamic culture and Europe had just begun its Renaissance, based in large part on the intellectual heritage of Islam.

Christian Europe of the 15th Century was poor, ignorant, politically fragmented, and save the Italian city-states, less developed than Islamic society. Yet, between 1492, when Spanish imperialism moved to the New World, and 1588, when the Spanish Armada was defeated, the expanding commerce of Europe began a move from the Mediterranean to the Atlantic that would unleash the forces of capitalism. The decline of the Ottoman Empire would mark the end of Islamic hegemony. While capitalist, industrial Europe joined with American capital to become world hegemonic, the Islamic world became a number of peripheral and semi-peripheral areas. Today, with the events of 9/11, the development of conflicts between Western and Islamic societies has been brought to the forefront of concern.

There is no singular explanation for decline of Islamic hegemony, the failure of modernization efforts, and eventually the rise of (fundamentalist) Islamisms and terrorist movements[1]. A complex interaction of economic, political and cultural factors needs to be studied. To frame this discussion, we draw on Weberian studies, the critical, dialectical traditions of the Frankfurt School and psychoanalytic insights[2]. We employ a comparative historical analysis of ideal typical articulations of Christianity and Islam as world religions oriented to salvation. There are, of course, vast differences within groups due to local traditions, classes, interactions with other cultures, history, etc. Yet, we will argue that contemporary terrorism needs to be understood in relation to certain broad social factors that have informed the decline of Islam since the 16th Century. One key factor is that just as the Reformation played a major role in the transformation of Christendom into modern Western Europe, the *failure* of Islam to have a Reformation would impose certain barriers to the embrace of rational modernity. Key political economic factors include Western domination and the rise of dictatorial governments in Islamic states. Eventually, Islamic societies responded proactively to the rise of the West through two strategies that have yet to be fully realized in Islamic states: 1) *Westernization* and 2) *Islamic Modernism.* (See Part II below.) The economic decline, military defeat and colonization of Islam vis-à-vis Christendom/the Modern West served to constrain the modern cultural and political development of Islam through three major internal moments:

1) *Limits to modernity.* The nature of Islamic theology, ethics, culture and law limited the impact of foreign ideas and/or presented indigenous barriers to the emergence of the economic, political and cultural rationality, especially after the 16th century. (See Part I below.)

2) *Religious conservativism.* In the face of various political or economic challenges, from the sacking of Baghdad in the 13th Century on up to the secular modernity of contemporary globalization that might change power and/or gender arrangements, there was a retreat to conservative forms of Islam, like Wahhabism or other worldly Sufism, that served to maintain tradition and resist social change. Wahhabism, a severely Puritanical form of Islam, emerged as the Ottoman fell in decline. It was embraced by the House of Saud to legitimate themselves as the guardians of the holy cities of Mecca and Media (and was used, in part, to maintain a Saudi imperial claim on oil wealth in the 20th century). More recently, in the face of modernity, we have seen the growth of Islamisms[3] (see Part II) and, in some cases, dramatic religious terrorism (see Part III).

3) *Ressentiment* of the West. Just as Nietzsche suggested that the marginalized Christian artisans of Rome saw themselves as morally superior to the rich, powerful and debauched Romans, so too do many Muslims see the secular West as morally degenerate compared to the "superior" morality and ethical practices of Islam, which promise a return to a righteous society and glorious rewards in heaven. (See Parts III and IV.)

Based on historical and current scholarship, this paper discusses some of the general causes of Islamic terrorism and possible outcomes. Fundamentalist traditions sometimes turn militant. To understand the rise of Islamic terrorism, the questions we now address are threefold: 1) how do conservative religious political/moral goals become translated into acts of terror? 2) how are these acts justified, especially when they result in large numbers of deaths to non-combatants—often the elderly, women and children? and 3) what are the possibilities for elimination of the causes of religious terrorism and moving beyond terrorism?

Part I: the Rise and Fall of Islam

The Origins of Islam

In the 7th Century, the conflicts between Persia and Byzantium fostered a southerly movement of trade routes through the deserts of Arabia that were largely populated by warring nomadic tribes ever involved in vendetta and counter-vendetta. Particularistic tribal religions stood as barriers to the expansion of the urban, merchant classes and threatened the security of caravans. These conditions would dispose the emergence of a unifying religion that would extend across many lands, uniting the populations, and securing the general conditions for aggressive commerce and trade. The trading classes were aware of Judeo-Christian monotheism yet felt scorned and, in turn, excluded from its teachings; yet they were wanting of a monotheistic religion (Armstrong 2001). Muhammad, an illiterate merchant, articulated a divine message, attributed to archangel Gabriel. As an emissary of Allah, he would become a charismatic prophet. The Quran, the word of Allah, God, became the foundation of a new faith that provided a monotheistic salvation religion rooted in both Jewish and Christian traditions of prophesy, incorporating their ethics and many of their customs. Muhammad, as a prophet and skilled arbiter, found a ready audience among the growing classes of merchants, whose status disposed an "elective affinity" for a salvation religion that would establish an "imagined community" of people united by faith, and that provided members with valorized, sacralized identities and a God-ordained ethical regulation of everyday conduct conducive to commerce. As Weber noted in the case of Protestantism, ethical standards between members of the religious "brotherhood" of a "world" religion, even if strangers, were an important basis for the conduct of business in large markets.

Salvation religions tend to be expansionist, seeking both to control how people behave in this world and to ensure entry into the next. In its formative period, Islam was typically spread by conquest or *jihad*, holy war. It is important to note that *jihad,* with variable meanings, would remain an essential element of Islam along with its five pillars of faith[4]. The central meaning of greater *jihad* was the inner struggle to live a spiritual life according to Quran and Hadith (holy teachings). Military conflict was considered a lesser *jihad.* In political economic terms, the lesser *jihad* empowered the expansion and defense of the largest empire of its time. Soldiers justified imperial conquests as a religious duty. For Islam, soldiers who died in *jihad*, martyrs, would gain automatic entrance to paradise[5]. For Islam, political control was more important than the conversion of the conquered. Indeed, compared to other religions, Islam was highly tolerant of Judaism and Christianity, which the Prophet saw as preceding his work. In Islamic societies, the monotheistic religions were sometimes celebrated in the same shrines. However, there was an active destruction of polytheistic folk religion and ways. There was a dialectic of Islamic imperialism in which violence was used to eliminate tribal parochialism and create and enforce religious universalism. The tolerance of the major monotheisms facilitated cultural exchange and political stability. Another factor in the expansion of Islamic political control is that converts were from powerful families (Schluchter 1999, p.79).

At the time of its origin in Mecca, the eschatological religion of Muhammad developed in pietistic urban conventicles prone to withdraw from the world: subsequently in Medina and in the evolution of early Islamic communities, the religion transformed into a wide-spread Arabic, status oriented, warrior religion (Schluchter 1999, p. 79).

> Muhammad was both an ethical prophet and a charismatic politico-military leader. He overcame tribal particularism by surpassing its polytheism and ritualism with monotheism and a legal ethic, and by transforming feuding tribes into a national-Arabic movement of conquest. . . .Mohamed was . . .not a marginalized prophet of doom, and certainly not a wandering charismatic preacher; instead, he was a religio-political leader who knew how to realize his intentions step by step, especially through the skillful use of time honored tribal practices of the creation and resolution of conflict. . . With the successful reception in Medina, the transformation of Islam from an eschatological religiosity into a political religion into a religion of national-Arabic warriors was inaugurated. (Schluchter 1999, p. 85)

Early Islam as a religion of knightly warriors had little room for sin, humility, or vocational asceticism. But Muhammad was also a merchant and encouraged the expansion of trade. "Under Muhammad, Arabian society made a respectable leap forward in social complexity and political capacity" (Bellah 1970) Islamic mercantilism grew, prospered and eventually supported centers of learning devoted to art, science, medicine etc.

Weber emphasized that there was generally a relaxed relationship in Islam between faith and reason (Schluchter 1999). While Islamic societies were tolerant of secular reason, more so than Christendom (initially), the Quran and Islamic law, *sharia*, defined morality in a traditional way that constrained political and economic behavior. That is, Islam gave license to philosophy, generally a pursuit of elites, and technical innovation, but not to moral life. In ethical terms, Islam, in most of its expressions, is a highly codified religion that is meant to oversee many aspects of everyday life, and whether and to what extent this was practiced is highly variable. Lawyers and administrators regulated traditional Islamic society, not a clergy. Jurism in Islam was not centrally litigated or legislated. It was engaged through interpretation and local decision. It was highly important for Islamic societies that social rationality was closely tied to the foundations of specific religious categories, beliefs, and exercises in relation to everyday life, commerce, and governance. More specifically, the legal codes of the Hanafi School, based in large part on what had been local traditions, would facilitate the rapid growth of Islamic commerce, but would eventually acquire a fixity that would act to prevent later generations from making revisions as conditions changed (Kuran 2001).

Islam Triumphant

Within 500 years, Islam had spread across vast tracts of North Africa, the Middle East, the Caucuses, India and parts of Asia from China to what is now Indonesia and Malaysia. As Islam initially spread, institutionalizing faith and laws, it established the conditions in which a new kind of society of merchants emerged. Economic trade was sponsored by religion in a number of ways. Supported by the flows of large populations making the *Hajj* (pilgrimage to Mecca), an extensive trade network helped sustain an Islamic world across many cultural boundaries. Arabic became the *lingua franca* for the realm. A banking network (with checking system/exchange) eventually formed. Islam was spread outside of the Arab world through trade by merchants, not by wars of conquest. The fairly universal (but flexible) Islamic law, *sharia*, also enabled the expansion of trade throughout the region. However, Islamic societies continued the tradition of religious justification, if not mandate, for political/territorial expansion, as in the case of the imperialist armies of Ottoman Turks (Levtzion 1999). It should be noted that as Islam grew, Christian soldiers tried to wrest the Holy land from the infidels. While they established some Crusader cities, Saladin ultimately cast them out the Holy Land. Ever since, there has been a degree of suspicion toward Christians. Notwithstanding, Islam became a far more tolerant religion than either Judaism or Christianity.

Culturally, in contrast to the European Enlightenment, for Islam, there were no contradictions between the life of faith and the intellect, reason, and science. Given Muhammad's injunction to study knowledge from many cultures, including practical knowledge, Islamic societies regarded worldly and sacred knowledge as complementary; worldly knowledge was useful and desirable. There was a drive in early Islamic societies to amass knowledge, starting with that of other civilizations (including Byzantine, Rome, Greece, Egypt, India, China and the ancient middle East). The theology and philosophy of Islam was strongly influenced by Neoplatonism and eventually Aristotelian metaphysics. Once amassed, knowledge, technology, science, philosophy, ethics, etc., were critiqued and elaborated. Eventually new forms of knowledge were created, including social theory[6], the advances of which were usually available, unfortunately, only to small circles of elites. The Golden age Islamic scholars of Baghdad, Cordoba, Arabic Egypt, etc. were renaissance thinkers, working simultaneously in the fields of medicine, science, philosophy, and theology. Islamic scientists developed the scientific experimental method and refined Indian mathematics and Chinese material arts and developed innovations in many of sciences: astronomy, medicine, physics, etc.[7] Muslims performed cataract surgery almost 1,000 years ago.

As the Golden age of Islam was nearing its end, the Medieval Catholicism sustained by dynastic rule held relatively closed, narrow cosmological worldviews and showed religious intolerance. Its "holy wars" were the pontifically blessed Crusades. From about the time that Islam emerged, till the Renaissance, the Church maintained the hegemony of the landed classes. Its promises of salvation appealed to knightly warrior elites while its magical practices and dramatic rituals and practices appealed to the uneducated, agrarian feudal peasants. With the growth of trade, ironically an unintended consequence of the Crusades, there came a growing merchant class of cosmopolitan traders centered in Italy, yet also found throughout the Mediterranean: the Venetian mini-empire covered a wide area. This newly affluent class would attempt to articulate a distinct identity, valorizing difference from either the feudal aristocrats or peasantry. Their artists and intellectuals "discovered" their heritage in the Greco-Roman era. (Muslim scholars had preserved much of the legacy of Greco-Roman philosophy, arts and science.) This "rebirth" or Renaissance fostered new expressions in art, perspectivism, literature, vernacular, science, astronomy, and philosophy. Humanism, the philosophical expression of the Renaissance, was a reaction to clerical orthodoxy and its heliocentric cosmology. The intolerance of Christianity may have forestalled a more gradual transition to rational society, a more gradual secularization of ethics and/or more tolerance of other religions.

The Renaissance opened a cultural space for new ideas, and this would eventually extend to theological critiques. This began when Humanism influenced theologians such as Erasmus. With the growth and spread of the merchant classes, as well as a rising free peasantry, there emerged potential bearers of a critical theology—as was indeed evident with the teachings of Jan Huss, whose "heresies" led to the stake. In the face of potential theological challenges, the Church became more rigid and dogmatic. But the growing merchant and free peasant classes would then be structurally disposed to alternatives to Roman Catholicism. The reaction of the Church to challenges was greater intolerance and orthodoxy. Eventually, Christian exclusivity from Holy Roman imperialism and exclusive religious claims and intolerance—including the extremes of the Inquisition such as the rejection of Galileo and Copernicus—led to the Reformation as a critique of the corruption and relative backwardness, rigidity, and theological conservatism of the Catholic Church. Whereas Huss had few supporters, between the changing class structure and availability of paper (from China via the Muslims) and moveable type, Luther became a major figure of the Reformation. Protestantism would have independent consequences for the growth of commerce and science. It would encourage the eventual rise of the European hegemon. The bourgeoisie would foster and embrace the Enlightenment whose doctrines were influenced by the rational traditions and sciences of Islam, as well as being reactions to the exclusivity and rigidity of Christianity as an inflexible realm of faith that resisted the development of secular reason.

The Decline of Islam: Retrenchment and Barriers to Modernity

Toynbee (1939-61), Spengler (1962) and other historians have suggested that civilizations grow, flourish, stagnate, fail to meet challenges, and eventually decline in the face of other civilizations. Such analyses do not specify why this happens, nor do they explain the meaning of "challenge," save in military terms. We argue that the same factors that led to the rise of Islam, dialectically understood, thwarted the emergence of modernity. As Toynbee (1939-61) suggested, when cultures limit variability and diversity, they lose their capacity to adapt to changing circumstances. How can this be explained sociologically in terms of classes and ideologies, etc.? In the face of challenge and threat, typically from actual or imagined competing classes or ideologies and challenges at cultural, institutional and personal levels, groups become more rigid, dogmatic and intolerant. We suggest that two moments of political economy be noted. First, as we suggested, the same legal codes that had enabled Islam to flourish in its early eras would thwart economic growth. Second, and perhaps due to the economic stagnation, there were military defeats and setbacks. In the face of these challenges, Islam retreated to orthodoxy.

Rokeach's (1960) now classical studies of dogmatism have shown how dogmatism, rigidity and absolute certainty are comforting positions in the face of challenge.[8] In his studies he found that at the time of social or theological challenges, the Catholic Church retreated to more orthodox, dogmatic positions.[9] We similarly suggest that in the face of various assaults or challenges to Islam, from the sacking of Baghdad by the Mongols to the Inquisition and expulsion from Spain, and more recently the decline of the Ottoman Empire in the 19th Century, Islamic societies and leaders repeatedly embraced more conservative positions, which for reasons to be discussed below, became entrenched cultural formations. When the central scholarly community of Baghdad was destroyed by the Mongol invasion, a center of liberal, diverse learning was lost. This happened again in the Iberian Peninsula. Cordoba had been one of the primary Islamic cultural/intellectual centers, where liberal forms of Islam thought and science were practiced and developed. With the consolidation of Aragon and Seville into a unified Spain, the rising Spanish merchant classes encouraged the Inquisition that cast out infidels. With the Inquisition, an ideological justification for purifying Christianity, competition with Muslim or Jewish merchants, was eliminated. Progressive alternatives to Islamic orthodoxy were lost and a need for solidarity and a sustaining ideology was needed. This resulted in retrenchment and cultural conservatism. By the time the merchant classes of Christendom became ascendant, and as Venice became a major economic power in the Mediterranean, the cultures and political economies of Islamic society began to stagnate and ossify. It might be recalled that in 1492, not only did Columbus reach the New World and begin to plunder its gold, but the Spanish Inquisition cast out the Muslims; this foreshadowed a gradual realignment of the world system as Christian Europe became a core and the Islamic world fell to peripheral and semi-peripheral status. Even within Islamic states, European and/or Jewish merchants and professionals began to play ever more important roles. While Islamic societies tried to incorporate some of the European scientific, technological and cultural innovations, social barriers proved too strong, the indigenous economies too weak, and the administrative apparatuses too inefficient, though more benevolent than in Europe.

There are a number of reasons why Christendom surpassed Islam. Given the nature of Sultanism and dynastic rule, patrimonial organization, a religious orientation rooted in a warrior ethic, and other factors outlined below, Islam presented formidable barriers to the economic modernization, qua the diffusion of instrumental rationality, individualism, the embrace of democratic institutions and rational, meritocractic bureaucratic administration[10]. We would suggest that seven factors limited the impact of foreign ideas and/or created indigenous barriers to the emergence of the economic, political and cultural rationality that enabled Christendom, and in turn, capitalist modernity, qua secular nationhood, administrative rationality and a culture of critique and equality:

1) *Economic barriers and the law.* For Weber, the great jurists establishing the legal traditions of Islam were more "legal prophets" establishing substantive-theological "stereotyped jurists law...that opposes secularization" than formal-juridical (rational) legal codes (Schluchter 1999, p.108). Sacred law eliminates the space for predictable legal procedures. The economic practices dictated by Quranic law, Kadi justice and Hanafi codes thus precluded large-scale economic enterprises and capital accumulation (Kuran 2001). Firstly, Islamic merchant trading associations, whether or not familial, could not assume the legal form of a corporation with juridical rights independent of the owners. Second, Islamic succession and inheritance laws meant that when one of the associates died, the partnership was terminated and inheritance was divided in egalitarian ways as opposed to European laws that allowed limited inheritance, e.g., a single person could inherit a share of an enterprise that nevertheless survived the loss of a partner. Thus, a business could continue to grow and amass fortunes long after the death of the founder(s). Indeed many of the

successful merchants of Italy were families such as the Medici's. But Islamic codes kept business small, limited and ephemeral, so no great merchant families emerged (Kuran 2001). Third, proscriptions on either long-term investments or short-term usury meant that financing of economic enterprises was limited. Thus, while one could invest in a particular venture and be repaid from profits, and while there was an extensive network of banks that enabled check cashing across the Islamic world, there was not much incentive to investment banking. Hence, borrowing was not rationalized. While Islam developed an extensive banking system, it depended on personal relationships and thus never achieved either the rationality of the later Western banking nor the economies of scale that would take place in the West to finance factories, railroads etc. Commerce was regulated by Quranic laws that would limit the growth of a secular, commercial, sphere; Muslim merchants were unable to practice the kinds of economic rationality, e.g., double entry book keeping or joint stock corporations as the Italian merchants whose commerce flourished[11]. Muslim merchants were unlikely to become bearers of a worldly ethic of practical action. Between the 12th and 15th Centuries, the diversity of occupations declined while military and bureaucratic occupations grew; Islamic economies then began to stagnate (Kuran 2001). The commercial-legal Hanafi codes that once promoted expansion and regional trade would both thwart economic growth at later periods and need to be jettisoned, as has been done in Turkey, Malaysia or Indonesia, or Egypt.

2) *Islam as a decentralized religion.* Islam, while a world religion, unlike Roman Christianity, was decentralized, without a singular supreme authority or centralized hierarchy. This enabled a number of competing learning centers and variations in local practices, and precluded a Reformation as a form of resistance to Church control (Collins 1998). As Islam remained compatible with both its merchant and warrior traditions, there did not emerge an oppositional class that would foster a public sphere, embrace a separation of Church and state and/or foster a systematic critique of religious dogma. Indeed, to this day, many Islamic states openly embrace *sharia* law while theological dissents (and many secular acts) are often met with *fatwas,* religious/legal decrees to maintain orthodoxy and censure threats to Islamic society. Without a Reformation, in spite of the advanced development of science, philosophy, technology and ethical-legal thought, an Enlightenment-based embrace of modernity and its secular institutions and politics was not forthcoming.

3) *A theology of determination.* It is important here to note the

differences between the theology of predestination in Protestantism and pre-determination in Islam. The former is based on problematic salvation in the next world and the latter on the guarantee of Allah's will in this. Thus, the power of Allah to impact this world disposed a fatalism that would stifle the attempt to control/dominate nature and other people inherent to capitalism, in which salvation anxiety provided an "inner determination" that impelled economic action qua this worldly asceticism, and a methodical orientation to everyday life in which each moment was part of a career. Thus guilt and turning inward were essential moments of Protestantism. Otherwise said, Islam did not generate that intense "salvation anxiety" that became a compulsive orientation to work seen as a morally based vocation, a sacralized career (*beruf*). Insofar as Islam fostered both a warrior ethic of paradise in heaven and a petty bourgeois orientation of booty on earth, there is an inherent avoidance of introspection. Save among elite scholars, there has been little tendency to locate causality from within. There is thus a tendency to locate causality from without and deny culpability from within. This is often seen in psychotherapy as denial, the inability to see oneself responsible for ones actions, but rather to attribute ones misfortunes to others. Thus the relative underdevelopment of Islam today is typically blamed on the West, Jews, or both. This is not to ignore the many injustices of colonialism, underdevelopment, geo-politics and globalization.

4) *Political centralization.* It is also necessary to note that whereas ascetic Protestantism was a rational bourgeois religion from the start, Islam began as a religion of ruling stratum, *Herrenreligion*, and to a large extent, despite its formal egalitarianism, it disposes the acceptance of Caliphism, Sultanism and/or other forms of dynastic rule, and more often than not, legitimates suppression of democratization and pluralism. In this way, there is little difference between God-ordained kings, presidents for life, and one party states. Both internal and external political forces exacerbated this trend. For example, following WWII, American policy in the Middle East, devoted to stopping communism, supported a number of dictatorial governments that, no matter how heinous, corrupt or duplicitous, were well rewarded if they opposed communism. Budding progressive, secular movements in Muslim countries, from socialism to nationalism, were both resisted by indigenous power arrangements and thwarted from without by American policy-read oil interests.

5) *Close relations of church, dynasties and commerce.* There was a seamless relation between mosque, political dynasties and the

merchant classes. Indeed many mullahs and imams either came from the merchant classes, as did Muhammad, or were themselves still actively engaged in commerce and trade. The merchant classes could not find themselves in conflict with the existing political arrangements in Islamic societies, partly due to the close regulation, sponsorship, and housing of markets by political and religious authorities. Thus, merchant classes would not become a powerful autonomous class as did the Europeans, nor would they stand in opposition to the ruling classes. Islamic societies, therefore, did not have social conditions disposing an ideological critique of dynastic rule or religion. There were generally no sources of resistance that might lead to the emergence of a public sphere that might be a locus for counter-hegemonic discourses of resistance, strategies of mobilization, and alternative visions.

6) *Conservatism and limits to diffusion.* In its maturity, in the face of challenges and weakened by "internal" strife, Islamic societies turned to orthodoxy and resistance to change. Indeed, in sharp contrast to early Islamic societies, later societies actively maintained various barriers to external cultural influences. While this reproduced Islamic cultures and preserved social arrangements, it created the conditions that resisted the incorporation of Western innovations from factories to nationalism, etc.[12] The highly advanced Islamic pursuit of science and philosophy ceased to develop. "Independent inquiry virtually came to an end, and science was for the most part reduced to a veneration of a corpus of approved knowledge." (Lewis 2002, p.79) Further, Christendom was largely identified with a defeated Byzantium and a vague land of barbarians beyond. At the same time, there was a great deal of ethnocentrism in many parts of Europe against the "evil Turks," a generic, often derogatory term toward all Muslims. In addition to having little interest in the Infidel lands, Muslims feared to live or travel there (Lewis 2002). These fears were sustained by religious edicts against living with the infidels. Hence, the Renaissance, Reformation and Enlightenment were relatively unknown in early modern Islamic societies and the European innovations in technology, philosophy and commerce little impacted Islam.

7) *Individualism and pluralism.* Perhaps one of the most important moments of modernity was the rise of the autonomous, self-interested individual with the capacities to adapt to new situations. For Weber individualism emerged with Protestantism when the believer faced his/her God by him/herself. Some suggest it began earlier when the Church institutionalized confession. Still others suggest that with the rise of bourgeois commerce and the emergence of childhood,

individualism was evident in the Renaissance and valorized by humanism. The importance of the individual in the West can clearly be seen in contrast to the value of the community (*umma*) in Islam. One of the central factors that hindered the spread of modernity in Islam has been the intolerance of individualism, the absence of a commitment to individual rights and personal freedom which serves to limit change and innovation. Consider how many academics are silenced, jailed or murdered in Muslim countries compared to the West, where radical critiques are typically ignored and relegated to obscure journals, book chapters and sociology classes.

Notwithstanding the defeat of Byzantine and rise of the Ottoman Turks who would eventually assume control over much of the Arabic world, Islamic societies began a long and gradual decline relative to ascendant Christendom. Islamic cultures, as we noted, had a number of inherent qualities that limited its capacity to modernize in the Western sense. The nature of Islamic theology, ethics, culture and law limited the impact of foreign ideas and/or the emergence of the economic, political and cultural rationality. Rather, shorn of its centers of liberal thought and toleration for pluralism, without an autonomous "public sphere" there was a retreat to more conservative forms of Islam. Henceforth, in the face of challenges, Islam often embraced orthodoxies such as Wahhabism or other worldly Sufism that served to maintain tradition/resist social change[13]. The barriers to changes, the retreats to conservative theologies, together with *ressentiment* to the West limited the flows of people and information with the morally inferior infidel cultures and the adaptation of their technologies and secular-rational forms of governance and organization. Societies that would embrace "Westernization" would prosper.[14]

Defeat and Domination

By the 17th Century, European military and economic powers from Russia to Portugal began to encroach upon Islamic hegemony. With the defeats in Vienna and Buda, Ottoman rule began to contract. By the 18th Century, European merchants often traveled to Muslim countries. Within Islamic states, European and/or Jewish merchants and professionals had begun to play ever more important roles in commercial life. But, rarely did Muslims come to Europe. (See Part II below for a discussion of 19th Century Islamic reactions to modernity.)

At the end of WWI, the Ottoman Empire, after a long decline, fell by virtue of its alliance with the defeated Axis powers. This was presaged by earlier defeats, such as by the expanding, modernizing Russia using more advanced naval artillery[15]. But at the end of the 19th Century, following the Tanzimat reforms, Mustafa Kemal Ataturk led a secular, nationalist revolution in which Turkey embraced Western modernism and established secular law—backed by its military—which has often intervened against traditionalist elements. The Europeans (British, French) colonized most of the Islamic Middle East. While modernity included many major social changes, neither the Europeans nor their sponsored intermediaries attempted to empower the Islamic people and encourage pluralistic democratic governance. Indeed, colonialism sustained both economic and political underdevelopment. Local authorities, dynastic or military, in turn gained wealth-sustaining autocracy (Lewis 2002).

The transformation of the once powerful, majestic Islamic world into fragmented, colonial, neo-colonial, or peripheral states with autocratic governments having little popular support, had a number of adverse effects, not the least of which was to foster the kinds of humiliations, powerlessness and dependencies that foster *ressentiment*, envy and rage (as is discussed in Part III below). Today, between rapid population growth, an obscene inequality generated by neo-liberal globalization and autocratic governments, there has been a general economic stagnation. In turn, the poor, unemployed and often even the more educated feel thwarted and/or humiliated. They often find compensatory solace and comfort in fundamentalist mosques where they embrace politicized, purified versions of Islam (see below). Many Muslims, finding means to transform the present blocked, turn to the "glorious past" to reclaim a glorious future: they embrace a powerful cultural meaning system within vulnerable Islamic societies that explains social problems on the basis of lack of religious fidelity and valorizes the universal Islamic community, *umma*, granting dignity and recognition (Tibi 1998). Islamic societies such as Egypt, Syria or Iran, with some commercial development (many cars, televisions, cell phones, skyscrapers, and the embrace of some Western technologies), remain highly traditional, as seen in their autocratic governments, unequal treatment of women, harsh penal systems and deplorable records on human rights[16]. On the other hand, Lebanon was, and is again becoming, a very educated, sophisticated, urbane society, in part due to having been a trading country since the Phoenicians, and in recent times, a "modern" banking center. Many Lebanese are actually Christians, not subject to the economic barriers of traditional Islam[17].

Part II. Islamic Responses to the West, Westernization, Modernism, Fundamentalism

As European power expanded in the 19th Century, there were attempts by Islamic societies to modernize. The introduction of newspapers and the telegraph by Europeans in the 19th Century made widely evident the "backwardness" of the "Oriental" Other. Two major strategies were developed to proactively respond to Western power and its expanding hegemony (Davidson 1998). First, leaders and intellectuals advocated *westernization* and secularization as the surest way to compete with Europe. This vein won out in terms of political power. As the west carved up the Islamic world into various states, indigenous leaders led the secularization of some Islamic societies, notably Turkey, promoting western education, law, science, etc. Much like the Japanese Restorationists, modernity was backed by the military. Second, a relatively small circle of intellectuals advocated an *Islamic Modernism*, arguing that Western methods and key institutions, legislatures, modern administrations, and banks, could be revised along the lines of Islamic law. This movement was neither able to influence the Westward leaning, secular political elites of the day nor the conservative Islamic religious authorities. These ideas did not reach the uneducated masses. Hence, Islamic development generally became polarized between Westernizing and conservative extremes.

Theorizing in the early 20th Century, Weber was personally troubled and theoretically concerned with the negative side of modernity, its rationalization of the world that dehumanized the person and reduced everything to what could be quantified. Economic striving, detached from a religious ethic, had become an empty striving for shallow materialism. A new industrial elite was emerging. A century after Weber wrote about the moral nullity of Western civilization, mass mediated consumerism, and privatized hedonism devoid of meaning have proliferated everywhere. The globalization of capital, secularization, and rapid social and cultural changes, together with population movements, has fostered both anomie and the attenuation of social ties. In the face of changes, crises and challenges, one of the typical responses has been the embrace of dogmatic, orthodox positions. In a similar way, countries with economic challenges often embrace authoritarian governments, if not fascism. Fundamentalism and terrorism are both reactions to and moments of resistance to the dominating aspects of modernity and the shallowness of secularism.

And, as discussed in Part III below, ressentiment mediated through radical fundamentalism can become part of the impetus for religious terrorism.

The Nature of Fundamentalism

One of the most important religious social transformations of the last century has been the gradual rise of fundamentalism, the embrace of anti-modern religious orthodoxies. Why has there been a rise of fundamentalisms? Jurgensmeyer (2001) notes that religious fundamentalism across various religious cultures is on the rise globally for three common reasons: first, radical conservative religious movements reject the liberal values of secular institutions and blame society's decline on the loss of religious inspiration; second, these radical religious movements refuse to accept boundaries of secular society which keeps religion a private observance and not the public sphere; and third, these conservative movements are seeking to restore religion as central to social life. As noted above, in the face of challenges, groups may become more dogmatic and intolerant. We have suggested that in response to challenges, ranging from the sacking of Baghdad to the expulsion from Spain to the decline of the Ottoman Empire, that Islamic leaders have repeatedly embraced more conservative positions[18]. This created conservative traditions as the basis for a conservative response to Western secular encroachments. This, however, is a general global cultural phenomenon in response to rapid social change, uncertainty, attenuation of social ties, challenges to ingrained value precepts, etc.

Fundamentalisms generally require unquestioning acceptance of transcendent religious precepts, a strict adherence to compulsory rituals and a subjugation of the self to higher powers. Fundamentalism may be defined as a conservative religious reaction to secular society that typically includes the following characteristics: Exclusive truth claims are typically based on a sacred text. It often has Manichean truth claims in which non-believers are constructed as immoral and an apocalyptic view of the world. Fundamentalism seeks to restore a glorious past from which people had strayed. Fundamentalism makes exclusive truth claims grounded in canonical religious, spiritual texts and seeks to recreate an idealized religious community while paradoxically embracing modern means: mass media, bureaucratic institutions, and destructive technologies in militancy. Christian,

Jewish, Hindu, and Islamic fundamentalisms more or less follow this pattern. Thus, fundamentalisms resist the usually hedonistic, secular, materialistic values of modernity. At the same time, fundamentalists are modernists in that they use elements of tradition in combination with modern methods—advanced technology, institutional forms, and instrumental rationality—to transform the political order (Tibi 1998).

Radical religious movements often position themselves to act in the public sphere as moral agents. From the viewpoint of religious radicals, it is not so much that religion has become political as much as politics has become religious. The reasons for this deep antagonism are not merely political. Secular modernity and its valorization of Reason has made an assault on religious values and worldviews that erode the impact and power of religious institutions, leading to a general crisis in religious belief. As secular society is suffering a crisis of morality and meaning, there is a space for religious critiques of secular modernity and transcendental alternatives. The West, celebrating the secular materialism of modernity, spread through a political economic imperialism and mass mediated consumerism, has created spaces for radical religious movements, both in the developed and developing countries.

Islamisms

Islamic fundamentalisms arose in various Islamic states. For example, Wahabbism was embraced in Saudi Arabia, as the Ottoman Empire declined in the later 18th and early 19th centuries. As Western power grew and the division of the Islamic world proceeded, Western interests encouraged the suppression of progressive movements in the Middle East, such as socialism or even nationalism. (Note that there have been intrinsic reasons why these Western ideologies were not embraced.) For example, the US has strongly supported the (oil rich) House of Saud, where Islam has turned increasingly conservative and militant in resistance. Islamic fundamentalism is a response to many factors, central among which are the domination by the West, the relative poverty and underdevelopment of the Muslim world, and the lack of political outlets to express discontents.

In the 20th Century, Westernization did not yield its promised results. Modernity failed Islamic states for a variety of reasons mentioned above, especially the conservatism of its religion, the underdevelopment inherent in colonialism and foreign sponsoring of local elites, the lack of education of the populace, and, the conservatism of religious leaders. Islamic states generally secured the wealth and power of the elites and sustained oppressive secular governments rather than seek expansions of democracy and human rights. With the failure of modernity to bring its promised benefits, conservative Islamic brotherhoods and movements, originally organized to address social justice issues, attempted to reinvigorate, reform and reestablish Islam as the basis for revitalized Islamic states. As westernizing strategies in Islamic states failed and/or were suppressed in the 20th Century, conservative religious responses grew more pronounced, generating various Islamisms, Islamic fundamentalist movements. Note that in many developing nations, secular *thought* and autonomous *institutions*, especially democratically elected legislative bodies and the executive, are not very well formed or advanced. Religious ways of life and social-political institutions hold more public power, especially in Islamic countries. Hence, there is a strong link between religious belief and resistance to Western hegemony among radical religious movements in the Islamic world. We also note that the rigid claims and orthodoxy of fundamentalism generally prevents a group from self-examination and critical reflection. This is *not* likely to change as long as the educational processes in the developing world remain tied to traditional religious institutions. Studying the Quran and/or Islamic studies does not much prepare the student for science, industry, commerce or critical thought.

Conservative Islamic movements have pursued three main ends in Islamic society: reformism, revivalism, and radical defense. The main interest of these movements is to reestablish the moral and political virtues of traditional Islamic society (Choueiri 1990). Islamism is modeled on the attempt to recapture Muhammad's early role of rebel in Mecca in criticizing moral corruption and need for lifestyle and political economic reforms grounded in religious mores. For revivalists, just as Muhammad challenged false gods and immoral ways instead of a righteous life, Islamism is seen as a path to justice and equality against the Western ways of corruption and worship of its false gods. Islamist ideological analysis offers these reasons for the decline of Islam: 1) Islamic society declined due to the departure from the practice of religious values and dictates; 2) This decay made possible the Western intrusion; and, 3) The solution is to revitalize and return to Islam by a) reintroducing the Shariah, Islamic law, while purging most Western cultural influences, but not science and technology and b) re-politicizing Islam, along lines of Muhammad's role as administrator and law giver in Medina.

The rise of Islamic fundamentalism was the result of many factors beginning with general factors that have also fostered the growth of Christian fundamentalism, Orthodox Judaism and even Hindu fundamentalism. But further, in Islamic societies, the barriers to modernity, mentioned in Part I above, have joined together with economic underdevelopment, traditional education, and the suppression of political dissent to dispose fundamentalism. Further, various Islamic institutions have provided cheap alternatives to public education, in which young boys learn strict conservative forms of Islam, as for example the *madrassas* of Pakistan funded by Saudi Arabia. Islamism has often been directly reproduced through strictly enforced civic codes in which "moral police" vigorously patrol the borders of virtue as in Saudi Arabia, Kuwait, Iran and the former Taliban controlled Afghanistan.

There have been wide variations in the extent to which Muslim societies have embraced Islamisms, and within particular societies there have been wide disparities in the appeal of Islamisms. For example, Afghanistan, under the Taliban, was extreme, even by fundamentalist standards. But so too was (is) Afghanistan one of the poorest, least educated societies in the world. In contrast, Pakistan was (is) not a fundamentalist country. After General Zia took power, he tried to impose fundamentalism from the top down. It had few adherents, not more than about five percent of the people, primarily among tribal groups—looked down upon in Pakistani society[19]. The Saudis financed *madrassas* that were accepted by subsequent governments in order to divert scarce funds to nuclear weapons programs, in response to India. Islamic fundamentalism was accepted by elements within Pakistani Security (the ISI) who used these schools to provide "volunteers" to fight against India in Kashmir as well as train US-financed *mujahadeen* that would fight a proxy war against Russia. In Algeria, a prolonged conflict between urban, Western modernists and rural fundamentalists has cost perhaps 200,000 lives. Although fundamentalism has been widely embraced in the Muslim world, and it often promotes hatred of infidels, the vast majority of fundamentalists do *not* become terrorists, and not all terrorists in Islamic societies are "holy warriors". Nevertheless, the world wide rise of fundamentalism, with its Manichean division of the world into those who are good and those who are evil, with it assertions of patriarchy and promises of redemption, creates an atmosphere in which terrorism can thrive.

Part III. Terrorism: From Ressentiment to Action

Religion and Ressentiment

Marx understood religion dialectically. Religion was an expression of the real pain and suffering engendered by the political economy, as well as an opiate that made that suffering tolerable, bearable, by providing compensations. Religion, as a hegemonic ideology, sustains domination by providing quite genuine social and emotional gratifications, creating a realm of hope outside the political economy. As Durkheim noted, collective rituals evoke the efflorescence of powerful emotions that celebrate and reinforce social solidarity. So too did Freud (1989) argue that religion, while an illusion resting on powerful unconscious longings for a benevolent father figure, could nevertheless evoke powerful feelings, "oceanic feelings" of unity with the universe recapitulating a blissful symbiosis with the mother. While religion may well assuage domination and yet sustain it with compensatory emotional experiences from either the group or the unconscious, as Weber would note, religion, providing a theodicy of the distributions of fortune articulated by virtuosos, nevertheless took particulars forms, with theologies that had an "elective affinity" with the status positions of its followers. Thus religious values and doctrines, guiding both everyday conduct and eschatological ends, provided its followers with affective gratifications and, indeed, hope.

Weber was highly influenced by Nietzsche, who called Christianity a "slave religion" in which there had been a transvaluation of the ethical (Stauth and Turner 1988). For Nietzsche, the dominated classes of Rome embraced Christianity, a slave "mentality" with its values of mercy, justice, forgiveness and compassion. Slaves would ask for their master's mercy and justice rather than plan the overthrow of their masters. Christianity represented a "transvaluation of the ethical"; the values of the strong and powerful, the expressions of will, bravery, conquest or indeed cruelty that had been considered "good" were redefined as "bad," indeed "sinful." Christianity defined "goodness" from the standpoint of the weak, the powerless, the alienated. Christianity traded docility and subordination for strength and power. But the renunciation of the "will to power," the subordination of the Dionysian for the Apollonian came at a cost—sickness of the soul and the contraction of the self to the banality of the pitiful masses.

In articulating a critical theory of religion, located in the Frankfurt School tradition of immanent critique, Siebert (2001) emphasized the contradictions between the promises of religion, often utopian, and the actual conditions of people's lives. In order to understand the relation of religion to material factors in the development of religious terrorism, we need consider the important role of *ressentiment,* as first articulated by Nietzsche, to note the allure and response of Christianity as a religion of subalterns:

> With the emergence of Christianity we have the successful slave-revolt in morality with its accompanying new set of values and virtues, and its underlying ascetic ideal. The slave revolt in morality begins when *ressentiment* itself becomes creative and gives birth to values: the *ressentiment* of natures that are denied the true reaction, that of deeds, esteemed, desired and possessed by the noble. It is the rejection of external goods such as honor and prestige, political power and influence, wealth, physical strength and beauty; and as well a disparagement of those virtues, especially courage and pride, characteristic of the Greco-Roman nobleman. . . . The goods and virtues associated with the despised nobility themselves come to be hated as evil. In the place of the negatively apprehended values, traits and devices found expedient for sheer survival of the weak are elevated to the status of goods and virtues. Thus, the weakness of the oppressed is transformed into virtue and the original power and strength of the noble is now considered evil and sinful. (Morelli 2001)

In other words, when superiors possess certain desirable actualities of power, wealth and dignity, as well as possibilities of freedom that are denied to subordinates, the latter will come to loath what they cannot have, materially, politically or morally, and instead will embrace denial and asceticism that become valorized. But this *ressentiment,* as a repressed form of envy/hatred of the Other, becomes turned on the self as a sickness, as self-hatred that consumes. As Nietzsche put it,

> *Ressentiment*: Everything hurts. Being sick in itself is a kind of *ressentiment.* The defensive and offensive instinct in man becomes soft—one does not know how to have done with anything—one does not know how to thrust back—everything hurts—men and things come importunately close—events strike too deep—the memory is a festering wound (1969 pp.33-4).

For the Christian subalterns of Rome, with the transvaluation of the ethical, their kingdom of God would be the next life—where the vile Romans were consigned to hell. As Greenfeld (1992) has argued, the *ressentiment* of the bourgeoisie toward dynastic rule impelled the rise of the Nation State that would empower people as citizens with dignity based on membership in an "imagined community". Similarly, religious terrorists may see terrorism as hope, as the only means to overcome their despised secular oppressors, find agency and even secure dignity in a "purified" state. Following Nietzsche, we suggest that dominated groups, lacking public means for the realization of will qua agency and empowerment, denied recognition and dignity, facing humiliations, experience *ressentiment,* which in turn disposes the embrace of religious fundamentalism, a vision of hope in attaining a "better world," often of restoring a lost "Golden Age" in which the "redeemed" faithful regain a lost sense of agency and dignity. For Nietzsche, the only way to overcome ressentiment was to give up the desire for vengeance—but the hatred of Other typically makes that impossible for all but the "*ubermench.*"

To bring meaning to the world and to control human passions, all societies develop frameworks of meaning and understanding to explain the nature of the world, prescribe ethical regulations of everyday life, explain injustice, and promise redemption. Religions typically provide a theodicy that explains the contradictions between the promises of God and worldly injustice. Further, these theodicies typically provide a course of amelioration from the abnegation of the world. "For Horkhiemer, religion or theodicy was the expression of the longing for the Infinite: for perfect justice. This perfect justice could never be realized in the secular history. Even if a better world would take the place of the present social disorder. . . the past misery would not be made good and the predicament and plight in the surrounding nature would not be superceded" (Siebert 2001, p.11).

Islamic Ressentiment

As Islam became culturally stagnant in the face of a growing Christendom, Christian Europe became economically, politically and militarily vastly superior to what had been a far more advanced culture. One cultural consequence was the development of a long-standing *ressentiment* against the upstarts, whose crusaders were cast out of the Holy Land, defeated in Constantinople, who would eventually colonize and or control much of the land that had been under Muslim rule. Until the 19th Century, Islamic societies mostly ignored the West. Following the end of colonial domination, despite the many Western educated leaders and intellectuals, none of the Muslim states were able to throw off the shackles of history, again fostering *ressentiment* to the West and attribution of blame almost verging on the paranoid. For example, many Muslims in places like Egypt accept the *Protocols of the Elders of Zion* and blame underdevelopment on Israel, the US or whomever.

This became even more pronounced following colonization and partitioning of the Islamic world by Europe and the failure of post-colonial Muslim societies to achieve widespread economic growth. Following WWII, there were vast changes throughout the world that impacted Islamic states. This began with the increasing importance of oil and the alliances between dynastic rule in the Gulf States and Western capital. In addition to Western economic domination, in autocratic governments—whether secular (Syria, Iraq, Egypt) or theocratic (Iran, Sudan)—the suppression of personal freedom and dissent has also maintained political barriers to economic growth. Then came the founding of Israel as an alien, secular, Zionist state. The *ressentiment* toward modern infidels was evident in 1937 when the Grand Mufti of Jerusalem rejected the Peel commission suggesting partitioning Palestine and granting a "homeland" to Western Jews. In 1947, the UN partitioned Palestine and Israel, leading to that war, as well as wars in 1967 and 1973. They ended in humiliating defeats in which a small, secular power triumphed over the armies of far larger, more populous countries. There were of course other events such as the seizure of the Suez Canal and the CIA-engineered overthrow of Mossadeq and installation of Shah Palevi in Iran that showed the political weakness of Islamic states. Western manufactured goods became more common, as well as Western companies providing these goods, attesting to the economic backwardness of their economies.

The conditions of modernity have fostered greater and greater *ressentiment*. One of the consequences of globalization has been the annihilation of time and space. Islamic cultures have been increasingly exposed to the secular values of the West, especially its shallow materialism, individualism and instrumental rationality that have challenged many traditional beliefs of orthodox Islam[20]. The diffusion (and appeal) of the popular culture of the West, with its narcissistic hedonism and sexual freedom, among the educated classes, especially youth, has been an affront to the culturally dominant conservative traditions of Islam[21]. Further, the growth of satellite television and/or

VCRs and media representations of the West have highlighted the value differences between Islam and the West[22]. Large numbers of Muslims have access to mass media (many have the internet). Many Muslims receive reports from family members who are part of the migrations and student sojourns to Europe and the US. Muslims witness how they are represented as subalterns in the West. "Orientalism" constructs the Muslim (and Islamic culture) as denigrated Other. S/he is seen as lazy, dirty (despite Islam's almost fanatical concerns with cleanliness), ignorant, treacherous, duplicitous, corrupt, violent and/or barbaric. Muslims everywhere see how blatantly their societies are materially poor compared to the West. They are well aware of the power of the US and the many injustices it fosters. They find that their religious values are challenged and, in response, they are more likely to defend their values, even as they often know it is hard to defend certain laws and practices, e.g., slavery, the treatment of women and autocracy. This disposes the embrace of fundamentalism that valorizes and sacralizes their culture that is denigrated by others. Nevertheless, fundamentalism, while rarely violent, may become used as its justification.

Varieties of Terrorism

Radical conservative religious movements have become linked to terrorism in places as diverse as the Middle East, Ireland, Japan, and the U.S. It is necessary to examine terrorism before further exploring the link between radical religion and the embrace of violence. It is difficult to define terrorism. One person's terrorist is another's freedom fighter. There are various types of egregious political violence that are sometimes conflated. Official documents on terrorism rarely define the term or differentiate it from other forms of violent political action, e.g., guerilla movements, ethno-nationalist conflicts or progressive movements that take direct action. Nations often brand opposition/resistance/demonstrations as "terrorist" to demonize and discredit those who might dissent

Ahmad (1998) offered a typology of five varieties of terrorism: state terrorism, religious terrorism, criminal terrorism, pathological terrorism, and secular oppositional, or political, terrorism. There are different motives for these. Some highly visible expressions of terrorism can be thought of as spectacles of violence, media events staged to dramatize an issue by gaining the attention of the world. Terrorism acts as both a symbolic message and supposed means of social change aiming at political transformation[23]. The terrorist act dramatically "advertises" the grievance to a larger community that may support their goals. Further, the "pain and suffering" inflicted is believed, at least by the terrorists, to avenge a prior injustice and/or attain the organization's goal.

Some terrorists seek to destabilize a regime through low intensity warfare that is often entwined with foreign policy of states, whether explicit or implicit. The types of terrorism can overlap. While terrorists are not typically members of official state organizations, the line between state terrorism and oppositional terrorism gets blurred at times as imperialistic states or state agencies (e.g., KGB, CIA, MI6 or ISA) often support terrorists to attain geo-political goals. For example, Ahmad notes that the United States has sponsored various types of terrorism and terrorist agents: the contras in Nicaragua, paramilitary death squads in El Salvador, and the Mujahadeen in Afghanistan. While a combination of factors such as hatred against oppressors, poverty and blocked opportunities may breed the conditions for terrorism, terrorist organizations nevertheless require resources provided by rich states, e.g., Iran's support of Hezbollah or rich individuals such as Bin Laden's support of Al Qaeda. The focus of Western political and corporate media discourse is on the types of terrorism against its states and/or its globalized political economy. Oppositional and religious terrorism are generally far less destructive than egregious state sponsored violence; 9/11 wanes pale compared to the 500,000 Huks slaughtered by Sukarno, 200,000 Guatemalans killed by US trained/financed death squads, or the 20,000 Argentines who "disappeared".

The spread of terrorism today is facilitated by technologies of media, communication (cell phones, Internet), and advanced means of lethal mass violence[24]. It is increasingly possible, perhaps inevitable, that radical terrorists may gain or develop weapons of mass destruction, whether biological, chemical or even nuclear. Oppositional terrorism, our focus, whether based on secular or religious political struggle, can be understood then as the actions taken by members of quasi-military organizations, more or less unified by a Manichean ideology of good friend and evil foe, where there are not innocents. They attack noncombatants, military or civilian, and/or the infrastructures of a "dominating power" in order to attain certain political or cultural goals or conditions.

Religious Terrorism

Political economic goals and values have long been cloaked with religious justifications and cosmological goals (Juergensmayer 2001). For example, at various historical moments, the Holy Land gave rise to three different monotheistic faiths that have often killed each other, in God's name. Indeed, the Holy War tradition of God-ordained combat that became *jihad* in Islam or Crusades for Christians originated in Judaism when God bid Joshua do battle against the Canaanites who ordered the soldiers to smite every last man, woman and child. Almost every ethical code proscribes the taking of life. Religions often preach mercy, kindness, charity and love of neighbor—because as Freud (1930) said our natural inclination is to do otherwise. This is clear in the Abrahamic tradition where "though shall not kill" was carved in stone, yet in the name of God, nation or worthy cause, there are a number of justifications to kill. Consider the many injunctions to smite the criminal, the enemy or the one who violates a religious code. There are religious justifications to smite gays, harlots, adulterers, etc. Nefarious Others who (would) do harm to the group, challenge its social hierarchies and/or violate its moral order must face "just punishment," *lex talianis.* As Durkheim noted, traditional societies, with mechanical solidarity, demand the most severe punishments. When religious fundamentalism becomes militant, what has been described as "clerical fascism", and embraces the use of force, it's exclusive truth claims, eschatology, and intolerance of sacrilegious Others often demands their death. Religious terrorism thus justifies and rationalizes inflicting death upon enemy infidels, unholy Others from within or without.

The development of religious terrorism is complex; historical legacies become intertwined with conservative reactions to modernity and political economy in such ways that *ressentiment*—mediated through cultural understandings and insults, political/social movements, and characterological factors, and sustained by certain individuals, organizations, networks and/or states—is manifested as recurring terrorist actions. Willingness to engage modern technologies, including weapons, creates the conditions for catastrophic religious terrorism.

Ressentiment and Religious Terrorism in Islam

Today, as a deviant "Other" to the hegemonic West, Muslims often experience humiliation and contempt, deprivations of dignity and recognition. Political economic domination, political centralization, capital's repression of secular lines of democratic resistance (liberal or socialist), and absence of a modernizing ideology, together with cultural isolation and denigration, have been major factors that have given rise to *ressentiment* vis-à-vis the West, Islamic fundamentalism, and the rise of religious terrorism. In almost every Muslim country there are a number of anti-Western organizations that would and do embrace terrorist means. For example, Al Qaeda, grounded in both Wahhabist philosophy and adamant militant resistance to the West, is situated throughout the Islamic world. This combination of ultra-conservative worldviews promoting self-sacrifice and militant resistance disposes religious warriors to become terrorist-martyrs, as was seen in 9/11.

While terrorism can be cloaked in the teachings of any religion, there are certain unique aspects of Islamic terrorism rooted in its own history and culture. Foremost is the articulation of *ressentiment*-based claims of moral superiority in the face of the material advantages and secular morals of the West. Thus certain aspects of Islamic traditions, lesser *jihad*, martyrdom and the primacy of *sharia,* are drawn upon to legitimate terrorist activities as Islam traditions of tolerance, equality and respect for difference are ignored[25]. Islam *ressentiment* is rooted in one of the basic polarities of our age, the dialectical conflict between modernity and tradition in the modern age, between religion and the secular. Just as the Catholic Church long resisted modernity (read: class interested culture of the rational bourgeoisie), so too has Islam resisted modernity on a number of levels, e.g., intolerance to any questions of either theological leadership or political leadership that rests on religious claims. Secular, democratic governance is not only feared by indigenous elites who would be quickly replaced, but the repression of modernist elements such as pluralism and intellectual/political dissent is often used by certain authoritarian secular leaders to justify the repressive nature of their regimes, claiming to the world that the alternatives might be fundamentalists. Laquer (2001) has suggested that the basis for the increased Islamic terrorism has been the failure of western ideologies such as secular nationalism to take hold, leaving an intellectual and political vacuum in which the only alternative forthcoming has been Islamism and terrorism—neither of which can ameliorate the lives of those who would embrace their doctrines (see also Juergensmeyer 2001, Kepel 2002).

In militant Islamisms, the moral superiority of Islam is framed in conservative theological terms and is expressed through political resistance articulated through terrorism, legitimated as a *jihad*, a holy war, against the secular West. However, for the US, Europe and Israel, the bombings of buildings, hotels, malls, discos, embassies, etc. in Lebanon, Kenya, Tanzania, Saudi Arabia, etc., the Palestinian *intifada*, the bombings of the WTC, the attack on the Cole and above all, 9/11, have been seen as acts of terrorists. While oppositional and religious terrorism has been used as a political instrument to attain certain goals for a long time and has often been cloaked in religious justifications, the legacies of Islam give its expressions of terrorism a distinctive hue. In particular, its early legacies of warrior-based *jihad* now inform contemporary articulations of holy war or "sacred terror" that renders holy warriors *mujahadeen*. But however brave and fearless these warriors may be, direct military attacks on the vastly more technologically advanced Western militaries is unthinkable. Thus, by the logic of holy war, in which all infidels are regarded as "enemy," there are no innocents. Attacks on civilian targets, including women, children and the elderly are seen as morally justified by radical conservative religious militarists. But as many would note, if America were to completely disengage itself from the Islamic world, if Israel ceased to exist, the conditions of the one billion Muslims would not only not improve, but would actually deteriorate.[26]

Part IV. The Social Psychology of Terrorism

Structural conditions and/or collective sentiments do not "impel" action per se. To understand oppositional terrorism, sacred or secular, we argue that subordination and *ressentiment* to superordinates is *necessary*, as are religious (political) justifications of violent means to attain moral or political ends. But these are *not sufficient* to lead actors to the passionate intensity of terrorism; powerful emotions are needed to realize value rational goals. What must happen for people to savagely kill "innocent" civilians or, indeed, martyr themselves to do so? We thus need to consider the relationships of *ressentiment* to the social psychology of identity and desire that dispose terrorism. This is not to reduce the social and political to the psychological, but rather to argue for the importance of psychosocial mediation using multiple levels of analysis, a critical interdisciplinary stance first articulated by the Frankfurt School that stood in the shadows of Marx, Nietzsche, Weber and Freud. As Nietzsche noted, under conditions of domination and *ressentiment* to the dominator, the will is turned upon the self, the person seeks revenge, and this leads to a sickness. In Freudian terms, when the outward expression of aggression is blocked, it turns upon the self as a self hatred that joins with the external forces to sustain and reproduce domination by thwarting and stifling the person, leaving him/her angry, depressed and/or symptomatic or otherwise incapable of resisting domination.

The work of Fromm (1941) remains a source of insight to explain how social conditions intersect with character to dispose an ideological stance that is more or less congruent with behavior; or more accurately, to show how ideologies are embraced if they legitimate certain actions or provide self enhancing feelings such as pride or dignity. Fromm, and later Adorno (1950), thus argued that some character types were typical of certain cultures or class locations, e.g., the authoritarian character, rule bound conformists, disposed to dominate subordinates and defer to superiors, showed certain characterological tendencies, especially in response to weakened social ties and structurally based powerlessness. Fromm argued that with the attenuation of social ties and greater powerlessness of the petty bourgeois classes at the time of the Reformation, and again with the post WWI conditions of Germany, there were three responses to what he called "mechanisms of escape," social forms of defense mechanism. These were submission to those deemed powerful, projection of aggression to those "outsiders" responsible for one's malaise, and legitimate aggression to those seen as responsible for one's misery. In other words, under stress, there was an "escape from freedom." For Fromm, the elective affinity of class-character was a crucial factor in understanding the appeal of Luther and the rise of Protestantism, and later, the appeals of Hitler and embrace of Fascism. Afary (2001), in her biographies of two Iranian women, Zahra Rahnavard and Marziyeh Dabbagh, who "paradoxically" embraced Ayatollah Khomeini's fundamentalism (patriarchy), suggested that Fromm's insights remain a useful paradigm linking history and the individual. More specifically, authoritarian personalities, intolerant of freedom and individualism, found gratification in 1) submission to rule bound doctrines and 2) the exercise of power over others.

If we look at the death, pain and human suffering that results from terrorist acts, whether shooting pro-choice doctors, planting bombs in cars, school buses or mailboxes or crowded public places, gunning down people in streets, crashing planes into buildings, or even the potential use of weapons of mass destruction, our first reaction is that the people who plan human slaughter and/or commit such deeds must be cold, heartless killers or deranged, maddened individuals. Most research suggests otherwise. Psychological profiles of terrorists have revealed that, in general, they are fairly typical of the groups from which they come, and these groups are especially prone sensitive to the consequences of domination. Indeed, terrorist organizations do not want unstable, psychotic individuals who may be unpredictable. Terrorists may be more assertive and outgoing, but there is little evidence of striking psychopathology or irrational hatreds (Post 1998). We suggest that the motives for terrorism are little different than the factors that dispose fundamentalism in general. Rather, these motives become more intense due to such factors as social location, age, and most often, a prolonged period of humiliation followed by socialization into a fundamentalist or terrorist organization, e.g., fundamentalist mosques, *madrassas*, Al Qaeda camps, Hamas camps, etc., where "total institutions" foster particular (intolerant) world views, and squelch alternatives or critical interrogation. What is being suggested is that terrorists are people who desire what most people want, but the conditions in which terrorists live foster limited options, as their social ties to the larger community are attenuated, their self realization and fulfillment become blocked by structural conditions, and these conditions generate emotions[27]. Between the humiliation of denigration, powerlessness in the face of domination, and hopelessness for the expected future, terrorism becomes a means to a goal that ameliorates *ressentiment* through revenge[28].

We are not "blaming the victim." As Nietzsche suggested and Fanon (1961) demonstrated, in the face of colonization and domination, the cultures and identities of the colonized were denigrated and deemed inferior compared to the more affluent and powerful colonizer. This of course leads to *ressentiment* and rage, but the subaltern's rage is often turned inward, upon the self. The violence done to the culture of the colonized, the "wretched of the earth," fostered self-hatred and self-destructive behavior such as crime, addiction or interpersonal violence. Terrorism serves to redirect this rage to the oppressor and thus empowers the person, to restore his/her dignity and honor—qualities highly valued in Islamic societies. Violence to the colonizer is not only cathartic, but becomes viewed as the means to overcome political, economic or cultural domination (Scatamburlo and Langman 2002). Projecting *ressentiment* outwards, a small number of radical fundamentalists, typically young, unattached, underemployed males, turn militant and turn to terrorism.

As Weber notes, rational action can either be oriented to instrumental rationality (*zweckrational*) or to realize values (*wertrational*). But Weber maintained a Kantian trifurcation of Reason, Emotion and Will. Nietzsche understood the unity of agency and desire, i.e., that people may practice certain actions, self-denial, or rational means to attain certain functional *or* ideological ends that, *at the same time*, secure powerful affective gratifications (Langman 2000). We suggest that just as psychopathology is often the extreme of normalcy, terror is one of the most extreme expressions of political, economic or cultural frustrations. Just as religion and/or nationalism may generate positive consequences, terrorism represents the other side of this dialectic. We start by assuming that a person's identity, his/her narrative of selfhood, is based on his/her membership in an identity granting community of meaning. This can range from the clique of the "popular kids" of an American middle school to a Nation-State, or even a universal community of faith, the *umma*, for Muslims. One of the consequences of modernity in general has been to erode traditional collective identities and provide the person with greater freedom and choice. As traditional communities and identities are first eroded and then denigrated, modernity does not provide compensatory alternatives.

Identity and Desire

As conscious scripts and narratives of selfhood, "self-identity" for Giddens (1991) is a mediating linkage between the individual, dynamically understood, and the larger society. One's identity is not simply a set of identifications, but is a reflexive, conscious locus of subjectivity, as it moves through the flow of social time and space seeking affective gratifications in the enactment of the routines of everyday life. But this is also the site where frustrations, humiliations or insults are experienced. Otherwise said, people seek emotional gratifications or the avoidance of frustrations. This is not a simple hedonism in that people will suffer great deprivations to sustain their identities. They may even give their lives. People: 1) seek membership and attachments in identity granting communities of meaning that provide social bonds and attachments; 2) strive for recognition and dignity granting statuses; 3) exercise agency in striving to overcome powerlessness; and 4) given a universal fear of death, seek a value system that provides explanations for pain, suffering and injustice, remedies and/or promises of amelioration, even if in the next life (Langman 2000).

1) *Community*: For most of human history, between the powerful bonds of an infant's attachments to caretakers, to family/clan work groups, to the periodic solidarity rituals of large groups, people are social creatures with needs to be part of a community. (And communities also grant identities, recognition and meaning; see below). For Freud, group life depended on "aim-inhibited cathexes."Later psychoanalysts, like Bowlby and Winnocott, have seen early bonding as the foundation of healthy development. Similarly, sociologists have long argued that collective rituals like religion, national celebrations etc., or interpersonal rituals serve to sustain community, solidarity and engagement. At the same time, capitalism, undergirded by Protestantism, served to attenuate social ties and connections. With globalization, this tendency became universalized and has even impacted peripheral societies, including most Muslim societies. Given our Western (Protestant) traditions of individualism, it is easy to slight the importance of community in traditional societies; and in the case of Islam, the community of faith (the *umma*) is sacralized. Between the political-economic impacts of globalization, and the mass consumerism that individualizes people as consumers (even if commodified, pseudo-individualism) social ties are attenuated, if not rent asunder. This social fragmentation is often resisted. In this way, fundamentalism can be seen as a way of resisting, rekindling and affirming those bonds. Terrorism would act as a penultimate expression; the terrorist might even perish to sustain his/her community, and if s/he died, the funeral would fortify and re-affirm the bonds of community.

2) *Recognition:* Following Hegel's understanding of the master-slave struggle for recognition as the basis for self-consciousness, a number of psychoanalysts and scholars have noted the importance of recognition as the basis of self esteem; some consider the pursuit of self esteem "honorific status," much more powerful a motive than sexuality. And indeed far more men have died for the sake of honor in combat than for the love of a woman. Following observations by Sennett and Cobb (1972), echoed by Honneth (1995) and Taylor (1998), struggles for recognition/dignity may be seen as central to both the person and his/her groups.

Conversely, shame and humiliation, assaults on honor and selfhood foster rage to assuage the insult. The failure to acknowledge unconscious shame leads to destructive conflicts and violence (Scheff, 1994). For Fanon, the only way to overcome colonization and the denigration of the self was through violence. We would say that his analysis applies to the neo-colonialism of the globalized political economy as well, although the oppressor is more difficult to identity[29]. Terrorism serves as a violent response to the violent conditions that deny recognition, honor and dignity.

3) *Agency:* A long line of philosophical critique, as articulated by Spinoza, Kant, Hegel and, Marx, suggested that active self-constitution, striving for realization and creating reality is an inherent human tendency. With Nietzsche, philosophy moved from epistemology to psychology. *Will*, now framed as agency, became a central quality of investigation. For Marx, alienation, the consequence of wage labor, externalized production. Commodity production stood as an external power, thwarting his/her agency, his/her humanity and selfhood. The humanly constructed systems of domination refluxed back upon the person to render him/her powerless. To understand humans as willful is to see people as active agents, who strive to make their everyday lives meaningful and to attain certain long-term goals and values.

Powerlessness, the denial of agency, is generally an extremely potent motive for individuals and groups. To be powerless is often humiliating and shame can be a powerful motive that fosters attempts to gain empowerment, to overcome domination. Indeed from slaves' cutting of limbs to escape the chains of servitude to masses enthralled with the empowering promises of a dictator, people seek empowerment. As Nietzsche suggested, to accept domination, to assent to slavery, leads to the sickness of a revenge denied. So too does fundamentalism dialectically foster subordination to power by establishing "micro-spheres" of empowerment that provide illusory realms of power. But at the same time, fundamentalism can shade into terrorism and provide realms of actual power; indeed, what can give a person more power than the power to take the lives of others, the very power of God.

4) *Meaning:* People have a fundamental need to make their lives meaningful. They need frameworks of meaning that provide anxiety reducing significance to one's life, ethical codes of regulation, a theodicy of the distributions of fortune, and above all, they need to assuage the painful reality of the inevitability of death (Becker 1973). For most of human history, religion has provided people with meaning and direction for their lives, and in many cases, hope for some kind of immortality. But again following Weber, the "disenchantment of the world" eroded the sacred and the realms of transcendent meanings. As religion waned in the West, nationalism emerged as a "modern"

political framework in which "invented communities" of granted identities, recognition, and above all, meaning. But insofar as nationalism was a secular, Western framework dependent on an autonomous public sphere, it has generally held little sway in the Muslim world. As globalization began to erode the basis of nationalism, a highly fragmented mass mediated popular culture of privatized hedonism became widely diffused. But participation in cultures of consumption of modernity is beyond the means for the vast majority of Muslims. At the same time, Western materialism and narcissism is offensive to Islamic values. Fundamentalism offers an alternative, a repudiation of secular Western ideologies that is easily available. Much like early Christianity provided compensatory *ressentiment*, so too does fundamentalism provide a palliative alternative to secular, Western meaning-systems based on hedonistic indulgence.

Character and Reactions to Domination

When domination is imposed from without and internalized at the level of character, when recognition, dignity and agency are frustrated or denied, when selfhood is humiliated and enfeebled, the person both reproduces the structural conditions of subalterity and thwarts resistance at the price of the person's actualization and fulfillment. As was noted, the waning of Islam, the rise of the Christian hegemon, and finally, colonization (or neo-colonization through local intermediary autocrats), fostered *ressentiment* and the desire for revenge. But that revenge would consume and destroy the self. Moving from Nietzsche to Freud, *ressentiment* based on domination, denigration, shame and humiliation of being inferior to a powerful Other can be interpreted in terms of insults to character and dignity, and frustrations/denials of desires for community, agency, recognition and meaning. This is typically handled in at least three intertwined ways:

1) Denial. Denial and external blame are typical ways of handling the shame and humiliation that might come from seeing oneself as culpable or inadequate vis-à-vis the Other. For example, the person fired had a horrible boss, the flunking student had unfair teachers. On a social level, this tendency to project one's shortcomings on other has long been studied in terms of scapegoating, prejudice, etc. In medieval times, ill fortune was blamed on witches, and many innocent women died. Perhaps nowhere was this as clear as Hitler's blaming the Jews and Jewish conspiracies for all of Germany's problems.

In terms of the issue at hand, we can see that denial, blame and projection are typical forms of explanation in Islamic societies. Poverty, illiteracy and scientific backwardness is due to either the infidels of the West, pro-Western leaders like King Hussein or Anwar Sadat, or an Israeli conspiracy. For example, when the WTC was attacked, a common story that appeared in Al Ahram (government newspaper), widely believed in Egypt and Saudi Arabia, blamed *Mossad.* The story claimed that 3,000 Jews were told to stay home from work at the WTC. Arabs were said to lack the capability for such an operation. It was almost 6 months later that the Saudis finally acknowledged that 15 of the 19 men were Saudi nationals, and even then most Muslims did not believe other Muslims did it. Such an account keeps a people from either looking within themselves or questioning their own leaders. Indeed, certain leaders typically blame others for general misfortune and not only deflect self-criticism but mobilize people to hate and condemn an outside party, and in the process, secure their own power and legitimacy. As most people know, or should know, conspiracy theories of history, while quite useless as explanations, are often quite useful for a leader or group to avoid self examination and/or avoid changes that might undermine power. Leaders have long found that scapegoating, casting blame on someone else, can mobilize support for a regime. To paraphrase Sartre, if the Israelis didn't exit, Muslim states would need to invent them[30].

2) Profound distrust. The limited economic opportunities on the one hand due to both internal and external factors, and the denial of recognition and dignity on the other, have colluded to foster structurally based blocked opportunities that in turn engender anger and rage and a sense of revenge to redress the humiliation. But insofar as much of anger is to the self, and it is denied, not acknowledged, it becomes expressed toward an external object. In psychoanalytic terms, there is a "splitting," a disavowal of dissatisfaction of what is within, and its attribution to that which is without is intensely distrusted and hated. In a similar vein, to loosely borrow from Melanie Klein, one of the most archaic forms of agency can be seen in projection/aggression evidenced in envy. More specifically, given the helplessness and dependency of infancy, there is frustration, and in turn, anger and resentment that are projected to the "bad object" that is both needed and yet is hated and must be destroyed. While for Klien this "paranoid position" is an inevitable part of infancy that is transcended, in later life, certain social conditions reawaken the primitive rage and destructive fantasies of early childhood. Scheler had noted that *ressentiment* is based on envy, but we are suggesting that this envy has powerful unconscious underpinnings. Following her insights, psychoanalysts like Kernberg or Kohut have theorized that narcissistic insults, primarily the lack of recognition of the self and/or failures to achieve dignity and esteem elicit narcissistic rage toward denigrated objects.

Thus, a number of scholars, from Wilhelm Reich to the more recent work of Scheff (1994), seem to suggest that a combination of humiliation and powerlessness can foster intense, irrational forms of hate, rage and indeed a willingness to die. But, to whom must that rage be expressed? In the case of Islam, distrust of and rage towards the West have become mediated through selective interpretations of Islam that denigrate the infidel[31]. As such, there is a profound distrust of the Western infidel and intense reactions to those who might seem to advance Western interests or ideas. Sadat was assassinated and Rushdie was condemned in a *fatwa.*

3) Rage, terror and death. These factors, given both very real and attributed injustices, foster intense anger and rage that would destroy the enemy Other. As Freud argued, there were two fundamental drives, Eros, the sexual impulse (libido) that would bind people through love, sexual or aim inhibited, and Thanatos, the Death Instinct (aggression) that would destroy and tear down. Freud's formulation should be seen as a poetic metaphor rather than an essentialist psychology. But following Freud's cultural psychology, Fromm (1967) argued that the domination of the subject led to impairments of self love, the thwarting of self constitution and realization that leads to the embrace of nihilism and necrophilia, the love of death and destruction whether of self or Other.[32] This attenuated attachments and capacities to love others, and becomes a constraint upon agency that can only be overcome through violence[33]. Perhaps we might also note Theweleit's (1989) study of the *Freikorps*, the veterans of WWI, petty bourgeois men without jobs or job prospects who disdained women and erotic love; they sought only war, death and destruction. To die in combat was preferable to living in peace. In sum, some who suffer from various forms of domination, social constraints, or limitations on agency may find community, meaning and identities in battle, death and devastation that provide compensatory forms of dignity and agency.

Insofar as both Islam and Christianity condemn suicide, there have instead emerged cults and rituals that celebrate, valorize and imitate death. Salvation religions that promise a better life offer a ready escape from domination and hopelessness in this life, death. Consider only the passion plays of medieval Christianity, or the various flagellant parades among Catholics and Muslims. Islam, as a warrior religion, celebrated the martyred warrior hero who died in holy combat. While Islam forbids both suicide and killing innocent civilians, some fundamentalist clerics have interpreted the Quran in ways that legitimate "sacred terrorism" through suicide missions such as shootings and/or bombings directed at civilians.

In sum, given decline, domination, and political economic distress, together with cultural insults, humiliations, degradations and despair, anger, rage and hatred is generated and channeled through the available means of resistance. This kind of rage can be mobilized through secular political channels, in which various extremist groups turn to life destroying terrorism, e.g., Bader Meinhof, Red Brigades on the left or the Contras on the right. But so too can terrorism become religiously interpreted to be God's will.

Terrorism and Identity

Young men in particular social/cultural locations are especially prone to certain social and political stresses and influences that foster their identities. The lower middle classes of Islam tend to be religiously observant, fearful of modernity, and resentful of their condition. The rage of the unemployed, subjugated and humiliated, is much the same whether in the ghettoes of America, the marginalized lower middle classes of rural America or the *souks* of the Middle East. Young men, without alternative sources of agency and respect, turn to compensatory identities of hate and violence preached in cults of death. The difference between the gangbanger, right wing militiaman and terrorist is a function of socialization, institutional support and a justifying ideology. In many Muslim societies, men and women do not date, have sex, nor can they marry unless and until they have jobs and/or means of livelihood. But most Muslim countries are showing demographic explosions, and even with modest economic growth, there are not enough jobs for the growing numbers of youth and declining per capita incomes for most. Without jobs or prospects, many unemployed or underemployed young men have nothing to do and nowhere to go. Yet they are welcomed into the mosques or *madrassas* where they learn a theology of anger that disposes terrorism. This is often the case in refugee camps. Palestinian camps such as Balata and Jenin are notorious spawning grounds for terrorists.

The situation of these dispossessed men stands in sharp contrast with media-constructed hegemonic global masculinities; the suited, forceful western businessmen and politicians express a dominant, celebrated masculine identity (Connell 2000). In most Muslim societies, the institutionalization of patriarchy has disposed a machismo demeanor; yet subaltern masculinities are insulted, humiliated. For young men without work and socialized into traditional Islam, *ressentiment* is not only a hateful envy in response to political-economic domination, but is also directed to racial/cultural subjugation and humiliation, this "emasculation" disposed hate and violence. According to Kimmel (2000), through disenfranchisement, and the loss of status, employment, and emasculation, in contrast to the empowerment of women in western societies, lower-middle-class men "may continue to feel a seething resentment against women, whom they perceive as stealing their rightful place at the head of the table, and against the governments that displace them." A central complaint by fundamentalists against the West is the brazen, immoral behavior of Western women. Note in this context that the Taliban regime attempted to restore masculinity and empower men, requiring the beard as the marker of masculinity, and to re-feminize and control women by exclusion from jobs, education, etc. Most Islamic terrorists, including the 9/11 terrorists, are men under the age of 25, caught in the tension between exclusion from modernity and the inability to realize traditional roles. The violence of terrorism, even if as a martyr, restores the sense of self.

In some cases, even members of the more educated classes embrace terrorist causes. As was noted in the press, the 15 Saudis of 9/11 were not uneducated teenagers of poverty and refugee camps but of the educated classes. Most had come from a rapidly changing region, one of the poorest in a now stagnating, declining Saudi Arabia. Even when living or studying in Europe, or because of it, exposed to prejudice and denigration as Europe's Other, they gravitated to fundamentalist mosques that provided them a sense of community and valorized identities. Islamism provided them with a solution to society's problems, pride in their heritage, and affirmed personhood/manhood. But along with that came hatred to the infidel so great they became sacred warriors facing death and martyrdom. The absolute certainty of Allah's rewards in the next life made earthly sacrifice a component of recognition and dignity that is often wanting in this world. Europe is a relatively closed society, especially to immigrants. Law enforcement officials have found extensive active terrorist networks in Europe, but not in America, for good reason. In this regard, Hundley (2002) notes, "Europe—with its burgeoning population of Muslim immigrants and relatively limited opportunities for them to gain access to the social and economic mainstream—has become a factory for turning frustrated men into religious fundamentalists and political fanatics." We might add that the general ethnic monocultural prejudice and racism of European societies is a remnant of the same type of exclusivity that led to the Reformation and the secular Enlightenment. In the face of economic retrenchment, Europe shows little welcome for "foreign" immigrants and workers.

From what has been said, in the face of *ressentiment*, emasculation and subalterity, becoming a terrorist gives compensations, a valorized identity, a sense of dignity, purpose, meaning, and hope, especially when conditions are hopeless. Consider by analogy the Jews who fought the Nazis in the Warsaw ghetto. Notwithstanding the futility of their efforts, they nevertheless held out against the *Wehrmacht* longer than did the Polish army. While many died, they did so with a sense of agency and dignity that will long be remembered. We suggest that the motives of the Warsaw Jews, secular or sacred, are not so different than the Islamic terrorists of today, secular or sacred. More specifically, if we consider the following articulations of desire: 1) *Membership* in a terrorist organization, from the time of schooling and/or recruitment to training camps to the planning/execution of missions, places one in a highly valued publicly esteemed, cohesive community. 2) Resting upon the legacy of the esteemed warrior, the terrorist finds *recognition* and *dignity* in his acts (on some occasions her acts). Some gain *pride* in this life (seculars), those who go on to the next (holy warriors) are remembered and esteemed by friends and family[34]. 3) Powerlessness, being without agency to shape one's own destiny, leads to an intense anger and hatred that is turned upon the self. But as a terrorist, by turning passivity into activity, *empowerment* and *agency* are realized, however destructive and inhumane may be the consequences. 4) Finally, given the historical legacies/current realities that engendered *ressentiment*, in the face of the rapid social changes of the modern world and attendant anomie, exposed to the empty materialism of the West with its "disenchantment of the world," terrorism, sacred or secular, provides a framework of values and meaning that saves one from insignificance, finitude and even the fear of death.

Islamic cultures provided their followers with various major identities or narratives of self such as the merchant, the warrior and the scientist-scholar. Weber emphasized the warrior tradition for a number of reasons, not the least of which is that in most cultures, warriors are more likely to be heroes than merchants or professors. This phenomenon long antedates Islam, let alone the modern culture industry. Identity formations, and the actions and routines they enact, may provide affective gratifications. But, under the conditions of social fragmentation, humiliation, domination, and meaninglessness, there is often frustration and regression. A readily available identity for a Muslim male is the warrior engaged in lesser *jihad* against infidels. In many ways, terrorism can be understood as a way of redeeming the self and returning the society to the time of its "Golden Age," a moment of both religious virtues and culture, free of external domination, where various gratifications can be found.

Part V. Globalization and the Dialectics of Terrorism

Following Weber, to end our historical and analytical discussions, we would like to consider some trends and possibilities since 9/11[35]. We suggest two potentials in the confrontation between the West and militarized fundamentalism. First, military and police networks may become highly intertwined and form a de facto global police force. We predict that the "War on Terror" is likely to lead to the gradual decline of large scale terrorist organizations, but will not eliminate terrorist acts in the context of guerrilla warfare in isolated locales nor potentially catastrophic terrorist acts of mass destruction by individuals and small groups. The military technologies of advanced capitalism dispose a potential for imperialist wars, and in turn, destructive terrorism as resistance, whether organized or random. Given the emergence of the Islamic Brotherhood of Egypt in the 1930s, the growth of Islamic fundamentalism in the past few decades, and the proliferation of religious terrorisms such as Hamas, Hezbollah, Abu Sayyif and, of course, the globalized terror network of Al Qaeda, it might well seem as if there is an emerging "clash of civilizations" and a protracted conflict between Christendom and Islam (Huntington 1996). We reject this thesis for many reasons. The Islamic states vary greatly in their traditions and interests. "Civilizations" include a number of classes and groups that are often very much in conflict, for example, the bazaari vs. intellectuals, westernizers vs. traditionalists, etc. The most deadly conflicts in recent times have been within and/or between Muslim countries: Iran-Kuwait, Iran-Iraq, Turkey-Kurds, or the civil war in Algeria. Moreover, national and regional politics today are very much caught up within various moments of economic, political and cultural globalization. This, however, is not to deny that Islamisms and the Right wing in the West often frame Islamic-Western conflicts in terms of a "clash of civilizations" whose rhetoric aggravates conflicts and legitimizes military mobilizations (Tibi 1998).

On the other hand, to counter the various adverse consequences of neo-liberal globalization, increasingly powerful global civil social institutions and global governance are emerging to create mechanisms that regulate the global economy and control the forces of militarization to foster peace, justice and equality. The project of modernity, with its emancipatory promises and rationalized institutions creates the possibilities for global democracy. Progressive movements, ironically, are often resisted by secular elites, who might lose power, as well as by religious fundamentalists.

Responding to Terrorism

To understand the root causes and possible outcomes of terrorism, it must be kept in mind (dialectically speaking) that terrorist movements, especially in the developing world, are not only resisting the undemocratic, exploitative face of globalization but are reacting to the long standing grievances and injustices based in the hundreds of years of political economic domination by European powers of other societies and their own workers. Religious movements, as movements formed at the interaction of cultural and national independence, are rooted deep in the psyche and history of dominated peoples. The roots of fundamentalism and hence terrorism are very deep. The ways the contradictions of modernity in a global age may play out is very complicated. There are progressive and reactionary ways to address the issues underlying the drastic consequences of globalization. The potentials of resistance are complicated by the flexible responses of global capitalism. Hence, the solutions to the injustices of global capitalism, if any, will probably be global in scope. The Al Qaeda network is one such global if reactionary response that indicates the necessity of attending to the root causes of the inequality and political domination that disposes the embrace of terrorism.

In the face of stagnant or declining fortunes, many young Muslims have turned to fundamentalism, and a small minority move on to terrorism. For the poor and less educated, and/or often educated in fundamentalist schools and madrassas, there are few job prospects that will allow them to fully participate in their own societies, e.g., to marry, have families and homes. Such men find community and solace in fundamentalist mosques where they can find dignity in religious virtue and devotion. Given the proximity to comparatively affluent Europe with its relatively open borders, many people go there to find jobs. And as we have seen, this includes many of the educated and more skilled who have trouble getting jobs either in their own stagnant societies and go to study or work in Western Europe. But with ten percent unemployed, the still relatively "homogeneous" European nations regard them as interlopers, with disdain and contempt. Unemployed or underemployed, given their credentials, such men too gravitate to fundamentalist mosques. In both cases, we see the spawning grounds of those who might become terrorists. The former take up guns and/or bombs and go on terrorist missions. The latter learn to make bombs, design and execute plots, and send the former on suicide missions.

These factors, individually or collectively, may bode ill for the future. As we have seen these conditions and attitudes create an atmosphere that condones terrorism as well as generates likely recruits. Islamic countries that are poor, undeveloped, and prone to seemingly ever more religious fundamentalism thus engender people willing to use terrorism on a mass scale. September 11 may be a preview to the use of weapons of mass destruction against civilian targets. The Al Qaeda network may well have cells in over 60 countries around the globe ranging from Somalia to Malaysia, alliances with a number of local terrorist organizations and perhaps the support of "rogue" states like Iran or Iraq. Such a network of cells, mosques and social welfare agencies spanning perhaps 60 countries cannot be easily or quickly dismantled. And with its careful planning, logistics and the autonomous nature of its cells, that may well include well-armed sleeper cells. There may well be more dramatic incidents of terrorist activities. We do expect that to happen.

On the other hand, there have been a number of recent developments that counter these developments and may well reduce terrorism. Kepel (2002) argued (before 9/11) that Islamism was becoming politically and morally bankrupt; *jihad* had exhausted itself and was in a state of retrenchment following repudiation of its excesses and the failure of theocracies (Iran, Taliban) to improve the living conditions for the masses. Indeed, in a decade or two, historians may look back at 9/11 as the heyday of Islamic terrorism. One unintended consequence of 9/11 has been to mobilize a concerted, worldwide effort against terrorism[36]. While this was perhaps spearheaded by the American retaliation against the Taliban, this effort was indeed underway long before 9/11. The highly unpopular Taliban were quickly overthrown in Afghanistan and the Al Qaeda network and training camps were seriously degraded and are unlikely to be reconstituted. It seems as if a great deal of intelligence was found in notebooks, computers and records of Al Qaeda and the Taliban that listed many terrorists and disclosed many plans leading to a number of arrests and confiscations of explosives, etc. in places like Malaysia and Singapore. Since that time, all over the world we have seen growing cooperation of intelligence agencies that have become far more diligent and aggressive in surveillance and arrest of terrorists. The day of this writing, Italian police stopped a plot to poison the water of Rome. There have also been hundreds of other arrests of terrorists linked to Al Queda in Germany, Belgium, Spain, France, England, Turkey, Malaysia, Indonesia and the Philippines, etc.

A number of governments that have in the past supported terrorism and anti-Americanism have made major changes in direction, often beginning before 9/11. Perhaps most important has been Pakistan, where President Musharraf was paid several billion dollars for withdrawing support from the Taliban, who were strongly supported by his own ISI (Pakistan's military intelligence). He then provided a great deal of logistical and intelligence support for the United States military campaign. He closed a number of fundamentalist mosques, changed the curricula of the *madrassas* and reduced the influence of the ISI.

Yemen, site of the Cole bombing, was relatively uncooperative in investigating the crime. But since 9/11, Yemen has embarked on an anti-terrorism campaign, replete with American military advisors. So too has Sudan, once home to Bin Laden, moved toward the US. In 1999, the Emir of Bahrain, Sheik Hamad bin Isa al-Khalifa, assumed the throne. He immediately opened the jails, released all political prisoners and allowed the return of political exiles. More recently, he declared himself king, but with plans to create a constitutional monarchy with democratic elections in which both men and women can run for office and/or vote.

The Saudis, who have indeed contributed to the problem of terrorism, are now facing problems of their own (see below). Some Princes have been raising questions about the need for changes. They are suggesting that more students should study banking, science, engineering and business administration. While millions of foreign workers have been sent home to give Saudis jobs, there have been voices for gradual changes of Saudi laws and practices. They have offered Israel recognition if it withdrew to its 1967 borders. (Ending the Israeli-Palestinian conflict would end one major irritant to many Muslims.) They have become more cooperative with US intelligence after 9/11. There have been louder calls for women's rights and even demonstrations. Teenagers and young people have found more and more creative ways to use cell phones and the Internet to plan rendezvous, out of the sight of the moral police.

Using state military and police networks to control terrorism yields a mixed outcome. With the increase in police and military expenditures and loss of civil liberties there is also is the attempt to recreate a safe world. We question the merit long term of a militarized response. Note the cases of Viet Nam, Ireland, Bosnia, and Palestine: violent suppression often leads to violent resistance rather than the intended outcomes. The "War on Terror" will probably lead to a decline in widespread terrorist organizations but not to the end of terrorism or resistance to imperialism.

Globalization as Both Oppressive and Liberating

Neo-liberal globalization, fostering greater and greater inequalities, has created vast wealth, most of which has gone to elites. While global capital has provided few job-generating investments in the Islamic countries, transnational corporations have nevertheless found/created large markets for their products and have developed various "exotic" sites for tourists. The mass media display an outside world of plenty while rich tourists from that world display their wealth. At the same time, Western media celebrate a secular, hedonist mass culture that is morally offensive to traditional Islamic values, ranging from autocracy to patriarchy. Insofar as globalization has infiltrated many of these countries, clerics and political leaders deplore, resist and condemn the self indulgent, erotic hedonism, and quite rightly fear that it will corrupt their culture and their cultural power may erode[37]. In part due to the factors noted, Muslim countries have not been incorporated into the new worlds of commerce. Even a "wealthy" country like oil rich Saudi Arabia has seen its revenues stagnate and its population explode, leading to a decline in per capita income from $22,000 to $8,000.

Across the Islamic world there are population explosions, unemployment, underemployment and mismatched skills, e.g., many college students graduate with degrees in Islamic studies—with no job prospects rather than science, technology or business administration. There is a generally unfavorable view of the US and its policies based on its hyperpower political-economic status, the geo-politics of oil, its support of tyrants, its uncritical support for Israeli treatment (occupation) of the Palestinians, and the materialistic culture. Many believe that the US is run by the Jews, if not by a Zionist conspiracy. A recent Gallup survey of over 9,000 residents of Pakistan, Iran, Indonesia, Turkey, Lebanon, Morocco, Kuwait, Jordan and Saudi Arabia found that more than half had an unfavorable view of the US. While some of that resentment is a displacement from dissatisfaction with local leaders, the fact remains that most people have a negative view of the US, not entirely undeserved.

Marx celebrated capitalist modernity as liberating; it rent asunder the personal ties of fealty and ended the idiocy of rural life that sustained the domination by kings, lords and bishops. Capitalism would create the seeds of a socialist society. In much the same way, globalization has liberating effects. It sows seeds of modernity that, if they sprout and flourish, can act in the Muslim world, much like the Reformation in Christendom, initiating a transformed religion that can both lead Islam into the modern world, and at the same time, recapture its own now often forgotten legacies of tolerance, justice, philosophy, and science.

In this light, what are some of the positive outcomes and developments since 9/11? At the most recent meeting of the pro-business World Economic Forum in New York, in the shadow of 9/11, such issues and critiques of alternative globalization movements were given attention by the elites of global capital. In contrast to previous WEF meetings, business, political and cultural leaders debated alternative globalization critiques of neo-liberalism[38]. At the same time, at the pro-union/social movement 2nd World Social Forum in Porto Alegre, Brazil, 50,000 participants, including representatives from around the globe, formulated structural strategies for democratic globalization.

We suggest that the events of 9/11 might contribute to the growth of a global civil society and new political structures to administer and enforce international law. Certain global trends interact with the response to terrorism. First, 9/11 and the "War on Terror" highlight the growing importance and power of regional and global political bodies and pacts such as the UN, EU, G-8, and NATO. While there are tensions within and amongst such bodies as well as protest movements against them, and while the US has often acted unilaterally, the U.N. and European states were involved in the initial legitimation of the "War on Terror" and have been very involved in the postwar organization of the government of Afghanistan, and in the peace keeping missions. Secondly, the gradual institutionalization of progressive treaties such as the International Criminal Court may well offer caution to even leaders of the industrial nations, who might sponsor terrorist organizations or engage in state terrorist acts. Third, with the growing pressure of net-mediated global justice movements, such as the World Social Forum, which produced statements strongly criticizing U.S. policy in Afghanistan and the War on Terror, we can see the beginnings of a transformation towards a global civil society to complement and challenge the U.N. and push for regulation and democratization of the global political economy.

In the light of these and other developments in reaction to globalization, we see possibilities for a struggle between neoliberal and social democratic forces ultimately yielding a more democratic global society. To accommodate critiques and challenges and still sustain profits, there may be a return to neo-Keynsian economics at a global level. This would seem to call for a global, social democratic welfare network state to moderate the domination of some states over others (constrain imperialism), alleviate poverty (moderate capitalism) and modernize education (modernize traditions). The growing calls for debt relief and increasing challenges to IMF/World Bank neo-liberalism should be noted. While various dystopian and utopian scenarios are possible, with a wide range of options in between, we suggest that although there may be risks of further terrorist attacks, the shock of 9/11, followed by the intervention in Afghanistan, War or Terrorism and the increased recognition of the global scope of governance and militarization, in the long run will encourage the world to embrace more global governance serving not only the elites, but all of humanity. In other words, 9/11 and subsequent developments may be a watershed, political and cultural moments that will lead to greater awareness of the adverse consequences of globalization that dispose globalized terror. Various alternative globalization movements, progressive NGOs, and now even some of the elites of globalization are suggesting ameliorative actions and strategies.

Conclusions

To understand the spread of fundamentalism, in this case Islamic fundamentalism, as a search for religious certainty and purity rooted in an imagined past, and violent terrorism as a rare but visible political means to restore that past, we must look at the historical roots of the phenomena. Military conquest and trade networks spread the hegemony of Islamic culture and its *shariah*-based codes for life, law and society from the Atlantic coasts of Iberia through to western China. The growing affluence of the Islamic world fostered great centers of advanced learning and culture. Within 500 years, Islamic civilization reached a level previously comparable only to India or China. Although Islam engendered a very advanced civilization, and indeed enabled the Renaissance in the West, the values and conditions that made the rise of Islam possible, together with various challenges and defeats from other societies, led to an erosion of its dynamism, to stagnation, dogmatism, and a turning inward and a waning of its hegemony. Lewis (2002) and others have asked, "What went wrong?"

In contrast to Islam, ascendant Protestant Christianity, freeing the person from the shackles of feudalism—with its rationalization of the economy, administration and legal systems, and a rejection of abnegation of the world, together with its subjective moment, "salvation anxiety," impelling an "inner determinant" for instrumental action—disposed the rise and proliferation of rational capitalism. This eventually led to the European subjugation of Islam and the reduction of Islamic societies to peripheral status, and in turn, ressentiment to the wealthy and powerful West. Within 500 years of the Reformation, Christendom, now including the US, achieved global hegemony and unprecedented economic, technological and military might. Following WWII, global hegemony was dominated by America.

In the face of modernity and political economic domination, the many assaults on traditional values and identities, and the homogenizing tendencies of globalization, in spite of the liberalization of beliefs and pluralism, there has been a worldwide embrace of fundamentalism. For Islamic fundamentalists, the secular governance, toleration, individualism and personal freedom (sexuality) of the West are abhorrent. Its materialistic culture is seen as shallow and godless, its toleration for democracy, human rights, gender equality and sexual freedom are heresies alien to Islamic traditions. Its mass mediated popular culture is an apostasy. Hence, in the face of economic, political and cultural challenges and *ressentiment*, for societies where the diffusion of globalization has been limited, as has been the case in many Muslim countries, there was a broad impetus for religious renewal.

Islamic societies, at the time of their Golden Age, practiced toleration, justice, pluralism and equality. But that past has also included internal factors that have acted as limits to the growth of modernity. Between fundamentalism and *ressentiment*, there has been violence against memory that stems from the need for revenge. The "invented" past of fundamentalism that would place the blame for social ills on ethical lapses and reclaim a glorious theocratic future provides compensatory identities and affective gratifications to its followers by paradoxically preaching dogmatism, intolerance, hatred, blame and violence, all of which sustain poverty and despair. For a marginal few in particular social locations of age, class and gender, there is an elective affinity for terrorism and the celebration of Death. *Ressentiment* meets the death instinct and joins with the ideology of a Holy war through resistance to external oppression that leads to unspeakable, violent acts. Religious terrorism is a dark moment of the collective soul, grounded in hate. It is a rigidly defensive ideology of retribution that reproduces the very conditions it would seek to ameliorate.

The options for Islamic societies are vexing. Secular westernization at the state level has been undone and/or resisted from within by Islamist reactions and by neo-colonial forces from without. In most Islamic states, efforts to elaborate Islamic modernisms, the pursuit of tolerance, compassion, and understanding, in syntheses of Islamic culture and modernity have either been suppressed or lacking a ready public. Yet there are traditions within Islam of metaphorical interpretations of the Quran, of free speech and diversities of interpretation. In recent years there has developed a cottage industry of Islamic scholarship examining the texts and the actual historical roots of the Quran and its evolution in early Islam (Stilles 2002). What must be noted is that most of this scholarship is located in Western universities; in most Muslim countries, questions that the Quran is anything other than the actual word of God, revealed by Gabriel, are typically met with *fatwas* and violence[39]. The transformations of Islamic fundamentalism, with its conservatism and literalism that would silence the clerical fascists who preach hate and destruction, which would recapture the vibrant heterodoxy and toleration of its Golden Age, made relevant to our global age, can only come from within Islam. In the West and in the more pluralistic and materially advanced Islamic states such as Lebanon or Turkey, hard compromises and creative syntheses are being worked out between modernization and tradition. Kepel (2002) has argued that we are on the cusp of a new, post-Islamist age in which the traditions of Islam become reconciled with the democratic and pluralistic side of globally based modernity.

It remains to be seen if the emancipatory, liberalizing forces of globalization will temper the adverse consequences of its neo-liberal forms that have unconsciously colluded with the reactionary elements within Islamic societies that prefer stability to democracy while many people suffer. The adverse moments of modernity, American geo-political interests and its mass mediated consumer culture are found everywhere in the world, in which time and space have been compressed. Throughout the world we have seen fundamentalism growing as a response to pains of globalized modernity. The unique culture, histories and legacies of Islamic societies have led to dislocations, humiliations and *ressentiments* that have been expressed in Islamisms, ethno-religious conflicts and terrorism that give voice to an oppressive modernity.

Perhaps more important than ideological debates over the nature of Islamic history is the future of reform in Islam. Kepel (2002) suggested that Islamist terrorism does not, nor can it produce its intended goals, and has become consumed with a fantasy of a world-wide triumph of radical Islam. Dreams of world domination generally lead to many deaths before they exit from the stage of world history. We are left with the dilemmas and solutions of Marx and Weber. To remedy the injustices of global capital, we must create global solutions through political solidarity across ever more permeable boundaries. To reform the nullity of modern civilization, now freed of any transcendental meaning and based on a frantic pursuit of profit gained through heartless, technical reason, we must base education and understanding on a critical, value-based reason, tolerant of a plurality of differences. The growing numbers of educated Muslim women suggest a gradual tempering of patriarchy, toleration for the individual and voices for justice. The development of the positive possibilities of modernity, social justice, equality, democracy, and pluralism are needed to balance or, hopefully, to transform oppression. In a global age, to survive terrorism with growing access to technologies of ever more lethal destruction, part of the solution requires that we allow public spaces for the social sources of forgiveness and kindness that reside in most moderate and progressive religious traditions, which also serve as bases for mobilizing alternative globalizations. Notwithstanding the media images of bloody bodies, masked gunmen, falling towers, suicide bombers and fanatical clerics, Islam societies have long traditions of toleration, pluralism, and hospitality to the Other. There are voices within Islamic societies that would reclaim these traditions, as well as progressive forces from without that would join with them in ushering in a new era.

Notes

1. Fundamentalism, as used here, means general conservative religious resistance to modernity, with instances in various religious. A common term for this in scholarship on Islam is Islamism.

2. There is a small cottage industry of Weberian studies of Islam, especially given Bellah (1970), Turner (1974) and the collection by Toby and Schluchter (1999).

3. There were of course many variations insofar as Islam was embraced from Africa to China.

4. The five pillars are faith, prayer five times per day, tithing, fasting, and the *hajj* — pilgrimage to Mecca.

5. Most interpretations suggest they will find 72 virgins waiting for them, but some translators say they will find golden raisins, a prized delicacy, not virgins (Stilles 2002).

6. For instance, Ibn Khaldun, was a brilliant a 14th Century Islamic historian and social theorist: "Recently, some sociologists have argued Ibn-Khaldun might be considered the founder of sociology because he developed important sociological concepts such as social forces, social facts, and social laws. His work emphasized both conflict and solidarity, thus being related to both functionalism and the conflict perspective. However, since he was largely unknown to most sociologists, his impact on the field has been minimal." From: http://www.missouri.edu/-socbrent/khaldun.htm

7.This website, http://www.islamnet.orgunder/Islam.Knowledgeand Science.htm, notes, "It is important to recall that in physics as in many other fields of science the Muslims observed, measured and carried out experiments. They must be credited with having developed what came to be known later as the experimental method."

8. Rigidity and orthodoxy in the face of ambiguity, fear or stress is a very typical reaction.

9. Note that in contrast to the openness of Vatican II that in response to the continuing expansion secularism and hedonism, the Catholic Church has become rigid in face of greater challenges over birth control, abortion, the ordination of women, etc.

10. The Turkish Janissaries, Christians, stood as a limiting case, while specifically trained for administration, they were nevertheless loyal to the Sultan rather than other notable families.

11. Kuran (2001) contrasted the operations of the Medici, Bardi, Peruzzi or Fugger enterprises with Islamic partnerships to indicate how and why the former led to intergenerational growth while the latter were unlikely to endure.

12. There are of course wide variations, Turkey, as a result of geography and history has large factories and encourages nationalism, its own, not that if its Kurdish

population. The UAE has a successful and growing airline. But as Lewis (2002) notes, save the oil industries, there is less production in Islamic countries than in tiny Finland where one company, Nokia, produces more cell phones than any other company.

13. There were of course many variations insofar as Islam was embraced from Africa to China.

14. In the 40+ years from the time Japan was opened to the West, there was an overthrow of its feudal system, the Tokugawa Shogunate, and it became a world power, defeating the Russian navy. Following WWII, many Buddhist, Confucian and/or communist societies would modernize and ascend.

15. Ironically, the canon technology originally developed by the Chinese was first introduced to Islam in the overthrow of Baghdad in the 13th century, and later improved. See *A Brief History of Rocketry,* http://science.ksc.nasa.gov/history/rocket -history.txt.

16. There are of course wide variations, e.g., women have more equality in "secular" Turkey, Iraq or Syria than in theocratic Iran, conservative Saudi Arabia, or Kuwait.

17. Similarly, the affluence of Malaysia is largely due to the Chinese, thus one of the factors that enables Muslim countries to prosper is ethnic and/or religious diversity

18. One may generalize that modern fundamentalism of the 20' Century, as a theologically based resistance to the threat of modernity is a historically specific moment of a tendency for religious doctrines to become more rigid, dogmatic and orthodox in face of challenge (see Marty 1994).

19. At the time of the American war against the Taliban, it was feared that the opposition by Pakistani fundamentalists would overthrow Musharef s pro-US government. Yet as it turned out, less than 5% of the population strongly opposed the US, mostly tribal Pashtuns ethnically related to the Taliban.

20. Again we must note that there are 50 Muslim societies/states with wide variation across and within states. While Turkey, Lebanon, Jordan and Bosnia may stand at one extreme of moderation, even in such places, the countryside is often far more conservative.

21. Of course much like the West, there had long been erotic art and literature, but not typically part of the popular culture.

22. It should however also be noted that in many Muslim societies, there are many people who enjoy the decadence and sexuality, e.g., the most popular program in Iran was Baywatch and within a short time of the fall of the Taliban, TVs and satellite dishes began to appear.

23. Terrorism more often than not fails to achieve its goal.

24. Consider the anthrax scare. A few days before this was written, Palestinians deployed a spiked form of C-4, as magnetized particles that destroyed an Israeli Merkava tank, the best armored tank in the world.

25. We should of course remember that this toleration for difference has varied by time and social class, etc. scholars are more tolerant than shepherds.

26. It's been suggested that the Saudi peace initiative was aimed at gaining Israeli investment and expertise.

27. This is not to ignore the terrorism of the chic in which people from privileged classes renounce their advantages and become terrorists, e.g., Bill Ayers, Patty Hearst or Osama Bin Laden

28. As is noted below, ressentiment cannot really be alleviated through revenge.

29. We will note that denial and blame are typically used to deflect considerations of one's self and thus much of the anger to the Great Satan, the US, and Almost as Great Satan, Israel, is an attempt to concretize the consequences of more abstract factors and INGO's such as the World Bank, IMF, WTO etc. This is of course not to deny the many oppressive and odious actions of the US and Israel.

30. This is not to slight the great injustices done to the Palestinians by the Israelis.

31. This pattern can be seen in many other religions, e.g., marginal status Christians embracing religious justifications for racism, sexism, and even the murder of secular "sinners" like abortion providers. One can read the Quran in ways that stress harmony and forgiveness as well as jihad to the infidel.

32. We are not suggesting a psychological basis for terrorism, indeed most studies suggest a "banality" of terror, most terrorists tend to be relatively normal people, free of evident psychopathologies.

33. It is worth noting that most terrorists tend to be unattached males, typically blocked or thwarted by limited alternatives, prejudices and/or injustices.

34. Hamas sacralizes it martyrs and commemorates their pictures and their deeds. Moreover, their families gain respect and are very well taken care of financially.

35. In 1920, Weber suggested that without a Protestant tradition of individualism and decentralized, democratically administered churches, Communist Russia, with its legacies of Tsarist and Orthodox hierocracies would itself become a huge, rigid bureaucratic state that would fall under its own weight.

36. It seems as if Osama Bin Laden will not rank with Hannibal, Alexander, Napoleon or Patton. It seems he expected a massive military response and ground invasion by US forces that would ignite anti- American sentiments everywhere.

37. Iran is a good case in point where the conservatives are fighting a losing battle with the modernists supported by growing numbers of young people.

38. See Lenora Todaro. "The WEF's Corporate Moguls Debate Their Role as Unelected World Leaders." *Village Voice,* February 8, 2002. Online: http://www.villagevoice.com/issues/0206/todaro.php.

39. In the West, close examination of the Bible and its historical roots was the prelude to the Reformation and Enlightenment.

References

Adorno, Theodore. 1950. *The Authoritarian Personality.* New York: Harper.

Afary, Janet. 2001, "Portraits of Two Islamist Women: Escape from Freedom or From Tradition". *New Left Review,* 19, Fall, 46-77.

Ahmad, Eqbal. 1998. "Terrorism: Theirs and Ours." Talk at the University of Colorado, October 12, 1998. Retrieved January 15, 2002, from Internet: http://www.indiatogether.org/talks/ahmad01.htm

Armstrong, Karen. 2001. "Was it Inevitable," in Hoge, James and Gideon Rose, Eds, *How did this Happen: Terrorism and the New War.* New York: Public Affairs.

Bellah, Robert. 1970. *Beyond Belief: Essays on Religion in a Post Traditional World.* New York: Harper and Row.

Becker, Ernst. 1973. *The Denial of Death.* New York: Free Press.

Choueiri, Youssef. 1990. *Islamic Fundamentalism.* Boston: Twayne Publishers.

Collins, Randall. 1998. *The Sociology of Philosophies: A Global Theory of Intellectual Change.* Cambridge, MA: Harvard University Press.

Connell, R.W. 2000. *The Men and the Boys.* Berkeley: University of California Press.

Davidson, Lawrence. 1998. *Islamic Fundamentalism.* Westport, CT: Greenwood Press.

Fanon, Frantz. 1961. *The Wretched of the Earth.* New York: Grove Press.

Freud, Sigmund. 1989. *The Future of an Illusion.* New York: W.W. Norton & Company.

Freud, Sigmund. 1930. *Civilization and its Discontents.* New York: W.W. Norton & Company.

Fromm, Erich, 1967. *The Anatomy of Human Destructiveness.* New York: Holt, Rinehart and Winston.

Fromm, Erich. 1941. *Escape from Freedom.* New York, Holt: Rinehart and Winston.

Giddens, Anthony. 1991. *Modernity and Self Identity: Self and Society in the Late Modern Age.* Stanford, CA: Stanford University Press.

Greenfeld, Liah. 1992. *Nationalism: Five Roads to Modernity.* Cambridge: Harvard University Press.

Honneth, Axel. 1995. *The Struggle for Recognition: The Moral Grammar of Social Conflicts.* Cambridge, MA: Polity Press.

Hundley, Tom. 2002. "Islamic Radicalism festers in Europe." *Chicago Tribune*, February 25, 2002.

Huntington, Samuel. 1996. *The Clash of Civilization.* New York: Simon and Schuster.

Jurgensmeyer, Mark. 2001. *Terror in the Mind of God: The Global Rise of Religious Violence.* Berkeley, CA: University of California Press.

Kepel, Gilles. 2002. *Jihad: The Trail of Political Islam.* Cambridge: Harvard University Press.

Kimmel, Michael. 2000. *The Gendered Society.* Oxford: Oxford University Press.

Kuran, Timur. 2001. "The Islamic Commercial Crisis: Institutional Roots of Economic Underdevelopment in the Middle East." Los Angeles, California: USC Center for Law, Economics and Organization, Research Paper, C01-12, Retrieved February 1, 2002 from Internet: http://papers.ssrn.com/sol3/papers.cfm?abstract id=276377

Langman, Lauren. 2000. "Identity, Hegemony and Social Reproduction", in *The Living Legacy of Marx, Durkheim and Weber, Volume 2*, New York: Gordian Knot Books.

Laquer, Walter. 2001. "Left, Right and Beyond", in Hoge, James and Gideon Rose, Eds., *How did this Happen: Terrorism and the New War*, New York: Public Affairs.

Levtzion, Nehemia. 1999. "Aspects of Islamization: Weber's Observations on Islam Reconsidered." In Huff, Toby, and Wolfgang, Schluchter, Eds., *Max Weber and Islam*, New Brunswick, N,J.:Transaction Publishers.

Lewis, Bernard. 2002. *What Went Wrong? Western Impact and Middle Eastern Response.* Oxford: Oxford University Press.

Marty, Martin. 1994. *Accounting for Fundamentalisms: The Dynamic Character of Movements*. Chicago: University of Chicago Press.

Morelli, Elizabeth Murray. 2001. "Ressentiment and Rationality." Paper presented at Twentieth World Congress of Philosophy, Boston, Massachusetts U.S.A., 10-15, August 1998. Retrieved January 15, 2002 from Internet: http://www.bu.edu/wcp/Papers/Anth/AnthMore.htm

Nietzsche, Friedrich. 1969. *On the Genealogy of Morals*. Translated by Walter Kaufmann and R. J. Hollingdale, New York: Random House.

Post, Jerrold. 1998. "Terrorist psycho-logic: Terrorist behavior as a product of psychological forces." In Reich, Walter, Ed., *Origins of Terrorism: Psychologies, Ideologies, Theologies, States of Mind,* Cambridge: Washington, D.C.: Woodrow Wilson Center Press.

Rokeach, Milton. 1960. *The Open and The Closed Mind,* New York: Basic Books.

Scatamburlo, Valerie and Lauren Langman. 2002. "Fanon Speaks to the Subaltern," In Jennifer Lehmann Ed., *Current Perspectives in Social Theory*, V. 21, pp 253-86, New York: JAI-Elsevier Press.

Scheff, Thomas. 1994. *Bloody Revenge: Emotions, Nationalism, and War.* Boulder, CO: Westview Press.

Schluchter, Wolfgang. 1999. "Hindrances to Modernity, Max Weber and Islam", In Huff, Toby, and Wolfgang, Schluchter, Eds., *Max Weber and Islam,* New Brunswick, N.J.: Transaction Publishers.

Sennett, Richard and Jonathan Cobb. 1972. *The Hidden Injuries of Class.* New York: Knopf.

Siebert, Rudolf. 2001. "The Critical Theory of Religion." Retrieved January 20, 2002 from Internet: http://www.wmich.edu/religion/siebert/CT_Intro.pdf

Spengler, Oswald. 1962. *The Decline of the West.* Trans. by C.F. Atkinson. New York: The Modern Library.

Stauth, George and Bryan Turner. 1988. *Nietzsche's Dance: Resentment, Reciprocity and Resistance in Social Life*, New York: Blackwell.

Stille, Alexander. 2002. "Radical New Views of Islam and the Origins of the Koran." *New York Times*, March 2, 2002. On Internet: 0http://www.nytimes.com/2002/03/02/arts/02ISLA.html

Taylor, Charles. 1992. *Multiculturalism and the Politics of Recognition.* Princeton, N.J.: Princeton University Press.

Theweleit, Klaus. 1989. *Male Fantasies*. Minneapolis: University of Minnesota Press.

Tibi, Bassam. 1998. *The Challenge of Fundamentalism: Political Islam and the New World Disorder*. Berkeley: University of California Press.

Toby, Huff, and Wolfgang Schluchter, Eds. 1999. *Max Weber and Islam.* New Brunswick, N.J.: Transaction Publishers.

Todaro, Lenora. "The WEF's Corporate Moguls Debate Their Role as Unelected World Leaders." *Village Voice*, February 8, 2002. On Internet: http://www.villagevoice.com/issues/0206/todaro.php

Toynbee, Arnold. 1939-61. *The Study of History*. London: Oxford University Press.

Turner, Bryan. 1974. *Weber and Islam*. London: Routledge & Kegan Paul.

Structural Determinants of State Involvement in International Terrorism

Satya R. Pattnayak
Thomas M. Arvanites

Abstract: *This analysis of international acts of terrorism reveals two interesting findings. First, state involvement is more complex than simply becoming a "source" or a "target" country. This study presents a typology that specifies four levels of state involvement (ideological source, facilitating source, immediate target, and ultimate target). Second, the data reveal quite clearly that a small number of countries consistently fall into one of the four levels of involvement. It is suggested that structural factors (e.g., level of relative deprivation among the population, nature of the political system, nature of the existing coercive control mechanisms, location in the world communication network, and level of racial/ethnic diversity in the population) are crucial in explaining specific state involvement in international terrorism.*

In recent years international terrorism has received much attention in the media. The general public has been made more aware of the perils of international terrorism by governments and politicians worldwide. Much of this increased awareness has been due to a dramatic jump in the number of recorded incidents of international terrorism during the past decade. There was an average of 482 acts (from Mickolus et al. 1989, xviii) of international terrorism per year during 1980-87, whereas during 1968-79, the figure was fewer than 300 (calculated from Mickolus 1980, 935-949). Moreover, there have been dramatic shifts in the distribution of terrorist events across major regions and individual countries. For example, although Western Europe and the Middle East still accounted for nearly 62% of all acts of international terrorism during the 1980s, there was ample evidence to suggest that, at least since 1986, Sub-Saharan Africa and the Asian-Pacific region are fast becoming happy hunting grounds for more mobile terrorist groups (See Mickolus 1989, xviii). This increase has influenced social scientific research on terrorism in general. Social scientists have been interested particularly in the structural characteristics of the countries involved in international terrorist incidents.

Existing Theories

A systematic, causal understanding of the occurrences of terrorist events worldwide has unfortunately been lacking in rigor. Thus far, broad theoretical attempts to understand international terrorism have been few and far between. It has been suggested that it is an illusion to suppose that social scientists have anything resembling an adequate theory of terrorism (Gibbs 1989, 334). Many economists advocate a "rational-choice" approach to study international terrorism (Laplan and Sandler 1987; Sandler and Scott 1987; Sandler, Enders, and Laplan 1991). Simply put, the rational-choice approach argues that terrorists only engage in those violent or violence-inducing behaviors that would optimize at least one of their goals. Faced with resource constraints (e.g., budgetary and time constraints) and risks involved (e.g., governmental deterrence and military backlash) terrorists pick a target that they perceive to have a high potential to minimize costs and maximize their gains. Assuming everything else constant, a change in the constraints would induce a change in terrorist behavior. This approach works on a simple premise: The increase in risks and punishments should negatively affect terrorism.

Its simplicity notwithstanding, this approach does not adequately explain why terrorists pick certain countries and not others. Despite an undoubted increase in state-led vigilance activities in major Western European countries, incidents continue to occur in those countries. Research on certain dominant structural features of Western European and other leading target nations for terrorist events should be an important priority of researchers.

Another dominant paradigm on international terrorism is the "social contagion" approach. This approach suggests that terrorist incidents may encourage similar developments in the neighboring countries through a process of diffusion and imitation (Heyman and Mickolus 1981; Fowler and Purkitt 1980). Assuming that nations located in a region may have certain cultural similarities, this approach fails to explain the occurrences of terrorism across regions. In other words, why do international acts of terrorism occur in countries that are culturally as far apart from each other as the United States is from Lebanon? Here again, a structural ingredient is missing in the existing literature on international terrorism. It is essential to earmark the existing dominant structural conditions of countries in which most terrorist events occur. Why are only certain groups of countries chosen as targets and why are only certain groups of nations identified as sources of terrorism?

In this paper we suggest that since more than one group of nations is involved, it is imperative to learn about their major structural characteristics as a basis from which one can assess the likelihood of a nation becoming a target or a source of international terrorist events. Keeping that in mind, this paper is organized into four parts. Part I attempts an operational definition of international terrorism. Part II elaborates on a theoretically conceivable typology of groups of nations. Part III examines the conditions under which a nation is more likely to be a source or a target nation. Finally, Part IV draws conclusions, focuses on the limitations of the structural approach, and suggests possible topics worth undertaking in future research on international terrorism.

Part I: Attempting an Operational Definition of International Terrorism

"A comprehensive definition of terrorism . . . does not exist nor will it be found in the foreseeable future. To argue that terrorism cannot be studied without such definition is manifestly absurd" (Laqueur 1977, 5). Gibbs has suggested that attempts to study terrorism without a definition are "no less manifestly absurd" (1989, 329). Clearly, an operational definition is necessary before any attempt is made to understand international terrorism in terms of causality. Building on the definition suggested by Gibbs (1989) we propose the following components of a working definition of international terrorism.

To begin, international terrorism involves more than one nation. Second, it entails nonsanctioned violence or threatened violence (against perceived injustice) undertaken by a group located in nation A and directed against human or nonhuman objects located in nation B. Third, the action or threat of action by groups in A is undertaken with the hope of altering or maintaining at least one aspect of relevant political decision-making in a different nation (Nation B) or nations (Nations C, D. . . .or N). Fourth, the action should not be intended to permanently defend some area in nation B, nor can it be considered conventional warfare. (For a discussion on terrorism in general, please see Gibbs 1989, 330-331.)

The four important components of the operational definition of international terrorism noted above need further elaboration. The first component makes it unquestionably cross-national. This excludes all acts of domestic terrorism along with all incidents of governmental backlash toward domestic terrorist groups. The second component is formulated to encompass all types of recorded incidents of international terrorism. Most recorded incidents of international terrorism are either kidnapping, some form of bombing, armed attack, hijacking, assassination, theft, or a threat to engage in any of the above. Each of these types of incident is either violent or a threat to engage in some form of violent behavior.

The third component underlines that the groups involved in international terrorism do possess a set of goals and work toward influencing at least one political norm in another nation. Basque terrorists, located in Spain, blowing up a train station in southern France to influence the French government's policies toward the Basque separatist movement in France provide an example of how the third component can be made operational. In reality, some international terrorist actions may specifically be committed in one country to influence at least one putative norm in a third country. For example, if a terrorist group located in Mexico, but inspired by the Iranian Revolution, engages in the destruction of American institutions in France, it satisfies the extension of the third component to a third country or nation.

Finally, the fourth component distinguishes terrorist events from incidents that may occur while nations engage in conventional warfare. In a situation of conventional warfare, nations or groups operating from the warring nations try to control some territory of the enemy. By the same logic, terrorist actions are not intended to achieve permanent or semipermanent defense of some territory of another nation.

Part II: Typology of Nations Involved in International Terrorism

By definition, any discussion on international terrorism involves at least two groups of countries. The first group can be called the source countries and the second the target countries. In theory and practice, however, there may be different types of sources and different types of targets. Based on the third component of our definition of terrorism, we conceptualize that four groups of nations can be part of a typology involving international terrorism. Groups A and B may be conceived to be the source countries and Groups C and D the target countries. Group A consists of countries construed to be the ideological source of terrorist events. For example, the success of the Islamic Revolution in Iran may prove to be the ideological source of many militant islamic terrorist groups operating outside Iran. In such a case, Iran becomes a Group A country. A Group B nation is the facilitating source of terrorist groups. For example, many international terrorist incidents in Lebanon were linked to groups whose members were either residents of or were operating from Mexico, Paraguay, or Argentina. In this case, regardless of whether the state authorities in Mexico, Paraguay, and/or Argentina deliberately encourage such activities or not, they become Group B countries.

Group C involves countries that are immediate targets of terrorist incidents. The incidents occur in the territories of Group C countries. Basque terrorists operating from Spain engage in incidents in France, in which case France becomes a Group C country. Group D includes countries that are ultimate targets of terrorists. By hitting a target in C, in many cases terrorist groups wish to influence some form of decision-making in Group D. If an American is kidnapped in Paris by a terrorist group and this act is intended to pressure the government of the United States to engage in some action that it otherwise would not, then the U.S. becomes a Group D country.

Since there can be four groups of countries involved in a given act of international terrorism, it is essential to sort out the various combinations among the groups.

- Possibility 1: Groups A, B, C, and D are distinguishable from each other.
- Possibility 2: Groups A and B can operate together as a single source whereas Groups C and D remain separate targets.

- Possibility 3: Groups A and B and Groups C and D can be collapsed together to form only two identifiable groups of countries, the former acting as both the ideological and the facilitating source, and the latter acting as both the immediate and the ultimate target.
- Possibility 4: Groups A and B can be distinguishable from each other whereas Groups C and D can operate together to form a composite target, both immediate and ultimate.

	Source Categories		**Target Categories**	
	Ideological source	Facilitating source	Immediate target	Ultimate target
1.	Group A	Group B	Group C	Group D
2.	Groups A+ B		Group C	Group D
3.	Groups A+B		Groups C+D	
4.	Group A	Group B	Groups C+D	

The major research question then becomes: Under what conditions is a nation more likely to be either a source or a target country? In other words, what specific structural features of each of these groups of nations make them a distinct analytic category? An answer to this research question can emerge only from a substantive understanding of the international terrorism data of the past years. For the present paper, we concentrate on the decade of the 1980s, specifically on 1980-87. Almost all of our data are from Edward F Mickolus *et al.* (1989), *International Terrorism in the 1980s,* Volumes I and II.

Part III: Structural Characteristics of Nations in Groups A, B, C, and D

Existing social scientific literature delineating the conditions under which terrorist movements may originate is abundant. Most social movement and revolutionary literature provides us ample causal variables that are also appropriate to considering terrorist group activities. Gurr's (1970) aggregate-psychological approach and Johnson's (1966) system-value consensus perspective complement each other in order for us to better understand the psychological, sociological, and political motivations necessary to engage in terrorist incidents. According to

Gurr (1970), a society characterized by a high level of relative deprivation and politicization of the discontent would witness violence against visible political targets. Relative deprivation symbolizes a state of mind in which there is an intolerable, perceived gap between people's goals and existing opportunities to attain them legally. According to Johnson (1966), countries experiencing a high level of relative deprivation are more likely to experience violent upheavals if a high level of value dissynchronization already exists. A high level of value dissynchronization entails great vulnerability to the intrusion of new values from abroad. In many cases, these new external values arrive in the form of fresh ideologies. In this line of thinking, every modernizing society is a potential source of international terrorism.

Many scholars have argued that high socioeconomic inequalities, high regime repression sustained by systematic political exclusion of certain groups, and a tight state control over the information network are necessary conditions for future terrorist activities (see Gal-Or 1986). Other researchers have maintained that these necessary conditions become sufficient to generate exports of terrorism, especially: if the nation was at some time a colony; has some obvious reasons to feel angry at a former colonial power for the past undoings; or has recently achieved a successful change in government through nonpeaceful means (Alexander and Gleason 1981; Schmid 1983).

Structural Characteristics of Group A Nations

Data from independent sources that would substantiate a list of Group A nations is lacking. For the purposes of this paper we use the classification of the U.S. State Department to identify the existence of such a group of nations as a distinct analytic category. Readers should not be surprised if they notice some inherent bias in the classification of certain countries as the ideological source of terrorism.

The State Department in numerous documents has identified a short list of nations that it believes to have been the main source of ideological inspiration for international terrorism worldwide. A survey of the State Department publications points to the following nations as the main source of international terrorism in the past decade: Iran, Libya, Syria, Cuba, South Yemen, and North Korea (United States Department of State 1990). In our typology of nations, this group will certainly qualify for inclusion in Group A. The paramount question is, what causes these countries to be in Group A? The group members have one very identifiable ideology to export. In the case of Iran and Libya it is their own version of Islamic fundamentalism. In the case of Cuba, Syria, South Yemen, and North Korea, the exportable ideology is some form of socialism.

Assuming that these countries are indeed the major ideological sources of international terrorism, we must underline some structural features they have in common. Several characteristics put these countries in a separate group. First, none of them is a democratic country. Second, there is a tight and exclusive state control over the media and the information network. Third, all these countries were formerly either colonies or semicolonies. Fourth, all these nations have had at least one successful transition of power in the past three decades through nonpeaceful means. The regimes periodically try to validate their legitimacy either by engaging in anti-Western rhetoric or by tacitly encouraging terrorist events abroad. The domestic frustration over the inability of these regimes to satisfy the range of societal demands is translated into an engagement in terrorist activities, where some groups look for obvious targets to hit. In most instances these targets are former colonial or present neocolonial powers.

The above characteristics may be necessary conditions for nations to be in Group A, but are perhaps not sufficient to induce some groups operating from their territories to look for terrorist targets. Table 1 illustrates an interesting point that must testify to the degree of coercive control these states possess over their populations. In each of the six nations except Iran, the number of armed personnel per 1,000 civilian population is extremely high. South Yemen, the nation with the lowest ratio among all Group A nations except Iran, had 17 armed personnel per 1,000 people in 1987, whereas France, with the highest ratio of armed personnel to civilian population among Western democratic nations, had only 10.1 in the same year. Iran's success with the Islamic Revolution in 1979, its militant population under the Khomeini regime, and its high-level ideological involvement against anything anti-Western may have acted as substitute mechanisms of societal coercive control against domestic terrorism. A high level of coercive control exercised by Group A states then increases the probability that international terrorism would take the place of domestic terrorism.

Table 1
The Number of Armed Personnel per 1,000 Civilian Population in Selected Countries

Country	1980	1981	1982	1983	1984	1985	1986	1987
North Korea	39.1	41.9	41.7	40.9	39.9	38.5	40.1	39.1
S. Yemen	12.0	11.7	12.3	12.0	12.6	12.2	14.9	39.1
Cuba	22.8	23.8	23.5	25.3	29.8	29.5	29.2	28.9
Syria	28.8	30.1	32.3	41.5	40.2	38.8	37.2	35.9
Libya	17.5	17.3	16.4	19.5	24.8	24.8	24.5	23.7
Iran	7.8	6.4	5.7	5.5	7.4	7.3	7.1	7.0
Netherlands	7.6	7.6	7.4	7.2	7.1	7.1	7.3	7.2
Canada	3.4	3.3	3.3	3.3	3.3	3.3	3.3	3.3
Spain	9.5	9.7	9.8	9.3	8.9	8.1	8.1	8.1
W. Germany	8.0	8.0	8.0	8.1	8.0	8.1	8.1	8.1
Paraguay	4.4	4.3	4.4	4.3	4.4	3.5	3.9	3.8
Guyana	9.4	9.2	9.2	9.2	9.2	9.1	7.3	6.5
Lebanon	5.5	6.1	6.4	6.1	5.8	6.4	10.9	11.1
France	10.7	10.6	10.6	10.6	10.4	10.2	10.1	10.1
United States	9.2	9.4	9.5	9.4	9.4	9.4	9.4	9.3
Israel	52.4	52.9	53.1	52.2	51.2	47.8	43.4	42.6

Source: *World Military Expenditures and Arms Transfers.* 1988. Washington DC: Government Printing Office.

Structural Characteristics of Group B Nations

It is not automatic that a Group A nation becomes a facilitating source nation in Group B. According to our typology of nations, delineated earlier, a Group B nation must facilitate the existence and operation of a terrorist group from its territory. Facilitation may take various forms.

A terrorist group may use passports and other legal or illegal documents of a Group B nation for travel and coordination purposes. A terrorist may also use a dummy name and register legally as a corporation or a club in the territories under the control of a Group B nation. Given the current international deterrence measures in place against a Group A nation in the event its sponsorship of a given terrorist act is established, terrorist groups may look to territories of other less secure countries from which to operate. This has been clearly demonstrated in Table 2.

Table 2
Major Facilitating Countries of International Terrorism
During 1980-87

	Total Number of Incidents	Percentage Share of the World Total
Spain	104	5.75
Paraguay	58	3.21
Netherlands	58	3.21
Canada	57	3.15
Cuba	56	3.10
Guyana	55	3.04
Mexico	54	2.98
United Kingdom	54	2.98
Colombia	51	2.82
Argentina	48	2.65
France	48	2.65
Brazil	46	2.54

Note: These figures are derived from the data that clearly link terrorist incidents to a facilitating source located in another nation. Of 3,856 total international terrorist incidents reported in Mickolus (1989) during 1980-87, only 1,809 incidents had documented links with another nation.

Source: Calculated from Mickolus, Edward F. et al. *International Terrorism in the 1980s*. 1989. Volume II. Appendixes 1 and 2.

According to the data presented in Table 2, very few of the international terrorist incidents recorded during 1980-87 could be traced to a Group A nation. Column 1 in Table 2 illustrates that the major facilitating source nations of international terrorist events during 1980-87 were Spain, the Netherlands, Paraguay, Canada, Cuba, and

Guyana. The deterrence measures implemented bythe U.S. and other allied nations against international terrorism have not been very successful in the past precisely because the ideological sources are different from the facilitating sources. The question is, what specific characteristics do these nations have that make them attractive facilitating sources for international terrorism?

A closer look at Table 2 would lead to the discovery that the leading nations in Group B are from two major regions of the world: Western/Southern Europe and Latin America. The Netherlands and Spain form an integral part of the European Common Market and Paraguay, Cuba, and Guyana are active participants in the Latin American Free Trade Area. Only Canada remains outside these two regions. These nations obviously provide better than average opportunities for terrorist groups to operate. Note that Cuba is also a member of Group A. It fits into the second and third possibilities, where both ideological and facilitating sources are the same. Cuba's high level of sustained animosity with the U.S. since the 1960s makes it a potential facilitating nation as well. Other than Cuba, all other members of Group B are characterized by a low ratio of military personnel to the civilian population, thus testifying to the existence of a state apparatus with at least one weak coercive control mechanism.

According to Table 1, the number of military personnel per 1,000 civilian population in Spain, the Netherlands, Paraguay, Canada, and Guyana are much lower than in any nation in Group A except Iran. There may be several additional reasons behind this trend. First, most of these nations are either weak states (Paraguay and Guyana) or open societies (the Netherlands, Spain, and Canada). A state is considered weak when it is unable to control the authority relationships among various social groups in civil society. An open society is characterized by free elections, free press, and an emphasis on due process of law. If the state is weak, then it becomes easier for terrorist groups to operate from their territories. In addition, in a weak state it perhaps becomes easier to corrupt government officials through bribes and/or other gifts.

On the other hand, if the society is open, then the response to terrorist group activities takes some time to materialize, as there are political ramifications. Societies such as the Netherlands, Canada, and Spain are open, democratic, and except for the Netherlands, are multi-ethnic societies. Any governmental retaliation against minorities who might be involved in terrorist operations carries deeper political meanings for subsequent elections. Additionally, the presence of ethnic and/or racial diversity enables foreigners to "blend in" to the population. Bornschier and Heintz (1979) ranked countries on the level of ethnic and linguistic fractionalization. On a scale of 0 to 1, Canada ranked above average with a score of .75. This may explain Canada's ranking among the top five Group B countries.

The facilitating state is either a weak state or is sustained by an open society. This dichotomy makes us entertain the possibility that other important structural factors may contribute to the facilitating state status. First, the nation's location in the international information network becomes significant. Whether terrorist groups are located in Paraguay or Canada, they are linked to an efficient informational network system that may be used to communicate with their counterparts globally. Second, with the exception of Cuba, a legal or an illegally counterfeit document from one of these countries increases the group's mobility. For example, a Spanish or a Dutch passport, or even a Canadian passport is sufficient proof to ensure the group's mobility in Europe and North America. A Paraguayan or a Guyanese document is sufficient to ensure mobility to the terrorist group across Latin America. A facilitating source nation then may also be chosen for its potential to ensure mobility from and within its boundaries in case of military retaliation.

Table 3
Major Immediate Target Nations of International Terrorism
During 1980-87

Year	Lebanon	France	W.Germany	U.S.	Spain	Greece	Italy
1980	44[a](9.[b])	45(9.)	19(4.)	47(9.)	13(3.)	31(6.)	24(5.)
1981	56(12.)	36(8.)	40(8.)	40(8.)	23(5.)	22(5.)	22(5.)
1982	35(8.)	49(12.)	46(11.)	48(11.)	10(2.)	20(5.)	26(6.)
1983	71(17.)	45(11.)	11(3.)	12(3.)	10(2.)	14(3.)	5(1.)
1984	79(17.)	42(9.)	19(4.)	9(2.)	25(5.)	17(4.)	13(3.)
1985	82(16.)	23(4.)	23(4.)	7(1.)	29(6.)	30(6.)	19(4.)
1986	96(18.)	41(8.)	17(3.)	14(3.)	35(7.)	13(2.)	11(2.)
1987	73(15).	27(5.)	20(4.)	6(1.)	27(5.)	9(2.)	13(3.)
'80-87	536(14.)	308(8.)	195(5.)	183 (4.7)	172 (4.4)	156 (4.)	133 (3.)

a =Total number of international terrorist incidents
b = Percentage of the yearly total of all international terrorist events (in parentheses)
Source: Calculated from Mickolus, et al. *International Terrorism in the 1980s*. 1989. Volume II. Appendixes 1 and 2.

Structural Characteristics of Group C Nations

Table 3 illustrates the list of Group C countries that were the leading immediate targets of international terrorism during 1980-87. Overall, Lebanon, France, and West Germany stood out to be the primary target countries. They were closely followed bythe U.S, Spain, Greece, and Italy. Except for Lebanon, all other leading Group C nations are open societies with democratic procedures and are located in Europe or North America. This brings us back to the important element of location, which was raised in the earlier section on Group B nations. The immediate target nations may have the potential to retaliate against terrorist groups, but their *willingness* to do so may be very different. These European nations and the U.S. have several strong constituencies of ethnic minorities. Moreover, except for Lebanon, the close ties that these nations have with the United States and United Kingdom may have made them major surrogate targets. European Common Market connections may be paramount in a terrorist group's consideration. It ensures high mobility and it is in the heart of the world communication network. Exposure of the events is almost guaranteed by the media, and exposure, in turn, helps publicize the political demands of the perpetrators.

Lebanon's presence in Group C may be considered a fluke. Lebanon's almost paralyzed state apparatus in the aftermath of the Israeli invasion in the early 1980s makes it more of an exception rather than a normal case study.

Several lesser known factors such as the degree of heterogeneity in the existing population may have to be taken into account. A substantial number of a given minority population already present in a nation makes that minority an obvious target for hiring by the terrorist groups. Minorities, especially if they belong to the same racial and/or ethnic group as the recruiters, are likely to be tempted by terrorist groups to be part of a scheme that guarantees an adequate monetary reward.

Structural Characteristics of Group D Nations

Data which clearly identify a group of nations as leading ultimate targets are lacking for the 1980s. Again, in an effort to identify this group as a distinct analytic category we used the data from the 1970s (taken from Mickolus 1980, xiv-xvii). We found that Israel, West Germany, France, and the United States were the leading ultimate target nations. There is no reason to believe that these countries have ceased to be so in the 1980s. Thus, they qualify to be in Group D.

It is beyond doubt that the potential military power of Israel, West Germany, France, and the U.S. to strike at the terrorist groups is perceived to be very high. Any estimate of their military and surveillance capabilities would testify to that effect. However, high potential to strike may not translate into actual striking power. Many of the reasons are nonmilitary. First, because they are open societies, any antiterrorist military action is likely to be slow due to the emphasis on debates and discussion. The separation of the legislative, executive, and the judiciary branches of government with the usual check and balance mechanisms to curb the absolute exercise of power makes immediate retaliation almost impossible. In the event of retaliation, enough precautions are normally taken to ensure civilian safety at the target location. A well established free press makes the risk of military retaliation even greater. In case anything goes wrong, the incumbent government is almost certain to be discredited for its supposedly merciless military retaliation. Considering the above, Group D nations are more apt to consider measures other than military. All of the above considerations perhaps carry more weight because three of these nations are also leading immediate targets of international terrorism (see Table 3).

Only Israel is not one of the leading immediate targets. This may be because of Israel's unquestionable high-level commitment to security. Israel is not a leading immediate target because of its great defenses against potential terrorist attacks on important institutions. Antihijacking measures are in place in every major airport. The installation of sophisticated metal detectors at major buildings has augmented security measures around the country. Additionally, the number of armed personnel per 1,000 civilian population (Table 1) in Israel is one of the highest in the world. The difference in becoming an immediate target nation or an ultimate target nation then may depend on how elaborate the security measures are around major civilian and noncivilian institutions.

Finally, each of the Group D nations described above is politically and economically close to countries that are the leading facilitating sources of international terrorism. Except for Cuba, all leading facilitating source nations have extensive trade and investment ties with West Germany, France, the U.S., and, to a lesser extent, Israel. These ties make the matter of effective retaliation politically impractical. Without established proof linking a Group A nation to a terrorist incident, an effective military retaliation becomes almost impossible. In the absence of such an option, nations in Group D would perhaps continue to rely on good will and trust in each other's promise to engage in efforts to curb international terrorism within their respective territories.

Part IV: Conclusions

We have attempted to understand how specific national characteristics are related to state involvement in terrorist incidents across nations. A number of social scientists have argued in favor of choosing "a small number of nations that provide maximum leverage in testing theoretical issues" (See Kuhn 1987, 726). It is normal to find similarities and differences among countries chosen to be members of a particular theoretically conceived group. Debates have been raised among researchers on how to interpret such findings theoretically. Slomczynski, et al. (1981), for example, argue that the differences among the members of the same group of nations may actually be lawful regularities, if put in a larger theoretical framework.

Although many scholars have attempted to interpret cross-national inconsistencies in terms of differences in history (see Chirot and Ragin 1975), attempts should be made to use differences in major structural characteristics to understand more general social processes. The present article is an attempt in that direction. However, an attempt is seldom free from limitations.

For one, this article does not attempt to distinguish among types of international acts of terrorism. For example, some nations may be better suited to bombings than to kidnapping or hostage-taking. Some nations may be considered a better location for assassination attempts than for aerial hijacking. A decision to select an immediate target country may very well depend on several subsidiary factors that are by-products of the existing state-led coercive control mechanisms. How elaborate the existing security laws are, how committed the security personnel are to implementing the existing laws, and how politically sensitive the issue of combating terrorism is, may turn out to be important factors determining the likelihood of a particular type of international terrorism in a nation at a given point in time. Briefly put then, the structural conditions that we delineated earlier are parent conditions that may increase the likelihood of a terrorist act if the subsidiary environment (e.g., who is in charge, who is supposed to detect, and who is supposed to carry out) is also in place. For example, the bombing of the Pan Am jet in 1988, although it was viewed by many as a response to the U.S. downing of an Iranian Airbus during the Iraq-Iran War, would not be explained by structural factors. In this paper, however, we focus only on structural conditions that we believe can be used to explain overall patterns of state involvement in international terrorism.

Acknowledging the above limitations, we make the following concluding statements. First, in order for a target nation to exist, the existence of a source nation is assumed. A nation could either be an ideological or a facilitating source. Note that without an ideological source, there is no need for a facilitating source. Therefore, an understanding of major structural characteristics of the ideological source nations is important. In the typology of nations delineated earlier, these nations are Group A nations. Most of them: (1) are either ex-colonies or semi-colonies; (2) experience a high level of relative deprivation among many societal groups; (3) are states that systematically practice political exclusion of certain groups; (4) are states that exercise tight control over the information and communication network; and (5) are states that implement elaborate coercive control measures over the civilian population.

A Group A nation may or may not be a facilitating source, which according to our typology falls under Group B. Based on the data on the past decade, only Cuba is considered to be both an ideological and a facilitating source nation. Most Group B nations: (1) are favorably located in the world communication network; (2) are weak states in terms of implementing coercive control measures or open societies with emphasis on due process of the law; (3) facilitate high mobility among potential terrorist groups because of their political links to other nations in the same region; and (4) are characterized by a high level of racial and/or ethnic diversities.

A nation, on the other hand, may be an immediate or ultimate target. An immediate target nation is a Group C nation and an ultimate target nation is a Group D nation. Normally, a Group C nation: (1) is favorably located in the world communication network, which guarantees publicity of the terrorist event; (2) is an open society; (3)

has the ability to retaliate but the willingness to do so is restrained for various political reasons; and (4) is characterized by a high racial/ethnic diversity in its population. Group D nations: (1) are normally open societies; (2) have a high potential to retaliate; (3) show concerns for civilian safety in case of retaliation; and (4) consider their political and economic relations with Group B nations important enough to preclude Group B's territorial inclusion in any military retaliation.

The emphasis on important structural conditions of nations in Groups A through D in our typology is exploratory in nature. We only hypothesize that the acts of international terrorism taking place in Group C nations are a function of a set of structural conditions prevailing in Groups A, B, C, and D. Whether they actually influence international terrorist events in Group C nations will have to be established through rigorous quantitative research in the future.

References

Alexander, Y and J. M. Gleason, eds. 1981. *Behavioral and Quantitative Perspectives on Terrorism.* New York: Pergamon.

Bornschier, V and F Heintz. 1979. A *Compendium of Data for World System Analyses.* Zurich: Sociological Institute of the University of Zurich.

Chirot, D. and C. Ragin. 1975. "The Market Tradition and Peasant Rebellion." *American Sociological Review.* 40:428-44.

Fowler, W. W. and H. E. Purkitt. 1980. "Trends in Terrorism 1968-79: An Analysis of Poisson and Contagion Models." Paper presented at the Annual Meeting of the International Studies Association, Los Angeles. March.

Gal-Or, N. 1986. *International Cooperation to Support Terrorism.* London: Crown Helm.

Gibbs, J. F 1989. "Conceptualization of Terrorism." *American Sociological Review.* 54:329-340.

Gurr, T 1970. *Why Men Rebel.* Princeton, NJ: Princeton University Press.

Hamilton, L and J. D. Hamilton. 1983. "Dynamics of Terrorism." *International Studies Quarterly.* 27:39-54.

Heyman, E. and E. Mickolus. 1981. "Imitation by Terrorists: Quantitative Approaches to the study of Diffusion Patterns in Transnational Terrorism." In *Behavioral and Quantitative Perspectives on Terrorism.* Y Alexander and J. Gleason, eds. New York: Pergamon. 175-228.

Johnson, C. 1966. *Revolutionary Change.* Boston: Little, Brown.

Kuhn, M. 1987. "Cross-National Research as an Analytic Strategy." *American Sociological Review.* 52:713-731.

Laplan, H. E. and T Sandler. 1987. *To Bargain or Not to Bargain: That is the Question.* Unpublished manuscript.

Laqueur, W. 1977. *Terrorism.* London: Weidenfeld and Nicolson.

Mickolus, E. F 1980. *Transnational Terrorism*: A *Chronology of Events,* 1968-1979. Westport, CT: Greenwood Press.

Mickolus, E., T Sandler, and J. Murdock. 1989. *International Terrorism in the 1980s:* A *Chronology of Events.* Volumes I and II. Ames, Iowa: Iowa State University Press.

Sandler, T and J. L. Scott. 1987. "Terrorist Success in Hostage-taking Incidents." *Journal of Conflict Resolution.* 31:35-53.

Sandler, T, W. Enders, and H. E. Laplan. 1991. "Economic Analysis Can Help Fight International Terrorism" *Challenge.* 10. January/February. 10-17.

Schmid, A. 1983. *Political Terrorism.* New Brunswick, NJ: Transaction Press.

Slomczynski, K. J. Miller and M. Kuhn.1981. "Stratification, Work and Values: A Polish-United States Comparison." *American Sociological Review.* 46:720-744.

United States Department of State. 1986. *Patterns of Global Terrorism.* Washington, DC: Office of the Ambassador at Large for Counter-Terrorism.

United States Department of State. 1990. *Gist.* Bureau of Public Affairs. January.

Counterterrorism Policy and the Political Process

Martha Crenshaw

Abstract: *America's counterterrorism policy has traditionally reflected the more general domestic political process. In that process, threatening events are filtered through the perceptions of political elites, who usually lack consensus. The decision-making process is, therefore, pluralistic, and power is diffused among the Executive Branch, Congress, FBI, CIA, National Security Council, and Department of Defense, as well as influenced by the media, interest groups, and communities of "experts" from professional consulting firms or think tanks. Implementation of policy decisions is affected by many factors, and decisions are often controversial due to rivalries among agencies with operational responsibilities. It is thus difficult for any Administration to develop a consistent counterterrorism policy based on an objective assessment of the threat of terrorism to America's national interests.*

American counterterrorism policy is not just a response to the threat of terrorism, whether at home or abroad, but a reflection of the domestic political process. Perceptions of the threat of terrorism and determination and implementation of policy occur in the context of a policy debate involving government institutions, the media, interest groups, and the elite and mass publics. The issue of terrorism tends to appear prominently on the national policy agenda as a result of highly visible and symbolic attacks on Americans or American property. However, the threat is interpreted through a political lens created by the diffused structure of power within the American government.[1]

In general, focusing events, such as crises or disasters, trigger attention to a problem by attracting the attention of the news media and the public.[2] Such sudden and harmful events, rare by definition, come to the notice of the mass public and policy elites simultaneously. In the case of terrorism, focusing events frequently come in clusters, so that it is often difficult to trace a specific policy response to a single event. The reaction to the Oklahoma City bombing, for example, is linked to perceptions of the 1993 World Trade Center bombing and the 1995 Aum Shinrikyo sarin gas attack on the Tokyo subways. Under the Reagan administration, the 1986 military strike against Libya was a response not just to the La Belle disco bombing in Berlin but to earlier attacks such as the TWA and Achille Lauro hijackings and the shooting attacks at the Rome and Vienna airports in 1985. Thus, sequences of events rather than single disasters typically serve as policy catalysts.

As Robert Johnson has emphasized, in the United States threatening events are filtered through a political process that is characterized by lack of consensus among political elites.[3] The decision-making process is disaggregated and pluralistic, and power is diffused. Because not all issues can be dealt with simultaneously, political elites—the president, different agencies within the executive branch, Congress, the media, interest groups, and "experts" in academia and the consulting world—compete to set the national policy agenda. They compete to select certain problems for attention, interpret their meaning and significance, conceive of solutions, put them into practice, and evaluate their outcomes. Despite the secrecy inherent in formulating and implementing policy toward terrorism, issues are developed, interests formed, and policies legitimized through public debates.[4] Decision makers with different identities and preferences define and represent problems, or frame issues, in order to gain public support for their positions. Furthermore, the selection and implementation of policy depend on the particularistic interests of the actors or coalitions that assume the initiative as much as consistent policy doctrine or strategy based on a broad national consensus about what can and ought to be done. Lack of coordination and fragmentation of effort are often the result.

The Politics of the Executive Branch

The political process within the executive branch is characterized by progressive expansion of the number of agencies involved; overlapping lines of authority among them; expansion of jurisdictions to encompass new issues; parochialism; and competition. No agency in the executive branch of the government wants an issue on the agenda unless it has an efficient and acceptable solution for it. Thus, public policy problems such as terrorism are typically linked to proposed solutions that are in turn linked to specific institutions within the government. How an issue is defined will typically determine which government institution has jurisdiction over it and can thus take charge of policy solutions, often with corresponding budget increases. (Spending on antiterrorism programs jumped from $61.7 million to $205.3 million in the fiscal 1999 appropriations.[5] Overall spending on terrorism is generally estimated at $7 billion per year.)

As the definition of the threat of terrorism changes, so too does jurisdiction. If the image of an issue can be changed, then its institutional venue may change accordingly. Issues can be partitioned among agencies, or different institutions can have more or less authority at various stages or sequences of a decision. For example, if terrorism is defined as a crime, it is a problem for the Department of Justice and the nation's law enforcement agencies such as the Federal Bureau of Investigation (FBI). However, if it is defined as warfare or as a threat to national security, responsibility shifts accordingly. The Central Intelligence Agency (CIA) and the military become central to the process. Nevertheless, the FBI did not lose its role. In 1986, major legislation established extraterritorial jurisdiction for crimes committed against Americans abroad, which has led to prosecutions in the World Trade Center bombing and East Africa bombing cases, along with others. Definition of the threat of terrorism as "bioterrorism" in the 1990s brought a host of new agencies into the jurisdictional competition, including Health and Human Services (HHS) and its Center for Disease Control. Previously, when the threat of "super terrorism" was interpreted as the danger of the acquisition of nuclear materials, the Department of Energy assumed a key role. In the 1990s, as the threat of terrorism came to be seen as a threat to the "homeland," not only did local and state governments enter the picture but the military was called on to provide "homeland defense." The Defense Authorization Act for Fiscal Year 1997 called on the Defense Department (DOD) to train local "first responders" and to establish response teams to assist civilian authorities should there be a terrorist incident involving weapons of mass destruction (WMD).[6] The result was Joint Task Force Civil Support, established in 1999.[7]

Responsibility for dealing with terrorism is widely distributed, and lines of jurisdiction tend to be blurred and overlapping, with no clear institutional monopoly of the issue. The U.S. government tried to deal with this problem by establishing the "lead agency" concept. The Department of State is the lead agency for responding to international terrorism, while the FBI is the lead agency for domestic terrorism.[8]

Nevertheless, the White House National Security Council (NSC) and the Department of State have traditionally competed for institutional control of the issue of international terrorism, and the FBI and the State Department sometimes clash. For example, Secretary of State Cyrus Vance resigned after his advice against a hostage rescue mission in Iran was overruled by the president and the NSC under National Security Adviser Zbigniew Brzezinski. Former Director of Central Intelligence Stansfield Turner described the relationship between the NSC and executive branch agencies as it affected the rescue decision:

> The National Security Adviser and his staff often are frustrated because they have no direct authority to carry out the President's decisions. That's the task of the bureaucracy, which frequently resists outside direction, even from the President. Bureaucrats are even more likely to resist what they suspect are directives from the National Security Council staff. A result of these tensions is that the staff of the NSC often attempts to sidestep the bureaucracy and do as much as possible on its own.[9]

Turner and the CIA also resisted the NSC's proposals for covert operations against Iran, seeing the dispute as a case of "the professionalism of the experts keeping the political leadership from undertaking ventures that would be embarrassingly unsuccessful."[10]

Rivalries between the NSC and other executive branch agencies also emerged under the Clinton administration. In April 1998, as a result of having read the Richard Preston novel, *The Cobra Event*, the president held a meeting with a group of scientists and Cabinet members to discuss the threat of bioterrorism. The briefing impressed Clinton so much that he asked the experts to brief senior officials in DOD and HHS. On May 6 they delivered a follow-up report, calling for the stockpiling of vaccines (an idea that was soon dropped). The *Washington Post* reported with regard to the stockpiling proposal that "Some administration officials outside the White House expressed surprise at how fast the president and his National Security Council staff had moved on the initiative. . . , noting with some concern that it had not gone through the customary deliberative planning process."[11] Critics noted that not all scientific experts were disinterested; some stood to gain financially if the government invested large sums in developing technology against bioterrorism.

In the investigation of the October 2000 bombing of the

destroyer U.S.S. Cole the State Department was said to be less than enthusiastic about the FBI's hard-line approach to Yemeni authorities[12]. While the FBI appealed to the president to demand that Yemen accept a central FBI role, the State Department countered by warning that the pressure would likely backfire.

Clinton's move to establish the position of a national coordinator for counterterrorism policy on the NSC staff also provoked opposition from within the executive branch. The *New York Times* reported that Clinton's May 1998 initiative "had provoked a bitter fight within the Administration, with the Departments of Defense and Justice opposing a key provision that critics feared would have created a terrorism czar within the White House."[13] As a result, Clinton created a national coordinator with limited staff and no direct budget authority. The *Washington Post* reported, "It is not clear how much real authority [Richard] Clarke will have. . . . The Defense Department successfully fought off proposals to give this coordinator a large staff and independent budget similar to those of the drug policy coordinator. . . . Clarke's appears to be essentially a staff job, reporting to National Security Adviser Samuel R. 'Sandy' Berger."[14]

Moreover, agencies may reject jurisdiction and try to exclude issues from the agenda, especially if they think that they do not have a solution or that the new task is not appropriate to their mission or routine. The DOD, for example, appears divided and ambivalent about its new role in homeland defense. As early as July 1995, some Pentagon officials were calling for an expanded military role in counterterrorism, but this view did not appear to reflect an internal consensus. In a speech to the Council on Foreign Relations in New York in September 1998, Secretary of Defense William Cohen prominently mentioned terrorism.[15] His description of the military mission, however, was vague; he said that the administration hoped to consolidate the task of coordination into one lead federal agency, and that DOD would provide "active support" for that agency's operation. Falkenrath et al. argued that the DOD is not "fully committed to this mission."[16] The military see "homeland defense" as law enforcement, which the military supports only if ordered and when possible. Essentially, in their view, it is a diversion and misuse of defense dollars, and they would prefer that the entire domestic preparedness program be shifted to the Federal Emergency Management Agency (FEMA). The military's reluctance is confirmed by John Hillen, who sees DOD as dominated by interservice rivalries rather than leadership from the president or the secretary of defense: "Today the services are interested in neither the White House's new wars (peacekeeping, terrorism, organized crime, and the like) nor the Joint Staff's futuristic technological blueprint. . . ."[17] The military really wants to fight wars that are like those of the past, only with upgraded equipment on all sides. In January 1999, press reports announcing Cohen's decision to seek presidential approval for a permanent DOD task force, with a senior officer, to plan for a chemical or biological attack on the U.S. quoted Deputy Defense Secretary John Harare as saying "Frankly, we're not seeking this job."[18]

Similarly, FEMA did not want to take charge of the domestic preparedness program.[19] FEMA officials opted out on budgetary grounds, fearing that the program would be inadequately funded, and thus be a drain on already scarce resources, and that the agency would then be criticized for ineffective implementation of the program. Since they could not afford the solution, they did not want to take on the problem.

In 1998, the decision to retaliate against the Sudan and Afghanistan also revealed disarray within the executive branch, a state of confusion and contentiousness that threatened to eclipse terrorism as the issue at the forefront of public debate.[20] The FBI and the CIA were accused of failing to share complete information on threats in East Africa with the State Department.[21] Disagreement surfaced between Washington and bureaucracies in the field. The ambassador to Kenya in December 1997, and again in April and May 1998, asked unsuccessfully for support from the State Department Bureau of Diplomatic Security for the construction of a new and less vulnerable building. The decision to retaliate was controversial. Some analysts in the CIA and the State Department Bureau of Intelligence and Research remained unconvinced of the reliability of the evidence linking Osama bin Ladin's network to the pharmaceuticals plant in Khartoum and informed the news media of their doubts after the cruise missile strikes. The FBI and the Defense Intelligence Agency were excluded from the decision. Apparently Chairman of the Joint Chiefs of Staff General Shelton objected to the original targeting plan and succeeded in reducing the number of targets.

Congressional Politics

Congress frequently plays a critical role in shaping the counter-terrorism policy agenda, without the constraint of necessarily having to present an integrated solution to the problem. Although the president typically has the most power to set the agenda, he depends on Congress to appropriate funds for the measures he proposes, and Congress can block issues or push forward others that the president has not chosen. Furthermore, executive branch agencies usually have their own channels of communication and influence with congressional committees. Congressional staffers and career bureaucrats often have extensive back-channel contacts. Individuals move back and forth between positions in Congress and in the executive branch. Thus, even if the president wants to keep an issue off the agenda or to minimize a problem, he may have to confront it because congressional actions have captured media and public attention. Confrontation is especially likely when the government is divided along partisan lines. The president cannot afford to appear to ignore a potential threat of terrorism, even if restraint might be the most appropriate and effective response. In the 1990s, the president and Congress often seemed to be engaged in a highly partisan politics of anticipatory blame avoidance.

Examples of congressional influence on critical policy decisions include President Reagan's decision to withdraw American troops from Lebanon in the aftermath of the 1983 bombing of the Marine barracks. Reagan was apparently dissuaded by congressional and military opposition encountered in the context of an upcoming campaign for reelection.[22] Initially Reagan resisted the idea of withdrawal, although the House Committee on Armed Services urged him to reconsider his policy and issued its own report critical of security at the Marine barracks. Reagan withheld the release of the DOD's Long Commission report for several days in order to limit the damage he feared it would create as a rallying point for opposition in Congress. Congressional responses from both Republicans and Democrats to Reagan's press conferences and speeches were lukewarm at best. Although the movement to reassess policy was largely bipartisan, House Speaker O'Neill assumed a prominent role in the debate, organizing the passage of resolutions calling for an end to the military presence in Lebanon, and Democratic presidential candidate Walter Mondale seized on withdrawal as a campaign issue. The State Department and the National Security Adviser opposed withdrawal, but

DOD and the Joint Chiefs favored it. In early January, Reagan sent his national security adviser, secretary of defense, and the chairman of the Joint Chiefs of Staff to speak with leading House Republicans. Nevertheless, Minority Whip Trent Lott stated publicly that the Republicans had told them that they wanted the Marines out by March 1985. Still, in his State of the Union address in January 1984, Reagan persisted: "We must have the courage to give peace a chance. And we must not be driven from our objectives for peace in Lebanon by state-sponsored terrorism."[23] Within two weeks of the State of the Union address, Reagan announced the withdrawal.

An earlier instance of congressional influence over policy occurred during the Ford administration. Secretary of State Kissinger ordered the recall of the ambassador to Tanzania, Beverly Carter, when he learned that Carter had played an active role in facilitating negotiations for the release of American students held hostage in Zaire. Kissinger took strong exception to this violation of the official policy of no concessions and reportedly intended to end Carter's State Department career, although Carter had expected to be appointed ambassador to Denmark. However, when the Congressional Black Caucus intervened on Carter's behalf, generating negative publicity for the State Department, Kissinger relented.[24] It was also helpful to Carter's defense that he was a former journalist.

In the 1990s, as Richard Falkenrath points out, one source of the difficulties of the domestic preparedness program was "its origin in a series of discrete, uncoordinated legislative appropriations and administrative actions," the result of ad hoc initiatives rather than strategic concept.[25] In 1996, for example, Congress began "earmarking" specific counterterrorism projects, such as providing $10 million for counterterrorism technologies for the National Institute of Justice in the Fiscal Year 1997 Department of Justice budget. The FBI counterterrorism budget was also dramatically increased, largely as a result of the Oklahoma City bombing. Congress also instructed the Departments of Justice and Defense to prepare long-term plans for counterterrorism, and established an independent National Commission on Terrorism to investigate government policy. Lawmakers are also concerned about lack of congressional oversight of administration efforts.

Outside the Government

Actors outside the government also try to shape the public policy agenda. Interest groups and communities of "experts," sometimes associated with professional consulting firms, or think tanks, seek access to decision makers in order to promote favored issues. They often accumulate the scientific or technical information about the problem that then causes decision makers to recognize it. They can promote a specific conception of an issue, such as the idea of a new, more lethal and irresponsible terrorism in the 1990s.[26] They contribute the "talking heads" who appear regularly on television news programs such as CNN. They may also be influential in shaping policy solutions because of their expertise.

Among interest groups, in the area of terrorism, business interests may oppose economic sanctions against state sponsors. Interest groups devoted to protecting civil liberties are likely to oppose measures that restrict individual freedoms, such as expanding the power of the FBI or the use of passenger profiling at airports. The American Civil Liberties Union, for example, has frequently opposed legislative initiatives such as assigning responsibility for domestic preparedness to the military. Along with conservative Republicans, civil liberties interest groups blocked the wiretapping provisions of the 1996 bill.

The families of victims of terrorism, as well as victims themselves, such as the former hostages in Lebanon, have mobilized to influence policy. They have lobbied the State Department as well as the White House and Congress, and gone to the courts to press their claims against Iran and Libya. For example, the Victims of Flight Pan Am 103 organization established a political action committee, a legal committee, an investigation committee, and a press committee. They lobbied the State Department, published a newsletter, picketed Pan Am offices, and met with the president and Congress.[27] They were instrumental in the creation of a presidential Commission on Aviation Security and Terrorism to investigate the bombing. They played an influential role in the 1996 Iran-Libya Sanctions Act of 1996.[28] Their intervention led to major changes in airline procedures for handling disasters.

During the Iran hostage crisis, the families of the victims formed the Family Liaison Action Group, which, according to Gary Sick, "played a crucial role in public and government perceptions throughout the crisis."[29] Sick adds that President Carter promised the families that he would take no action that would endanger the lives of the hostages, although Brzezinski was pressing for a decisive response that would protect national honor.

The early development of counterterrorism policy was influenced by interactions between individual government agencies and specific interest groups. The debate over the Airport Security Act of 1973 shows how insider-outsider coalitions form.[30] The government players included Congress, the Departments of Transportation, State, and Justice, and the Federal Aviation Administration (FAA). The outside actors were the Air Line Pilots Association (ALPA), the Air Transport Association of America (ATAA), and the Airport Operators Council International (AOCI). In the jurisdictional dispute between Justice and the FAA, the ATAA and AOCI preferred the FAA, while ALPA preferred Justice. In fact, Justice did not want jurisdiction. While the interest groups wanted the federal government to take responsibility for airport security measures, the Department of Transportation and the FAA wished to rely on local law enforcement.

All of these actors use the news media to articulate and disseminate their views not only to the public but to other elites. Government officials (or former officials) are the main source of information for reporters, as well as for Congress, sometimes openly and sometimes through strategic leaks. Leaks to the press can be a way of conducting internal battles as much as informing the public. The media's attraction to drama and spectacular events also makes it hard for the government to ignore an issue when policymakers assume that public opinion will track media attention. But the news media do not set the agenda, according to John Kingdon: "The media's tendency to give prominence to the most newsworthy or dramatic story actually diminishes their impact on governmental policy agendas because such stories tend to come toward the end of a policy-making process, rather than at the beginning."[31] The media tend to be responsive to issues already on the agenda, to accelerate or magnify them, rather than initiate attention. They report on what the government is doing or not doing.

Jeffrey D. Simon agrees.[32] He argues that the media image of crisis is due to the way presidents and their aides handle events; the press depends almost exclusively on authoritative official sources. Government officials set the tone through background briefings and off the record interviews as well as public speeches and press conferences.

Presidents, not reporters, make hostage seizures into personal dramas. On the other hand, Brigitte Nacos argues that government policy is exceptionally sensitive to the news media and to public opinion, especially during hostage crises.[33] Yet the tone of general mass media coverage of U.S. counterterrorism policy is positive.[34]

Conclusions

It is unlikely that the politics of the domestic policy process will change. Thus, expectations for the future should be grounded in the assumption that the trends described in this article will continue. Terrorist attacks, especially spectacular incidents causing large numbers of casualties or targeting important national symbols, will contribute to putting the issue on the national policy agenda. They focus public attention on the threat of terrorism. However, policy will be developed within a general framework of diffusion of power. Multiple actors, inside and outside government, will compete to set the agenda and to determine policy through public debate, conducted largely in the news media. Each actor, whether an executive branch agency, Congress, or an interest group, wants to forge a national consensus behind its particular preference. Due to pressures from Congress, the president will not be able to set the agenda for counterterrorism policy with as much freedom as he can in other policy areas. Where the president dominates is in the rare use of military force, but these decisions may also be controversial within the executive branch. Implementation of policy decisions will also be affected by controversy, due to rivalries among agencies with operational responsibilities. Thus it will be difficult for any administration to develop a consistent policy based on an objective appraisal of the threat of terrorism to American national interests.

Notes

1. Despite its significance, little systematic attention has been paid to the politics of the counterterrorism policy process. William Farrell's early book, *The U.S. Government Response to Terrorism: In Search of an Effective Strategy* (Boulder, CO: Westview Press, 1982), analyzed the organizations behind counterterrorism policy. David Tucker, *Skirmishes at the Edge of Empire: The United States and International Terrorism* (Westport, CT: Praeger, 1997), is also relevant, particularly Chapter 4 (pp.

109-132). Paul Pillar's *Terrorism and U.S. Foreign Policy* will also help fill this gap (Washington, DC: Brookings, 2001).

2. Thomas A. Birkland, *After Disaster: Agenda Setting, Public Policy, and Focusing Events* (Washington, DC: Georgetown University Press, 1997).

3. Robert H. *Johnson, Improbable Dangers: U.S. Conceptions of Threat in the Cold War and After* (New York: St. Martin's, 1997), Chapter 2, "American Politics, Psychology, and the Exaggeration of Threat," pp. 31-48.

4. The classic work is John W. Kingdon, *Agendas, Alternatives, and Public Policies,* 2nd ed. (New York: Harper Collins, 1995). See also Frank R. Baumgartner and Bryan D. Jones, *Agendas and Instability in American Politics* (Chicago: University of Chicago Press, 1993) and Deborah A. Stone, *Policy Paradox: The Art of Political Decision Making* (New York: W.W. Norton, 1997).

5. See Congressional Quarterly *Weekly Report*, 16 January 1999, p. 0151.

6. See Richard A. Falkenrath, "Problems of Preparedness: U.S. Readiness for a Domestic Terrorist Attack," *International Security* 25(4) (Spring 2001), pp. 147-186. See also Martha Crenshaw, "Threat Perception in Democracies: 'WMD' Terrorism in the U.S. Policy Debate," presented to the 22nd Annual Scientific Meeting of the International Society for Political Psychology, Amsterdam, 18-21 July 1999.

7. It has 82 members and an annual budget of $8.7 million, and is expected to increase to 121 people by 2003. It is based in Virginia, as part of the U.S. Joint Forces Command. In the event of a request from local or state government authorities, it would probably take direction from FEMA. See James Dao, "Looking Ahead to the Winter Olympics, a Terrorist Response Team Trains," *The New York Times*, 11 April 2001.

8. However, the Federal Emergency Management Agency (FEMA) has jurisdiction over "consequence management," which is in effect disaster response policy in the event of a domestic attack, especially one involving mass casualties.

9. In *Terrorism & Democracy* (Boston: Houghton Mifflin, 1991), p. 39.

10. Ibid., p. 81. Brzezinski set up an NSC committee to oversee covert actions because the CIA estimated that prospects for success were low. The CIA then vetoed the list of operations the NSC suggested, but Brzezinski was reluctant to take the dispute to the president.

11. 21 May 1998, p. Al.

12. See John F. Burns, "U.S. Aides Say the Yemenis Seem to Hinder Cole Inquiry," *The New York Times*, 1 November 2000.

13. 26 April 1998.

14. 23 May 1998, p. A3.

15. For the text of the speech, see (http://www.defenselink.mil/news/Sepl998).

16. Richard A. Falkenrath, Robert D. Newman, and Bradley A. Thayer, *America's Achilles Heel: Nuclear, Biological, and Chemical Terrorism and Covert Attack* (Cambridge, MA: MIT Press, 1998), p. 263. See also Falkenrath, "Problems of Preparedness," p. 162, who says that the military see this role as a distraction from their core mission.

17. "Defense's Death Spiral," *Foreign Affairs* 78(4) (July/Aug. 1999), p. 4.

18. *The New York Times*, 28 January 1999; also *The Hartford Courant*, with *Washington Post* byline, 1 February 1999.

19. See Falkenrath, "Problems of Preparedness," p. 163.

20. On this subject, see James Risen, "To Bomb Sudan Plant, or Not: A Year

Later, Debates Rankle," *The New York Times*, 27 October 1999, and Seymour Hersh, "The Missiles of August," *The New Yorker*, 12 October 1998, pp. 34-41.

21. See Report of the Accountability Review Boards: Bombings of the US Embassies in Nairobi, Kenya and Dar es Salaam, Tanzania on August 7, 1998, 11 January 1999. Available at (http://www/zgram.net/embassybombing.htm). See further details from the classified report in James Risen and Benjamin Weiser, "Before Bombings, Omens and Fears," *The New York Times*, 9 January 1999. According to this account, the Kenyan authorities arrested a group of suspects but the CIA Station Chief declined to interview them.

22. This section relies on research assistance by Karen Millard. See press reports such as Lou Cannon, "Political Pressure for Marine Pullout Likely to Increase," *The Washington Post*, 29 December 1983; Martin Tolchin, "House Leaders Urge New Study of Beirut Policy," *The New York Times*, 3 January 1984; and John Goshko and Margaret Shapiro, "Shultz Asks for Support on Lebanon; Holds Hill Parleys as Pressure for Withdrawal Grows," *The Washington Post*, 27 January 1984.

23. See text in *The Washington Post*, 26 January 1984, p. A16.

24. See *The New York Times*, 14, 18, and 20 August 1975. Kate Whitman assisted with the research of this case.

25. Falkenrath, "Problems of Preparedness," p. 149.

26. For example, Ian O. Lesser et al., *Countering the New Terrorism* (Santa Monica, CA: Rand Corporation, 1999). The study was commissioned by the Air Force.

27. See Steven Emerson and Brian Duffy, *The Fall of Pan Am 103: Inside the Lockerbie Investigation* (New York: G.P. Putnam's Sons, 1990), especially pp. 221-225.

28. See Gideon Rose's account of the politics of the legislative process in his chapter on Libya in Richard N. Haass, ed., *Economic Sanctions and American Diplomacy* (New York: Council on Foreign Relations, 1998), pp. 129-156, especially pp. 142-144. See also Patrick Clawson's chapter on Iran, pp. 85-106.

29. See his chapter, "Raking vows: The domestication of policy-making in hostage incidents," in *Origins of Terrorism*, edited by Walter Reich (Washington, DC: Woodrow Wilson Center and Cambridge University Press, 1990), pp. 238-239.

30. Joel Rothman assisted with research on this debate. See U.S. Senate, Committee on Commerce, Subcommittee on Aviation, *The Anti-Hijacking Act of 1971*. Hearings. 92nd Cong., 2d sess., 1972.

31. Kingdon, *Agendas, Alternatives, and Public Policies*, p. 59.

32. *The Terrorist Trap: America's Experience with Terrorism* (Bloomington: Indiana University Press, 1994), especially Chapter 7, "Media Players," pp. 261-308.

33. *Terrorism and the Media* (New York: Columbia University Press, 1994).

34. Measured by references to international terrorism in *the Readers' Guide to Periodical Literature* 1968-1998. Database available upon request.

Federal Habeas and the Death Penalty:

Reflections on the New Habeas Provisions of the Anti-Terrorism and Effective Death Penalty Act

Jordan Steiker

Abstract: *When the Alfred P. Murrah Federal Building in Oklahoma City was bombed in 1995, it was the worst case of domestic terrorism in America's history. The horrific event led to the enactment of a landmark antiterrorism statute. Not surprisingly, several of the statute's provisions strengthen federal power in extraordinary and unprecedented ways to counter the threat of terrorism. But other provisions radically restrict the ability of federal courts to enforce the federal constitutional rights of state prisoners. How could Congress miss the apparent irony of responding to the destruction of a federal courthouse with its own assault on federal judicial power? This article argues that the role of federal habeas corpus has changed substantially over the past three decades. Whereas federal habeas had emerged during the Warren Court as a general forum for supervising state court compliance with constitutional norms, it has now become primarily a forum for death penalty litigation. Congress appears to have recognized this transformation, and the antiterrorism statute confirms that Congress views federal habeas through the lens of the death penalty rather than the lens of federalism. This article explores the costs of the "capitalization" of habeas and the subtle relationship between federalism, federal habeas, and the death penalty.*

On 19 April 1995, a massive bomb placed in a rental truck exploded in downtown Oklahoma City, ripping apart the Alfred P. Murrah Federal Building and killing 168 people inside. Timothy McVeigh and Terry Nichols were subsequently convicted for their involvement in the bombing and sentenced to death and to life imprisonment, respectively. McVeigh apparently planned the attack as some sort of revenge for the federal government's siege of the Branch Davidian compound in Waco, Texas, two years before.

Within days of the first anniversary of the Oklahoma City bombing (and the third anniversary of the Waco catastrophe), Congress enacted the Anti-Terrorism and Effective Death Penalty Act (AEDPA). Much of the AEDPA expands federal power in extraordinary ways. On the immigration side, the AEDPA makes it easier to remove aliens suspected of terrorism and to exclude persons with ties to alleged terrorist organizations from entering the United States or receiving financial support. On the domestic side, the legislation continues the movement toward the federalization of crime and toward the enhancement of federal law enforcement powers. Federal law enforcement officers now account for nearly 10 percent of all law enforcement officers nationwide (Strossen 1997), and the number of offenses within the federal criminal justice system has never been greater.

In many respects, then, the congressional response to the Oklahoma City bombing was to advance precisely the agenda that McVeigh and Nichols apparently feared: to expand and nurture the ever growing federal criminal machinery. For conservative dissenters whose rallying cries are Ruby Ridge and Waco, the AEDPA reinforces fears about the lurking threat of jackbooted government thugs.

At the same time that Congress fed the federal leviathan, though, it radically curtailed federal judicial power to grant federal habeas corpus relief to state prisoners. In addition to imposing a new limitations period for filing federal habeas petitions and restricting the availability of successive petitions, the AEDPA altered the most central feature of the federal habeas statute: the substantive standard for granting relief.[1] Prior to the AEDPA, the governing statutory language was quite bare, authorizing habeas relief for inmates held in violation of the Constitution, laws, or treaties of the United States. The federal courts had construed this language as requiring federal courts to undertake de novo review of state court determinations of federal law.[2] Under the AEDPA, however, federal courts are required to focus not on the federal lawfulness of an inmate's custody but, rather, on the state court's resolution of an inmate's federal constitutional claims. A habeas court can grant relief only if a state court's decision rejecting the merits of an inmate's claims is contrary to, or an unreasonable application of, clearly established federal law. The net effect of this change is to require the federal courts to leave unredressed reasonable but wrong state court legal determinations concerning the federal constitutional rights of state prisoners.[3]

For those interested in the theory and practice of American federalism, the AEDPA presents an enormous puzzle. On the one hand, the AEDPA abundantly illustrates Congress's willingness to augment the size, power, and significance of the federal law enforcement bureaucracy. In this respect, the AEDPA is of a piece with other statutes that move ever closer to establishing a general congressional police power. On the other hand, the habeas provisions appear to honor the finality concerns of state criminal justice systems and the comity concerns of state courts. In this light, the habeas reforms of the AEDPA seem to be one of the very few examples of congressional respect for the notion of limited federal government.

One crass explanation for the AEDPA's apparent schizophrenic attitude toward federalism is to insist that Congress is much more concerned with its own power than with federal power generally. To borrow from Justice O'Connor's critique in a federalism case,[4] Congress's underdeveloped capacity for self-restraint is simply not implicated in battles involving the power of the federal judiciary vis-à-vis states; or, to put it more bluntly, Congress is quite comfortable embracing federalism-based limits on the judiciary that it would never impose on itself.

Though likely true, this explanation fails to capture a related but importantly distinct phenomenon: in contemporary political discourse, the debate over the scope of federal habeas is less about federalism than it is about the death penalty. This fact is obviously reflected in the title of the legislation itself, and given that the most significant reforms of the AEDPA apply equally to death and non-death penalty cases, one wonders why the legislation is not called something like the "Anti-Terrorism and Anti-Federal Habeas Act."

It should not be surprising, though, that the congressional response to domestic terrorism—even terrorism inspired by those critical of expansive federal power (though I do not argue that McVeigh and Nichols were themselves committed to some version of federalism)—is to ensure the viability of the death penalty. The most extreme crimes in this country invariably ignite calls for a more robust death penalty, and Congress has not shied away from affirming its commitment to the ultimate punishment. At the symbolic level, Congress continues to increase the number of federal offenses punishable by death, though the federal death penalty remains an insignificant part of the death penalty machinery nationwide (with considerably less than 1 percent of death row inmates produced by federal prosecutions) (NAACP 2000, 122-23).[5] The habeas reforms, on the other hand, are likely to have a real impact on the effectiveness of the death penalty, if that is measured in terms of the ability of states to carry out executions and to do so in an expeditious fashion.

The Capitalization of Federal Habeas Corpus

The most interesting question, then, is not about the apparent irony of Congress's destroying federal habeas in response to the destruction of a federal courthouse. Rather, it is how the debate about federal habeas became a debate about the death penalty. It has not always been so. Federal habeas first attracted significant public debate during the 1960s, when the federal courts first assumed a significant role in regulating state criminal justice systems. Prior to the 1960s, federal habeas for state prisoners was relatively inconsequential as a practical matter because the range of federal rights enforceable in state proceedings was extremely limited. Until the United States Supreme Court began to apply the Bill of Rights against the states via the due process clause, state prisoners seeking relief in federal court could challenge state practices only on the ground that the latter were so unfair or arbitrary as to deny due process. When the Court made clear in 1953 that the legal claims of state prisoners should be addressed de novo on federal habeas, Justice Jackson complained of a "haystack" of petitions[6] that in today's terms looks like an anthill; the 541 petitions filed in 1951 had become 12,000 by 1990 (Mecham 1991).

As the Supreme Court "constitutionalized" criminal procedure in the 1960s and extended to state prisoners virtually all of the protections of the Fourth, Fifth, Sixth, and Eighth Amendments, the scope and availability of federal habeas became extremely consequential. For many state inmates, the Court's declaration of new rights occurred after their convictions had already become final, so vindication would have to come, if at all, in postconviction proceedings. Because a large number of states did not offer comprehensive postconviction remedies, these inmates brought their claims, often pro se, directly to federal court via federal habeas corpus. The disruption to state criminal justice systems was substantial, as the federal courts retroactively enforced many (though not all) of the constitutional guarantees that had recently been extended to state prisoners.

By the late 1960s and early 1970s, federal habeas seemed like an essential component of the Warren Court "revolution" in federalizing criminal procedure. But by the late 1970s and to the present day, the typical beneficiary of federal habeas had changed dramatically. Over the past quarter-century, the courts' relatively solicitous attitude toward pro se filings during the Warren Court era has given way to more sporadic and cursory review. The increasing reluctance to vindicate the claims of pro se petitioners is reflected in part by the enormous growth of intricate procedural obstacles to federal habeas review (Steiker 1998). Exhaustion, procedural default, and nonretroactivity rules make it extremely unlikely for uncounseled petitioners to receive "merits" review of their underlying constitutional claims (much less relief). At the same time, in the past two decades Congress established an unprecedented right of court-appointed counsel for state death row inmates challenging their conviction or sentence on federal habeas. As a result of these two developments, virtually all of the meaningful contemporary federal habeas litigation involves capital defendants represented by federally funded lawyers.

Moreover, a good portion of the litigated claims in federal habeas concerns doctrines unique to capital punishment law under the Eighth Amendment. When the Court first subjected state death penalty schemes to federal constitutional scrutiny in the early 1970s, the popular perception was that the Court was deciding the constitutional rightness or wrongness of the death penalty as a punishment. In 1976, though, the Court made clear that the death penalty was a permissible punishment so long as states developed adequate systems for ensuring its reliable and equitable administration.

The notorious subsequent history reveals the development of extremely intricate, difficult-to-apply doctrines that have plunged states and petitioners into a morass of confusing litigation concerning states' obligations in their administration of the death penalty (Steiker and Steiker 1995, 371-403). The most conspicuous example of how the Court's substantive Eighth Amendment jurisprudence has generated protracted litigation is in the Court's insistence that states channel or guide sentencer discretion to ensure evenhanded, consistent treatment of capital defendants while also insisting that states permit sentencers to exercise unbridled, uncircumscribed discretion to withhold the death penalty based on "individualized" (usually mitigating) factors. Over the past 20 years, literally dozens of cases in the United States Supreme Court (and hence hundreds of cases in the lower federal courts) have involved challenges to state schemes on the grounds that they provide either insufficient guidance or insufficient discretion (or both) to capital sentencers.

Federal habeas, then, has become less a broad forum for

enforcing the federal rights of state prisoners generally than the inevitable battleground for enforcing or overturning state death sentences and elaborating the meaning of the Eighth Amendment in capital cases. The drafters of the AEDPA undoubtedly understood this when they equated "effective death penalty" with diminished federal habeas corpus.

Should we embrace the "capitalization" of federal habeas, and what are its costs? First, we should recognize that by shaping federal habeas doctrines with death row inmates as the norm, both the Court and Congress have put federal habeas out of the reach of virtually all noncapital inmates. The new one-year filing deadline imposed by the AEDPA,[7] for example, is simply not suited to the typical indigent, pro se, non-death-sentenced inmate, especially when viewed in light of the Court's strict procedural default and exhaustion requirements.

One could make a case that the old federalism model of federal habeas is no longer viable and that the practical unavailability of federal habeas in noncapital cases is entirely justified. On this view, the strongest arguments for federal supervision over state court adjudication of federal rights have diminished or disappeared entirely.

For example, it was commonly asserted in the 1960s that the federal courts would have greater expertise in applying the criminal procedure provisions of the Bill of Rights against the states at least in part because federal courts had been applying such protections in federal criminal cases for almost two centuries. Now, though, state courts have had almost four decades of experience with constitutional criminal procedure and in fact are more likely to address such issues on a routine basis.

Moreover, the claim that state courts are particularly hostile toward federal rights made more sense in the context of the general legal upheaval wrought by the Warren Court. By the mid-1960s, the Warren Court legacy had come to include not just incorporation and a newly expansive view of the rights of criminal defendants but also the recognition of privacy rights and more expansive speech rights, a greater commitment to separation between church and state, and, above all, an attack (albeit restrained) against legally enforced segregation in schools and other institutions. Today, the Rehnquist Court does not represent the same sort of threat to localist concerns, and the ideological divide between federal and state judges is more complicated and nuanced than the Warren Court models would suggest. Indeed, many state courts have provided greater rights than those required by the federal constitutional floor.

These arguments, though, prove too much. They do not explain the current state of affairs in which uncounseled state inmates have a legal right but no genuine opportunity to seek habeas relief in federal court. The prospect that vindication of constitutional rights depends entirely on the fortuity of having the means to secure counsel runs counter to basic democratic and egalitarian commitments in our law. Perhaps the altered legal and structural landscape of the present era invites reexamination of the central premises of federal habeas (and reevaluation of the virtues and vices of federalism in this context), but the new landscape hardly justifies preserving on paper rights we are unwilling to make effective.

On the capital punishment side, the costs are slightly different. Death row inmates have lawyers, and the gatekeeping doctrines that essentially bar noncapital inmates do not completely shut the door to capital petitioners. To make the death penalty more effective, Congress chose to restrict rather than eliminate federal habeas review. Whatever one's view about the optimal level of federal review, this choice has distinctive costs.

Federal Habeas Corpus, Federalism, And the Death Penalty

Most obviously, litigants on federal habeas spend extraordinary and disproportionate resources determining whether the federal courts can reach the merits of federal claims. Although the court-driven and congressional reforms of habeas impose significant procedural obstacles to relief, the reforms are invariably accompanied by intricate exceptions. As a result, instead of litigating, for example, whether an inmate's counsel performed below constitutionally mandated minimum standards, the parties debate whether the inmate adequately preserved the claim in state court and, if not, whether exceptional circumstances ("cause and prejudice" or "miscarriage of justice") nonetheless justify reaching the merits of the claim. The efficiency secured by such reforms is not to be found in the preservation of scarce federal judicial resources, as it is clear from published opinions that federal judges must spend no less time (and considerably more intellectual energy) navigating the maze of procedural rules than they would interpreting the underlying constitutional norms.

An outside observer of the American system of appeals and postconviction remedies in criminal cases, particularly our apparatus for entertaining the constitutional claims of state prisoners, would likely be astonished. We appear to have an unparalleled taste for expensive procedural safeguards and yet an extraordinary reluctance to have those safeguards make a difference in terms of constitutional norm enforcement. We want to nod in the direction of the Great Writ (and are willing to bear great administrative costs in doing so), but, at the end of the day, we want our executions to be carried out as well. To borrow from the old saw about our nation's capital (combining southern efficiency and northern charm), contemporary federal habeas combines southern efficiency and (when it comes to the death penalty) southern charm.

In addition, by slowly closing but not fully shutting the door to federal habeas review, Congress has managed to preserve the appearance of extensive federal supervision over state death penalty practices even though in fact the scope of federal remedies has become quite limited. As most lawyers know, federal habeas courts do not revisit a sentencer's ultimate decision to sentence an inmate to death rather than imprisonment. But as most lawyers do not know (unless they are involved in federal habeas practice), the federal courts also no longer decide whether the processes leading to an inmate's sentence were constitutional. That is the question that the United States Supreme Court asks in the extremely rare cases it chooses to hear on direct review. Instead, in accordance with the modifications of habeas to enhance the death penalty system's effectiveness, the habeas court asks whether the Supreme Court had previously made clear what the Constitution requires and, if so, whether the state court unreasonably departed from such clear commands.

Supporters of the death penalty, including prosecutors and executive officials, routinely insist that they (and therefore we) should be more comfortable with the punishment because of the numerous layers of searching review. But it is neither true nor fair to insist, as most proponents do, that two sets of courts have exhaustively scoured the record looking for error. In short, the very existence of federal habeas, even in its increasingly truncated form, unjustifiably alleviates anxiety about the accuracy of state court capital proceedings.

Ultimately, these considerations suggest that federal habeas should either be eliminated or revived. If, in the end, robust federal habeas review treads excessively on legitimate state law enforcement interests, we should not continue to erect expensive, time-consuming obstacles to such review simply to indulge the fiction that state prisoners have a meaningful opportunity to vindicate federal constitutional claims. If, on the other hand, federal enforcement of federal law contributes sufficiently to the protection of constitutional norms to justify bearing those costs, we should resist efficiency-based reforms such as those found in the AEDPA.

As I have argued elsewhere, productive federal habeas reform should take account of the hybrid nature of the federal habeas remedy: federal habeas provides both an appellate forum for record legal claims litigated in state court and an original forum for nonrecord claims that often require additional factual development (Steiker 2000, 1728). By disaggregating these appellate and original functions, and insisting the record claims be resolved soon after direct review (perhaps in the federal courts of appeals rather than the federal district courts), federal habeas could significantly reduce the finality and comity costs of the status quo. At the same time, the central resource-consuming and norm-defeating procedural obstacles of current habeas law, such as the nonretroactivity and reasonableness-review doctrines, could be withdrawn, allowing for both timely and meaningful federal resolution of federal claims.

These sorts of changes are unlikely to emerge unless the United States Supreme Court and Congress swap their current orientations toward federal habeas. Unlike Congress, the Court is well aware of the federalism implications of federal habeas, and the Court's decisions routinely and self-consciously locate the debate surrounding the proper scope of habeas within a larger dialogue on federalism. Given this focus, it is not surprising that the Court seems more attentive to the costs rather than the benefits of the federal enforcement of federal rights. If the Court were to recognize, though, that federal habeas has become primarily a capital punishment forum, it could recalibrate federal habeas in light of the goals of its capital punishment jurisprudence.

One prominent theme in that jurisprudence is the requirement of heightened reliability in capital cases (Steiker and Steiker 1995, 379). That commitment should not tolerate the deferential review reflected in the current nonretroactivity and reasonableness-review doctrines. Heightened reliability should encompass not only the procedures states must adopt in capital prosecutions but also the mechanisms in federal court for ensuring that states honor the principle.

Congress, on the other hand, should think of federal habeas not solely in terms of the death penalty but also in terms of federalism. Congress's high regard for its own responsibility in enforcing civil rights law should extend beyond the usual contexts to the area of criminal justice. Just as Congress recognizes that national resources are often necessary to fulfill national antidiscrimination commitments (to guarantee equality for women and for racial and religious minorities), it should recognize the role of the federal courts in securing compliance with the protections for criminal defendants embedded in the Bill of Rights and the Fourteenth Amendment.

To answer a question raised by this article—Did the Oklahoma City bombers succeed?—the Oklahoma City bombers did not succeed. Federal law enforcement power grew in the wake of the bombing, and the bombers' terroristic act offered poignant support for such expansion. Martyrdom has been shifted, or at least shared, as the victims of Oklahoma City are now inextricably linked to the Waco tragedy. But the political reaction to Oklahoma City embodied in the AEDPA should at least prompt us to assess the complicated relationship between federal habeas, capital punishment, and federalism. Congress and the Court should revisit the current state of federal habeas with a clearer picture of what federal habeas accomplishes (or fails to accomplish) and at what cost. The pure federalism paradigm that captured a particular moment in history should be reexamined to determine what role, if any, federal courts should play in securing federal constitutional rights, with special attention to the practical significance that habeas review holds for the implementation of the Court's death penalty law.

Notes

1. See Pub. L. No. 104-132 § 104, 110 Stat. 1214,1218-19 (codified at 28 U.S.C. § 2254(d)).

2. See, for example, *Brown v Allen*, 344 U.S. 443, 503-08 (1953) (opinion of Justice Frankfurter) (articulating de novo standard).

3. See *Williams v Taylor*, 526 U.S. 1050 (1999) (construing new standard of review under the AEDPA).

4. See *Garcia v. San Antonio Metropolitan Transit Ass'n*, 469 U.S. 528, 588 (1985) (O'Connor, J., dissenting).

5. NAACP 2000 indicates that 24 of 3691 death row inmates were sentenced

to death in federal (nonmilitary) proceedings; an additional 7 death row inmates were sentenced in federal military proceedings.

6. See *Brown v. Allen*, 344 U.S. 443, 537 (1953) (Jackson, J., concurring in the result).

7. See 28 U.S.C. § 2244(d)(1) (new limitations provision).

References

Anti-Terrorism and Effective Death Penalty Act. Pub. L. No.104-132.110 Stat. 1214 (codified in scattered titles of U.S.C. (Supp. IV 1998)).

Mecham, Ralph L. 1991. *Annual Report of the Director of the Administrative Office of the United States Courts.* Washington, DC: Administrative Office U.S. Courts.

NAACP (National Association for the Advancement of Colored People). Legal Defense and Education Fund Inc. 2000. *Death Row, U.S.A.* New York: NAACP

Steiker, Carol and Jordan M. Steiker. 1995. Sober Second Thoughts: Reflections on Two Decades of Constitutional Regulation of Capital Punishment. *Harvard Law Review* 109:355-438.

Steiker, Jordan. 1998. Restructuring Post-Conviction Review of Federal Constitutional Claims Raised by State Prisoners: Confronting the New Face of Excessive Proceduralism. *Legal Forum* 1998:315-47.

_____. 2000. Habeas Exceptionalism. *Texas Law Review* 78:1703-30.

Strossen, Nadine. 1997. Symposium: Justice and the Criminal Justice System, the Fifteenth Annual National Student Federalist Society Symposium on Law and Public Policy—1996: Panel VI: Feds Fighting Crime: When and How: Criticism of Federal Counter-Terrorism Laws. *Harvard Journal of Law and Public Policy* 20:531-41.

The Internet: A Terrorist Medium For the 21st Century

Kelly R. Damphousse
Brent L. Smith

Abstract: *This article examines use of the Internet by violent protest groups that focus either on hatred of people (e.g., Jews, women) or opposition to policies (e.g., abortion, immigration), tracing changes in their communication methods since 1980. A background on pre-Internet communication practices and the origins and functioning of the World Wide Web is given. Using a 1995-96 content analysis of Web pages, it is shown how the Internet allows these groups a greater capacity to communicate, bring together like-minded individuals, level written attacks against enemies, raise funds, and carry out terrorist acts. The potential for cyberterrorism is assessed, and citizen counterterrorism activity on the Internet is described. It is concluded that the Internet will provide important insights into the nature and function of protest groups.*

This chapter investigates the use of the Internet by two types of violent protest groups: (a) those that hate certain types of *people (e.g.,* blacks, Jews, women) and (b) those that oppose certain types of *policies (e.g.,* affirmative action, abortion rights, immigration). Although the ultimate focus of each may differ, the two certainly overlap some in terms of behavior, strategy, membership, and etiology (Lofland, 1996). The term *protest group* is used to refer to both potential and active terrorist groups. It would be incorrect, for example, to refer to a group of militia members as terrorists until they have actually performed some act of terrorism. At the same time, these protest groups are still interesting to study because of their marked potential for (a) engaging in terrorist acts or (b) providing for others the incentive to engage in violence.

How the members of these groups communicate with each other and with outsiders (potential members, financial supporters, targets) has been a topic of interest in the past. New technology, such as the Internet, however, has allowed protest groups to communicate with greater ease. This chapter traces how communication by protest groups has changed in the past two decades. The analysis begins by reviewing common practices used before the advent of the Internet. Then it describes how the Internet came about and the history of how protest groups have made use of the technology. After that, it discusses how the new technology not only allows for an increased capacity to communicate but also makes possible the threat of "cyberterrorism," using the World Wide Web as a tool of terror. Finally, the chapter addresses one unintended consequence of protest group use of the Internet: the establishment of citizen counterterrorism activity on the Internet.

Previous Communication Practices

Protest groups in general, and terrorist groups in particular, engage in behaviors designed to send messages to outsiders. Violent behavior, for example, has been considered an attempt by terrorist groups to call attention to some problem that needs to be fixed (Herman, 1982; Rubenstein, 1987). It has been suggested that terrorism could not exist without communication (Schmid & Graaf, 1982). Acts of terror by protest groups can be considered indirect efforts at communication that use the news media to inform the public about the motives of the group in an effort to give "violent voice to the voiceless, and to awaken their sleeping brethren to the necessity of mass action" (Rubenstein, 1989, p. 323).

Less extreme, though more direct, measures have also been taken by protest groups to get their message out. In general, this tactic is referred to as *propaganda* (Wright, 1990). Propaganda is used by protest groups to inform the general public or more specific groups about some problem in an effort to make them "feel the urgency, the necessity of some action, its unique characteristics, . . . [and] what to do" (Ellul, 1969, p. 208). Traditionally, protest groups have used the printed word—via leaflets, fliers, posters, and newsletters—to inform others about their cause (Wright, 1990). More recently, protest groups have used faxes to communicate with each other and with selected outsiders, such as the media and academics. Two problems with the use of these media are the relatively high cost and the limited scope of coverage. There is little "bang for the buck" when much of the material is discarded by uninterested members of the public.

Protest groups experimented with the use of shortwave radio for a time and still continue to do so, to a lesser extent, but access to a larger audience was still restricted. The next advance that allowed greater access to the general public was made possible by the increased popularity of nationally syndicated talk radio programs. Talk radio first allowed members of protest groups to discuss their concerns with a host and, presumably, a national audience. Conservative talk radio shows that allowed, as well as fostered, the discussion of topics that angered groups of individuals blossomed in the late 1980s. Still, access to a wide audience by the protest groups was somewhat limited, as was the information that could be provided. Even worse, the information was also limited in that it was in verbal format that was both easily discarded or forgotten. Although members of protest groups were able to communicate readily with each other and with a limited sympathetic audience, they were still unable to get their message to the "uncommitted audience" (Wright, 1990).

The Information Revolution

The advent of the World Wide Web (WWW) in the mid 1990s provided protest groups with access to a communication arena that was in printed format, relatively inexpensive, and accessible to almost anyone in the world. To the extent that antigovernment groups were among the first to use the Internet for propaganda, the information revolution coincided with the conservative revolution in an ironic twist. The Internet was developed in the late 1960s by the federal government (U.S. Department of Defense) to allow for the sharing of computer files between research scientists located around the country. The irony was that the project initially developed by the federal government was now being used by protest groups to encourage the government's downfall.

Protest groups were not latecomers to the computer age. In fact, discussion lists (listservs), bulletin board systems (BBSes), and news groups (e.g., alt. activism.militia, alt. society. anarchy) had been actively used by protest groups in the decade before the WWW came into existence. *Listservs* make use of the Internet's e-mail system as a means of communication. Usually, a moderator operates a "site" where members of the "list" can send e-mail messages. Everyone who has subscribed to the list receives the message onto their computer as an e-mail message and has opportunity to respond. In *news groups,* messages (articles) are posted to servers. With few limitations, anyone who has access to the news group can read the messages. These slow-motion communication processes are now being replaced by real-time applications called multi-user dungeons (MUDs) and Internet relay chat (IRC), which allow groups of individuals to communicate instantly with each other by way of their computers.

These early computer links were important for the planning and transmission of information between group members. But this medium was accessible only to a limited audience, mostly people who were active computer users and interested in the topic. The advent of the WWW changed the importance of the Internet for protest groups. For the first time, activists had access to people from all walks of life who were potential members, supporters, and contributors to their cause. Unfortunately for the protest groups, potential enemies also had access to the information they made public.

How protest groups and their opponents use the WWW is discussed in the following sections. But before detailing the activities of protesters on the WWW, it is necessary to provide some background regarding how the WWW makes communication via the computer more accessible to a larger group of people.

How the WWW Works

As described above, the WWW is based on the Internet system established in the late 1960s. Before the WWW, knowledge of several software programs was required to perform different tasks, such as sharing files and sending e-mail. Compatibility problems emerged because of the diversity of programs used to share information. The creation of the WWW solved this problem through the use of *hypertext markup language (html). Hypertext* is a system that allows different parts of a document, even those housed in a different computer, to be accessed by the click of a mouse button. The link between any two computers is also simplified because the "language" is readable by all computers.

This system was made even more accessible in 1993 when *browsers* were developed that allowed computer users to interact with other computers through a graphical interface. With the Mosaic browser, and subsequently others like Netscape and Microsoft Explorer, users were able to access the picture-based pages created by other users on their servers. Increasingly, the graphical interface of the "home pages" are being supplemented with sound and video. Excerpts of speeches and videos, for example, can be easily accessed by users. Individuals with little computer acumen are able to create home pages that can be viewed by anyone in the world with access to the Internet. With the decreased cost of personal computers, increased access onto the Internet via companies like Compuserve and America Online, increased modem speed, and increased knowledge, activity on the Web has grown dramatically. From 1993, when there were virtually no home pages, to the beginning of 1997, the growth of the Web has virtually exploded. There are now nearly five million home pages.

On these home pages, the host/creator can present information to an audience that can download a copy to their own computers or print for future use. Finding a home page can be relatively simple. Companies such as Alta Vista and Yahoo have created *search engines* that serve as databases containing the addresses of all the home pages on the Web. The engines continuously search the Web for new sites and updates to old sites and then catalogue each site by category. Search engines allow users to use *key word searches* to find pages pertaining to certain topics. For example, a search using the term *terrorism* would return a list of all the home pages that use the term. Typical searches last anywhere from a few seconds to half a minute. Simply clicking on one of the links provided by the search engine sends the user to the appropriate page.

Once the home page is accessed, the user is able to click on buttons, icons, and underlined text (links) that take the user to other areas of the same site or to other sites. For example, a typical white supremacist home page may link the user to other white supremacists, with links to music groups that hold similar views, and to a collection of news items the host has been gathering that reflect a similar political or social agenda. Following these links, along with the search process described above, represents the act of "surfing the Web" and provides much of the accidental access to individual home pages.

Method of Study

The data presented below were compiled during a 2-year research project (1995-1996) designed to examine how protest groups use the Internet for communication purposes. The initial project began by the researchers conducting WWW searches via Yahoo for the virtual presence of specific known terrorist groups such as the Ku Klux Klan (KKK) and the Armed Forces of National Liberation (FALN, after its Spanish name).

It is not enough to search for *terrorism* because protest groups do not always have the word *terrorism* in their home pages, so the search must be more creative. For example, a recent search on *terrorism* yielded 68 links, most of which pertained to news stories about terrorists. A search on Yahoo for *Aryan,* however, yielded nine pages all directly related to Aryan Nations groups. More than 3,700 pages with the word *Aryan* were found on Alta Vista. Other locations were found by conducting searches for militia groups and by following links from one site to another. For example, one site maintained by a white supremacist group may have links provided to several other locations (home pages) that share the same interests. Many of these links were followed to the new location. Each location that was located was "bookmarked" for ease of later access and then visited monthly during the 2-year period. In this way, it was possible to track the way these violent protest groups use the Internet and the WWW.

The Internet as a Tool for Protest Groups

The Internet, especially the WWW, can be used by protest groups in five ways. First, the inexpensive and potentially broad access to millions of people allows protest groups to present propaganda explaining their position to people who are passive and uncommitted or just "dropping by." In this case, the expected audience is the potential new members, who have not yet "seen the truth." Second, the Internet provides information to like-minded people about specific topics of concern. The Internet allows people who might never have met otherwise to communicate with each other about topics that anger them. Third, the Internet allows angry protest groups to level written attacks on the objects of their anger. Thus, persons who are targets of a protest group's written venom may be subjected to these diatribes. Fourth, protest groups can use the Internet to request financial assistance from the general public. Fifth, and most ominous, the Internet can be used to *perform* acts of terrorism. The potential threat of cyberterrorism has been causing increased concern (Collin,1996). Each of these potential uses is described in the sections that follow.

Propaganda Machines

The WWW offers an outstanding opportunity for protest groups to proselytize potential members because so many people have access to the information. Most sites examined for this research had sections that described why the host was angry. In these sections, the host appealed, through the use of vivid imagery, to the reader's sensitivity. Most sites suggested America was worse off now than in the past because of some problem (e.g., immigration, gay and minority rights, excessive taxation and government control). Anecdotal evidence was often provided. Like the moral entrepreneurs of other moral panics (Victor, 1993), these hosts often appealed to readers' emotions through use of atrocity stories, e.g., one site suggested that the events in the Waco "holocaust" were part of a continuing pattern of attacks by federal law enforcement agencies against the citizenry. To further alarm its audience, the host provided links to autopsy reports of the Waco burn victims. These files showed the coroner files and photographs of people who were killed in the fiery end of the siege. Other pages offered similarly vivid stories:

> As I was preparing to mail this double issue of "The Watchman" an event took place in the Chicago area which demands comment. Three black animals butchered a White woman and her young White children, one by torture and then cut her open to remove the half-breed baby she was pregnant with. A seventeen month old mulatto male was also spared. It seems that they were using her as an incubator to breed a light-skinned child, and decided to eliminate her, having no further need for her reproductive ability. The one who removed the little bastard was a negress nurse who used her medical training to carry out her part in the crime. I do not know all of the circumstances surrounding the event but it is becoming more apparent with every day that passes that unless the White Race rises up against their tormentors in a consuming fury, we will instead be consumed by them. I do not hate these people as individuals but only a fool would believe that we will ever live together in peace. Events like this, as well as Waco, the Randy Weaver massacre and Oklahoma City portend a darkening future for America and it is becoming increasingly clear that unless heroic measures are taken without delay, there will be no future for us or our children. (http://www2.stormfront.org/watchman/index.html [1996, November 24])

At the same time, protest group propaganda on the WWW often tries to show the readers they have been deceived into a complacency (false consciousness) that threatens to destroy them. The following quote, which appeared on the home page called "The Patriot's Soapbox," demonstrates this line of reasoning:

> If there is one thing I want to accomplish by publishing these thoughts on the Internet, it is to stimulate you American slaves out there to WAKE UP and become sovereign Americans again. While you were slumbering, watching television, drinking beer, being amused, your "servants" captured and enslaved you, and became your "masters." You could be free, but you are entangled in a web of deceit: lies, fictions and frauds committed by your friendly public servants and their attorneys. (http://www.geocities.com/CapitolHill/1781 [1997, February 10])

The takeover of the Japanese ambassador's residence in Lima, Peru, by rebels from the Tupac Amaru Revolutionary Movement (MRTA) at the end of 1996 is a further example of how terrorist groups use the WWW to get their messages out to the people of the world. During the crisis, Tupac Amaru militants who were participants in the hostage taking provided interviews and statements to the outside world via their European home page in three languages (http://burn.ucsd.edu/ats/mrta.htm). They also provided a video clip showing the terrorists preparing for their mission.

Communication Devices

One fear about the growth of the Internet is that it allows many people who would never have met to be able to communicate with each other. Thus, a person in Idaho who hates African Americans can create a home page to exhibit this hatred. A person living in Florida can visit this home page and read the material placed there. Further, if the Florida reader is impressed with the page, the reader might add the Idaho address to a list of hot links. This action would allow people who visit the Florida page to find and access the Idaho page easily. The importance of the Web for this capacity is exhibited in the following quote:

> For those of you who are surfing the net, you can access the CAUSE web page at http://www.cheta.net/cause. The net is the most powerful free speech forum that has ever existed. Support all efforts to keep it uncensored. Wild claims of your children being carted away by internet pedophiles, etc. are meant to frighten the unaware. The powers that be are terrified by the internet because they are no longer in control of the information that you can receive. Through the internet one can set up a web page and state his opinion to the world, literally. Everyone in the world who is interested in that subject can then access that page and read that opinion for themselves. How unbelievable! We no longer have to wait to be told what someone or some group is saying. We can now get it straight from the horse's mouth. Well, expect the world control freaks to move to crush this situation. (http://207.15.176.3:80/cause [1997, February 10])

The greatest potential for communication is that people who are interested in a topic and see something that is potentially of interest to other fellow believers can almost instantly make that information available. The information and the interpretation are then made available to all.

Some protest groups use the Internet as a method of communicating with the group as a whole. For example, the Republic of Texas—a secessionist group whose aim is to reclaim Texas from the federal government and overturn the de facto (state) government—holds its meetings all over Texas. Because all members cannot attend every meeting, the minutes of the meetings are published on the home page. At the same time, the group publishes all its press releases and its interpretations of previous events. Although most information housed here appears to be more for storage and public access, this information distribution can also be conducted for emergency purposes. When the group's "ambassador" was arrested by federal agents, for example, an urgent alert was placed on the Web, asking citizens to call local, state, and federal law enforcement agencies demanding his release. (http://www.rapidramp.com/Users/marine/rmtaken.htm [1996, May 5]).

Further efforts at the coalescing of like-minded individuals and groups have evolved into a Web page with a more social than political agenda. The Aryan Dating Page allows men and women who are white and heterosexual to meet over the Web. Pictures of available and interested men and women, as well as their personal information, are also made available by Alpha Headquarters, an Aryan rights group (http://www.alpha.org/lifestyles/lifestyles.html [1997, February 10]). In addition, one can access Resistance Records, a recording company that produces music suitable for those with pro-Aryan attitudes. Its home page advertises that the company is "Forging a new destiny for White Power music: For Blood, Soil, Honor, Faith & Folk" (http://www.resistance.com/founder.html [1997, February 10]).

Virtual Graffiti

As we have shown, the nature of Web use is such that happening upon some home page is usually not a planned event. In fact, one problem with performing research on the Web is that, in the act of following links from one page to another, the researcher can get distracted by interesting side links. Thus, a user can end up far removed from where he or she had ever intended to go. This feature of the Web works to the advantage of protest groups who want to inflict harm on others through the written word or artwork. Thus, an African American may have happened upon the Alpha, or Aryan, home page in December 1996 and seen the following messages scrolling at the bottom of the screen:

> African American, what a joke, why not just call them what they are? NIGGERS!
>
> America for Whites, Africa for blacks, ship those apes back to those trees, send them niggers back!
>
> Ring that bell, jump for joy, White mans day is here, no more nigger civil rights, led by queers!
>
> Who needs Niggers?

In a similar vein, the Alpha home page and other Aryan-type pages proclaim allegiance to a sacred 14-word code of honor that is portrayed prominently on most of the pages: "We Must Secure the Existence of Our People and a Future for White Children!" T-shirts, posters, and bumper stickers showing the 14 words in different formats are readily available over the Web.

But race is not the only feature that Aryans attack on the Web. One page, "White Aryan Resistance Hate Page (WAR)," exhibits cartoons and a joke book attacking gays ("Life isn't easy for the modem gay activist. . . . For one thing, there's all those heavy protest signs to carry around.") and Jews ("What's the difference between a Jew and a Pizza? . . . "Pizzas don't scream when you put them in the oven."). The use of stereotypical humor is a common phenomenon appearing on many of these sites.

Support Activities

One of the most common protest group activities on the Web is the attempt to garner funds from the audience. The pleas used in these sections are mainly addressed to fellow believers and stress the lack of good equipment and funding. Often, the funding request is associated with a desire to be a better service to the user:

> Many people have told us how they can not access our web site much of the time, this is due to lack of funding. Our web site is run on an old and slow machine which allows only two people at any time to be on the site. The site is now receiving between 50 and 100 users per day with not a second of idle time. That 50-100 per day can be improved to hundreds of white people per day world wide accessing great writings of white leaders and learning more about the movement for White Power. We must upgrade and improve our equipment a.s.a.p. Every white man or woman who can not access our site may not return to try again becoming a lost soul. (http://www.alpha.org [1997, February 10])

> There is such great potential for ALPHA with the proper financial foundation. Our opposition at the ADL and NAACP receive millions of dollars in donations form their members and supporters, yet the supporters of our cause fail to see just how important financial contributions are to a growing organization. Keep in mind that ALPHA has no clout when applying for a loan at the local bank, yet the ADL has a working budget of millions of dollars to spread lies. (http://www.alpha.org [1996, November 10])

> ALPHA needs help from all our brothers who use and enjoy our web site. For the past 50 years groups of Aryan men and women throughout the world have been working for the cause of White Power, and now it is YOUR turn to assist us. Your financial donations can help the white youth of the

> earth make sense out of what has happened to their world. ALPHA, although not registered as such, is a non-profit organization. Every cent received from people goes right into the movement. (http://www.alpha.org [1997, February 10])

At other times, efforts at fund-raising display the personal hardships endured by the host that are the result of efforts to be a good citizen.

> Your prayers and financial support are urgently needed at this time. I am currently under tremendous attack and the threat of criminal prosecution. In the last six months I have lost my disability allowance, had many of my belongings stolen by the feds and am being driven from my home of 18 years. I have six children and staggering legal bills. Without a miracle, I am going under, and if the feds have their way, to prison. I have given my life to this struggle on faith, without regard to the consequences to my self or even my family. Our future is in God's hands and they are attached to your forearms. We are unable to cash checks without using a bank account that could be seized at any time by the feds. Postal Money Orders made out to Wendy Watkins are best and they protect your privacy as well. Please help us to survive and continue the struggle for His Kingdom at the Watchman. (http://www2.stormfront.org/watchman [1996, August 10])

Even international terrorist groups, such as Peru's Shining Path (Sendero Luminoso), have Web sites where supporters seek to export the revolutionary message ("Welcome to a REAL revolution in cyberspace!") while the groups seek financial support by hawking revolutionary products like T-shirts, posters, and videos (http://www.csrp.org/index.html [1997, February 10]).

The Web as a Weapon

The possibility that the Web will be used to conduct acts of terrorism has increased dramatically since its inception. Indeed, because corporations that are the victims of computer crime are wont to deal with virtual invasions discretely, it is likely that much more cyberterrorism is occurring than is currently known. Protest groups using the WWW to perform acts of terrorism pose four possible threats. First, protest groups can access other home pages and either deface them or change them to provide alternative information. Already, several examples of this have occurred. Perhaps the most infamous recent incident was the defacing of the home page of the Central Intelligence Agency (CIA): On September 18,1996, the home page of the CIA was vandalized by a Swedish protest group called Power Through Resistance. The group changed the title of the page to "Central Stupidity Agency" and added several links to nongovernment home pages, like Playboy. Although no sensitive material was available to the attackers, the fact that individuals on another continent were able to sabotage this computer link is evidence of the potential for remote activity. Earlier, hackers had renamed the Department of Justice home page the "Department of Injustice."

Second, protest groups can impair, or at least threaten to impair, vital government or corporate communication processes. It is not difficult, for example, to imagine a protest group "hacking" its way into the computer system that controls the power supply to an area and then threatening to cut off power unless some demand is carried out. In fact, such a problem has been occurring in Japan, where groups attacked the commuter train computer system (Devost, Houghton, & Pollard,1996). The threat is even greater if one considers the impact such a threat would have on the operation of a nuclear facility. The relative ease of impairment of other computers is evidenced by the large growth in computer viruses, which infect computers with programs designed to destroy software or data, in the past several years.

Third, protest groups could directly access financial institutions and perform account transfers. The extent to which this has already occurred is not clear. Fourth, governments are increasingly concerned that information housed on their computers may be accessed by unauthorized individuals. In 1994, a British youth was arrested for suspicion in a case in which a military base in New York was impaired for more than a month (Wilson, 1996). Two potential problems exist here. First, intelligence information may be gained more easily by opposition groups. Second, and perhaps more deadly, false or illegitimate commands could be delivered to military forces, ordering them to unwittingly perform some terrorist act.

The problems associated with virtual attacks perpetuated through the Internet have created a new industry of software protection referred to as firewalls. These programs are designed to allow only legitimate users access to the information housed on corporate or agency computers (Alpert, 1996). In general, firewalls are designed to inspect each attempt to access a computer network. Those users who attempt to get into the network without authorization are rejected.

Summary

The World Wide Web is being used by protest groups in the United States, as well as throughout the world, to deliver their message in ways never dreamed possible before 1980. Access to the Web has allowed protest groups to attempt to proselytize more individuals than ever before. They have also become better able to communicate with each other for political and social ends. And they are in a better position to attract funding from people with whom they would not otherwise have contact. The most serious threat, however, appears to be the potential of actual terrorist acts committed via the Web. The presence of protest groups on the Web has spawned a new aspect of terrorism/counterterrorism previously never imagined—the explosion of citizen counterterrorists.

Citizen Counterterrorists

Counterterrorist efforts of the past have traditionally been composed of two types of organizations. First, government agencies, the military, and special task forces have been charged with the mandate of gathering intelligence about potential terrorist groups. Second, some social/civic groups have created formal organizations whose function is to publicize the operations of protest-type groups. The Klanwatch project of the Southern Poverty Law Center and the Anti-Defamation League, for example, focus on making available information about the KKK and anti-Semitic activities. In fact, these two organizations have continued these activities in cyberspace, operating home pages that describe activities of protest groups. Also available at these home pages are opportunities to purchase literature describing the history of the militia groups and other protest groups.

What is unique about the advent of the WWW on the Internet, however, is the proliferation of home pages spawned by private citizens who have dedicated portions of their home pages to documenting links to both pro- and antiterrorism pages. A common example of civilian counterterrorism on the WWW is the "Police Officer's Internet Directory" home page, hosted by a Boston police officer. This page has little independent commentary but many links to pro- and antiprotest groups (e.g., hate groups, terrorists, radicals). The commentary supplied by the host is limited to suggesting that the 17 sites provided on the page are offensive and may be unpleasant to view.

One of the most progressive of these counterterrorism pages is called "The Militia Watchdog," which grew out of a Usenet FAQ (frequently asked questions). In this location, the host (a writer who is an expert on the history of the militia in America) tracks news about protest groups and provides links to, and commentary about, the home pages of various protest groups. The page provides Patriot profiles (thick descriptions of contemporary militia groups), essays (e.g., description of gun show activities), collection of news articles about terrorists (e.g., the *Militia Follies),* and special reports (e.g., election 1996 coverage). Interest in the home page is exhibited by statistics provided by the host that suggest the number of accesses to the page by visitors, or *hits,* per month grew from around 4,000 in January 1996 to almost 9,000 by May 1996. In fact, the various pages on this site had been accessed more than 100,000 times in the 5-month time period. During the Freemen standoff in Montana, more than 2,000 hits were made on the Freemen page at this Web site.

Perhaps the most interesting development along these lines is the formation of counter-counterterrorism on the Web. At least two home pages have been created that challenge the information provided on the "Militia Watchdog" and other similar pages:

> [The author of the Militia Watchdog] is feeding the paranoia of the mass population, fueled by the news media, that the patriots and militias are somehow planning to commit terrorist acts. [He] and his traitorous counterparts in the government in the media have yet to prove there to be a link between the militias and Oklahoma City Bombing. Having recently reviewed footage of the initial 2 hours following the bombing in Oklahoma City, simple things I noticed REFUTE the claims to a 4800 pound truck bomb full of cow manure! Rather, the basic evidence supports an INTERNAL blast blowing out from INSIDE the building. (http://www.execpc.com/warning/dogpound.html [1996, November 10])

Clearly, the use of the WWW by protest groups and those who oppose them is a new phenomenon that bears continued observation. The impact of citizen counterterrorists on the propaganda and fund-raising efforts of the protest groups is uncertain at this time. The fact that counter-counterterrorism home pages have begun to spring up is evidence that the effect is beginning to be noticed.

Conclusion

The creation of the Internet and the WWW has been referred to as the beginning of the information revolution. How fitting, then, that the political revolutionaries of our time are among the first to make the most creative use of it. It is interesting that the term *leaderless resistance* may take on a new meaning in this age of generating information and then making it available to the world. Serious implications await discussion concerning the liability of those whose home pages—filled with anger, hate, and protest—become the catalyst for some violent action by an unknown actor. The Oklahoma City bombing, for example, has been compared with activities described in William Pierce's *The Turner Diaries* (Macdonald, 1978), which is now also available on the Web (www.geocities.com/Athens/Acropolis/1406 (1996, November 10]).

In essence, individuals who operate home pages perform essentially one-way communication with other people. The information provided on the WWW is a special case. Much like leaflets of old, the information is distributed to individuals only indirectly; that is, propaganda about the excesses of government or some other threat are distributed rather anonymously so that the reader and the writer may never meet. The author of the information in the home page can rightfully claim that he or she did not intend for the reader to take any specific action. Information provided via a home page may be used to stimulate or legitimate terroristic activity. It is certain that the Internet in general, and the WWW in particular, will come to play an important role in our understanding of protest groups and how they function in our society.

References

Alpert, B. (1996, November 25). On fire: Fear of hackers should keep the computer firewall market smokin'. *Barons, 76*, 15-17.

Collins, B. (1996, September). *The future of cyberterrorism: Where the physical and virtual worlds converge*. Paper presented at 11th Annual International Symposium on Criminal Justice Issues. Available: http://www.acsp.uic.edu/ OICJ/ CONFS (1996, September 9).

Devost, M., Houghton, B., & Pollard, N. (1996). Information terrorism: Can you trust your toaster? *Terrorism Research Center* [On-line]. Available: http://www.terrorism.com / terrorism/itpaper.html (1997, February 10)

Ellul, J. (1969). *Propaganda: The formation of men's attitudes*. New York: Knopf.

Herman, E. (1982). *The real terror network: Terrorism in fact and propaganda*. Boston: South End.

Lofland, J. (1996). *Social movements organizations: Guide to research on insurgent realities*. Hawthorne, NY: Aldine de Gruyter.

Macdonald, A. (1978). *The Turner diaries*. Hillsboro, WV: National Vanguard Books.

Rubenstein, R. (1987). *Alchemists of revolution: Terrorism in the modern world*. New York: Basic Books.

Schmid, A. & Graaf, J. (1982). *Violence as communication: Insurgent terrorism and the Western news media*. Beverly Hills, CA: Sage.

Victor, J. (1993). *Satanic panic: The creation of a contemporary legend*. Chicago: Open Court.

Wilson, D. (1996). 40 million potential spies. *CNN Interactive News*. Available: http:/www.cnn.com (1996, May 23)

Wright, J. (1990). *Terrorist propaganda: The red army faction and the provisional IRA, 1968-86*. New York: St. Martin's.

Warnings Versus Alarms: Terrorist Threat Analysis Applied to the Iranian State-Run Media

Sean K. Anderson

Abstract: *State-sponsored terrorism is a form of coercion, backed up by the threat and use of violence, to achieve political ends. These terrorist tactics also involve signaling of intentions and responses between the terrorist sponsor and those whom it targets. Accordingly this study examines Iranian state sponsorship of anti-U.S. terrorism in the period 1980-1990 using quantitative content analysis of official Iranian state-run media to determine whether Iranian support for terrorist and insurgent actions against United States targets in the period March 1980 to March 1990 has reflected deliberate Iranian state policy or else has proceeded more spontaneously from various groups either within Iran or elsewhere. The method used in this study of establishing correlations between the incidence of anti-U.S. terrorism and the official communications of the presumed state sponsor can be used more generally for making threat assessments based, in part, on the public communications of state sponsors of terrorism.*

Terrorism as Political Communication

Much of the study of terrorism as a form of political communications has focused on the problems of the co-optation or manipulation of the Western news media by terrorist groups.[1] Other studies have focused on the "contagion effect," that is, the notion that media coverage of terrorist events greatly magnifies the influence of terrorism on mass society as well as possibly inspiring imitation by others.[2] In his study of government negotiations with hostage-takers and possible deterrence measures, John L. Scott has documented the use of such signaling and deliberate communications by terrorists.[3] In order to assess the coverage by the Western news media in its reporting of transnational non-state terrorist actions, Michael J. Kelly and Thomas H. Mitchell carried out a content analysis of the coverage by prominent western newspapers of 158 terrorist attacks in the period 1968-1974. Their finding was that the news media's focus on the violence and criminal aspects of the terrorist events tended to overshadow the purported grievances or political demands of the terrorists, so limiting the effectiveness of terrorism as a strategy of political communication.[4]

The first comprehensive study of terrorism as a form of political communication, particularly through its exploitation of the mass media to convey particular messages to specific audiences, was Alex P. Schmid and Janny de Graaf's work *Violence as Communications: Insurgent Terrorism and the Western News Media.*[5] Their model sees this communication process as involving three parties: the terrorist actors, who send a message by inflicting violence on their immediate victims, which generates a news event by which their message is conveyed to an ultimate target.[6] While their discussion was confined to non-state terrorist groups and to the news media of liberal democracies, in principle this analysis can be extended to explain the use of terrorism as communications by state sponsors of terrorism. The model must be adjusted to recognize that facts that there is now one additional "sender" of messages using another level of communication as well. In addition to the sponsored group, whose communications consist of the terrorist deed itself as well as attendant communiques, there is the state sponsor which can signal its intentions through diplomatic offices and state-owned mass media organs. The other refinement is that whereas the non-state group must depend largely on the free press of liberal democracies, which may ignore or distort their intended message, the state sponsor has at its disposal telecommunications and publishing resources which will broadcast precisely those messages and nuances that the regime wishes to make known. Whereas the non-state insurgents's terrorist attack alone initiates the political communications process, in the case of state sponsorship the political communications may begin through threats or demands directed at an ultimate audience even before any terrorist action occurs. Should its threats remain unheeded or its demands unfulfilled, the state sponsor can punish the uncompliant target audience by ordering the sponsored group to carry out the terrorist attack which, in turn, reinforces the political message to the nation-state or group being attacked. This expanded model involves also a third level of communications, namely the covert information and instructions exchanged between the sponsoring state and its agents, but these are not the subject of this study.

States or groups sponsoring terrorism can benefit from this psychological warfare only if they are perceived as having the initiative and power to bind or to unleash the terrorist menace. On the other hand they will not want to become so unambiguously and directly identified as the source of the terrorist actions as to legitimize direct retaliation against themselves. Therefore sponsors of terrorism would tend to associate themselves indirectly with pending terrorist actions through generalized threats, innuendos, or conferral of tokens of legitimacy upon the sponsored terrorist groups. Once the terrorist actions have been carried out the sponsor tends to disclaim any responsibility, prior knowledge or direct control over the sponsored groups, so maintaining its plausible desirability. Thus typically state-sponsored actions would be preceded by veiled threats or indirect statements of intention and warning and would be followed by official denials of culpability.

The communications model assumes that terrorism, being inherently political, cannot be understood apart from the environment of politics in which its sponsors, agents and targets communicate and interact. Due to the penetrating force of global mass communications and relative ease of transit across national frontiers in this age, the political environment of terrorism has become transnational in scope. Terrorism thus takes place as part of a transnational political dialogue involving demands or threats, expectations of compliance, and enforcement of threats to ensure future compliance. Analyzing the content of this enveloping public dialogue is therefore one approach to understanding the nature of a phenomenon that usually cloaks itself in obscurity and deception.

Contending Explanations for Anti-U.S. Terrorism

At the outset this study must note that there is little scholarly consensus over the causes and nature of terrorism in general or of Middle Eastern terrorism in particular. In a survey of the major rival explanations of terrorism Martha Crenshaw identified two major poles of explanation. First there is an anthropological approach which seeks to explain terrorism in terms of community support for such actions, rather than in terms of the responsibility of specific groups or governments, and which holds that historical "root causes" are the essential sources of terrorist motivations. Crenshaw identifies the second of the two "poles of the explanatory debate" as what she termed the *strategic choice* approach which attributes responsibility for terrorism to specific actors who choose to use terrorism as one of a number of alternative strategies to seek present and ongoing political ends.[7]

Two examples of such anthropological analysis, one directed at explaining Middle Eastern terrorism generally and another discussing Iran's Islamic revolutionary statecraft specifically, are found in the community-support model of William O. Beeman, an Iranian area specialist and anthropologist, who had earlier applied the rudiments of this model to an analysis of the behavior of Iranian decision-makers.[8] An example of the contrary strategic choice approach is Joseph Kostiner's analysis of Iranian state-sponsored terrorism in response to the Iran-Iraq war in which terrorist pressures against Iraq's former Arab allies were found to be part of the overall strategy for fighting Iraq.[9] The analysis of Iran's special operations capabilities by William H. Burgess III similarly contended that Iran's special operations were under a unified command and had been developed within the context of an overall strategic plan extending even into the period beyond the cessation of hostilities with Iraq.[10] The same assumption that Iran behaves as a unitary actor executing a comprehensive strategy is to be found in Alvin H. Bernstein's analysis of Iranian low intensity warfare directed against the United States.[11]

An intermediate position, which can be designated as the factional politics model, holds that the contending factions within Iran view foreign and military policy as simply other theaters in which to pursue what are essentially domestic political quarrels through "one-up-manship" and pre-emption of rivals' preferred policies in the international arena. Bruce Hoffman's RAND study of trends in Iranian sponsored terrorism identified several cases of terrorist actions which appeared to have been sponsored by political groups within Iran without the support or prior knowledge of those government leaders in Iran who had formal authority for such actions.[12] Hoffman, however, also cited several incidents that conform more closely to the strategic choice model and suggests that factional influence in state sponsorship of terrorism has largely subsided. Farhang Jahanpour and John Calabrese, in separate articles dealing with Iranian domestic and international politics, maintained that factional politics has quite suppressed any coherent and consistent foreign policy, including policies regarding Iranian sponsorship of terrorism abroad. Both of these observers denied that the Iranian state held any monopoly of control over such external surrogates as Hizballah.[13] In a detailed study of incidents involving Iranian political factions engaging in free-lance sponsorship of terrorism James Weinrauch also advocated a factional interpretation of Iranian politics.[14]

A more subtle distinction between a state strategic choice model and a factional politics model has been made by Iranian area specialists Shahrough Akhavi and Nikola Schahgaldian. Akhavi maintained that while Iranian factions are split largely over social and economic domestic policies that they are united on "cultural" issues, such as the status of women in Islam, education policy and minorities.[15] In contrast with Akhavi, who believes the solidarity of Iran's religious leaders to be rather brittle, Schahgaldian stresses the resiliency of clerical cohesiveness and their ability to subsume their differences when their common interests are at stake.[16]

Other Iranian area specialists appear to concur that the role of Iranian factional politics is now confined largely to Iranian domestic politics. James A. Bill explained factionalism in the Islamic Republic as stemming from the internal difficulties and external threats that Iran experienced during the early period following its revolution. Accordingly James A. Bill predicted that the disruptive power of factionalism would decline as the consolidation of the state continued and as the extremists among the factions came to experience a form of revolutionary "burn-out."[17] In a more recent work Rouhollah Ramazani maintained that state consolidation is reducing the role of factions in Iran's foreign policy to relative insignificance.[18] Both James A. Bill and Rouhollah Ramazani believed that Iranian involvement in terrorism has been due more to the disruptive power of the factions than to deliberate strategic choice on the part of the Iranian state.

The three contending explanations for apparent Iranian support of anti-U.S. terrorism are, to recap, the following: First, there is the anthropological, community-action approach that views instances of anti-U.S. terrorism as the spontaneous work of Muslim activists acting under the inspiration of an Islamic resurgence and not tied to the policy or actions of any given nation-state. Second, there is a factional politics model that views anti-U.S. terrorism as the work of factions or groups within Iran acting without the sanction of the Iranian state. Finally, there is the state sponsorship model in which the Iranian state has sponsored terrorist groups outside Iran to carry out anti-U.S. terrorism as part of an overall political strategy. The communications model can be used to resolve which of these models best fits the available evidence.

In studying incidents of international terrorism as instrumental political action this study regards the actions under consideration as forms of communication to better describe and explain Iranian-sponsored anti-U.S. terrorism. These communications emanate from within a political context in which other features of more conventional political and diplomatic activities are present. Apart from its originating within a national context of political dialogue and/or conflict, terrorism as a political instrument also seeks to pressure certain ultimate target audience(s) through its direct attacks on other immediate targets. If the Iranian state is the sponsor of such actions its statements of intention and warning should be found in the Friday Prayers sermons, the decrees of the Supreme Religious Jurisprudent (*vali-yi faqih*), and presidential or Foreign Ministry declarations. Editorials by the state-controlled radio-television, or the Islamic Republic News Agency, or by the quasi-official daily newspaper *Ittilaʿāt* also would reflect the views of the government. If a given faction is the sponsor of an action its statements of intention and warning might be found in the parliamentary speeches of key factional leaders who happen also to be Majlis members, in editorials by factionally-aligned newspapers, or in protests organized by such factions. Another indication of factional, as opposed to state, inspiration of terrorism might be found in indications of internal political dissonance reflected in official and non-official media.

This study sampled Iranian state communications using the categorical coding techniques of content analysis and it also employed quantitative analysis to determine whether significant associations could be found between certain categories of statements and terrorist events. Systematic sampling of communications reduces the number of representative communications by purported sponsors of terrorism to a more manageable mass. Categorical classification and coding schemes in content analysis serve to reduce the role of the researcher's own subjectivity and possible bias in the selection and identification of significant communications. Finally, applying standard measures of association for the nominal data and of correlation for the interval data derived from the content analysis seeks to clarify the relationship between proposed explanatory variables and the terrorist phenomenon being studied.

Key Definitions: Terrorism and State-Sponsorship

Terrorism differs from ordinary criminal violence not merely because it involves "politically-motivated violence" but mainly in its targeting and intended effects. Terrorism seeks deliberately to target largely non-combatants as its victims and to cultivate terror among both victims and spectators not as the primary end in itself but as means to capture the attention of others who are the terrorists' ultimate target audience and to force them to respond in some manner.

One definition that incorporates both the intended psychological impact of terror on spectators and the nature of the target was developed by Edward F. Mickolus in constructing his chronology *International Terrorism in the 1980s*:

> [International/transnational terrorism] is the use, or threat of use, of anxiety-inducing, extranormal violence for political purposes by any individual or group, whether acting for or in opposition to established governmental authority, when such action is intended to influence the attitudes and behavior of a target group wider than the immediate victims and when, through the nationality or foreign ties of its perpetrators, through its location, through the nature of its institutional or human victims, or through the mechanics of its resolution, its ramifications transcend national boundaries.[19]

This definition is substantially similar to that used by the RAND Corporation.[20] As both the Mickolus and RAND databases of international terrorism use functionally equivalent definitions both databases are used to substantiate cases of Iranian-sponsored anti-U.S. terrorism. In defining terrorism in terms of violence directed at non-combatants, this study does not count most instances of attacks upon U.S. peace-keeping forces as cases of terrorism.[21] Nor are mere "threats of use" of anxiety-inducing, extranormal violence unaccompanied by violence counted as *bona fide* instances of terrorism. To avoid the ambiguity between threats as intentioned public communications and *threats* as covert, objective dangers this study reserves the word "threat" to refer only to projections of malicious harm willed upon others by sponsors of terrorism or to their own perceptions of such harm being willed upon them by their opponents.

Sound methodology also requires deleting instances of threats from incidents forming the dependent variable because the independent variables here are operationalized by statements of official and non-official entities within Iran that indicate either perceptions of threats against the Islamic revolution or projections of threats by such groups against external enemies. Counting threats both as indicators of impending terrorism and also as terrorist events in themselves would obscure the distinction between the dependent variable of anti-U.S. terrorism and the independent variables, which include threat statements made by state sponsors or their sponsored groups.

Sponsorship of international terrorism is here defined as the support of agents, including non-nationals of the sponsoring power, whether individuals or groups. Such support is counted as *state sponsorship* when it receives either the explicit sanction, or else tacit approval, of the ultimate legal and political authorities of the sponsoring regime who, in either case, have sufficient knowledge and approval of the types of activities by its agents and who maintain effective control over these agents. The operational definition of state-sponsorship of terrorism used in this study is the same as that developed by the RAND corporation:

> "state-sponsored terrorism" is defined as the active involvement by foreign governments in training, arming, and providing other logistical and intelligence assistance—as well as sanctuary—to terrorists for the purpose of carrying out violent acts on behalf of that government against its enemies. State-sponsored terrorism is therefore defined as a form of surrogate warfare. Incidents are identified in the [RAND] Chronology as state sponsored based on published accounts detailing or alleging the specific involvement of a foreign government in the attack, the nationality and nature of the target, the *modus operandi*, and past evidence of that government's involvement in such attacks.[22]

Methods of Research and Analysis

The dependent variable consists of cases of anti-U.S. terrorism in the period 1980-1990 for which there is strong evidence of Iranian sponsorship, whether by state or sub-state actors, that has been materially corroborated by multiple and diverse witnesses. The independent variables, which are to be generated through a systematic content analysis of public official Iranian political communications, include a) perceptions of external threats shared by Muslim fundamentalists, b) indications of threats by persons or offices representing the Iranian state projected against the United States, and c) evidences of factional struggle or discord within the Iranian state. The dependent and independent variables are examined for any significant statistical relationships that will identify the most plausible source of the political communications associated with terrorist threats.

Identifying the Dependent Variable

Two major sets of chronologies of international terrorism were separately developed, one by Edward F. Mickolus, spanning 1980-1987, and the other being the RAND Chronology of International Terrorism, spanning 1980-1988. These contain rather complete summaries of both circumstantial and substantive evidence of sponsorship derived from multiple and diverse sources. The substantive agreement found between the Mickolus and RAND chronologies underscores the external validity of the approach used independently by both groups of researchers. For instance, if one examines only attacks by suspected pro-Iranian terrorists on U.S. targets for the period 1980-1987, RAND confirms 29 out of 37 incidents reported by Mickolus, which represents 78.4 percent agreement.

Both chronologies provide summaries of the essential details of each case so allowing users to sort these cases further according to the criteria of state sponsorship mentioned earlier and to eliminate the more doubtful cases. Other public reports, such as those contained in the *New York Times*, *Iran Times International*, and the U.S. Department of State's annual report(s) *Patterns of Global Terrorism*, and the annual chronologies published by RAND provided multiple and diverse sources for identifying cases in the period 1988-1992 not jointly covered by the Mickolus and RAND chronologies.[23]

The RAND chronology, "International Terrorism Incidents Which May Involve Iranian Perpetrators," covered some 233 cases from 1980 to 1988. In the RAND report, *Recent Trends and Future Prospects of Iranian Sponsored International Terrorism* (RAND/R-3783-USDP), this selection had been in turn narrowed down to a subset entitled "International Terrorist Acts Committed by Shi'a Extremists," which included 160 cases from 1980-1987.[24] An inspection of the Mickolus chronology covering the same period also yielded 160 cases of terrorist events committed by Shi'ite terrorists.[25] Multiple and diverse sources similar to those used by Mickolus and RAND provided 31 more cases for the period 1988-1992 extending beyond the RAND and Mickolus chronologies. These 191 cases included 149 attacks directed against non-U.S. targets, attacks by groups not supported by Iran, and intra-mural attacks committed by rival Shi'ite militias, none of which were counted as cases of the dependent variable. These 42 remaining cases involving targeting of U.S. interests by presumed Iranian or extremist Shi'ite perpetrators, were further sorted to select just those cases for which there were substantial reasons to assume Iranian sponsorship, whether by the Iranian state or some faction within the Iranian state.

The multiplicity, diversity and reliability of the sources separately used by the compilers of the Mickolus and RAND chronologies is reflected in the construction of each database. Both the RAND and the Mickolus databases have been independently built up from primary and secondary sources, most of which originate in the same universe of open source materials.[26] These materials include literally hundreds of domestic and foreign news sources, as well as chronologies developed by the Federal Bureau of Investigation, the Nuclear Regulatory Commission, those compiled by various United States embassies, and also other official documents of the United States government and foreign governments.[27]

Therefore whenever the Mickolus and RAND chronologies have both reported the same event as an anti-U.S. terrorist event, one then has independent verification of that event using what are substantially the same definitions and criteria of evidence both for terrorism, and for state sponsorship. All cases for which dual confirmation in the Mickolus and RAND databases was lacking (or lacking comparable diverse and multiple witnesses), have accordingly been eliminated from consideration as instances of the dependent variable. The class of terrorist attacks has been further narrowed by eliminating all instances of mere threats from the class of incidents and also eliminating most cases involving U.S. or Allied troops in war-like situations.

Following this step-wise elimination of dubious or inconclusive cases, Table 1 (see p. 266) listed only those cases for which dual confirmation of Iranian sponsorship exists.[28] This list includes all cases (N=24) of the dependent variable to be explained in this study.

Threat-Indicators by Content Analysis

Content analysis can produce measures of threat perceptions, threat projections, and factional strife in the form of interval frequency and volume data which can then be analyzed by standard statistical tests of association or correlation with the dependent variable to determine which, if any, of the independent variables has a statistical association that may illuminate the sources of anti-U.S. terrorism. Content analysis has been defined as, "any technique for making inferences by systematically and objectively identifying specified characteristics of messages."[29] The research design used for data collection and content analysis is elaborated in what follows.

The communications model of terrorism implies that sponsored terrorist actions will be substantially correlated with preceding increases in levels of public statements by the responsible state or sub-state actors. Such statements could indicate the sponsors' perceptions of external threats, or else their own projections of threats against external targets, or else give evidence of factional strife within the regime.

A positive correlation between succeeding terrorist incidents and the index of state projections of threats against its targets supports the model of state sponsorship. The sponsoring state would be producing the prior threatening statements as part of its political dialogue with its external enemies. Should its enemies appease its demands no terrorist action would follow but otherwise such actions could be expected as the next stage of political communication.

If only the index of factional strife within Iran shows any significant positive correlation with succeeding terrorist incidents, this would be taken as support for the factional politics model. Terrorism here would be regarded as an externality effect of a factional political controversy under way within Iran.

If only the index of threat perceptions shows any significant positive correlation with the dependent variable this would be taken as indicating that anti-U.S. terrorism by Islamic fundamentalists is essentially independent of Iranian domestic politics and its accompanying discourse. In this case the ultimate cause of anti-U.S. fundamentalist terrorism would be found in the root causes that give rise to the Islamic resurgence throughout the Middle East rather than in the actions or policies of any given state. Both the terrorist acts outside Iran and the statements of threat perceptions being made in Iran would be separate effects being independently produced by the Islamic resurgence world-wide Such reactive terrorist actions would primarily signal their perpetrators' displeasure over perceived U.S. threats to Islam quite autonomously of any grand strategic plan, direction, or material help from Tehran.

Data Sources and Sampling

The theory of terrorism as a form of political communication holds that the same politics that lead the state sponsor to order terrorist acts will also lead it to signal its intentions through its mass media organs. Therefore the content analysis will be carried out on samples of running record, public domain documents reflecting that stream of political discourse.

Records of regularly-appearing Iranian publications are available from quasi-official Iranian-compiled sources, such as the leading Persian-language Tehran newspapers or magazines. Of the various major Iranian Persian-language publications, *Ittilaʿ āt*, *Kayhan*, and *Jumhuri-yi Islami* have continued to be published throughout the period of interest (1980-1990). *Ittilaʿ āt* and *Kayhan* are the two major Tehran dailies and while both are under government editorial supervision the former, older paper *Ittilaʿ āt* is regarded as the semi-official Iranian government mouth-piece. Accordingly *Ittilaʿ āt* has been chosen as the main Iranian running record source since it would reflect the official state threat perceptions or projections most clearly of these three. It is also used to measure factional discord insofar as the official newspaper of record would be best situated to acknowledge all significant factional strife, or other forms of potential or actual opposition.

The *sampling units* are those minimum observations that are independent of each other to be examined, isolated, and recorded. The *recording units* are those separately analyzable parts of the sampling unit or, as Holsti says, a recording unit is "the specific segment of content that is characterized by placing it in a given category."[30] By choosing recording units that are smaller than the sampling unit one can eliminate from the content analysis those portions of the sampling unit that are inessential to the content analysis. As *Ittilaʿ āt* consists of daily issues, the actual sampling unit was the front page of each issue while the recording unit was each headline with attached story or photograph, since lead stories alone merit front page treatment whilst Iranian governmental policy guides the editors of *Ittilaʿ āt* in choosing and assigning space to headlines and any accompanying story.

The choice of recording units depends on the substance of interest, or "content," defined by one expert as "that portion of the symbolic material that needs to be examined in order to characterize a recording unit."[31] Alternative types of content include (1) certain words, (2) certain themes, (3) characters or actors, (4) sentences, or (5) paragraphs.[32] Given the focus of this study on the relation between political perceptions and their relation to sponsorship of terrorism the thematic unit appears the most obvious choice because, as Holsti says, "for many purposes the theme is the most useful unit of content analysis. It is almost indispensable in research on propaganda, values, attitudes, beliefs, and the like."[33] The themes chosen, namely perceptions or projections of threats, will be elaborated in greater detail in the discussion of content categories and coding schemes. The coder or analyst must decide whether the greater portion of each report is dominated by the themes of threat perception, threat projection, or factionalism and to assign each report to no more than one exclusive category. In reviewing each front-page of an issue of *Ittilaʿ āt* entire articles will be counted as the recording units insofar as each headline determines the overall theme of the article.

The sheer volume of material contained in the *Ittilaʿ āt* running record requires some form of systematic sampling.[34] Such sampling involves the selection of cases, usually beginning from some arbitrarily-selected starting point, such that each succeeding case that is selected is separated from the former case by approximately equal intervals, whether the interval is measured in calendar time or else by numbers of intervening issues. For the purposes of this study Ayatullah Khomeini's pronouncement ordering the "exportation of the revolution" on 21 March 1980 has been chosen as the starting point. Rather than using a fixed interval of days from that starting point, however, this study will use regularly-spaced single issues selected for each month of the Persian solar calendar as its sampling points in the case of *Ittilaʿ āt*.[35]

Coding Schemes and Content Categories

The categories to be used are, 1) Threat Perceptions: perceptions of threats by outsiders, 2) Threat-Projections: threats directed at outsiders, and 3) Factional Strife statements indicating perceived internal threats to the regime.

In each of these three cases a "threat" means an action or attitude or event that is, or is at least viewed as being, *deliberately willed*, with a *malicious intention* by a *human agency*, whether this agency is an individual person, group, organization, government or nation.

To recap, then, "threats" in general involve public statements, a) that entail past, present or future *harm* to someone or something, and, b) are *deliberately willed* by another person or group of people, and, c) that proceed from blameworthy or *malicious intentions.*

Threat-Perceptions are those threats which are seen as directed by non-Iranians or by enemies of Islam against Iran, Iran's revolution or regime, Islam, or against the Muslims in general.

Threat-Projections are those warnings or threats by Iran directed against governments, groups or persons outside of Iran viewed as enemies of Iran or of Islam.

Factional Strife Statements are those statements that either indicate perceptions of threats coming from persons or groups within Iran or else which are warnings directed at such groups or persons.

Articles matching the above categories would be the recording units selected from the sample of front-pages of *Ittilaʿāt*. In addition the percentage of front-page space occupied by each *Ittilaʿāt* recording unit would also be measured in square centimeters of reduced photocopy to provide some relative measure of intensity or editorially-assigned stress to recording units that goes beyond a mere frequency count to produce a volume measure that is also referred to as an "attention score."[36]

Data Validity

To test the external validity of the categorization procedure at least two coders must independently carry out a content analysis on samples of literal translations of the Persian-language materials derived from *Ittilaʿāt* (N=58). The following composite reliability coefficient allows the agreement between coders to be measured as follows:

$$\text{Composite Reliability} = \frac{N(A)}{1 + [(N - 1)(A)]},$$

where N = the number of coders and A = the average proportion of agreement between coders.[37]

According to Kassarjian when coders are dealing with materials in their native language the lowest reliability measure that is generally considered acceptable is 80 percent while figures above 85 percent can be considered quite satisfactory.[38]

Three independent coders were given a Reliability Check Packet containing the sample (N=58) of the reports to be analyzed as well as instructions for using the categories. These instructions contained both the descriptions of the content categories, along with examples for illustration, and the decision-rules for classifying the recording unit. Examination of the three independently coded samples materials yielded a reliability coefficient of 90.4 percent, well within the standard of 80 percent agreement. Once the external reliability of the coding procedure was verified the 120 sampling units were coded, the results are shown in Table 2 (see p. 272).

Interpretation of *Ittilaʿāt* Content Data

While statistical associations of themselves do not sufficiently demonstrate any purported causality, nonetheless lack of any significant statistical association between the dependent variable and one of the independent variables would sufficiently demonstrate that the null hypothesis corresponding to a given state sponsorship, factional, or autonomous reaction hypothesis could not be rejected. Together the three independent variables developed from content analysis of the running record of *Ittilaʿat* and the dependent variable were statistically analyzed to reveal associations supporting either a reactive interpretation of such terrorism or else supporting an alternative pro-active model.

A reactive interpretation would hold that these anti-U.S. terrorist actions stemmed from the reaction of the Islamic resurgence at large to perceived threats from the United States or the West. Such an interpretation assigns a minimal role to the Iranian state in planning or directing such terrorism for it suggests that, at most, Muslim militants may take their inspiration from the Iranian example but that the Iranian state does not bear responsibility for their actions.

A pro-active interpretation suggests a more deliberate recourse to terrorism in which Iranian sponsors initiate and retain control over actual operations. One pro-active interpretation, the state sponsorship model, assigns most of the responsibility for terrorism to Iranian state actors while another pro-active interpretation, the factional politics model, assigns most responsibility to non-state actors. To determine which model best describes and explains the terrorist phenomenon the researcher needs to identify the sources of significant communications related to terrorism and to measure the strength and direction of their association with terrorist events.

The *Ittilaʿāt* data, being percentages of front-page space devoted to each variable, consist of interval level measurements. The assumption that the editorial policy of *Ittilaʿāt* is guided by governmental policy implies that the space and prominence given to each headline or article would be in some sense directly proportional to its perceived or intended importance within Iranian officialdom. Any possible association between the independent variables based on the *Ittilaʿāt* data and the dependent variable could be analyzed using tests of association appropriate to interval data, such as simple and multiple regressions. Such tests would reveal not only the strength of each variable's association with the dependent variable and direction of association but also allow the analyst to see how the various independent variables interact in affecting the dependent variable.

Sound statistical analysis also requires recognition of the relative timing of the variables because the political communications model places terrorism within a sequence of signals and responses. A terrorist act may be undertaken reactively to retaliate for a perceived wrong or else be intended pro-actively to enforce some earlier made demand or to intimidate other targets in the future. In either case a terrorist act may well be preceded by a warning or even a series of warnings, perhaps an earlier warning to force a target to obey one's demands and a later warning just prior to the action to reinforce the message that the target's disregard for previous warnings is going to be punished. To incorporate this temporal dimension into these tests one must test for association, not just between the contemporaneous values of the dependent and independent variables, but also between the dependent variable and several lagged values of the independent variables in preceding time periods.

The impact of threat-perceptions and the credibility of threat-projections are both sensitive to the passage of time. Threats will be more credible in the future and more likely to command future compliance if they are carried out relatively quickly, that is, within a matter of days, weeks or months from the time they are made. In the communications model a threat projection and its subsequent fulfillment could be separated by several weeks or even months and still remain credible. A major terrorist action, such as the construction and deployment of the truck-bomb used against the U.S. Marines in Beirut, as well as the political and diplomatic preparations among the Iranian, Syrian and Lebanese participants, required several months from the time Iranian authorities first threatened a "regional reaction" against the deployment of multi-national U.S. and French forces within Lebanon to the time of the actual bomb attack.[39] While it is difficult to delineate precisely what passage of time will totally depreciate the credibility of a threat-perception or projection, the expiration of one year has been selected in the following analyses as the cut-off for examining lagged values of independent variables. For most people the passage of an entire year psychologically represents the completion of a full cycle of the natural order. A threat that remains unfulfilled for more than a year is usually just forgotten.[40] Therefore the following analyses examine the associations of the dependent variable with contemporaneous and lagged monthly values of the dependent variables only up to the preceding twelfth month.

Results of Statistical Analysis

As the *Ittilaʿāt* data are in the form of percentages, and hence are parametric measures, they can be statistically analyzed using regression analysis, which can provide measures of the strength of association, coefficients of correlation, and measures of how the independent variables contribute together to explaining the variation in the dependent variable. The dependent variable, however, is measured solely as discrete terrorist events. If, however, one uses three-month moving averages of both the dependent and independent variables, the measure of the dependent variable is transformed to a percentage measure which can be used in an ordinary least-squares regression model.

A stepwise multiple regression algorithm was used with the three-month moving average of anti-U.S. terrorist events as the dependent variable with present and lagged values from month (t-0) to month (t-12) for the three-month moving average of each independent and lagged variable. The regression algorithm retains in the regression equation only those independent and lagged variables that are significant at the 5.0 percent level of confidence. The final regression model is presented in Figure 1 following:

Figure 1: Regression of Iranian State-Sponsored Anti-U.S. Terrorist Attacks Upon Content Variables Derived From *Ittila'at* Data

Variable		B	Standard Error	T-Value
Factional Strife	t -10**	1.22	0.30	4.001
Threat Projection	t - 9**	1.08	0.33	3.324
Threat Projection	t - 6*	0.76	0.36	2.151
Threat Projection	t - 4*	0.92	0.36	2.578
Constant*		-0.12	0.05	-2.195
R^2	= .29		F Value = 11.678	
Adjusted R^2	= .26		Signif F = .0000	

* P < .05
** P < .01

The final regression model contains none of the lagged values of the threat perception variable. This suggests that anti-U.S. terrorist attacks have not been reactive in nature, being in some way a defensive action by Muslim fundamentalists against perceived threats from the United States or the West. The most significant variable appears to be the ten-month lag of the Factional Strife variable: for every 1.0 percent increase in the measure of Factional Strife one should expect about a 1.22 percent increase in anti-U.S. terrorist incidents ten months later. This is consistent with the factional strife theory which views Iranian sponsorship of anti-U.S. terrorism as being a spill-over effect of factional struggle within Iran and quite possibly the work of sub-state groups within the Iranian state rather than the Iranian state itself operating as a unitary actor.

However there are three other variables which are all lagged values of the Threat Projection variable, at nine months, six months, and four months respectively. All of them are positively correlated with following incidents of anti-U.S. terrorism. The six-month lagged value of the Threat Projection alone accounts for 12.5 percent of the variation of the dependent variable while all three lagged values together accounted for 16.8 of the total variation. These positive correlations are consistent with the state sponsorship model in which the Iranian state acts as a unitary actor in making its threat projections and subsequently carrying them out. The existence of more than one significant lagged value of the threat projection variable is also consistent with a communications model of terrorism in which the state sponsor may repeat its threats before actually carrying them out.

How can one reconcile evidence for both the factional strife and state sponsorship models? Since the positive and significant correlations with the lagged values of the threat projection variable seem to indicate unequivocal evidence of state sponsorship the positive correlation with the lagged factional strife variable cannot easily be understood as indicating factional as opposed to state control over sponsorship of terrorism. A more simple explanation of the sequence and significance of the factional strife and threat projection variables is that the threat projections which follow the rise in the factional strife indicator reflects efforts by the Iranian state to distract its supporters from their various divisive intramural issues and controversies by directing their energies and attentions pro-actively against external enemies. This is an example of what Schmid and Graaf called "deflecting public attention from a disliked issue by bombing it from the frontpages,"[41] as well as an example of morale-boosting and solidarity-building through concentration upon an external enemy.

This interpretation belies the other interpretation of the relationship of factionalism within the Iranian regime to external terrorism which viewed substate factional actors as using terrorism overseas as a way of preventing more moderate elements within the regime from adopting more pro-Western policies.

These four variables together explain about 26.4 percent of the total variation in anti-U.S. terrorist actions under presumed Iranian sponsorship which itself is rather remarkable when one reflects that only public-domain data are being used to generate this regression. This means that one can explain slightly more than one-quarter of the total variation in anti-U.S. terrorism presumed to be sponsored by Iran merely by reading the newspaper *Ittilaʿāt* and keeping track of the amount of space devoted on its front pages to threat projections and indications of factional struggle within Iran using the content analysis and statistical approach used in this study.

Using the communications model outlined in this research and by following similar sampling and statistical procedures, analysts within the United States intelligence community could probably explain even higher proportions of variation in the dependent variable by incorporating in these variables classified data derived from signal intelligence or human sources that could give even clearer indications of threat perceptions, strategic intentions or internal factional disputes. Alternatively refinements in the categorical coding and sampling procedures applied merely to public domain materials alone might also improve the closeness of fit summarized in the adjusted R-Squared statistic.

The final optimal regression model contained only lagged values of two of the variables. As it happened to turn out, no contemporaneous value of any of the three original variables proved to have any significant association with the dependent variable. Such a fortuitous finding fulfills one the expectations implicit in the political communications model, namely, that terrorist actions should follow high observed values of those proposed threat-projection variables that are found to have a statistically significant association with terrorism.

The lack of any contemporaneous value for an independent variable in the final estimated model has some additional practical implications as well. This optimal regression model happens to be a time series model using exogenous variables, that is, it could be used to forecast future terrorist actions using only present and past measurements of the significant independent and lagged variables. If these regression results give evidence of some pro-active Iranian state involvement in anti-U.S. terrorism it is also likely that the planning or timing of future anti-U.S. terrorist actions would also be related to the prior history of such terrorist actions undertaken by the same sponsor(s) in the past. In other words a much more accurate predictive model capable of explaining even a larger proportion of the variation in anti-U.S. terrorist attacks might be generated using lagged values of the dependent variable, that is, measures of previous anti-U.S. terrorist attacks, along with the lagged values of the independent variables already used.

This study did not seek to create such a predictive model because such autoregressive models, in effect, beg the question of what originally accounted for the history of prior terrorist acts that is then being used to predict, but no longer to explain, future terrorist actions. This observation regarding the feasibility of creating such an autoregressive time series model is made here only to point out that if the quantitative analysis of public domain communications data gathered by content analyses can explain one-quarter of the known variation in Iranian-sponsored anti-U.S. terrorist attacks it could also lend itself to practical applications in forecasting, and so possibly forestalling, future incidents of such terrorism.

Conclusions

One definite conclusion to be derived from this statistical analysis is that the reactive model is not supported by any of the statistical evidence. Anti-U.S. terrorist actions do not increase as spontaneous reactions to perceived threats from either the United States or the West in general. Rather than terrorist actions arising automatically through the community-wide mobilizing force of the Islamic resurgence, which is supposedly the inevitable outcome of impersonal historical and cultural root causes and grievances, a more simple explanation consistent with the foregoing analyses would be that such terrorist actions result from the deliberate calculations and decisions of certain identifiable individuals or groups associated with the Islamic Republic of Iran.

The real contending explanations are then two pro-active models, the factional politics model and the state sponsorship model. The present analysis seems to give threat projections a predominant positive and significant role. While the analysis seems to indicate that factional indicators were significant, though less significant than the threat projection variable, they act rather to motivate subsequent efforts at regime consolidation in part through intensified anti-U.S. mobilization and propaganda, including “armed propaganda” in the form of terrorist actions.

For law enforcement and national security officials the

foremost practical implication of the results of this study is that it outlines a technical means to analyze the political communications of regimes or groups suspected of sponsoring terrorism in order to assess threats or warnings of impending terrorist actions.

The policy implication of this study may be of more concern to administrators of U.S. foreign policy, namely, that factionalism within Iran neither pre-occupies nor distracts this regime from carrying out its external terrorist agenda. If the anthropological, community action model were correct then U.S. national security policy could do little to deflect or deter the effects of the Islamic resurgence. If the factional politics model accounted from most of the anti-U.S. terrorism the United States would face the dilemma of seeking to punish the radicals within Tehran at the cost of undermining the position of alleged "moderates" within the Tehran government. However, as Jerrold Post indicated in his study of terrorist group structure and locus of authority, when state sponsored terrorism is that outcome of strategic choice then retaliatory policies that reduce the marginal utility of terrorism to the sponsoring state are both effective and morally justified.[42] The current study concludes that the Iranian state bears responsibility for the anti-U.S. terrorist actions committed in the period 1980-1990. The most prudent policy implication would appear to be that if Iran does not desist from its state sponsorship of terrorism, whether against the United States, against Israel, or against other nations, the United States should continue to impose international isolation upon Iran, and other state sponsors of terrorism, and so deprive such regimes of access to foreign aid, trade credits, and technology necessary for their national goals and regime survival.

Acknowledgment

Funding for reproduction of this article was provided through a dissemination grant by the Faculty Research Committee of Idaho State University.

Table 1

Terrorist Acts Against U.S. Targets
Committed Under Presumed Iranian Sponsorship
21 March 1980–21 March 1992

Incident Number References of Mickolous and RAND	Tactic	Nationality of Target	Date	Place
1. 80072203 19800723	Assass.	Iranian	22/07/80	U.S.A.

RAND cites as evidence of sponsorship FBI and NSA electronic surveillance of cash transactions between U.S. assassins of anti-Khomeini activist, Ali Akbar Tabataba'i and pro-Khomeini Iranians.

2. 80073102 19800731	Assass. (attempt)	Iranian	31/07/80	U.S.A.

Attempted assassination of Tabataba'i's associate, Shah-Rais, follows death threats by pro-Khomeini Iranians. Signal intelligence links identities of attackers to same group as in No. 1 (80072203/19800723).

3. 82071901 19820719	Kidnap.	American	19/07/82	Lebanon

David Dodge held in Iran during later part of captivity until freed in July of 1983.

4. 83041801 19830418	Car-Bomb	American	18/04/83	Lebanon

Hizballah accepted responsibility for this action in an open communique issued on 16 February 1985 which also confirmed the group's identity with that of Islamic Jihad which previously had claimed responsibility. U.S. electronic surveillance and National Technical Means produced evidence of Iranian and Syrian intelligence cooperation in planning and execution of the U.S. Embassy bombing.

Table 1 (continued)

Incident Number References of Mickolous and RAND	Tactic	Nationality of Target	Date	Place
5. 83102301-02 19831023 A1 B04 F241, 19831023 A1 B04 F059	Car-Bomb	American French	23/10/83	Lebanon

Counter-force nature of targeting of U.S. Marine barracks and French military headquarters makes classification as terrorist act questionable. Evidence of Iranian and Syrian involvement provided by U.S. electronic surveillance and National Technical Means linking Islamic Jihad with Iranian and Syrian intelligence and technical support. As *modus operandi* was same as terrorist incident No. 4 (83041801/19830418) this incident is included as being part of a pattern of terrorist activity. Moreover the event had a powerful impact on an ultimate U.S. civilian target audience causing a reversal of U.S. policy in Lebanon which, presumably, was the effect intended by the sponsors and perpetrators of these bombings.

6. 83121203-10 19831212	Car-Bomb	American French	12/12/83	Kuwait

Claim of responsibility by Islamic Jihad and *modus operandi* same as in incidents Nos. 4 (83041801, 19830418) and 5 (83102301-02,19831023 A1 B04 F241, 19831023 A1 B04 F059). Subsequent trial of surviving Kuwaiti and Iraqi perpetrators revealed membership in Islamic Al Daʿwa Party, an Iraqi Shiʿite fundamentalist group enjoying Iranian material and moral support. One of the convicted, Mustafa Bahreddin, was also the brother-in-law of Imad Mughniyah, an Arab member of the Islamic Revolutionary Guards Corps contingent in Lebanon and the mastermind of the 23 October 1983 bombings in Lebanon.

7. 84011801 19840118 A1 B06 F001	Assass.	American	18/01/84	Lebanon

Islamic Jihad claims credit for murder of Malcolm Kerr, President of the American University of Beirut.

Table 1 (continued)

Incident Number References of Mickolous and RAND	Tactic	Nationality of Target	Date	Place
8. 84031601 19840316 A1 B01 F001	Kidnap, Murder	American	16/03/84	Lebanon

Islamic Jihad claimed responsibility for abduction and also for subsequent murder of William Buckley on 4 October 1985, supposedly in revenge for Israeli air attack on P.L.O. headquarters in Tunis. His remains were returned on 26 December 1991.

Incident Number References of Mickolous and RAND	Tactic	Nationality of Target	Date	Place
9. 84050801 19840510 A1 B01 F000	Kidnap	American	06/05/84	Lebanon

Benjamin Weir was kidnaped by Islamic Jihad in May 1984. His release on 14 September 1985, apparently as a result of the McFarlane-North initiative to sell TOW missiles to Iran in August 1985 (*Tower Commission Report*, B25-B28, B140).

Incident Number References of Mickolous and RAND	Tactic	Nationality of Target	Date	Place
10. 84092001 19840920 A1 B04 F023	Car-Bomb	American	20/09/84	Lebanon

Partly successful suicide car-bomb attack similar to incidents Nos. 4 (83041801, 19830418), 5 (83102301-02,19831023 A1 B04 F241, 19831023 A1 B04 F059) and 6 (83121203-10, 19831212) for which Islamic Jihad claimed responsibility. Islamic Jihad had threatened to carry out such an attack on 8 September 1984 while on 15 September 1984 U.S. military intelligence warned of indications of such an impending attack.

Table 1 (continued)

Incident Number References of Mickolous and RAND	Tactic	Nationality of Target	Date	Place
11. 84120402 19841204 A1 B03 F007	Hijacking Murder	American	04/12/84	U.A.E.

Islamic Jihad hijackers murdered two U.S. employees of the Agency for International Development in Kuwaiti jetliner held at Tehran's Mehrabad airport. The hijackers were later overpowered by Iranian security guards. Circumstances suggest at least factional Iranian support for hijackers. Iranian rescue operation and reported intention to try hijackers have been cited by some as *prima facie* evidence of a lack of Iranian state involvement with the hijackers however Iranian authorities refused all extradition requests by Kuwait and details of supposed trial of hijackers have never been released.

12. 85010802 19850108 A1 B01 F000	Kidnap	American	08/01/85	Lebanon

Rev. Lawrence Jenco was abducted in January 1985 by Islamic Jihad. He was released on 27 July 1986 as part of the Reagan administration's covert deal to sell arms to Iran.

13. 85031601 19850316 A1 B01 F000	Kidnap	American	16/03/85	Lebanon

Terry Anderson was taken hostage by Islamic Jihad in March 1985 and released on 4 December 1991.

14. 85052801 19850528 A1 B01 F000	Kidnap	American	28/05/85	Lebanon

David Jacobsen was abducted by Islamic Jihad and released on 2 November 1986 as part of the Reagan administration's covert deal to sell arms to Iran.

Table 1 (continued)

Incident Number References of Mickolous and RAND	Tactic	Nationality of Target	Date	Place
15. 85060902	Kidnap	American	09/06/85	Lebanon

Thomas Sutherland was kidnaped by Islamic Jihad in June 1985 and released on 18 November 1991.

16. 85061404, 19850607 A1 B03 F001	Hijacking Kidnap, Murder	American	14/06/85	Greece

TWA flight 847 Athens to Rome was hijacked by Islamic Jihad members. Originally 104 U.S. citizens were held hostage, the remaining 41 of whom were released by 30 June 1985. During this event, the hijackers murdered one U.S. serviceman, Robert D. Stethem, found among the American passengers.

17. 86090903 19860909 A1 B01 F000 I000	Kidnap	American	09/09/86	Lebanon

Frank Reed was kidnapped by the "Revolutionary Justice Organization" in September 1986 and released on 30 April 1990.

18. 86091203 19860912 A1 B01 F000 I000	Kidnap	American	12/09/86	Lebanon

Joseph J. Cicippio was kidnaped by Revolutionary Justice Organization, believed to be another name for Islamic Jihad, and later released 2 Dec. 1991.

19. 86102102 19861021 A1 B01 F000 I000	Kidnap	American	21/10/86	Lebanon

Edward Tracey was kidnaped by Revolutionary Justice Organization, and later released on 11 August 1991.

Table 1 (continued)

Incident Number References of Mickolous and RAND	Tactic	Nationality of Target	Date	Place
20. 87012402 19870124 A1 B01 F000 I000	Kidnap	American	24/01/87	Lebanon

American professors Robert Polhill, Alan Steen, and Jesse Turner, and U.S. resident, Mithileshwar Singh, were kidnapped by "Islamic Jihad for the Liberation of Palestine," believed to be another alias of Islamic Jihad. Singh was released 3 October 1988; Polhill, on 22 April 1990; Turner on 22 October 1991; and Steen on 3 December 1991.

21. 87041001 19870409 A1 B07 F000 I000	Conspir.	American Israeli	10/04/87	Turkey

Turkish police arrested four members of Islamic Jihad, including one Iranian and one Lebanese, in connection with a conspiracy to bomb U.S. military and diplomatic installations in Turkey. The Lebanese member of this team provided details confirming Iranian sponsorship of Islamic Jihad and of that group's identity with the Hizballah militia of Lebanon.

22. 87061702 19870617 A1 B01 F00 I000	Kidnap	American	17/06/87	Lebanon

In June 1987 U.S. journalist Charles Glass was abducted by The Organization of the Oppressed on Earth but escaped on 18 August 1987. NBC News reported 1 July 1987 that U.S. signal intelligence interception of messages between the Iranian Embassy in Damascus and Hizballah offices in Lebanon provided "conclusive evidence that Iran had ordered the kidnapping" of Charles Glass.

Table 1 (continued)

Incident Number References of Mickolous and RAND	Tactic	Nationality of Target	Date	Place
23. L.A Times	Kidnap	American	17/02/88	Lebanon
Lt. Col. William R. Higgins, a U.S. Marines Corps officer serving in the UNIFIL forces in southern Lebanon, was kidnapped by "Organization of the Oppressed on Earth," an alias of Hizballah.				
24. L.A. Times	Murder	American	31/07/89	Lebanon
Lt. Col. William R. Higgins murdered on 31 July 1989. His remains were returned on 23 December 1991.				

Table 2

Measures of Independent Variables Derived From Content Analysis Of *Ittila'at* Samples 21 March 1980–21 March 1992

Date	*Ittila'at* Issue no.	Terrorist Event	Obs. No.	Threat Percept.	Threat Project.	Fractional Strife
03/30/80	16106	0	1	00.00	00.00	34.20
05/03/80	16131	0	2	23.38	00.00	09.03
05/31/80	16154	0	3	19.83	00.00	17.50
07/01/80	16178	2	4	00.00	00.00	20.57
08/23/80	16220	0	5	01.80	02.72	02.08
09/01/80	16228	0	6	02.40	00.00	13.52
10/02/80	16252	0	7	10.52	00.00	00.00
11/01/80	16275	0	8	00.00	10.27	00.00
12/01/80	16299	0	9	00.00	13.25	05.52
12/31/80	16324	0	10	15.97	00.00	02.48
01/31/81	16348	0	11	12.59	00.00	21.04
03/01/81	16372	0	12	00.00	12.68	08.93
03/30/81	16391	0	13	08.08	00.00	13.59
04/30/81	16416	0	14	04.41	00.00	14.05
05/31/81	16441	0	15	09.88	00.00	14.79

Table 2 (continued)

Date	*Ittila'at* Issue no.	Terrorist Event	Obs. No.	Threat Percept.	Threat Project.	Fractional Strife
07/02/81	16466	0	16	06.30	00.00	10.94
08/01/81	16491*	0	17	00.00	00.00	01.70
07/01/81	16515	0	18	00.00	00.00	70.70
10/07/81	16545	0	19	01.90	00.00	10.29
11/01/81	16565	0	20	29.28	00.00	12.41
12/01/81	16590	0	21	00.00	14.47	00.00
12/31/81	16615	0	22	00.00	17.98	04.67
01/30/82	16639	0	23	10.54	00.00	08.40
03/01/82	16664	0	24	00.00	00.00	04.52
04/03/82	16685	0	25	00.00	06.67	00.00
05/01/82	16709	0	26	00.00	00.00	00.00
05/31/82	16735	0	27	00.00	33.68	04.16
07/01/82	16759	1	28	12.56	35.17	02.24
08/01/82	16783	0	29	07.49	00.00	06.01
10/02/82	16833	0	30	15.49	00.00	01.28
Mehr 1361		0	31	(missing observations)		
Aban 1361		0	32	(missing observations)		
12/02/82	16883	0	33	00.00	00.00	07.87
01/01/83	16906	0	34	00.00	52.44	03.77
01/31/83	16931	0	35	06.17	07.41	53.61
03/01/83	16956	0	36	00.00	00.00	43.07
03/30/83	16975	1	37	00.00	00.00	14.68
05/01/83	17000	0	38	14.32	00.00	17.85
06/01/83	17024	0	39	00.00	04.94	04.83
07/04/83	17049	0	40	00.00	00.00	12.76
08/02/83	17073	0	41	15.85	00.00	04.70
09/01/83	17098	0	42	00.00	00.00	03.35
10/03/83	17123	1	43	23.70	00.00	03.13
10/01/83	17146	0	44	00.00	09.06	04.44
12/01/83	17171	1	45	00.00	04.52	00.00
01/01/84	17195	1	46	16.11	00.00	00.00
01/30/84	17220	0	47	00.00	08.00	00.00
03/01/84	17246	1	48	08.46	18.07	00.00
04/03/84	17267	0	49	10.06	00.00	16.51
05/01/84	17289	1	50	00.00	00.00	16.96

* Figure obscure

Table 2 (continued)

Date	*Ittila'at* Issue no.	Terrorist Event	Obs. No.	Threat Percept.	Threat Project.	Fractional Strife
05/31/84	17314	0	51	50.41	00.00	03.85
07/02/84	17338	0	52	10.21	32.28	00.00
08/01/84	17363	0	53	00.00	19.56	00.00
09/01/84	17387	1	54	00.00	28.63	14.94
09/29/84	17411	0	55	00.00	05.17	30.87
11/01/84	17439	0	56	18.73	02.44	00.00
11/29/84	17461	1	57	06.21	17.07	08.77
01/01/85	17488	1	58	00.00	22.75	00.00
02/02/85	17515	0	59	06.61	29.55	00.00
03/02/85	17538	1	60	01.64	15.25	05.14
04/06/85	17560	0	61	16.21	32.94	04.85
05/01/85	17581	1	62	00.00	14.51	00.00
06/02/85	17607	2	63	00.00	06.06	00.00
07/01/85	17629	0	64	00.00	00.00	49.30
08/01/85	17654	0	65	08.35	06.59	00.00
09/01/85	17679	2	66	10.12	00.00	00.00
10/01/85	17702	1	67	02.59	00.00	00.00
11/02/85	17729	0	68	00.00	08.51	18.48
12/01/85	17751	0	69	02.49	00.00	00.00
01/01/86	17778	0	70	02.98	02.52	04.20
02/01/86	17804	0	71	00.00	00.00	00.00
03/01/86	17839	0	72	00.00	12.73	00.00
04/05/86	17850	0	73	04.89	40.17	00.00
05/01/86	17872	0	74	01.83	06.44	00.00
06/01/86	17897	0	75	05.78	17.56	00.00
07/02/86	17922	0	76	00.00	03.74	00.00
08/02/86	17946	0	77	00.00	39.99	08.22
09/01/86	17970	0	78	00.00	00.00	04.71
10/01/86	17993	0	79	00.00	19.87	05.63
11/01/86	18018	0	80	00.00	19.87	00.00
12/01/86	18042	0	81	00.00	24.54	00.00
01/01/87	18069	1	82	00.00	02.37	20.29
02/01/87	18095	0	83	00.00	08.74	00.00
03/01/87	18118	0	84	00.00	00.00	00.00
04/04/87	18137	1	85	15.59	15.33	24.00
05/02/87	18160	0	86	14.91	21.68	00.00

Table 2 (continued)

Date	*Ittila'at* Issue no.	Terrorist Event	Obs. No.	Threat Percept.	Threat Project.	Fractional Strife
06/01/87	18185	1	87	00.00	15.15	31.20
07/01/87	18210	0	88	00.00	28.30	12.73
08/01/87	18235	0	89	79.75	07.41	00.00
09/01/87	18261	0	90	00.00	21.93	00.00
10/01/87	18286	0	91	00.00	11.28	10.73
11/01/87	18310	0	92	00.00	05.93	13.49
12/01/87	18335	0	93	00.00	00.00	00.00
01/02/88	18362	1	94	32.43	00.00	00.00
02/01/88	18388	0	95	00.00	00.00	00.00
03/01/88	18412	0	96	03.67	01.73	00.00
04/04/88	18430	0	97	00.00	00.00	17.22
05/01/88	18453	0	98	01.94	22.78	00.00
06/01/88	16478	0	99	00.00	00.00	00.00
07/02/88	18502	0	100	20.09	02.14	00.00
08/01/88	18527	0	101	01.54	00.00	00.00
09/01/88	18552*	0	102	00.00	00.00	06.67
10/01/88	18576	0	103	03.83	00.00	42.80
11/01/88	18600	0	104	00.00	00.00	00.00
11/15/88	18612	0	105	00.00	00.00	00.00
12/15/88	18638	0	106	00.00	00.00	00.00
03/01/89	18700	0	107	22.83	00.00	19.88
03/15/89	18711	0	108	00.00	00.00	50.04
04/03/89	18721	0	109	06.29	00.00	12.73
04/15/89	18731	0	110	06.36	00.00	33.85
07/01/89	18788	0	111	00.00	02.68	01.31
07/31/89	18813	0	112	00.00	00.00	03.76
08/15/89	18824	1	113	08.33	00.00	00.00
09/16/89	18851	0	114	00.00	02.13	07.56
10/15/89	18875	0	115	00.00	04.84	15.51
11/15/89	18900	0	116	01.72	00.00	00.00
12/16/89	18926	0	117	10.83	01.22	04.27
01/15/90	18952	0	118	09.14	05.16	00.00
02/15/90	18976	0	119	04.61	06.67	00.00
03/15/90	18999	0	120	13.78	00.00	08.47

* figure obscure

Notes

1. Alexander, Yonah, "Terrorism, the Media and the Police," *Journal of International Affairs, 32* (Spring/Summer 1978), pp. 101-13.

2. For a discussion of the contagion hypothesis, see Richard P. Y. Li and William R. Thompson, "The Coup Contagion Hypothesis," *Journal of Conflict Resolution, 19* (March 1975), pp. 63-88 and H. L. Nieburg, *Political Violence: The Behavioral Process*, (New York: St. Martin's Press, 1969), p. 30.

3. Scott, John L. *The Deterrence of Terrorism: Terrorist Rationality and Government Signaling*. Unpublished dissertation. University of South Carolina, 1990, pp. 6-9.

. 4. Kelly, Michael J., and Mitchell, Thomas H., "Transnational Terrorism and the Western Elite Press," *Political Communication and Persuasion, 1*:3 (1981), pp. 289-290.

5. Schmid, Alex P., and de Graaf, Janny, *Violence As Communication: Insurgent Terrorism and the Western News Media*, (London and Beverly Hills: SAGE Publications, 1982).

6. Ibid., p. 15.

7. Crenshaw, Martha. "The Logic of Terrorism: Terrorist Behavior as a Product of Strategic Choice," in Walter Reich, ed. *Origins of Terrorism: Psychologies, Ideologies, Theologies, States of Mind.* (Cambridge: Cambridge University Press, 1990), pp. 7-24.

8. Beeman, William O. "Iran's Religious Regime: What Makes It Tick? Will It Ever Run Down?," *Annals of the American Academy of Political and Social Science, 483* (January): 73-84, and also, "Terrorism: Community Based or State Supported," *American-Arab Affairs, 16* (Spring, 1986): 1-8.

9. Cited in "The Political Uses of Terrorism in the Middle East," in *The Politics of Terrorism: Terror as a State and Revolutionary Strategy*, ed. Barry Rubin, (Lanham, Maryland: University Press of America, 1989). pp. 29-65.

10. Burgess, William H. III. "Iranian Special Operations in the Iran-Iraq War: Implications for the United States," *Conflict, 8*, 1 (1988): 22-40.

11. Bernstein, Alvin H. "Iran's Low-Intensity War against the United States," *Orbis, 30*, 1 (1986): 149-167.

12. Hoffman, Bruce. RAND/R-3783-USDP, *Recent Trends and Future Prospects of Iranian Sponsored International Terrorism.* (Santa Monica: Rand Corporation, 1990), see especially pp. 15-19.

13. Jahanpour, Farhang. "Iran I: Wars Among the Heirs," *World Today, 40*, 10 (October 1990): 183-187; Calabrese, John. "Iran II: The Damascus Connection," *World Today, 40*, 10 (October 1990): 188-190.

14. Weinrauch, James. "Iran's Response to U.N. Resolution 598: The Role of Factionalism in the Negotiation Process," *Arab-American Affairs, 31* (Winter 1989-90): 15-28.

15. Akhavi, Shahrough. "Elite Factionalism in the Islamic Republic of Iran," *Middle East Journal, 41*, 2 (Spring 1987): 181-201, see especially pp. 192-194.

16. Schahgaldian, Nikola B. RAND/R-3788-USDP, *The Clerical Establishment in Iran.* (Santa Monica: Rand Corporation, 1989), pp. 83-85.

17. Bill, James A. "Power and Religion in Revolutionary Iran," *Middle East Journal, 36*, 1 (1982): 22-47.

18. Ramazani, Rouhollah K. "Iran's Foreign Policy: Contending Orientations," *Middle East Journal, 43*, 2 (1989): 202-217.

19. Mickolus, Edward F., Todd Sandler, and Jean M. Murdock. *International Terrorism In the 1980s: A Chronology of Events, Volume I, 1980-1983.* (Ames, Iowa: Iowa State University Press, 1989), Vol. II, p. xiii.

20. Gardela, Karen and Bruce Hoffman. RAND/R-4006-RC, *The RAND Chronology of International Terrorism for 1987.* (Santa Monica, CA: Rand Corp., 1990), pp. 1, reproduced here for comparison: "In RAND's continuing research on this subject, terrorism is defined by the nature of the act, not the identity of the perpetrators or the nature of the cause. Terrorism is violence, or the threat of violence, calculated to create an atmosphere of fear and alarm. These acts are designed to coerce others to take actions they would otherwise not take or to refrain from taking actions that they desired to take. All terrorist acts are crimes. Many would also be violations of the rules of war, if a state of war existed. This violence or threat of violence is generally directed against civilian targets. The motives of all terrorists are political, and terrorist actions are usually carried out in a way that will achieve maximum publicity. The perpetrators are members of an organized group, and unlike other criminals, they often claim credit for their acts. Finally terrorist acts are intended to produce effects beyond the immediate physical damage they cause: long-term psychological repercussions on a particular target audience. The fear created by terrorists, for example, may be intended to cause people to exaggerate the strength of the terrorists and the importance of their cause, to provoke governmental overreaction, to discourage dissent, or simply to intimidate—and thereby enforce compliance with their demands."

21. Exceptions to this rule include the case of the hostage-taking and subsequent murder of Lt. Col. William Higgins, a U. S. Marines Corps officer serving with United Nations peace-keeping forces in Lebanon, and the bombing of the U.S. Marines barracks at Beirut Airport on 23 October 1983. As the mission of Lt. Col. Higgins was more of a diplomatic than military nature he was clearly targeted for hostage-taking due to his role as a representative of the U. S. in Lebanon. The method of attack used by the bombers of the U.S. Marine contingent linked it to a pattern of similar attacks on U.S. diplomatic facilities in Lebanon. This attack created a tremendous psychological impact on its ultimate target audience of the U.S. public and so achieved the political objective intended by the sponsors of the attack of forcing the Reagan administration to abandon direct military support of the Lebanese government.

22. Gardela and Hoffman, idem., p. 7, footnote 11.

23. The Mickolus chronologies reproduce much of the material that he and his associates included in the *International Terrorism: Attributes of Terrorist Events* (ITERATE) database they developed on behalf of the United States Central Intelligence Agency. This source is accordingly used for selection of cases from 1980 to 1987. *The RAND Chronology of International Terrorism* is also used to confirm terrorist cases in the period 1980-1987. The RAND Corporation has published parts of this chronology for the years 1986, 1987 and more recently 1988. (See Gardela, Karen and Bruce Hoffman, RAND/R-3890-RC, *The RAND Chronology of International Terrorism for 1986*, Santa Monica, California: Rand Corporation, 1990, and also, Gardela, Karen and Bruce Hoffman, RAND/R-4006-RC, The *RAND Chronology of International Terrorism for 1987*, Santa Monica, California: Rand Corporation, 1991.) Although in 1990 RAND also published the RAND report, *Recent Trends and Future Prospects of Iranian Sponsored International Terrorism*, (RAND/R-3783-USDP), a study of Iranian sponsored international terrorism drawing on its chronology covering the years

1979 to 1988, it had not published the yearly chronologies for the period 1979 to 1985 at that time. (See Hoffman, Bruce, RAND/R-3783-USDP, *Recent Trends and Future Prospects of Iranian Sponsored International Terrorism*, Santa Monica: Rand Corporation, 1990). On request the RAND Corporation supplied this researcher with an abstract from its chronology of international terrorist incidents for the period 1979 to 1988 for which there was some probability of Iranian involvement.In response to an inquiry on 22 December 1992, the author of the RAND study on Iranian sponsored international terrorism, Bruce Hoffman, who is also Associate Director of the Strategy and Doctrine Program of the RAND Corporation, sent this researcher this abstract on 11 February 1992, which was labelled *Abstract From RAND Chronology of International Terrorism Incidents Which May Involve Iranian Perpetrators, 1979-1988.* I wish to thank him and his associate, Ms. Karen Gardela, for their kind efforts and helpfulness in this regard.

24. Hoffman, Bruce. RAND/R-3783-USDP, Recent *Trends and Future Prospects of Iranian Sponsored International Terrorism.* (Santa Monica: Rand Corporation, 1990), (Figure 1., p. 17).

25. That both chronologies each yielded 160 cases is coincidental and does not indicate a perfect one-to-one correspondence between both sets of cases. The Mickolus chronology often lists multiple events under a single incident number. For instance, the ten car-bombings carried out in Kuwait City on 12 December 1983 against U.S., French and Kuwaiti targets were listed under incident number 83121203-10, the "831212" indicating date of event by year, month and day, the "03" indicating the use of car-bombing, and the "-10" indicating that ten such events are counted as one incident. If one counts the separate events subsumed under such hyphenated incident numbers the actual number of events covered by the Mickolus chronology is actually 189 incidents.

26. Gardela, Karen and Bruce Hoffman. RAND/R-4006-RC, *The RAND Chronology of International Terrorism for 1987.* (Santa Monica, California: Rand Corporation, 1990), pp. iii.

27. Mickolus, Edward F., Todd Sandler, and Jean M. Murdock. *International Terrorism In the 1980s: A Chronology of Events, Volume I, 1980-1983.* (Ames, Iowa: Iowa State University Press, 1989), Vol. II, p. xii.

28. The only exception was the kidnapping of Thomas Sutherland which was listed as incident no. 85060902 in the Mickolus chronology but not listed in the *RAND Chronology of International Terrorism Which May Involve Iranian Perpetrators (1979-1988)*, referred to earlier in endnote 3, provided to this researcher. As sufficient independent confirmation of Sutherland's capture by Islamic Jihad existed this event was also been included in Table 1.

29. Holsti, Ole, *Content Analysis for the Social Sciences and Humanities* (Reading, Massachusetts: Addison-Wesley, 1969), p. 601.

30. Holsti, op. cit. p. 116.

31. Krippendorff, Klaus. *Content Analysis: An Introduction to its Methodology* (Beverly Hills: SAGE Publications, 1980), p. 59.

32. Johnson, J., and R. Joslyn. *Political Science Research Methods* (Washington, D.C.: CQ Press, 1986), p. 208.

33. Ole Holsti, ibid.

34. Krippendorff, op. cit., p. 67.

35. The researcher has attempted to select samples for each Persian month corresponding to the 1st or 15th day of the Gregorian calendar months. This has not

always been possible due to missing issues in collections of newspapers published in Iran during the post-revolutionary period. When gaps have appeared in the running record of Ittilaʿāt's publication due to any given day's coinciding with Friday, the weekly rest-day, other holidays, or due to gaps in library collections of Ittilaʿat then the nearest issue following the first or the preceding last day of the previous month is used instead if the following day is unavailable. Although this would permit two days to be sampled from one Gregorian month, e.g. 1 October 1993 and 31 October 1993, because the Persian calendar solar months correspond to the Zodiacal signs rather than the Gregorian demarcation of months this would mean two Persian solar months would be sampled, in this case the days corresponding to 9 Mehr 1372 and 10 Aban 1372.

36. Budd, Richard W., "Attention Score: A Device for Measuring News Play," *Journalism Quarterly, 41* (Spring 1964), pp. 259-62.

37. Holsti, Ole, *Content Analysis for the Social Sciences and Humanities* (Reading, Massachusetts: Addison-Wesley, 1969), p. 137. Each reliability coefficient can in turn be assigned a confidence level depending on the total numbers of judgments used to arrive at the average proportion of agreement. William C. Schutz, provides tables specifying such confidence intervals for coefficients as low as 80 percent and as high as 95 percent in his "Reliability, Ambiguity and Content Analysis," *Psychological Review, 59* (March 1952): 124-126. The Ittilaʿāt coefficient of 90.4 percent with 174 judgements indicated at least 80 percent agreement at a .01 level of confidence.

38. Kassarjian, Harold H. "Content Analysis in Consumer Research," *Journal of Consumer Research, 4* (June, 1977): 14.

39. Barely two months before the October bombings in Beirut the semi-official daily Jumhuri-yi Islami ran an editorial entitled, "Washington Maneuvering Amongst Gun-Powder Kegs," which contained explicit warnings against the U.S. becoming militarily involved in the Lebanese civil war. ("Islamic Republican Party Organ Claims U.S. 'Maneuvering Amongst Gun-Powder Kegs,'" Tehran, *TEHRAN TIMES* in English, 22 August 1983, p. 2, JPRS-84456, p. 136.) This editorial was also published in English translation in the *Tehran Times* which functions also as a semi-official newspaper. Following the bombing of the U.S. Embassy in West Beirut the semi-official daily Ittilaʿat ran an editorial praising the bombing, ("Paper Says U.S. Embassy Burned in 'Flames of the Wrath of Area's Nations,'" Tehran ETTELA'AT in Persian 21 April 1983, pp. 2, 22, JPRS-83560, p. 168.) Although the Iranian government officially denied having any involvement with this incident later on Muhsin Rafiqdust, who was the Minister of the Islamic Revolutionary Guards Corps at the time of the 23 October 1983 bombings, candidly admitted that Iran supplied both the explosives and the direction needed to carry out these bombings. "Interview with Muhsin Rafiqdust," Risalat, 20 July 1987.

40. Thus when the World Trade Center was bombed on 26 February 1993, the second anniversary of Iraq's defeat in Operation Desert Storm, very few people made any immediate inference that this event was in any way a fulfillment of the earlier statements by Iraqi government officials in the period 24-30 December 1990 that had threatened a wave of terrorist attacks against any nation that attacked Iraq. These threats were made in the Iraqi regime's official newspaper *Ath Thawrah* (Baghdad), Editorial, 30 December 1990, which were also relayed by the Iraqi News Agency in its commentary of 30 December 1990.

41. Schmid and Graaf, op. cit., pp. 53-54.

42. Post, Jerrold M., "It's Us Against Them: The Group Dynamics of Political Terrorism," *Terrorism, 10*, 1 (1987), p. 34.

Presidents Held Hostage: The Rhetoric Of Jimmy Carter and Ronald Reagan

Carol Winkler

Abstract: *Hostage crises have had negative effects on two presidents, crippling reelection bids and executive effectiveness. The public never forgave Jimmy Carter, but allowed Ronald Reagan to leave office the most popular president since Franklin Roosevelt. This analysis argues that presidential rhetoric is a key variable which explains the public's discrepant response. Recognizing the constraining effect of presidential rhetoric on future words and actions, this study posits that Carter's early rhetorical choices placed him in an untenable posture with the public, while Reagan's early choices allowed him sufficient flexibility to retain a successful image. The study concludes that Carter's rhetoric heightened the sense of crisis, associated him with repeated failures, intimated that he had no other solutions, and precluded traditional arguments for allaying public concern. Reagan's rhetoric discouraged public scrutiny, preserved argumentative options for diffusing public frustration, and maintained consistency with his promise to bring criminals to justice.*

In modern times, hostage crises have had a disproportionate impact on the foreign and domestic affairs of the United States. Although the actual number of victims has been relatively small, the potential that any American could be seized at any time has raised the public's anxiety far beyond what would be consistent with the actual threat.

Nowhere has the impact of hostage incidents been felt more severely than on the domestic political front. Each of two presidential administrations has suffered significant political blows for its handling of hostage situations. Political commentators blamed the Iranian hostage crisis for the failure of Jimmy Carter's 1980 bid for reelection.[1] More recently, Reagan's approval rating as president dropped more than 20 points, within weeks of the breaking of the Iran-Contra story.[2]

In the face of such adversity, the two presidents emerged differently. Jimmy Carter was unable to regain his credibility with the American public, while Ronald Reagan recovered to leave the office more popular than any president since Franklin Delano Roosevelt.

The most obvious explanation for such a discrepancy would be that Reagan was more effective in resolving hostage crises. But by many standards, the reverse is true. During the Reagan era, more citizens were held hostage,[3] and victims remained in captivity for longer periods of time.[4] Arguably, the hostages even suffered harsher treatment, as hostage takers took the lives of their victims—an extreme never broached during the Carter presidency.

Since the actual handling of hostage crises does not explain the public's reactions to Reagan and Carter, other variables must have been operating. Understanding these variables is critical given that public approval of a president is instrumental to effectiveness while in office and may determine chances for a second term.

This study posits that presidential rhetoric during hostage crises is a key variable in understanding the public's discrepant response to the last two presidents. This analysis argues that the rhetorical choices made early in the Iranian hostage crisis constrained Jimmy Carter into an untenable posture with the American public. Ronald Reagan's early choices, by contrast, allowed him sufficient flexibility to retain a successful image for resolving hostage crises.

The constraining nature of rhetoric on future rhetoric and future actions is well documented. Doris Graber[5] explained that

> the force [of verbal commitments] springs from the notion that it is morally obligatory or politically expedient to abide by publicly expressed positions and implied promises. Besides, abandonment of stated positions is deemed costly because it is apt to entail losses in credibility and prestige which may impair the defaulting parties' political effectiveness.

Statements made during hostage crises are particularly likely to have the force of verbal commitments. The need for public information during hostage situations is high. The innocence of the victims ensures that the public can identify with their fellow Americans suffering the horrors of captivity. Jan Schrieber has noted that hostage takers foster this identification and heighten the horror of their seizures by making their attacks random.[6] The advantage to the hostage takers is obvious: they increase public anxiety to pressure public officials to obtain the hostages' release.

Despite the need for information and reassurance about the hostage crises, the amount of information provided to the public is quite low. Generally classified as a national security matter, presidents are reluctant to make any comment about Americans held hostage. Historically, the period from August 1968 to June 1975 is illustrative. Brian Jenkins and his coauthors recorded that during this time period, actual seizures of American citizens averaged one every five months, while attempts were made every three months.[7] During this same period, the presidents commented publicly on only four incidents.[8]

Even when presidents have discussed hostage incidents with the public, they have limited the information they have divulged. While the amount of detail has varied from president to president, all have refused to speculate about the date of hostage release and to specify what precise actions they were taking to resolve the crises.[9]

When the need for information is great and the amount of information is small, the public is left with little choice but to seek reassurance and understanding from available sources. The president becomes a likely focus of directed attention, because he has access to all the intelligence regarding the crises and the power to make the decisions that will influence the fate of the captive citizens. Jeffrey Simons noted that the president is the most dominant force during hostage crises: "the media alone cannot create or dampen the perception of a national crisis over an act of terrorism. Despite the enormous growth of media influence over the last two decades, presidents still take the lead in molding public opinion."[10]

An examination of the rhetoric of Jimmy Carter and Ronald Reagan illustrates how the rhetorical choices made early in hostage crises have a constraining impact on future rhetoric and future actions. Specifically, the presidents' definitions of the hostage situation and their definitions of the nation's response have implications for their future words and actions.

Definitions of the Hostage Situation

Jimmy Carter and Ronald Reagan used opposing strategies for defining the hostage situations occurring during their administrations. Carter maintained the Iranian hostage crisis was a unique event. As early as November 1979, Carter characterized the holding of embassy personnel as "unprecedented in human history."[11] Later, Carter explained why:

> Well, this is an unprecedented and unique occurrence. Down through history, we have had times when some of our people were captured by terrorists or who were abused, and there have obviously been instances of international kidnapping which occurred for the discomfiture of a people or a government. So far as I know, this is the first time that such an activity has been encouraged by and supported by the government itself, and I don't anticipate this kind of thing recurring.[12]

Ronald Reagan considered all hostage situations during his administration as anything but unique. For him, all hostage takers were terrorists, and all terrorists were criminals. After the TWA hijacking, Reagan referred to the hostage-takers as "assassins" and called for the allies to prevent travel to countries where such "lawlessness [was] rampant."[13] After the *Achille Lauro* incident, he called for extradition of the hostage takers "to a sovereign state that would have the jurisdiction and could prosecute them as the murderers that they [were]."[14] When discussing the hostages in Lebanon, Reagan's rhetoric was more subdued, but he used the label *kidnappers* repeatedly to reinforce the criminal element of the hostage takers' actions.

The opposing strategies of the two Presidents had significant implications as each hostage crisis progressed. By maintaining that the Iranian government's role in the hostage crisis was unique, Carter encouraged the world community to denounce the actions of Iran collectively. The narrow interpretation afforded the international community an opportunity to avoid the traditional question of freedom fighter versus terrorist in the Iranian hostage crisis. Accordingly, on December 4, 1979, the Security Council of the United Nations passed Resolution 457 calling for the release of the hostages, and on December 15, the International Court of Justice at the Hague ruled that Iran should release the hostages and return the diplomatic properties of the United States.

Labeling the crisis unique, however, was not without consequence for the Carter administration. Carter's definition arguably had the inadvertent effect of heightening the sense of crisis in the situation. Stressing the unique aspects of the crisis invited the public to examine the situation closely in order to understand the unique phenomenon that the country faced. Accordingly, the media focused more attention on this incident than on any other hostage situation in the history of this nation—one network counted each of the 444 days of continued confinement. Such focused attention and examination did nothing but lead to increased frustration as effort after effort failed to achieve the release of the hostages.

Besides raising frustrations about the Iranian hostage crisis, Carter's rhetorical stance also precluded traditional avenues for responding to public concern. Facing mounting anxiety about hostage crises, Carter's predecessors had lowered expectations by referring to the length of time required for their predecessors to resolve hostage incidents successfully. When the North Koreans captured the crew of the *Pueblo,* for example, Lyndon Johnson analogized the requisite time for the crew's release to the seven months of negotiations required to obtain the release of the RB-47 pilot in 1960.[15] When Carter took the position that the Iranian hostage crisis was unique, he excluded the relevance of past efforts to resolve similar situations. Consistent with this lead from their President, the public never afforded Carter seven months to achieve the release of the hostages; within four months, a majority of the public disapproved of his handling of the crisis.[16]

The uniqueness of the crisis not only constrained Carter from publicly relying on lessons learned from previous hostage crises, but it also constrained him from arguing that his words and actions would have an impact on future presidents. Relying on the future impact of their rhetoric, other presidents justified not making concessions to terrorists on the grounds that to do so would create a dangerous precedent for future terrorist attacks. Richard Nixon was the first to elaborate on the precedent-setting effect of his rhetoric. At the funeral of Cleo Noel and George Curtis Moore, two hostages who died minutes after a proclamation that the United States would not meet the hostage takers' demands, Nixon explained that "[T]he hostage-takers knew and we knew that in the event we had paid blackmail in this way, it would have saved their lives, but it would have endangered the lives of hundreds of others all over the world, because once the individual, the terrorist, or others, has a demand that is made, that is satisfied, he then is encouraged to try again."[17] Virtually all presidents since Nixon maintained the same position, with Ronald Reagan being the most recent: "If we permit terrorism to succeed anywhere, it will spread like cancer, eating away at civilized societies and sowing fear and chaos everywhere."[18]

By arguing that the Iranian hostage crisis was unique and the likelihood of recurrence low, Carter rhetorically excluded the possibility that his words would have a major precedent-setting effect.

But at the same time, he could not appear to be willing to give in to Iran's demands. The result was that Carter reiterated that making concessions was wrong but justified the position on philosophical rather than pragmatic grounds. In a representative statement of the position, Carter stated, "We've upheld the principles of the Nation. There are some things that I could not do in order to secure the release of the hostages if it means embarrassing our country or apologizing for something which we have not done or bringing our Nation to its knees to beg those terrorists to do what they ought to do under international law and in the realm of human compassion."[19]

Carter's principled stance was difficult to sustain as the crisis continued. Because his rhetoric had forfeited the argument of pragmatic benefits, Carter could not weigh the potential savings of hundreds of future victims against the current suffering of 53 hostages. Instead, he had to rely on the absolutist moral stance of not embarrassing the nation that likely wore thin as the hostages remained in captivity and were the object of continued psychological and physical abuse.

By labeling all hostage takers "criminals," Ronald Reagan broke sharply from the rhetorical stance of Jimmy Carter. Hostage takers in Reagan's rhetoric were far from being unique; they shared the fundamental characteristic of having kidnapped innocent citizens. The public need not examine the peculiarities of each hostage situation. Motivations for the kidnappings were secondary, rendering the terrorists' causes inconsequenpal in the public discussion of the crises.

Reagan's rhetorical choice helped preserve the public image of his administration's interaction with terrorists. If all the hostage takers were criminal and guilty of kidnapping, the United States, by implication, was the innocent victim. The label rhetorically excluded the possibility that the United States might have contributed to the taking of the hostages, either directly through questionable foreign policy initiatives or indirectly through unwise alliances that provoked hostility.

This assumption of the United States' innocence helps explain why the Iran-Contra affair uniquely eroded Reagan's credibility with the American public. Throughout his first six years of office, Reagan appeared invulnerable to major slides in popular approval. But in those same six years, his rhetoric had encouraged the public to assume that all hostage takers were criminals who committed acts which threatened the very foundations of civilized society. Thus, when the United States appeared to be trading arms for hostages, the government no longer seemed committed to bringing criminals to justice. Instead, the administration looked as if it had surrendered to the criminal element, rendering Reagan himself ineffective.

In the last year and a half of his presidency, Reagan was able to restore his public image with reassertions of his unwavering commitment to bringing the hostage takers to justice. Repeatedly, Reagan denied accounts that his administration had sold weapons to those responsible for the kidnappings of American citizens. Instead, he claimed to be dealing with a moderate element of Iran that might be persuasive in obtaining the hostages' release.[20] Reagan's air raid on Libya in April 1986 reinforced the perception that his administration was still committed to punishing those responsible for terrorist attacks.[21]

Despite making Reagan vulnerable to public opposition, his depiction of all hostage takers as members of the same group had positive implications for how the public responded to the length of the hostages' confinement. Unlike Carter, Reagan's stance encouraged the applicability of past instances as a test of presidential performance. If previous presidents had taken a year or longer to resolve hostage crises, fairness would dictate that Reagan not be held responsible for continuing crises. By such a standard, Reagan's handling of the early hostage crises, the TWA and *Achille Lauro* hijackings, was successful because these crises were resolved in a matter of weeks. The hostages in Beirut suffer more protracted confinement, but they still face imprisonments comparable to those in the nation's recent memory.

If all hostage takers are alike, both the past and the future of terrorism are relevant concerns for present day decision making. Never encouraging the constraints that operated on the Carter administration, Reagan had the flexibility to maintain that his responses to current hostage crises would have an impact upon future terrorist acts. Reagan employed the strategy in the TWA crisis when he stated, "We must not yield to the terrorist demands that invite more terrorism."[22] This line of argument encouraged the public to consider the consequences of future suffering and deaths of American citizens before clamoring for a quick resolution to current crises.

Definition of the United States' Response

Ronald Reagan and Jimmy Carter were as different in their responses to hostage takers as in their depictions of the terrorists. Objecting to Gerald Ford's handling of the *Mayaguez* incident,[23] Jimmy Carter insisted that he would exhaust diplomatic and economic options before consideration of a military response against Iran. In an interview with foreign correspondents, Jimmy Carter articulated his policy:

> We do intend to exhaust not only our own diplomatic and economic action . . . but also to exhaust the common effect of concerted action on the part of our allies, which we have requested very clearly both privately and publicly. And following that, we will be required to take additional action which may very well involve military means.[24]

Ronald Reagan's rhetorical stance assured the public that hostage takers would be brought to justice, but did not specify how this would be accomplished. Unlike Carter, Reagan offered no details about when military force would be considered a viable option for responding to terrorism. When questioned by reporters whether he had ruled out the use of a military option during a particular crisis, Reagan refused to comment.[25] His only specification concerned who would be brought to justice. Relying upon an analogy to the court system of the United States, Reagan required proof that a particular nation or individual was guilty before he would require punishment for taking American citizens hostage.[26]

Jimmy Carter's approach aided him with the public in the beginning days of the Iranian hostage crisis. Initially, the strategy embodied the spirit of his campaign promise of "minimum secrecy in government!"[27] Revealing that he planned to exhaust diplomatic and economic options before consideration of military responses exposed not only the conclusions of the executive branch, but its decision-making processes as well. Such an approach drew a sharp contrast to the recent secrecy ever present in the Nixon administration.

Drawing the distinction, however, had devastating consequences for Carter as the Iranian hostage crisis continued. Promising the public that he would exhaust diplomatic and economic avenues placed Carter in the position of justifying that all conceivable options for a diplomatic or economic solution had been attempted. To fulfill his promise, Carter engaged in an unprecedented barrage of presidential rhetoric concerning a hostage crisis, and with each speech, Carter raised the issue that was eroding his approval ratings as president.

Carter's rhetoric not only raised an unpopular issue, but it personally associated him with numerous failed attempts to achieve the hostages' release. Demonstrating that he was exhausting non-military options, Carter publicly ordered economic sanctions to be placed on Iran[28] and personally indicated when he was embarking upon new stages of negotiations.[29] As the public architect of these initiatives, Jimmy Carter failed when the Iranians did not release the hostages.[30]

Rhetorically, Carter's failure was complete when he exhausted all of the options he had outlined to obtain the hostages' release. By April 1980, Carter had admitted that he saw no other diplomatic or economic alternatives. At a news conference, he stated, "if this additional set of sanctions that I've described to you today and the concerted action of our allies is not successful, then the only next step I can see would be some sort of military action, which is the prerogative and the right of the United States under these circumstances."[31] When Carter ordered the rescue mission, his prior rhetoric told the public that they could assume that diplomatic and economic options were exhausted. When the rescue mission failed, no options remained. Approval of his handling of the crisis plummeted,[32] and the public responded by replacing Carter with a president who might have other options for bringing the hostages home.

Ronald Reagan became that president, promising the American public that he would not only bring the hostages home, but also see that the hostage takers would be brought to justice. After labeling the hostage takers criminal, Reagan had an obligation to seek out and punish those responsible for seizures of innocent American citizens. As chief executive, he assumed the responsibility of enforcing the law and removing forces that threatened the foundations of a civilized society.

Reagan reinforced the public perception that he would act to punish terrorists with his criticisms of Jimmy Carter's handling of the Iranian hostage crisis. During the 1980 presidential debates, Reagan called for a congressional investigation into the Iranian hostage crisis to determine if the Carter administration had actually exhausted all options for obtaining the hostages' release. By criticizing Carter for not pursuing all avenues, Reagan implied that he, by contrast, could be trusted to do so.

The TWA crisis offered the first opportunity for Reagan to demonstrate how he would bring the hostage takers to justice. When Reagan failed to apprehend and punish those responsible for the TWA hijacking, he became vulnerable to public attack. News reporters began asking what, if any, differences existed between how he and Carter had attempted to resolve hostage crises.[33]

Reagan responded by using even more confining rhetoric than he had previously. He drew a distinction between the TWA and Iranian hostage crises. He argued that Carter knew who was responsible for holding the embassy personnel in Iran, but that he was unsure of the responsible parties in the TWA hijacking. He told reporters that "you have to be able to pinpoint the enemy. You can't just start shooting without having someone in your gunsights."[34] By drawing this distinction, Reagan implied that he would bring future perpetrators to justice, once he had reliable information concerning who was responsible for the acts.

The *Achille Lauro* incident provided Reagan just such a scenario. Four hijackers, plus two Palestinians allegedly responsible for the incident, were taken into custody following the forced landing at Sigonella Air Base. The United States not only knew who had planned and carried out the hijacking, but also what countries had aided the group during the incident. With his own preconditions for a successful resolution of a hostage crisis in place, Reagan was left with little choice. Needing the prosecution of the hijackers in order to keep his word to the American public, he called for extradition of the criminals to the United States.

The risks Reagan was willing to take to remain consistent with his prior promises to the American public demonstrate the constraining effect of his early rhetorical choices. Primarily, Reagan gambled with U.S.-Egyptian relations. Egyptian President Hosni Mubarak said that the forcing down of an Egyptian airliner was an "act of piracy," and "unheard of under any international law or code."[35] Mubarak claimed that the incident had caused "coolness and strain" in relations between Egypt and the United States and said that it would obstruct the Middle East peace program.[36]

Summary and Conclusions

Initial public responses made by presidents to hostage situations take on the force of verbal commitments with the American public. Delivered during periods of high public anxiety and low public information, presidential rhetoric becomes the natural focus of the public's attention. The president, as the individual equipped with all available information on the hostage situation and the authority to make decisions about its outcome, guides the public's expectations about the crises.

With such focused attention on their verbal pronouncements, presidents are reluctant to abandon their stated positions. The result is that the presidents' rhetoric becomes a framework for their future words and actions during the crisis. In some instances, the words constrain the presidents into an untenable position with the American public. In others, the rhetorical framework suggests opportunities for retaining or recovering public approval.

This analysis suggests that the early rhetorical choices of Jimmy Carter prompted the public to judge him a failure, while the early statements of Ronald Reagan allowed the public to view him as a success. Specifically, how the presidents defined the hostage situations and the United States' subsequent response influence how the public interpreted their handling of hostage crises.

Jimmy Carter's rhetoric contributed to his failure by heightening the public's sense of the crisis and by excluding options for diffusing public concern. In order to remain consistent with his early rhetorical stance, Carter brought the crisis to the public's attention repeatedly. In doing so, Carter became associated with recurrent failures in the diplomatic and economic arenas and ultimately intimated that he had no further alternatives for achieving the hostages' release. With growing disenchantment, Carter's rhetoric precluded traditional presidential arguments used to forestall public judgment. Instead, his rhetoric encouraged the public to carefully scrutinize the unique event that became a major failure of his administration.

By contrast, Ronald Reagan's early rhetorical stance allowed the public perception that he had been successful in dealing with hostage takers. Reagan discouraged public curiosity of hostage crises and governmental responses by treating all hostage takers alike. As long as Reagan maintained the image that his administration was pursuing the criminals vigorously, he remained consistent with his stated promise tc bring the hostage takers to justice. Reagan could credibly argue that terrorists were being punished with references to the imprisonment of the captors of the *Achille Lauro* and the bombing of Libya. Only in the Iran-Contra affair, when the administration blurred its distinction between the criminal acts of the perpetrators and the noble acts of the state, did the former president risk public disfavor.

This analysis is not intended to argue that presidential rhetoric alone explains why Carter failed and Reagan succeeded in the public's eyes. Certainly other factors, such as media coverage and overall credibility of the presidents, contributed to the public's evaluation. When these other factors are considered, however, interactive effects with presidential rhetoric should not be ignored. Differences in media coverage, for example, might be explained by the fact that Carter's rhetoric invited close scrutiny, while Reagan's stance discouraged a detailed examination. Differences in overall approval ratings might have occurred because Reagan made rhetorical choices that did not hamper him severely in his public interactions, while Carter's choices destined him to fail.

Notes

1. See, for example, George Will, "Lessons Unlearned," *Washington Post,* Nov. 6, 1980, *p. A 19.*

2. "Reagan's Job Performance," *The Gallup Report 261* (June *1987): 22.* Reagan's approval rating fell from 63% in July *1986* to 40% in February *1987.*

3. Rett R. Ludwikowski, "Political and Legal Instruments in Supporting and Combatting Terrorism: Current Developments," *Terrorism 11* (1988): 201.

4. The maximum period of confinement under the Carter administration was 444 days. During the Reagan administration, hostages remained in confinement for more than three years. For specific dates of capture, see Martha Ann Overland, "New Approach to Mideast Terrorism," *Editorial Research Reports* 2 (26 Aug. 1988): 437.

5. Doris A. Graber, *Verbal Behavior and Politics* (Urbana, Ill.: University of Illinois Press, 1976), pp. 66-67.

6. Jan Schreiber, *The Ultimate Weapon: Terrorists and World Order* (New York: William Morrow and Co., 1978), p. 39.

7. Brian Jenkins, Janera Johnson, and David Ronfeidt, "Numbered Lives: Some Statistical Observations from 77 International Hostage Episodes," *Conflict 1* (1978): 98.

8. Richard Nixon publicly commented on the capture of Cleo A. Noel and George Moore by the Black September Organization and on the release of John Downey, Richard Fecteau, Robert McCann, Joeseph Patrick McCormack, Hugh F. Redmond, Jr., and John Paul Wagner. Gerald Ford made public statements relating to the capture of the Mayaguez crew and of United States Army Colonel Ernest Morgan.

9. Carol Winkler, "Argumentative Topoi in Presidential Responses to Hostage Situations: Truman to Reagan" (Ph.D. dissertation, University of Maryland, College Park, 1987), pp. 156-167.

10. Jeffrey D. Simons, "Misunderstanding Terrorism," *Foreign Policy* 67 (Summer 1987): 109.

11. Jimmy Carter, "The President's News Conference on November 28, 1979," *Public Papers of the President,* Nov. 28, 1979, p. 2167.

12. Ibid., p. 2168.

13. Ronald Reagan, "The President's News Conference of June 18, 1985," *Weekly Compilation of Presidential Documents* 21 (1985): 806.

14. Ronald Reagan, "Informal Exhange With Reporters," *Weekly Compilation of Presidential Documents* 21 (1985) : 1226.

15. Lyndon Johnson, "The President's News Conference of February 2, 1968," *Public Papers of the President,* Feb. 2, 1968, p. 158.

16. "Presidential Popularity: A 43 Year Review," *The Gallup Public Opinion Index* 182 (Oct./Nov. 1980): 13.

17. Richard Nixon, "Remarks at a Ceremony Honoring Slain Foreign Service Officers," *Public Papers of the Presidents* (1973): 170.

18. Ronald Reagan, "Remarks to Citizens, Chicago Heights, Illinois," *Weekly Compilation of Presidential Documents* 21 (1985): 859.

19. Jimmy Carter, "Remarks and a Questions and Answer Session at a Town Meeting: Merced, California," *Public Papers of the President,* 4 July 1980, p. 13 1.

20. See, for example, Ronald Reagan, "Interview with Foreign Television Journalists," *Weekly Compilation of Presidential Documents* 24 (1988): 633; Ronald Reagan, "Presidential News Conference of June 11, 1987," *Weekly Compilation of Presidential Documents* 23 (1987): 653; and Ronald Reagan, "Interview with White House Correspondents," *Weekly Compilation of Presidential Documents* 23 (1987): 445.

21. Grant Wardlaw, "Terror as an Instrument of Foreign Policy," in *Inside Terrorist Organizations,* ed. David Rapoport (New York: Columbia University Press, 1988), pp.241-42.

22. Ronald Reagan, "Remarks at the Annual Convention of the United States Jaycees," *Weekly Compilation of Presidential Documents* 21 (1985): 817.

23. See interview conducted with Jimmy Carter in Reginald Ross Smith, "A Comparative Case Analysis of Presidential Crisis Decision-Making: The Pueblo, The Mayaguez, and the Iranian Hostage Crisis," (M.A. thesis, Emory University, Atlanta, 1984), 143-44.

24. Jimmy Carter, "Interview with the President, Question and Answer Session with Foreign Correspondents," *Public Papers of the President,* Apr. 21, 1980, p. 670.

25. Ronald Reagan, "Informal Exchange with Reporters," *Weekly Compilation of Presidential Documents* 21 (1985): 802.

26. Reagan, "The President's News Conference of June 18, 1985," 807.

27. Jimmy Carter, *Why Not the Best* (Nashville, TN: Broadman Press, 1975), 169.

28. Jimmy Carter, "Sanctions against Iran," *Public Papers of the President,* Apr. 7, 1980, p. 611.

29. See, for example, Jimmy Carter, "Remarks at a White House Briefing for Members of Congress," *Public Papers of the President,* Jan. 8, 1980, p. 40; and Jimmy

Carter, “Remarks and a Question and Answer Session at the American Society of Newspaper Editors Convention,” *Public Papers of the President,* Apr. 10, 1980, p. 638.

30. Jimmy Carter was unique among modern presidents in his willingness to associate himself with diplomatic and economic avenues of resolving hostage crises. See Winkler, “Argumentative Topoi,” pp. 218-20.

31. Jimmy Carter, “The President’s News Conference of April 17, 1980,” *Public Papers of the President,* Apr. 17, 1980, p. 707.

32. “Presidential Popularity: A 43 Year Review,” p. 13.

33. Reagan, “The President’s News Conference of June 18, 1985,” p. 810.

34. Ibid., p. 807.

35. “Mubarak Denounces Interception of Airliner by the United States as Piracy,” *New York Times,* Oct. 13, 1985, Al.

36. Ibid.

Terrorism and the Print Media: The 1985 TWA Hostage Crisis

Brigitte Nacos
David P. Fan
John T. Young

Abstract: *Terrorists are said to seek the attention of the public, the recognition of their grievances, and even respectability and legitimacy. This paper examines the question, to what extent do the mass media facilitate these goals? Analyzing the coverage of the 1985 TWA hostage crisis by three leading U.S. newspapers, we found that the press facilitated the attention-getting desires of the terrorists very generously. The terrorists were also quite successful in getting their causes and grievances reported, while they had only limited success in gaining coverage that might have helped their efforts to gain respectability and legitimacy.*

On June 14, 1985, TWA flight 847 from Athens to Rome left the Greek capital after a long delay on the ground. When the Boeing 727 was finally airbound, the 104 Americans and 49 other persons aboard seemed relieved. About ten minutes after take-off, two young Lebanese Shi'ites, waving hand grenades and guns, took command of the jetliner, forcing pilot John Testrake to fly to Beirut, to Algiers, again to Beirut, and once more to Algiers, before a final landing on a runway of Beirut airport. During the second stop in Beirut, the gunmen brutally murdered Robert Stethem, a 23-year-old Navy diver, and threw his body onto the tarmac. While releasing the majority of passengers and crew members, the terrorists—in alliance with the Amal militia and its leader Nabih Berri—led 37 of the remaining American hostages to a number of hideaways in Beirut and continued to guard three crew members aboard the TWA jet. After 16 days of high drama, the Americans were freed—with the understanding that the demand of the terrorists was met in that Israel was to release a large group of Shi'ite prisoners.

During the ordeal, the developments surrounding the hijacking and the fate of the hostages dominated the news in the United States. And even before the episode ended, coverage of the incident by the three over-the-air television networks (ABC, CBS, and NBC) and the Cable News Network (CNN) was widely discussed and/or criticized by public officials, political experts, and media critics. After analyzing the way television covered this terrorist incident, one research team suggested that "the Shi'ites [the terrorists and their Amal militia allies] got the networks to carry their political message back to America."[1] It was furthermore concluded that this kind of coverage "might be called terrorvision."[2] Many media critics agreed that the TV networks gave those responsible for the hijacking and their sympathizers an opportunity "to dominate U.S. television."[3] A content analysis of the early evening news broadcasts by the over-the-air networks established that ABC dedicated an average of 68%, CBS 62%, and NBC 63% of their respective air time to the TWA hostage crisis, a finding which led to the conclusion that the extent of the coverage "was staggering."[4] And during a House Foreign Affairs subcommittee hearing about network coverage of the TWA hijacking a few weeks after the incident, Ben Bagdikian pointed out that much of the coverage at issue had been "excessive for strictly self-serving, competitive reasons and in the process [had] . . . obliterated other important news."[5] The panel members encouraged the electronic media to establish voluntary guidelines for reporting on possible future terrorist incidents out of growing concern that TV coverage had at times interfered with American foreign policy principles. According to Zbigniew Brzezinski, "television tends to transform what is essentially a political issue into a personal drama. It prevents the Government from dealing with the situation as a political problem and forces it to think of it as a personal problem."[6]

While much as been said and written about the way television reported the TWA hostage crisis (and similar incidents such as the Iranian hostage crisis), the print press has not been scrutinized in the same fashion. One press critic seemed to speak for many when he remarked that he had "no complaints about print coverage."[7] The focus on television may be rooted in the belief that in the United States more people are informed by television than by the print press. Survey results confirm that Americans watch television more regularly than they read newspapers.[8] Still, 1667 newspapers with a combined circulation of 62.8 million are published daily around the United

States.[9] Given such a large circulation and the assumed influence of leading newspapers on the news judgment of other media organizations, on Washington decision makers and other elites, and on public opinion, the print press ought not be excluded when media coverage of terrorist incidents is studied.

Why Terrorists Want Media Access

Terrorism experts tend to agree that terrorists use the free press of liberal states to publicize their causes, their demands, and their threats. According to Walter Laqueur, "[t]he media are the terrorist's best friend. The terrorist's act by itself is nothing, publicity is all."[10] Yonah Alexander has argued that through the media terrorists seek "attention, recognition, and legitimacy."[11] But are terrorists successful in achieving their three publicity goals? According to Alexander, "there seems to be a close relationship [between media coverage of terrorist acts and public attitudes], at least in terms of greater awareness [on the part of the public]."[12] Characterizing media coverage as the lifeblood of terrorists," John O'Sullivan took this point a step farther: He identified three major goals on the part of terrorists and argues that they manage to realize them by "unwitting media assistance."[13] According to O'Sullivan, the media is of great importance to terrorists for the following reasons: (1) they want to spread fear and anxiety and do so simply by getting the media to cover their terrorist actions: (2) they want their views, their demands, and their philosophies publicized and achieve this by getting the media to broadcast or print what the terrorists' positions are; and (3) they want respectability and legitimacy and tend to gain in this respect by being interviewed and getting media response by holding press conferences. While O'Sullivan sees this "problem of legitimacy" in terrorism coverage in general, he identifies it as especially "acute" in relevant television reports.[14]

This article is based on a study which investigated the suggested connection between media reporting and the advancement of terrorists' goals by examining the coverage of the TWA hostage crisis by three leading U.S. newspapers—*The Washington Post, The New York Times,* and *The Los Angeles Times.* We chose the two East Coast newspapers because they are widely regarded as the most influential American publications, both in domestic and international affairs, while the *Los Angeles Times* was picked as the most influential West

Coast newspaper. Moreover, the contents of these three papers were available through the Nexis data base, enabling us to do a computer-assisted content analysis.

Content Analysis by Computer

American newspapers reported the hijacking of TWA Flight 847 on June 15, 1985, the day after the terrorist drama began, and the release of the hostages in their editions of July 1. Accordingly, we retrieved from the Nexis data base all items that concerned any aspect of the hostage incident and were published by *The Washington Post, The New York Times,* and *The Los Angeles Times* from June 15 to July 1, 1985. We found a total of 629 stories that appeared during the 17 days in the three newspapers.

To test the thesis that terrorists seek attention, recognition, and respectability/legitimacy through the press and achieve the desired coverage to one degree or another, we analyzed the content of the text in a multistep manner using the InfoTrend computer program and its "method of successive filtrations" developed by David P. Fan.[15]

Attention Goal

Every paragraph in the print press (like every second of air time in the electronic media) devoted to the coverage of terrorist incidents assures terrorists attention. Therefore, in the first step, we counted each paragraph in the complete TWA hostage crisis coverage of the three newspapers. The idea behind this is that everything published relating to the hijacking helped the Shi'ite terrorists to get the attention of the American public. Whether the coverage was critical of the hijackers or not does not matter because, as Marc A. Celmer has pointed out, terrorists "are not seeking approval or disapproval for their actions but public awareness."[16] Accordingly, it did not matter whether an article reported that President Reagan had condemned the terrorist act and had warned the hijackers or that the families of hostages were praying for the well-being of their loved ones—everything helped the attention-getting scheme of the terrorists. Table 1 details how much space, in paragraphs, the three newspapers devoted to the complete TWA Crisis coverage during the 17-day period.

Table 1
Complete Coverage of TWA Hijacking From
June 15 to July 1, 1985 (Attention)

	Paragraphs	Stories
Washington Post	4101	191
New York Times	4548	248
Los Angeles Times	3513	190
Total	12,162	629

The number of stories and paragraphs published during the 17-day period reveals the TWA hostage crisis got great play in each of the newspapers, which devoted an average of 11 *(Washington Post* and *Los Angeles Times)* or 14 *(New York Times)* stories a day to this news. Whereas the three television networks dedicated an average of more than 60% of early evening broadcasts to the TWA crisis, we can ask similarly, how extensive was the coverage by the three newspapers proportionately? To get an idea of the volume of coverage, we examined the first sections of the three publications. Just as communications researchers often analyze early evening broadcasts of the television networks only—even though there are nationwide morning news broadcasts and, in the event of fast-breaking developments such as the TWA crisis, frequent network news specials—we took a closer look at the newspaper sections that carry the bulk of the domestic and international news of the day *(The Washington Post* and *The New York Times* mark their first section A; *The Los Angeles Times* calls it part 1). We counted pages in these sections that carried any news items about the hostage crisis and compared the result with the number of all relevant pages in the first news section, excluding only sports, cultural, society, or other nonrelevant news in this context, as well as full-page advertisements. We found that during the 17-day period *The Washington Post* carried TWA crisis news (from full pages to one item concerning the hostage news developments) in an average of 31% of its section A, *The New York Times* in 28% of section A pages, and *The Los Angeles Times* in 23% of pages in its part 1. Looking only at pages that exclusively carried news items about the crisis (i.e., pages with or without partial ads), they still represented a significant amount of all pages in the national/international sections: 18% in *The Washington Post,* 19% in *The New York Times,* and 15% in *The Los Angeles Times.*

Special Attention Goal

We added the subcategory of "special attention" to the three categories offered by Alexander/O'Sullivan to suggest that terrorists might get the special attention of readers (or listeners-viewers of the electronic media) when they are mentioned by name or by characterization. The point here is that each naming or characterization of terrorists magnifies the attention they receive, and this, it can be argued, enhances their ability to spread their message of fear and anxiety. Thus, we also examined only those paragraphs of the text that contained the names or characterizations of the terrorists and their sympathizers, for example, hijacker(s), captor(s), terrorist(s), party of God, and so on. The number of paragraphs likely to assure the terrorist *special* attention was significantly smaller than in the attention category and represented in all three newspapers less than 40% of the complete TWA hostage incident (see Table 2).

During the hostage crisis it was suggested that the press "played into the hands of the hijackers" by keeping news of the drama on the front pages.[17] Indeed, all three newspapers covered the hostage crisis every day on their front pages during the 17-day period. *The Washington Post* carried an average of 3.2 front page stories per day during this period, *The New York Times* 2.8, and *The Los Angeles Times* 2.9. In addition, on most of those days, each of these newspapers published crisis-related photographs on their front *pages—The Washington Post* on 16, *The New York Times* on 15, and *The Los Angeles Times* on 11 of the 17 days. Articles on the front pages of newspapers amount to preferred placement because they are more likely to be read than stories published on inside pages.[18] Such placement also has an agenda-setting function by indicating to readers which of the day's news stories are the most important. In this respect, too, the argument can be made that the print press coverage assured terrorists and their sympathizers special attention.

Recognition Goal

Under the headline "Hijackers Free 64, Set New Deadline," *The Los Angeles Times* reported on its front page on June 16, 1985 that the terrorists "set a new deadline for meeting their principal demand, the release of Arab prisoners." The same story, carrying the dateline

Algiers, contained the following lines: "The hijackers, believed to be Shia Muslims, also pledged to free 10 more passengers if Cyprus turns over to Syrian authorities a prisoner they identified as Araf Erria. . . . The hijackers told the Algiers control tower, 'We are ready to die if our demands are not met'." If one subscribes to the Alexander/O'Sullivan thesis that terrorists want the public to recognize their demands, their reasons, their positions, and their human predicament, then lines like the ones cited seem to indicate the press, just by reporting objectively about a terrorist incident, facilitates this particular goal. The reader of the quoted paragraphs learned of two demands: the release of Arab prisoners by Israel, and the release of a Shi'ite from imprisonment in

Table 2
Paragraphs Mentioning Terrorists or Their Sympathizers by Name or Characterization (Special Attention)

	Number of Paragraphs	Percentage of All Paragraphs About TWA Hostage Crisis
Washington Post	1541	37.6
New York Times	1794	39.4
Los Angeles Times	1203	34.2
Total	4438	36.5

Table 3
Paragraphs Revealing Positions Articulated by Terrorists or Their Sympathizers (Recognition)

	Number of Paragraphs	Percentage of All Paragraphs Published about TWA Crisis
Washington Post	397	9.7
New York Times	413	9.1
Los Angeles Times	344	9.8
Total	1,154	9.5

Cyprus. Furthermore, the reader was informed about the terrorists' willingness to die for their cause, which may well have resulted in the recognition that the hijackers themselves were not in an enviable situation, that they must have serious grievances and strong convictions to do something so dramatic about it. Most reports about the status of the hostage situation contained similar sentences. The following is another example: In a *Washington Post* article, a young Amal member with obvious sympathies for the hijackers was quoted as having said, "If people [in southern Lebanon] are saying they are sorry, they are lying. . . . They think this is the only way to fight Israel—to get America."[20]

To identify only paragraphs which qualify for the recognition category, we excluded all text except for those paragraphs reporting what the terrorists themselves or their sympathizers, such as Amal leaders Nabih Berri and Akef Haidar, said, demanded, announced, threatened, explained, stated, etc. This way, we identified all paragraphs which reported something about the terrorists' positions. The number of paragraphs falling into the "recognition" category was significantly smaller than those in the "special attention" and dramatically smaller than in the "attention" category. In all three newspapers less than 10% of the complete TWA hostage crisis coverage consisted of paragraphs that could be understood as furthering the goal of the terrorists to inform the public through the press of their side of the story (see Table 3).

Respectability/Legitimacy Goal

"Two young gunmen met with journalists at the airport transit lounge after striding from the red and white T.W.A. jet," *The New York Times* reported in a front-page story.[21] Other newspapers covered the airport news conference held by the terrorists responsible for the hijack drama and for the brutal killing of Robert Stethem. If one subscribes to the Alexander/O'Sullivan thesis that terrorists hope to gain respectability and indeed legitimacy through media coverage of news conferences and interviews they themselves or their allies and sympathizers grant, then the report about the gunmen's airport news conference can be understood as an example for achieving one part of that goal.

It was not the hijackers themselves but rather members of the Amal militia, namely its leader Nabih Berri, who initiated most news conferences and responded to most interview requests by journalists during the hostage crisis. In one front-page story, *The Los Angeles Times* reported, for example, "In his press conference, Berri suggested a series of complex maneuvers with the remaining hostages that would meet concerns f their safety while satisfying the hijackers' demands, which he has supported."[22] The three newspapers reported again and again what Berri or other Amal leaders or rank-and-file members said and suggested and demanded during their press conferences and in interviews. Often, the print press referred to television interviews with Berri and others who supported the hijackers. On one occasion, for example, *The New York Times* reported, "Mr. Berri said in an interview with CBS news that he was ready to send the American hostages to Switzerland if the Israelis sent the detainees there, too."[23] Even articles that mentioned the controversy about the television networks' practice to interview sympathizers of the terrorists live and to broadcast press conferences staged by the captors with a number of hostages might well have worked toward the terrorists' goal. As O'Sullivan has explained it: "Even if the terrorist comes off badly [in the coverage], . . . he will achieve his aim by being treated as someone whose contribution to public debate is worthy of attention. He becomes by degree a politician."[24]

Thus, in our final content analysis, we filtered out all paragraphs but those which reported about "terrorists," "hijackers," "Amal," "Berri," etc., being "interviewed," giving a "press conference," "meet[ing]" the media, etc. The text that remained fit the "respectability/legitimacy" category.

As Table 4 demonstrates, only a very small fraction of the complete coverage of the TWA terrorist incident fit this last category—from 1.05% in *The Washington Post* and 1.12% in *The New York Times* to 1.39% in *The Los Angeles Times.* Taken together, the three newspapers referred in only 1.18 % of the space they devoted to the hostage crisis to terrorists or their sympathizers being interviewed or having given news conferences.

Conclusion

The coverage of the TWA hostage crisis was strikingly similar in *The Washington Post, The New York Times,* and *The Los Angeles Times.* Our study leaves no doubt that newspaper coverage of this terrorist incident was very extensive and thus assured the terrorists and their sympathizers a great deal of the attention and, to a lesser degree, the special attention of their target audiences—the American public and the American government. The three newspapers did not dedicate as high a percentage of their major domestic/foreign news sections as did television network news to covering the developments surrounding the hostage drama. In pointing out this difference, however, one must also consider that the time limitations on television news broadcasts are

Table 4
Paragraphs Reporting about Press Conferences or Interviews with Terrorists or Their Sympathizers (Respectability/Legitimacy)

	Number of Paragraphs	Percentage of All Paragraphs Published about TWA Crisis
Washington Post	43	1.05
New York Times	51	1.12
Los Angeles Times	49	1.39
Total	143	1.18

much more severe than are the space restrictions on newspapers. A president of CBS News once had the transcript of one half-hour early evening broadcast set in type to compare its volume with that of a leading newspaper: the transcript text filled less than two columns of a *New York Times* front page.[25]

Even if the networks had devoted their complete news broadcasts in the early evenings during the duration of the TWA crisis to this event, the spoken words of their broadcasts would have filled only a fraction of the column inches newspapers devoted to this topic. Because of its audiovisual effects and its ability to broadcast live, television may well have had a special impact on viewing audiences that newspapers did not have on readers, but that is a consideration apart from the question of how extensively the two types of media covered the TWA episode.

If, as critics have charged, the extent of television coverage in the TWA hostage crisis case was excessive or staggering, newspapers seem to deserve similar criticism. While the newspaper coverage generously facilitated the attention-getting desires of the terrorists, those who committed the TWA hijacking were not quite as successful in getting their demands, their cause, their grievances, and their human predicament covered by the press. We found that the three newspapers contained such information in less than 10% of their crisis coverage paragraphs. This was a significantly smaller percentage than for the attention and special attention categories, but it was still a considerable amount of news that might have advanced the recognition desire.

Terrorists may try to gain respectability and even legitimacy by inviting media coverage that is said to have the potential to influence their target audience in this respect, but our study shows that in the TWA case the hijackers and their allies had only limited success in this area as far as the coverage of the three newspapers was concerned: Little more than 1% of all relevant paragraphs fit this category.

A Washington Post-ABC News poll during the TWA hostage crisis seemed to indicate one change in public opinion: On June 17, 1985, 31% of those polled agreed and 53% disagreed with the statement that "the United States should reduce its ties to Israel in order to lessen the acts of terrorism against us in the Middle East." Five days later, 42% agreed and 41% disagreed with the same statement.[26] While we did not attempt to study in detail the impact of the TWA crisis coverage on public opinion, the recognition that there is a link between media reports and public opinion[27] is, of course, a major reason for the interest in the way television and newspapers cover the news, especially during crises.

Notes

1. Edwin Diamond, "TV and the Hostage Crisis in Perspective. The Coverage Itself: Why It Turned Into 'Terrorvision,'" *TV Guide,* Sept. 21, 1985, p. 10.

2. Ibid., p. 6.

3. "TV: Does It Box in President in a Crisis?" *U.S. News & World Report* (July 15, 1985): 23.

4. William C. Adams, "The Beirut Hostages: ABC and CBS Seize an Opportunity," *Public Opinion* (Aug./Sept. 1985): 45.

5. "Closer look at network coverage of TWA flight 847," *Broadcasting* (Aug. 5, 1985): 60.

6. Neil Hickey, "The Impact On Negotiations—What the Experts Say," *TV Guide,* Sept. 21, 1985, p. 22.

7. "Does TV Help or Hurt?" *Newsweek* (July 1, 1985): 37.

8. Robert S. Erikson, Norman R. Luttbeg, and Kent L. Tedin, *American Public Opinion* (New York: MacMillan Publishing Co., 1988), pp. 219-20.

9. Information provided to authors by the American Newspaper Publishers Organization, in July 1988.

10. Yonah Alexander, "Terrorism, the Media, and the Police," in *Terrorism Threat, Reality, Response,* ed. Robert Kupperman and Darrell Trent (Stanford, Calif.: Hoover Institution Press. 1979), p. 332.

11. Ibid., p. 335.

12. Ibid.

13. John O'Sullivan, "Media Publicity Causes Terrorism," in *Terrorism,* ed. David L. Bender and Bruno Leone (St. Paul, Minn.: Greenhaven Press, 1986), pp. 68-74.

14. Ibid.

15. David P. Fan, *Predictions of Public Opinion from the Mass Media: Computer Content Analysis and Mathematical Modeling* (New York: Greenwood Press, 1988).

16. Marc A. Celmer, *Terrorism, U.S. Strategy, and Reagan Politics* (New York: Greenwood press, 1987), p. 10.

17. Sam Zagoria, "Playing Into Hijackers' Hands," *The Washington Post,* June 26, 1985. p. A22.

18. Leo Bogard. "The Public's Use and Perception of Newspapers," *Public Opinion Quarterly* (Winter 1984): 716-17.

19. "Hijackers Free 64, Set New Deadline," *The Los Angeles Times,* June 16, 1985, p. 1, part 1.

20. Edward Walsh, "Crisis Reflects Shiite Rivalries," *The Washington Post,* June 26, 1985, pp. 1 and A 16.

21. John Kifner, "In Beirut, Hooded Men Tell of Captives' Release," *The New York Times,* July 1, 1985, p. l.

22. Charles P. Wallace, "Berri Frees Ill Hostage, Offers to Move Others, Suggests Western Embassy or Syria for 3rd Party Role," *The Los Angeles Times,* June 27, 1985, p. 1 part 1.

23. Bernard Gwertzman, "U.S. Aides Say Hostage Release Would Free 766 Held in Israel, Formal Link of Steps Bared," *The New York Times,* June 21, 1985, p. 1.

24. O'Sullivan, "Media Publicity Causes Terrorism," p. 73.

25. Austin Ranney, *Channels of Power* (New York: Basic Books, Inc., 1983), p. 46.

26. Barry Sussman, "Poll Finds Rising Sentiment for Distancing U.S. From Israel," *The Washington Post,* June 26, 1985, p. A17.

27. See, for example, Benjamin I. Page, Robert Y. Shapiro, and Glenn R. Dempsey, "What Moves Public Opinion?" *American Political Science Review* 81(1) (March 1987): 23-43.

Political Psychology as a Lens for Viewing Traumatic Events

Cheryl Koopman

Abstract: *A burgeoning area of scientific inquiry uses psychological perspectives to understand traumatic events. This research has led to the identification of psychological symptoms and disorders frequently experienced in response to traumatic events. Many of the events having traumatic effects on large numbers of persons are of interest to political psychologists. Such events include the Holocaust, war, terrorism, captivity, torture, political migration, living as a political refugee, and assassination. Some interpersonal forms of trauma such as rape also may be viewed with a political perspective. Although a number of studies have examined psychological consequences of political events, this area of inquiry is rarely explicitly considered within the domain of political psychology. Adopting an explicitly political psychology perspective on traumatic events may enrich our interdisciplinary understanding of these events and inform the design and evaluation of intervention programs to reduce psychological distress resulting from these events.*

Political Psychology and Traumatic Events

Political psychology may be an important and often underutilized perspective for viewing traumatic events. The term "traumatic events" is being used generally here to refer to any experience, either within or outside of the range of normal experience, which would be expected by most people to be extremely stressful to persons having to endure its effects. Some definitions of the traumatic event identify specific, intense emotions such as horror or helplessness whose occurrence in response to the event identifies its traumatic quality (American Psychiatric Association, 1994). As I will argue further here, the potential value of using political psychology perspectives to gain greater understanding of a traumatic event is derived in part by the potential benefits of using the insights gleaned from this discipline to help prevent or attenuate either the occurrence of the actual traumatic event itself or of the negative psychosocial consequences occurring in its aftermath. Furthermore, the potential value of using this perspective to better understand traumatic events is underscored by the great magnitude and frequency of traumatic events in the world, given that such events seem to be on the increase in the latter twentieth century (Wilkinson, 1983) and continuing in magnitude into the beginning of the twenty-first century. Also, the importance of this perspective is derived from considerable evidence that such events result in devastating consequences for the quality of many individuals' lives and of the social context (Gale & Hauser, 1988; Orstein & Ehrlich, 1991; Schell, 1982; Smoke, 1984).

The relative lack of research-based and other literature applying the perspectives of political psychology to many types of traumatic events may be due to the lack of understanding of how both political and psychological perspectives can be integrated in analyzing and studying these events. For traumatic events which have obvious political causes, psychological perspectives are of less obvious relevance than are political perspectives, although the integration of psychological with political perspectives is gaining in legitimacy. We focus here on psychological effects of political traumatic events, although other types of questions could be addressed in examining the interface of traumatic events with psychological and political perspectives, such as inquiring about the political effects of psychological trauma.

There is a growing political psychological literature on the psychological effects of the Holocaust, both World Wars, Vietnam, the Gulf War, and other international events. For illustration purposes, selective insights that this literature has gleaned will be mentioned here. There are also forms of traumatic events with political causes that affect the populace directly, such as torture and acts of terrorism, that have received relatively less systematic study, although recently there has been increased attention to investigating factors associated with psychological consequences of torture (e.g., Sarraj, Punamaki, Salmi, & Summerfield, 1996). Also, the 1995 bombing of the federal building in Oklahoma City and the 1993 bombing of the World Trade Center in New York City have been subjects of investigation into psychological consequences (e.g., North, Nixon, Shariat, et al., 1999; Ofman, Mastria, & Steinberg, 1995). Furthermore, there are events such as deaths of major political leaders which occur within a political context and have political consequences, whether their causes are viewed as politically-motivated or not, for which there is little literature from a political psychological perspective. Many other traumatic events are probably overlooked by political psychologists because these events do not have obvious political causes, but could be argued to have political as well as psychological dimensions in their prevention and/or palliation, such as natural disasters such as fires and human-made disasters such as chemical waste spills. Finally, there is only a limited literature integrating both political and psychological perspectives to investigate acts of violence against individuals (e.g., rape), probably due to psychological perspectives being of more proximate salience than political perspectives to the actual events. By developing further our understanding of the political psychology of traumatic events, we may identify better strategies for preventing or ameliorating the negative effects of such acts.

Identifying the Questions and Standards for Research

By describing these types of traumatic events in the context of considering them for investigation in political psychology, two major questions arise about the boundaries of political psychology. One question that arises is: "*What kinds of research questions about traumatic events are legitimate for inclusion within the sphere of investigation of political psychology*?" Vertzberger (1997) contributes to this dialogue by identifying six hypotheses from a political psychology perspective that can be tested in the aftermath of collective political trauma, which he examines in the context of the assassination of Israeli Prime Minister Yitzhak Rabin. A second question is: "*What are appropriate standards for evaluating scholarly work using political psychological perspectives to examine traumatic events*?" The answers to these two questions will not be resolved here, but these questions are briefly addressed to signal their importance for future investigations in this area.

Approaches for understanding political events from a psychological perspective include examinations of the psychological consequences and/or psychological causes of political events. Because of the limitations in the research on traumatic events, I will focus this review on using psychological perspectives to understand the consequences of traumatic political events.

Most of the literature specifically focused on the traumatic nature of political events examines the psychological effects occurring during or in the aftermath of an event. There are three related risks in bringing a psychological trauma perspective to bear on understanding political events. First, by describing psychiatric disorders that occur in response to a traumatic event such as to combat stress in war, the individuals most greatly affected can appear to be psychopathological, responsible for their own suffering, and therefore undeserving of others' compassion or help (Becker, 1995). For example, many veterans who served in the Persian Gulf War of 1991 who have experienced symptoms of Gulf War Syndrome complain that these symptoms are being overly attributed to their individual vulnerability to psychological stress rather than to the possibility that they suffer from having been exposed to severe environmental conditions (e.g., toxic chemicals). A second risk of evaluating the negative psychological consequences of an event is that a scientifically complete analysis of the consequences of an event must also recognize the individuals who endured the event yet who do not appear to be negatively affected, as Suedfeld (1997) argues. Thirdly, if the negative psychological consequences of a traumatic event are not adequately described and understood, this may negatively affect decisions concerning palliation of the consequences of the event (e.g., restitution to torture survivors), or of the prevention of such an event in the future (e.g., the decision to use torture to extract political information). With these caveats in mind about examining psychological trauma consequences of political events, I wish to briefly describe the emergence of a growing literature relevant to this topic.

Posttraumatic Stress Disorder

Since early in the twentieth century, it has been observed that many soldiers who serve in war combat develop a pattern of symptoms that are now referred to in the Diagnostic Statistical Manual—Fourth Edition (APA, 1994) as posttraumatic stress disorder (PTSD). This diagnosis has been heavily influenced by its origins in describing combat soldiers for the purposes of being able to help them to complete their tour of duty and to help them to become re-integrated into civilian society after the war. This diagnosis requires the occurrence of a traumatic stressor, such as a combat experience in which lives were lost or threatened, and to which the person reacted with helplessness, fear or horror, and includes frequent experiencing of three kinds of psychological symptoms: re-experiencing of the traumatic event, avoiding reminders of the traumatic event, and hyperarousal/anxiety. Other kinds of symptoms can also be present, such as depression, guilt, and substance abuse, but those are not required for the diagnosis. A particularly important characteristic distinguishing this diagnosis from most others is that it specifies an event to which the person is reacting, an event that anyone might find difficult. For example, in contrast, major depressive disorder and generalized anxiety disorder are two psychiatric diagnoses that do not specify a stressor.

Acute Stress Disorder

Acute stress disorder is another psychiatric disorder of direct relevance for describing the traumatic consequences of political events, also described in the DSM-IV (APA, 1994). This diagnosis is similar to that of PTSD in identifying a traumatic event to which the person reacted with fear, helplessness or horror, and it also requires experience of re-experiencing the traumatic event, avoiding reminders, and hyperarousal/anxiety, but it differs in two fundamental respects: 1) it describes responses occurring in the immediate aftermath of the traumatic event which persist for at least two days within the first month after the traumatic event's occurrence; and 2) it includes a great emphasis on dissociative symptoms, which are not highlighted in the PTSD definition. This diagnosis, only recently recognized in the DSM-IV, developed in response to the findings of empirical studies of a variety of types of traumatic events, natural and human-created, which resulted in a fairly clear pattern of symptoms clustering within affected individuals (reviewed by Koopman, Classen, Cardeña & Spiegel, 1995; Spiegel, Koopman, & Classen, 1994). The relationship of acute stress disorder to PTSD is suggested by several studies. One with a political context, on Vietnam veterans' recall of their combat experiences (Marmar et al., 1994) found that veterans' recall of their dissociative experiences during and immediately following combat stress was strongly predictive of current PTSD, assessed decades later. This relationship was also shown in other studies, including a study using a prospective design of survivors of the Oakland/Berkeley, California firestorm (Koopman, Classen, & Spiegel, 1994).

Acute stress disorder is related to another diagnosis, acute stress reaction, which is included in another diagnostic classification scheme, more widely used in Europe and known as the International Classification of Diseases and Related Health Problems, Tenth Edition (ICD-10). Acute stress reaction is similar to ASD in describing severe psychological symptoms occurring in the immediate aftermath of trauma, but it differs in that its timeframe only includes up to two days following the event.

Both ASD and acute stress reaction may have relevance to understanding psychological reactions during crisis decision-making, because they both describe reactions occurring while the effects of learning about the traumatic event are still unfolding and which may impair the quality of the decision-making. The dissociative symptoms may be particularly responsible, being characterized by a lack of integration of perceptions, identities and/or memories (Spiegel & Cardeña, 1993). Without adequate ability to integrate information contained within perceptions, identities and memories, a decision-maker may miss critical information about the crisis and its possible solutions. It has been estimated that 12-25% of people who are exposed to a disaster display grossly inappropriate behavior (Kinston & Rosser, 1974), and that alcohol use tends to increase in disaster's aftermath (Berah, Jones, & Valent, 1984; Madakasira & O'Brien, 1987). Also, research on the survivors of a fire in Boston (Lindemann, 1944) observed that some people made irrational decisions in the disaster's aftermath, such as about finances. Among prisoners of Nazi concentration camps, failing to conduct a daily inspection of one's body for lice risked a high likelihood of contracting typhus, and it was observed by prisoners that those who seemed to show denial of such dangers of everyday life often died prematurely (Eitinger & Major, 1993).

Additional research findings indicate that acute stress reactions may interfere with safe handling of a crisis. In the research on reactions to the Oakland/Berkeley firestorm (Koopman, Classen & Spiegel, 1996), we found that people who reported greater dissociative symptoms in the aftermath of learning about the firestorm were also significantly more likely to cross police barricades to try to get closer to the firestorm, particularly if their house was being destroyed in the fire, an irrational act from the perspective of the authorities who erected the police barricades. Furthermore, these same persons were significantly more likely to eat as a distraction, to fail to evacuate their home or pack their important possessions if they were in danger of losing their home, and to engage in other activities such as staring at the fire. However, these findings seem to contrast with those of Klingeman and Kupermintz (1994), who found that during the 1991 Gulf War, people who had been held in a sealed room in Israel were able to help other persons and implement safety measures even if they were using blunting methods of coping.

In addition to the importance of ASD in affecting the individual's immediate quality of life, decisions, and actions, ASD is also important because its symptoms are a powerful predictor of those individuals who will develop later PTSD. This has been demonstrated by the results of several recent studies, in a study of Vietnam combat veterans (Marmar et al., 1994), in a study of hospitalized accident survivors (Shalev, Peri, Canetti, & Schreiber, 1996), in our study of employees working in an office building where a lone gunman shot 14 persons (Classen, Koopman, Hales, & Spiegel, 1996), and in our firestorm study (Koopman et al., 1994).

Psychological Consequences of Traumatic Political Events

The literature on psychological responses during and after traumatic political events is uneven, focusing perhaps the most upon the effects of the Jewish Holocaust and on combat experience in war than on other types of political trauma. Even where the most research has been done, there is still a need to learn much more. I will briefly summarize some of the findings of studies on psychological effects of the Holocaust. Then I will even more briefly discuss psychological reactions to other kinds of traumatic political events, including war, torture, being held in captivity, terrorism, becoming a political refugee or migrating due to political trauma, political assassination, and rape. These brief discussions are not intended to comprise a comprehensive overview, but rather to indicate the kinds of conceptualizations and research questions that have been the focus of studies of psychological reactions to traumatic events. Furthermore, these summaries focus on research findings regarding the psychological effects of these kinds of political traumatic events on the general public, rather than on political decision-makers.

Psychological Effects of the Holocaust

There is considerable writing about the experiences of individuals who endured the Holocaust. The Holocaust was a political event that caused immense human suffering and death, suppressing, persecuting, arresting, and executing millions of persons whom the Nazis deemed to obstruct their political agenda, including Jews, gypsies, homosexuals, socialists, persons who abetted these political fugitives, and others. There were also traumatic experiences among the groups of partisans who fought the Nazi regime, whose psychological reactions to this experience have not been scientifically studied (Eitinger & Major, 1993). Studies have been conducted of persons imprisoned in the concentration camps, of persons who had family members taken to the concentration camps, and of persons who went into hiding, so we have considerable knowledge about the psychological effects of these experiences.

Published studies on the effects of the Holocaust generally have a number of conceptual and methodological limitations. They have focused more on the psychological effects than on social effects (Kleber & Brom, 1992). Journalistic accounts have been criticized because most published observations were made by persons not formally trained in scientific methods, although the number of persons making similar observations adds considerably to the credibility of such reports (Kleber & Brom, 1992). The studies of survivors and of their children seldom used random samples of a clearly defined group and also were criticized because they did not include an appropriate comparison group and because their measures were either too impressionistic or used standardized psychological measures which may not have been appropriately sensitive to the specific problems of the survivors (De Graaf, 1975: Kleber & Brom, 1992). Also, studies of psychological effects of the Holocaust and other societal traumatic events are criticized for conceptual limitations, such as using psychopathological terminology to describe the individuals who have endured extreme deprivation and suffering (Becker, 1995), and failing to give adequate recognition to the survivors' resilience in creating new lives for themselves after the Holocaust with so little negative effects considering the magnitude of the trauma undergone (Suedfeld, 1997).

However, despite such methodological and conceptual limitations, a general picture emerges from the research. During the initial weeks in the concentration camps, many people who were not immediately put to death had to face extreme conditions that often included starvation, cold, physical abuse, threat of death, and witnessing the beatings and deaths of others. People facing such conditions often developed what is referred to as the "Mussulman state," in which they became robot-like, mentally impaired, sluggish, and no longer adaptively coped (Helweg-Larsen, Hoffmeyer, Kieler, et al., 1952, cited in Eitinger & Major, 1993 and in Kleber & Brom,

1992), which usually led to their deaths. Suicide of prisoners was observed in the camps, although it is unclear how prevalent it was (Eitinger, 1993). In the early stages of living in the concentration camp, common experiences were hypervigilance, emotional numbing, apathy, selfishness, denial, a preoccupation with food, and depression about losing friends and family (Cohen, 1953; Eitinger & Major, 1993). However, over time, long-term prisoners tended to recognize more fully the reality of their situation and also to become more actively resistant toward the leadership of their concentration camp (Cohen, 1953; Luchterhand, 1971, 1980). Camp prisoners who had held a career in a helping profession, such as priests, physicians, nurses, and social workers, who continued to focus their attention on helping other persons, and other persons who found ways to continue their sense of identities and values seemed to fare the best psychologically (Eitinger, 1964; Kral, 1951). Finding meaning despite the horrendous conditions of living in the camp was an important factor in being able to cope with it (Frankl, 1959). Many prisoners continued to hold onto hope that they would survive and be able to return to their former lives (Eitinger & Major, 1993). Some people behaved aggressively toward other prisoners, although it is not clear how common was the "identification with the aggressor" phenomenon described by Bettelheim (1943), (Eitinger, 1964). Many prisoners derived some sense of control over their daily lives by making small decisions such as scheduling the eating of their tiny portions of food and attending to their personal hygiene (Eitinger & Major, 1993).

After being released from the concentration camps, a pattern of psychological symptoms which became known as (post) concentration camp syndrome (Herman & Thygesen, 1954), KZ syndrome (Bastiaans, 1970, cited in Kleber & Brom, 1992) and survivor syndrome (Niederland, 1961) was described, although psychological research was initiated slowly due to a social climate of denial and other factors (Kleber & Brom, 1992). The psychological symptoms identified by these and other researchers (e.g., Chodoff, 1966; Eitinger, 1964; Hoppe, 1971; Krystal, 1968) included: fear, nightmares and sleep disturbances, recurrent intrusive memories of the traumatic experience, chronic despair, irritability, psychosomatic complaints and reduced psychological resilience, such as problems shown in everyday functioning. The longer the time spent in a Nazi annihilation camp, the greater the severity of sleep disturbance and frequency of nightmares assessed 45 years later (Rosen et al., 1991). Also, a number of psychological themes were identified by Robert J. Lifton in his interviews of Holocaust survivors (1980), including: survivors guilt, "death imprint" (vivid memories of reminders of the deaths of other persons), psychological numbness, a complete reversal of norms and values that the Holocaust manifested, and a search for the meaning of the traumatic events. Furthermore, Keilson (1979, cited in Kleber & Brom, 1992) observed the additional traumatization undergone by concentration camp survivors, which led to their disillusionment of returning to their former neighborhood and realizing that their former home was destroyed or occupied by strangers, that the majority of their family and friends had perished (Eitinger, 1964), that they had permanently lost their home, community, and all of their possessions, and that they could not return to their former lives (Eitinger & Major, 1993). Also, survivors often entered hastily into marriages that they later terminated and threw themselves into their work (Ostwald & Bittner, 1968). Many survivors did not have a chance to fully discuss their experiences with others, partly due to other persons' reluctance to hear about such extreme trauma. Even among survivors who sought psychotherapy, a "conspiracy of silence" often occurred in which the camp experiences were not discussed (Danieli, 1981).

A somewhat unresolved area of research is the extent to which the survivors and their families showed long-lasting negative effects of the Holocaust. Impaired sleep was found to be a problem 45 years after the Holocaust had ended (Rosen, Reynolds, Yeager, Houck, & Hurwitz, 1991). In the long-term, the life circumstances (marital status, income, and health) of Holocaust survivors may be more predictive of their emotional well being than are their experiences in the Holocaust, although when life stress occurs in later life, survivors may become more depressed (Karel, Kahana, & Kahana, 1988). There appear to be transgenerational effects of the Holocaust on the second generation, born to the survivors of the Holocaust (Rose & Garske, 1987; Solomon, Kotler, & Mukulincer, 1988), and there may even be Holocaust effects manifesting in the third generation as well (Sigal, Dinicola, & Buonvion, 1988). Family patterns of child rearing may have been affected, characterized by failure to encourage children's autonomy (Freyberg, 1980; Sigal, Silver, Rakoff & Ellin, 1973) or too little emotional expressiveness (Nadler, Kav-Venaki & Gleitman, 1985). However, other researchers have not confirmed these findings (Leon, Butcher, Kleinman, Goldberg & Almagor, 1981; Rose & Garske, 1987). Notably, the effects of the Holocaust seem to reverberate through sensitizing the children of persons who were affected by the Holocaust to new traumatic events: Zahava Solomon and colleagues

(1988) found that two to three years after their participation in the 1982 Lebanon war, Israelis who were injured in combat had higher rates of PTSD if their parents had been involved in the Nazi Holocaust than did those whose parents had not gone through this earlier traumatic experience.

Even the field of political psychology is affected by the Holocaust in ways that are not normally apparent. At the 1996 meeting of the International Society of Political Psychology (ISPP), members who were survivors of the Holocaust participated in a panel, organized and chaired by Peter Suedfeld, in which participants described their individual life experiences during and subsequent to the Holocaust. In discussing their experiences, participants in this panel identified a number of conceptual links between their personal life experiences and research questions examined in their work as political psychologists, links that often had not been explicitly articulated prior to planning their remarks for this panel.

Military and Civilian Reactions to War

Posttraumatic stress disorder (PTSD) as a psychiatric diagnosis grew from a long history of systematic observations of the psychological difficulties experienced among men who had been involved in military combat (Engel et al., 1993; Grinker & Spiegel, 1945; Solomon, Mikulincer, & Benbenistry, 1989). Military doctrine has long recognized a syndrome of experiences identified as "soldier's heart" in the Civil War, as "shell shock" in World War I, as "war neurosis" or "combat exhaustion" in World War II, most recently identified as "posttraumatic stress disorder" in Vietnam veterans (Kleber & Brom, 1992; Weathers, Litz, & Keane, 1995).

Among a representative sample of 1,600 Vietnam war veterans, 15.2% were found to meet criteria for PTSD (Kulka, Schlenger, Fairbank, et al., 1990), raising the question of how to identify which persons are at greatest risk for developing PTSD if serving in combat. One obvious factor is the intensity of the trauma to which they are exposed. More severe combat exposure (e.g., being injured, seeing others die, engaging in violence) is found to be associated with a greater likelihood of developing PTSD (Sutker, Uddo, Brailey, Vasterling, & Errera, 1994). Although dissociative symptoms are not included in the PTSD diagnosis, experiencing dissociative symptoms at the time of the combat trauma is a significant predictor of which combat veterans develop PTSD (Marmar et al., 1994). This suggests that psychological changes occurring at the time of combat trauma can profoundly interfere with later resolution of the painful emotions associated with the traumatic event. Another predictor of which combat soldiers will develop PTSD is a childhood history of sexual or physical abuse (Bremner, Southwick, Johnson, Yehuda, & Charney, 1993; Engel, Engel, Campbell, McFall, Russo, & Katon, 1993). Also, developing PTSD from participating in a war can result in greater distress when the next one occurs, even if the person is not directly involved in the next war, as found among female Vietnam veterans after the onset of Desert Storm (Wolfe, Brown, & Bucsela, 1992). Research has been mixed in determining whether PTSD is greater among veterans of ethnic minority backgrounds (Ross & Wonders, 1993). PTSD may be greater among veterans of ethnic minority backgrounds because they are more likely to be given military assignments that expose them to more intense forms of combat.

Much of the research on PTSD among combat veterans has been done in the United States, especially focusing on the experiences of veterans who served in the Vietnam War. Combat stress reactions have also been the focus of considerable research in Israel and in West Europe, although this kind of research is lacking on soldiers originating from other geographic areas, such as East Europe and Vietnam (Kleber & Brom, 1992). Zahava Solomon and associates have done a series of studies on Israeli soldiers, such as a study (1986) in which they found that combat stress reactions (CSRs) among soldiers in the 1982 Israel-Lebanon War were associated with greater intensity of combat exposure and less perceived social support from officers. Also, Solomon (1989) found that among combat soldiers serving in the 1982 Lebanon war, stress symptoms declined over a three-year period after the end of the war, with the greatest decline in symptoms reported in the third year.

Another possible psychological effect of war experience is the development of a long-term use of illicit drugs. In examining Vietnam veterans, the amount of combat exposure is significantly related to recent drug use, even after statistically controlling for demographic factors and the use of drugs during service in the Army (Reifman & Windle, 1996).

Research has also examined effects of military conflict on civilians. Even if not physically involved in military conflict, civilians can have very strong fear about their vulnerability to attack. In a study of war-related admissions for hospital emergency care during Gulf War missile attacks of Israel, 78% of those who died were thought to have died from fear itself or from physical injuries attributed to actions stemming from fear, as they had not been physically touched by the war, compared to 22% who had been hit by the missiles or by flying debris (Bleich, Dycian, Koslovsly, Solomon, & Weiner, 1992). Among Israelis who evacuated during the missile strikes, 80% of those assessed a week later met all symptoms criteria for PTSD (Solomon, Laor, Weiler, et al., 1993), suggesting that a majority of persons in the immediate aftermath of encountering such war-related stress may experience symptoms that would be considered pathological if they persist.

Children's reactions to war and military conflict have also been a subject of research. For example, research on the effects of heavy shelling of East Beirut preschool children in 1989 found their later behavioral problems to be greater than a demographically similar "control group" of children in a Lebanese city where there was no shelling (Zahr, 1996). Furthermore, this study found that the children who lived in the area of heavy shelling seemed to be somewhat psychologically protected from the effects of this trauma if they lived in a more positive and functional home environment.

Psychological Reactions to Terrorism, Captivity, and/or Torture

Terrorism is explicitly political, being intended as a tool of persuasion to obtain political ends. Its psychological consequences on the populace are analyzed differentially according to whether persons are directly threatened or victimized by terrorism or by whether they are affected by living within a societal context where its possibility looms. Among persons whose lives are directly touched by acts of terrorism, the psychological consequences of terrorism have been examined in studies focusing on reactions to specific instances. For example, a study by Michelle Slone (2000) found that exposure to television news coverage of terrorism, compared to a control condition, induced greater anxiety in Israeli adults. In another study, 59 Israeli adolescents were examined 17 years after surviving an incident in 1974 in which they were seized and taken hostage in 1974 by armed Palestinians, and in which they also witnessed the killing of 22 other hostages as well as witnessing the wounding of many hostages, or even being wounded themselves (Desivilya, Gal, & Ayalon, 1996). This study found that 17 years after the event, 61% of the survivors were experiencing five or more posttraumatic symptoms within the last month, and the remaining 39% of them were experiencing at least four posttraumatic symptoms, indicating that no one was symptom-free even after years had passed since the event. For example, 68% reported hyperalertness, 61% reported sleep disturbances, and 63% reported intrusive images and thoughts.

Psychological effects of torture and other ill treatment have been examined in a study of Palestinian political prisoners by Sarraj and associates (1996). In 1992-93, the researchers examined the severity of posttraumatic stress symptoms among 550 males from the Gaza Strip who had been imprisoned by the Israelis for political purposes for durations of 6 months to 10 years. Most of the respondents (77%) reported intrusive re-experiencing of the traumatic experiences, such as through dreams and intrusive thoughts; 43% reported hyperarousal; and 34% reported withdrawal from normal activities and numbness. Both the frequency of torture and other forms of ill treatment (e.g., sensory deprivation, physical abuse, witnessing torture) and also the duration of imprisonment were associated with the severity of posttraumatic stress symptoms. Also their experience of further life stress in their lives following release from imprisonment further predicted the severity of their experience of posttraumatic stress symptoms. It is notable that in another study, focusing on torture survivors in Turkey, and comparing them with non-tortured persons, being a political activist seemed to have a protective effect in reducing the traumatic psychological effects of being tortured, perhaps because they held belief systems that gave meaning to the torture (Basoglu, Paker, Ozmen, et al., 1996). Given that no government openly admits that it condones or practices torture (Vesti & Kastrup, 1995), it is challenging to conduct research on the psychological effects of torture. However, given that over 150 countries still use torture and/or inhuman or degrading treatment or punishment by state officials (Amnesty International, 2000), it is imperative to better understand its psychological and social consequences.

Psychological Reactions of Political Refugees/Migrants

Political refugees and migrants have often experienced or had to live with the fear of experiencing the kinds of traumatic stress already discussed—genocide, international or civil war, terrorist acts, being held in captivity and/or tortured. For example, in a sample of Cambodian refugees living in the United States, 48% of the subjects had been physically assaulted and/or raped, 62% had a friend killed when trying to leave Cambodia, and 58% had a family member killed when trying to leave Cambodia (Carlson & Rosser-Hogan, 1991). In addition to having to cope with memories of traumatic events upon leaving their homes, in becoming political refugees/migrants, people have to face a number of additional stressors in giving up their residences, sources of income and sustenance, and social networks. Political refugees have the additional burden of tremendous uncertainty in gauging what their futures hold; also, they have little control over their daily lives. Immigrants to a new country have to cope with a number of new stresses even if they have not migrated as a result of persecution, terror or war (Shuval, 1993). These often include learning a new language and new customs, developing a new social network, and finding employment that requires learning new skills or accepting menial work. Furthermore, their social network in the country that they left must adjust to their departure as well, so two sets of people are affected by the migration. For political refugees, the decision to leave does not reflect personal choices as much as societal forces that mandate leaving to avoid persecution or death. For children and elderly political refugees, there is even less of a sense of choice in the migration than there is for most adults (Shuval, 1993). In the social setting to which people migrate, they are likely to come into contact with its most problematic aspects, such as poverty and xenophobia, adding further to their burden. For those migrants who move for political reasons, memories of traumatic events such as torture, loss of a family member, or a situation in which they feared death or injury may haunt them.

Reactions to Political Assassination

Seasoned journalists have reported fairly severe acute stress reactions in the immediate aftermath of witnessing an execution of a criminal for committing a heinous crime (Freinkel, Koopman, & Spiegel, 1994). Therefore, it is not surprising to find that the public reacts with strong feelings in the immediate aftermath of a major national leader such as Prime Minister Rabin (Vertzberger, 1997). Even a partly fictitious dramatic portrayal of the assassination of President John F. Kennedy shown in the Oliver Stone movie "*JFK*" seems to have at least a temporarily demoralizing effect on its viewers (Butler, Koopman, & Zimbardo, 1995). In a study of reactions to the 1994 assassination of Mexican Presidential Candidate Colosio, we found that about half of the variance in acute stress reactions in the immediate aftermath of the assassination was associated with three variables—perceived impact of the assassination, exposure to a previous, unrelated traumatic event (a gasline explosion two years previously), and to emotional coping (Maldonado, Page, Koopman, Butler, Stein, & Spiegel, in press).

Rape as a Political Form of Trauma

Rape may be conceptualized as a form of trauma with political dimensions, even if not motivated by explicitly political decision-making (Russell, 1975). Sometimes rape is officially or unofficially encouraged in war and civil strife as a political tool, such as has been reported in Bosnia-Herzegovina (Arcel, 2000). Rape in the political context has been overlooked in much of the dialogue about ensuring human rights as a political goal. Only recently has the United States officially adopted the policy of viewing rape in the context of war as a violation of human rights. However, it can be argued that it is legitimate to extend the conceptualization of rape as political to instances outside of the context of decision-making by political leaders (Mezey, 1994). Countries vary considerably in the prevalence of rape. Frequent occurrences of rape may be conceptualized as indications of a societal ideology of gender inequality and male supremacy (Russell, 1975). Rape has striking psychological consequences in its aftermath. Research in the United States found that in the immediate aftermath of rape (mean of 12.6 days post-assault), nearly all (94%) of the women who had been assaulted met criteria for PTSD, which decreased to 65% of the women when assessed at a mean of 35 days post-assault, and to 47% at a mean of 94 days post-assault (Rothbaum, Foa, Riggs, Murdock, & Walsh, 1992). These percentages show how enduring the traumatic impact of a rape can be for many of the victims.

The Need for Further Research

The effects of traumatic political events on individuals need to be more systematically examined. One area for future research is to assess a greater variety of outcomes than has been previously examined, such as examining the effects of political events on traditional and nontraditional indicators of psychological stress, including ASD, PTSD, and also effects on the family (e.g., divorce, child abuse, intimate partner abuse), occupational impairment (unemployment, underemployment, lack of presenteeism), and health (e.g., alcoholism, illness, longevity). Another area in which more research is needed is to more systematically examine the dimensions of the traumatic event and its context to more fully understand the factors that exacerbate or alleviate negative psychosocial and health consequences. Furthermore, research is urgently needed to evaluate the effects of mass media coverage of traumatic political events as well as of community based interventions such as brief psychoeducational crisis intervention and PTSD screening on preventing and attenuating the traumatic effects of political events.

References

American Psychiatric Association. (1994). *Diagnostic and statistical manual of mental disorders* (4th edition). Washington, D.C.: American Psychiatric Association.

Amnesty International. (2000). *Take a step to stamp out torture*. London: Amnesty International Publications.

Arcel, L.T. (2000). Deliberate sexual torture of women in war: The case of Bosnia-Herzegovina. In Shalev, A.Y., Yehuda, R., & McFarlane, A.C. (Eds.), *International handbook of human response to trauma* (pp. 179-193). New York, NY: Kluwer Academic/Plenum Publishers.

Basoglu, M., Paker, M., Ozmen, E., Tasdemir, O., Sahin, D., Ceyhanli, A., Incesu, C., & Sarimurat, N. (1996). Appraisal of self, social environment, and state authority as a possible mediator of posttraumatic stress disorder in tortured political activists. *Journal of Abnormal Psychology*, *105*, 232-236.

Becker, D. (1995). The deficiency of the concept of posttraumatic stress disorder when dealing with victims of human rights violations. In Kleber, R.J., Figley, C.R., & Gersons, B.P.R. (Eds.), *Beyond trauma: Cultural and societal dynamics* (pp.99-109). New York: Plenum Press, 1995.

Belle, D. (Ed.). (1982). *Lives in stress: Women and depression*. Beverly Hills, CA: Sage.

Berah, E.F., Jones, H.L., & Valent, P. (1984). The experience of a mental health team involved in the early phase of a disaster. *Australian and New Zealand Journal of Psychiatry*, *18*, 354-358.

Bleich, A., Dycian, A., Koslovsky, M., Solomon, Z., & Weiner, M. (1992). Psychiatric implications of missile attacks on civilian population. *Journal of the American Medical Association*, 268, 613-615.

Bremner J.D., Southwick S.M., Johnson D.R., Yehuda R., Charney D.S. (1993). Childhood physical abuse and combat-related posttraumatic stress disorder in Vietnam Veterans. *American Journal of Psychiatry*, *150*, 235-239.

Butler, L.D., Koopman, C., & Zimbardo, P.G. (1995). The psychological impact of viewing the film "JFK": Emotions, beliefs, and political behavioral intentions. *Journal of Political Psychology, 16*, 237-57.

Cardeña, E., & Spiegel, D. (1993). Dissociative reactions to the Bay Area earthquake. *American Journal of Psychiatry, 150*, 474-478.

Carlson, E.B., & Rosser-Hogan, R. (1991). Trauma experiences, posttraumatic stress, dissociation, and depression in Cambodian refugees. *American Journal of Psychiatry, 148*, 1548-1551.

Chodoff, P. (1966). Extreme coercive and oppressive forces: Brainwashing and concentration camps. In S. Arieti (Ed.), *American Handbook of Psychiatry*, Vol. III, New York: Basic Books.

Classen, C., Koopman, C., Hales, R., & Spiegel, D. (1996). Acute stress reactions as a predictor of post-traumatic stress symptoms following office building shootings. Unpublished manuscript.

Cleary, P.D. (1987). Gender differences in stress-related disorders. In R.C. Barnet, L. Biener, & G.K. Baruch (Eds.), *Gender and stress.* New York: Free Press.

Cohen, E. A. (1954). *Human Behavior in the concentration camp.* London: Jonathan Cape.

Danieli, Y. (1981). *Therapists' difficulties in treating survivors of the Nazi Holocaust and their children.* Ph.D. dissertation, New York University.

De Graaf, Th. (1975). Pathological patterns of identification in families of survivors of the Holocaust. *Israel Annals of Psychiatry and Related Disciplines, 13* (4), 335-363.

Desivilya, H.S., Gal, R., & Ayalon, O. (1996). Extent of victimization, traumatic stress symptoms, and adjustment of terroristic assault survivors: A long-term follow-up. *Journal of Traumatic Stress, 9*, 881-889.

Eitinger, L. (1964). *Concentration camp survivors in Norway and Israel.* London: Allen and Unwin.

Eitinger, L., & Major, E.F. Stress of the Holocaust. (1993). In Goldberger, L., & Breznitz, S. *Handbook of stress: Theoretical and clinical aspects* (pp. 617-640). New York: Free Press.

Engel, C.C., Jr., Engel, A.L., Campbell, S.J., McFall, M.E., Russo, J., & Katon, W. (1993). Posttraumatic stress disorder symptoms and precombat sexual and physical abuse in Desert Storm veterans. *Journal of Nervous and Mental Disease, 181*, 683-688.

Frankl, V.E. (1959). *From death-camp to existentialism.* Boston, Beacon Press.

Freinkel, A., Koopman, C., & Spiegel, D. (1994). Dissociative symptoms in media execution witness. *American Journal of Psychiatry, 151*, (9), 1335-1339.

Freyberg, J.T. (1980). Difficulties in separation-individuation as experienced by offspring of Nazi Holocaust survivors. *American Journal of Orthopsychiatry, 50*, 87-95.

Gale, R. R., & Hauser, T. (1988). *Final warning: The legacy of Chernobyl.* New York: Warner Books.

Grinker, R. R., & Spiegel, J. P. (1945). *Men under stress.* Philadelphia: Blakiston.

Hillman, R.G. (1981). The psychopathology of being held hostage. *American Journal of Psychiatry, 138*, 1193-1197.

Hoppe, K.D. (1971). The aftermath of Nazi persecution reflected in recent psychiatric literature. In N. Krystal & W.G. Niederland (Eds.), *Aftereffects in individuals and communities* (pp. 169-205). Boston: Little, Brown and Company.

Kinston, W., & Rosser, R. (1974). Disaster: Effects on the mental and physical state. *Journal of Psychosomatic Research, 18b*, 437-456.

Kleber, R.J., & Brom, D., with Defares, P.B. (1992). *Coping with trauma: Theory, prevention, and treatment.* Amsterdam, the Netherlands: Swets en Zeitlinger, Publishers.

Klingeman, A., & Kupermintz, H. (1994). Response style and self-control under Scud Missile attacks: The case of the sealed room situation during the 1991 Gulf War. *Journal of Traumatic Stress, 7*, (3), 415-426.

Koopman, C., Classen, C., Cardena, E., & Spiegel, D. (1995). When disaster strikes, acute stress disorder may follow. *Journal of Traumatic Stress, 8*, 1, 29-46.

Koopman, C., Classen, C. & Spiegel, D. (1994). Predictors of posttraumatic stress symptoms among survivors of the Oakland/Berkeley, Calif. firestorm, *American Journal of Psychiatry, 151*, 6, 888-894.

Koopman, C, Classen, C., & Spiegel, D. (1996). Dissociative responses in the immediate aftermath of the Oakland/Berkeley firestorm. *Journal of Traumatic Stress, 9*, 3, 521-540.

Kral, V.A. (1951). Psychiatric observation under severe chronic stress. *American Journal of Psychiatry, 108*, 185-192.

Krystal, H. (Ed.) (1968). *Massive psychic trauma.* New York: International Universities Press.

Kulka, R.A., Schlenger, W.E., Fairbank, J.A., Hough, R.L., Jordan, B.K., Marmar, C.R., & Weiss, D.S. (1990). *Trauma and the Vietnam War generation: Report of findings from the National Vietnam Veterans Readjustment Study.* New York: Brunner/Mazel.

Leon, G.R., Butcher, J.N., Kleinman, M., Goldberg, A., & Almagor, M. (1981). Survivors of the holocaust and their children: Current status and adjustment. *Journal of Personality and Social Psychology, 41*, 503-516.

Lifton, R.J. (1980). The concept of the survivor. In J.E. Dimsdale (Ed.), *Survivors, victims, and perpetrators: Essays on the Nazi Holocaust* (pp. 113-126). Washington, D.C.: Hemisphere.

Lindemann, E. (1944). Symptomatology and management of acute grief. *American Journal of Psychiatry, 101*, 141-148.

Luchterhand, E.G. (1971). Sociological approaches to massive stress in natural and man-made disasters. In H. Krystal & W.G. Niederland (Eds.), *Psychic traumatization: Aftereffects in individuals and communities* (pp. 29-55). Boston: Little, Brown and Company.

Luchterhand, E.G., (1980). Social behavior of concentration camp prisoners: Continuities and discontinuities with pre- and postcamp life. In J.E. Dimsdale (Ed.), *Survivors, victims, and perpetrators: Essays on the Nazi Holocaust* (pp. 259-284). Washington, D.C.: Hemisphere.

Madakasira, S., & O'Brien, K. (1987). Acute posttraumatic stress disorder in victims of a natural disaster. *Journal of Nervous and Mental Disease, 174*, 286-290.

Maldonado, J., Page, K., Koopman, C., Butler, L.D., Stein, H., & Spiegel, D. (in press). Acute stress reactions following the assassination of Mexican Presidential Candidate Colosio. *Journal of Traumatic Stress.*

Marmar, C.R., Weiss, D.S., Schlenger, W.E., Fairbank, J.A., Jordan, B.K., Kulka, R.A., & Hough, R.L. (1994). Peritraumatic dissociation and posttraumatic stress in male Vietnam theater veterans. *American Journal of Psychiatry, 151*, 902-907.

Mezey, G. (1994). Rape in war. *Journal of Forensic Psychiatry, 5*, 583-598.

Nadler, A., Kav-Venaki, s., & Gleitman, R. (1985). Transgenerational effects of the Holocaust: Externalization of aggression in second generation Holocaust survivors. *Journal of Consulting and Clinical Psychology, 53*, 53, 365-369.

Niederland, W.G. (1961). The problem of the survivor. *Journal of Hillside Hospital, 10*, 233-247.

Nolen-Hoeksema, S., & Morrow, J. (1991). A prospective study of depression and posttraumatic stress symptoms after a natural disaster: The 1989 Loma Prieta Earthquake. *Journal of Personality and Social Psychology, 61*, (1), 115-121.

North, C.S., Nixon, S.J., Shariat, S., Mallonee, S., McMillen, J.C., Spitznagel, E.L., & Smith, E.M. (1999). Psychiatric disorders among survivors of the Oklahoma City bombing. *JAMA: Journal of the American Medical Association*, 755-762.

Ofman, P.S., Mastria, M.A., & Steinberg, J. (1995). Mental health response to terrorism: The World Trade Center bombing. *Journal of Mental Health Counseling: Special Issue: Disasters and Crises: A Mental Health Counseling Perspective, 17*, 312-320.

Ostwald, P., & Bittner, E. (1968). Life adjustment after severe persecution. *American Journal of Psychiatry, 124*, 1393-1400.

Reifman, A. & Windle, M. (1996). Vietnam combat exposure and recent drug use: A national study. *Journal of Traumatic Stress, 9*, 557-568.

Rose, S.L., & Garske, J. (1987). Family environment, adjustment and coping among children of Holocaust survivors: A comparative investigation. *American Journal of Orthopsychiatry, 57*, 3, 332-344.

Rosen, J., Reynolds, C.F., Yeager, A.L., Houch, P.R., & Hurwitz, L.F. (1991). Sleep disturbances in survivors of the nazi Holocaust. *American Journal of Psychiatry, 148*, 62-66.

Ross, M.C., Wonders, J. (1993). An exploration of the characteristics of post-traumatic stress disorder in reserve forces deployed during Desert Storm. *Archives of Psychiatric Nursing, 7*, 265-269.

Rothbaum, B., Foa, E., Riggs, D., Murdock, T., Walsh, W. (1992). A prospective examination of post-traumatic stress disorder in rape victims. *Journal of Traumatic Stress, 5*, 455-475

Russell, D.E.H. (1975). *The politics of rape*. New York: Stein & Day.

Sarraj, E., Punamaki, R., Salmi, S., Summerfield, D. (1996). Experiences of torture and ill-treatment and posttraumatic stress disorder symptoms among Palestinian political prisoners. *Journal of Traumatic Stress, 9*, 595-606.

Shuval, J.T. (1993). Migration and stress. In Goldberger, I., & Breznitz, S. (Eds.), *Handbook of stress: Theoretical and clinical aspects* (pp. 641-657). New York: The Free Press.

Sigal, J.J., Silver, D., Rakoff, V., & Ellin, B. (1973). Some second generation effects of survival of the Nazi persecution. *American Journal of Orthopsychiatry, 43*, 320-327.

Sigal, J.J., Dinicola, V.F., & Buonvion, M. (1988). Grandchildren of survivors: Can negative effects of prolonged exposure to excessive stress be observed two generations later? *Canada Journal of Psychiatry, 33*, 207-212.

Slone, M. (2000). Responses to media coverage of terrorism. *Journal of Conflict Resolution, 44*, 508-522.

Smoke, R. (1984). *National security and the nuclear dilemma*. Menlo Park, CA: Addison-Wesley.

Solomon, Z., Laor, N., Weiler, D., Muller, U.F., Hadar, O., Waysman, M., Koslowsky, M., Ben-Yakar, M., & Bleich, A. (1993). The psychological impact of the Gulf War: A study of acute stress in Israeli evacuees. *Archives of General Psychiatry, 50*, 320-321.

Solomon, Z., Kotler, M., & Mikulincer, M. (1988). Combat-related posttraumatic stress disorder among second-generation holocaust survivors: Preliminary findings. *American Journal of Psychiatry, 145*, 7, 865-868.

Solomon, Z., Mikulincer, M., & Benbenistry, R. (1989). Combat stress reaction: Clinical manifestations and correlates. *Military Psychology, 1*, 35-47.

Solomon, Z., Mikulincer, M., & Hobfoll, S.E. (1986). Effects of social support and battle intensity on loneliness and breakdown during combat. *Journal of Personality and Social Psychology, 51*, 1269-1276.

Spiegel, D., Koopman, C., & Classen, C. (1994). Acute stress disorder and dissociation. *Australian Journal of Clinical and Experimental Hypnosis, 22*, (1), 11-23.

Suedfeld, P. (1997). Reactions to societal trauma: Distress and/or eustress. *Political Psychology, 18*, 849-861.

Sutker, P.B., Uddo, M., Brailey, K., Vasterling, J.J., Errera, P. (1994). Psychopathology in war-zone deployed and nondeployed Operation Desert Storm troops assigned graves registration duties. *Journal of Abnormal Psychology, 103*, 383-390.

Vertzberger, Y.Y.I. (1997). The antinomies of collective political trauma: A pre-theory. *Political Psychology, 18*, 863-876.

Vesti, P., & Kastrup, M. (1995). Refugee status, torture, and adjustment. In Freedy, J.R., & Hobfoll, S.E. (Eds.), *Traumatic stress: From theory to practice* (pp. 213-235). New York: Plenum Press.

Weathers, F.W., Litz, & Keane, T. (1995). Military trauma. In Freedy, J.R., & Hobfoll, S.E., (Eds.), *Traumatic stress: From theory to practice* (pp. 103-128). New York: Plenum Press.

Wilkinson, C.B. (1983). Aftermath of a disaster: The collapse of the Hyatt Regency Hotel skywalks. *American Journal of Psychiatry, 140*, 1134-1139.

Wolfe, J., Brown, P.J., Bucsela, M.L. (1992). Symptom responses of female Vietnam veterans to Operation Desert Storm. *American Journal of Psychiatry, 9*, 676-679.

Zahr, L.K. (1996). Effects of war on the behavior of Lebanese preschool children: Influence of home environment and family functioning. *American Journal of Orthopsychiatry, 66*, 401-408.

Author Notes

This paper grew out of discussions at two roundtables on the political psychology of trauma at the 1996 meeting of the International Society of Political Psychology held in Vancouver.

Acute Psychiatric Responses to the Explosion at the World Trade Center: A Case Series

JoAnn Difede, William J. Apfeldorf, Marylene Cloitre, Lisa A. Spielman, Samuel W. Perry

Abstract: *This article describes the acute psychiatric responses of nine survivors (aged 25-45 years) of the 1993 terrorist explosion at the World Trade Center in New York City. The subjects completed a structural clinical interview, the SCID. Most of this self-referred sample had posttraumatic stress disorder (PTSD). The cluster of symptoms that comprise a PTSD diagnosis did not seem to capture the subjective experience of these trauma survivors. The four subjects who had a past psychiatric history experienced a recrudescence of their symptoms. It is suggested that acute interventions for trauma survivors might be an examination of how trauma survivors' fundamental beliefs about themselves, the world, and others have been affected by the event to effectively integrate the experience and obtain symptom relief.*

On February 26, 1993, a bomb exploded in the underground parking lot at the World Trade Center (WTC). This was one of the most serious terrorist attacks to occur in the United States. Of the approximately fifty-five thousand people who occupied offices in the WTC, an estimated thousand people were trapped for up to 9 hours. Six people were killed and approximately 700 people suffered smoke inhalation and minor injuries.

The explosion at the WTC highlighted how little is known about the acute mental health effects of terrorism. Few studies have specifically addressed the natural history of PTSD and comorbid disorders following terrorism; thus, there is little information available on who is vulnerable and how the effects will appear (Abenhaim et al., 1992; Bell et al., 1988; Curran et al., 1990; Loughrey et al., 1988; Shalev, 1992).

The purpose of this report is to describe acute psychiatric responses to the explosion at the WTC. All those interviewed were referred for evaluation at our Anxiety Disorders Clinic through a referral network organized by the Office of the New York City Commissioner of Mental Health. Patients were evaluated with a structured clinical interview, the SCID (Spitzer and Williams, 1985; Williams et al., 1992) at 1 month following the incident and again 1 year later, if available.

Case summaries are provided below with the intent of providing information that may be useful to those who treat and study the survivors of future incidents.

Participant 1 was a 33-year-old single white woman with no psychiatric history. As a result of the explosion, she had multiple fractures that required extensive physical therapy. She was diagnosed with PTSD and reported a heightened sense of vulnerability, helplessness, and difficulty sleeping as her chief complaints. She was very angry that anyone would try to harm her and had begun to doubt the trustworthiness of others. She acknowledged that she believed in a just world, stating that she felt that if she was good, nothing bad would happen to her. However, the bombing led her to begin reexamining her "assumptions about life." She no longer found her work as a successful executive meaningful and questioned if she wanted to continue along her career path. She was also in a relationship, of several years duration, that she had begun to question. Six months after the explosion, she received a 16-week cognitive-behavioral intervention.

At follow-up, she did not have PTSD. However, she had quit her job, broken up with her boyfriend, and moved from the New York City area to "start her life over again." She contacted us almost 3 years after the incident to indicate that she had married, resumed her career in a related industry, but at a "slower pace," and was "doing very well."

Participant 2 was a 29-year-old married Hispanic woman with no prior psychiatric history. Two first-degree relatives who also worked at the WTC were injured during the explosion; one of whom died subsequently from a health problem that may have been exacerbated by smoke inhalation from the explosion. She received a diagnosis of PTSD and also reported a heightened sense of vulnerability, fear, and helplessness as her chief complaints. She, too, reported being very angry and bewildered that anyone would try to harm her because she had never done anything bad. She acknowledged feeling vulnerable and being more aware of her mortality, stating that "you hear about bad things happening, but you never think it's going to be you." At follow-up, she was diagnosed with a generalized anxiety disorder. Although she was given a referral for treatment at her initial evaluation, she did not seek treatment until after her mother died, a year later. She received a 24-week course of cognitive behavioral treatment for her GAD and PTSD. She, too, had moved from the New York metropolitan area, following her treatment, to "start over."

Participant 3 was a 30-year-old single man with no prior psychiatric history who had been active in rescuing others from the building once he himself had escaped. He received medical treatment for smoke inhalation. His stated reason for coming to the clinic was to see if he could be of any help to us because he knew we were interested in how people were coping with the incident. He reported feeling aimless since his involvement in the rescue effort and had fantasies of rescuing others after imagined disasters, but he did not feel afraid or vulnerable. He reported a history of unsatisfying relationships with women but expressed the desire to "settle down." He had no Axis I diagnosis. He was apprized of how psychotherapy might help him sort out his relationship problems but rebuffed the suggestion. At follow-up, he still worked at the WTC and had been in another failed relationship. He did not have an Axis I diagnosis. He again dismissed the suggestion of psychotherapy to address his acknowledged problems in intimate relationships.

Participant 4 was a 38-year-old married white woman with a history of panic disorder. She presented with an exacerbation of these symptoms as well as PTSD. Her chief concern was her panic symptoms. She did not report a sense of vulnerability or helplessness as among her principal concerns. She reported that her panic symptoms, which had been in remission for about 1 year, began the day after the bombing. Although she noted that she had had more panic attacks at work in the WTC than at other locations, she did not connect it to the explosion. At follow-up, she had pursued both psychotherapeutic and pharmacologic treatment. Upon reevaluation with the SCID, she no longer had panic disorder or PTSD. She had separated from her husband. However, about 2 and 1/2 years after the event, she contacted us asking for a referral, stating that her panic attacks had returned and that she had difficulty leaving her home. She had recently quit her job, of several years, at the WTC without having secured other employment, because she had begun to perceive a connection between her multiple somatic complaints and her fear of another terrorist incident. When she sought the consultation, she was in the process of making plans to move out of state so that she could be closer to her family who had offered financial support until she could "get her feet back on the ground."

Participant 5 was a single white woman with a history of major depression. She presented with major depression as her primary problem, although she, too, received a diagnosis of PTSD. The theme of her interview was a revocation of the sense of isolation and lack of support she felt from her family dating back to the death of one of her parents, 20 years earlier, during her adolescence. She reported that she had felt more support from a stranger than from her family following the WTC bombing and that this realization seemed to evoke a heightened sense of loneliness and isolation, conflicts with her family, and memories of the loss of her parent. At follow-up, she had been in treatment for almost 1 year. Although her depression and PTSD had improved with antidepressants and psychotherapy, she experienced a transient reemergence of her PTSD symptoms at the 1-year anniversary of the explosion.

Participant 6 was a 29-year-old married Hispanic woman with one child. She had a history of major depression and PTSD (secondary to childhood sexual abuse) but had never received psychiatric treatment. She presented with major depression as her primary problem but was also diagnosed with PTSD. She reported feeling isolated because her husband did not understand her experience at the WTC and seemed unconcerned about its effect on her. Additionally, she had a reemergence of flashbacks and intrusive images of her childhood sexual abuse. Follow-up information was not available.

Participant 7 was a 25-year-old single white college educated man with no prior psychiatric history who experienced smoke inhalation from the explosion. He was diagnosed with PTSD and generalized anxiety disorder. His chief complaints were of difficulty sleeping and nightmares where he would wake up to images of the explosion. He, too, believed that others did not understand his experience and minimized the impact it had on him because he did not appear injured. Follow-up information was not available.

Participant 8 was a 32-year-old single black woman who lived with her teenage daughter. She had no prior psychiatric history. Her primary concern was the fear she experienced in anticipation of returning to work at the WTC. She reported that she was unable to sleep, would lie awake thinking about returning to the WTC building, and that she had started to have two to three alcoholic drinks per night to fall asleep. She also reported vivid nightmares and a sense of isolation as among her primary problems. She was diagnosed with PTSD. Follow-up information was not available.

Participant 9 was a 45-year-old single black man who had served in the Vietnam War. He had a history of PTSD secondary to the Vietnam war and of major depression. His chief complaints were of feeling insecure, isolated, and jumpy. Additionally, he began to have intrusive images of his war experiences. He was diagnosed with PTSD and major depression. Follow-up information was not available.

Discussion

Not surprisingly, most of our small self-referred sample had PTSD. Our results are consistent with those of other studies of terrorism (Abenhaim et al., 1992; Bell et al., 1988; Curran et al., 1990; Loughrey et al., 1988; Shalev, 1992). Although no conclusions can be drawn about rates of acute psychiatric disorders following terrorism since our sample was small, self-referred, and treatment-seeking, a few observations are noteworthy.

First, the cluster of symptoms that comprise a PTSD diagnosis did not seem to capture the subjective experience of these trauma survivors. Patients reported that their beliefs about themselves and the world had been shattered; although most reported unbidden vivid sensory images of their trauma (e.g., intrusive symptoms), these symptoms did not seem to be their primary source of distress. The participants seemed most distressed that their fundamental beliefs, regarding themselves (invulnerability, immortality), the world (predictability, controllability, and safety), and others (trust, safety, isolation), that had shaped their lives had been disconfirmed. Most notably those interviewed reported that their belief in their invulnerability and immortality had been destroyed and that their lives felt out of control. They also reported that the world did not seem safe and that others no longer seemed trustworthy. Many were angry that their notions of a just world had been violated. This seemed to be particularly true for those with a strict religious upbringing

Cognitive theories of PTSD suggest that exposure to information during a trauma that is contradictory to one's fundamental beliefs may be associated with the development of PTSD symptoms

(McCann et al., 1988). Thus, a cognitive framework may be of heuristic value in explaining the relationship between these terrorist survivor's subjective experience and PTSD symptoms. The cognitive content elicited was consistent with five areas of functioning that are reportedly disrupted by victimization: safety, trust, power, esteem, and intimacy (McCann et al., 1988).

The reports of our patients also suggest that the phenomenology of PTSD may be organized along the lines of Yalom's existential themes (Yalom, 1981) of death, freedom, isolation, and meaninglessness, as Speigel (1988) has suggested. Three people moved from the NYC area directly attributing the decision to their experience, expressing a need to "start over again." All reported that others did not understand the profound impact that their experience at the WTC had had on them. They consequently felt isolated from their social networks at a time when support was crucial to their adaptation. Concerns about death were frequently raised, leading some to question the course that their lives had been on before their trauma.

The four people who had a past psychiatric history experienced a recrudescence of their symptoms. For example, a woman with a history of panic disorder presented with an exacerbation of these symptoms as her primary problem. Although also diagnosed with PTSD, her chief concern was her panic symptoms. While all the participants touched on existential issues, those with a prior history emphasized themes consistent with their prior psychiatric problems. The individual who had lost a parent during childhood presented loneliness and disconnection from her family. A woman with a history of childhood sexual abuse (prior PTSD and major depression) also presented with loneliness and interpersonal conflict with her husband. Additionally, both patients with a history of PTSD experienced a reemergence of intrusive images from their earlier traumas. It is noteworthy that their experience at the WTC evoked reexperiencing symptoms from previous traumas whose specific characteristics had little in common with the WTC bombing. Our experience suggests that a thorough psychiatric history should be taken even during the acute posttraumatic phase, when the exigencies of the trauma aftermath might dictate otherwise, to facilitate identification of those who may develop problems other than PTSD.

Our experience, conducting comprehensive interviews with this small group of trauma survivors, suggests that acute interventions might be guided by an examination of how trauma survivors' fundamental beliefs about themselves, the world, and others have been affected by the event to effectively integrate the experience and obtain symptom relief.

Acknowledgments

The authors thank Marlin R. Mattson, M.D. and Isaac Monserrate, ACSW for their assistance.

References

Abenhaim L, Dab W, Salmi LR (1992) Study of civilian victims of terrorist attacks (France 1982-1987). *J Clin Epidemiol 45*(2):103-109.

Bell P, Kee M, Loughrey GC, Roddy RJ, Curran PS (1988) Posttraumatic stress in Northern Ireland. *Acta Psychiatr Scand 77*: 166-169.

Curran PS (1988) Psychiatric aspects of terrorist violence: Northern Ireland 1969-1987. *Br J Psychiatry 153*: 470-475.

Curran PS, Bell P, Murray A, Loughrey G, Roddy R, Rocke LG (1990) Psychological consequences of the Enniskillen bombing. *Br J Psychiatry 156*: 479-482.

Loughrey GC, Bell P, Kee M, Roddy RJ, Curran PS (1988) Posttraumatic stress disorder and civil violence in Northern Ireland. *Br J Psychiatry 153*: 554-560.

McCann IL, Sakheim DK, Abrahamson DJ (1988) Trauma and victimization: A model of psychological adaptation. *Counseling Psychol 16*: 531-594.

Shalev AY (1992) Posttraumatic stress disorder among injured survivors of a terrorist attack. *J Nerv Ment Dis 180*(8):505-509.

Spiegel D (1988) Dissociation and hypnosis in post-traumatic stress disorders. *J Traum Stress 1*(1):17-33.

Spitzer RL, Williams JBW (1985) *Structured clinical interview for DSM-III-R (SCID)*. New York: New York State Psychiatric Institute, Biometrics Research.

Williams JBW, Gibbon M, First MB, Spitzer RL, Davies M, Borus J, Howes MJ, Kane J, Pipe JG, Rounsaville B, Wittchen HU (1992) The structured clinical interview for DSM-111-R: Multisite test-retest reliability. *Arch Gen Psychiatry 49*: 630-636.

Yalom ID (1981) *Existential psychotherapy*. Basic Books, New York.

Relationship of Physical Symptoms to Posttraumatic Stress Disorder Among Veterans Seeking Care for Gulf War-Related Health Concerns

Charles C. Engel, Jr., Xian Liu, Brian D. McCarthy, Ronald F. Miller, Robert Ursano

Abstract: *Studies of the relationship of posttraumatic stress disorder (PTSD) to physical symptoms in war veterans consistently show a positive relationship. However, traumatic experiences causing PTSD may correlate with other war exposures and medical illnesses potentially accounting for those symptoms. We analyzed data from 21,244 Gulf War veterans seeking care for war-related health concerns to assess the relationship of PTSD to physical symptoms independent of environmental exposure reports and medical illness. At assessment, veterans provided demographic information and checklists of 15 common physical symptoms and 20 wartime environmental exposures. Up to seven ICD-9 provider diagnoses were ranked in order of estimated clinical significance. Using bivariate and multivariate analyses, we found that veterans diagnosed with PTSD endorsed an average of 6.7 (SD = 3.9) physical symptoms, those with a non-PTSD psychological condition endorsed 5.3 (3.5), those with medical illness endorsed 4.3 (3.4), and a group diagnosed as "healthy" endorsed 1.2 (2.2). For every symptom, the proportion of veterans reporting the symptom was highest in those with PTSD, second highest in those with any psychological condition, third highest in those with any medical illness, and lowest in those labeled as healthy. The PTSD-symptom count relationship was independent of demographic characteristics, veteran-reported environmental exposures, and comorbid medical conditions, even when symptoms overlapping with those of PTSD were excluded. It was concluded that PTSD diminishes the general health perceptions of care-seeking Gulf War veterans. Clinicians should carefully consider PTSD when evaluating Gulf War veterans with vague, multiple, or medically unexplained physical symptoms.*

Introduction

Epidemiological studies have consistently found that persons with PTSD describe more physical symptoms than those without PTSD. Studies of Vietnam veterans (1, 2); Israeli combat veterans (3, 4);

communities (5); urban young adults (6); women with histories of sexual assault, criminal victimization, and Vietnam combat (7-9); gastroenterology clinic attendees (10); disaster victims (11-14); and firefighters (15) have suggested links between trauma or PTSD and various physical health complaints. Davidson et al. (5) examined a community-based sample of North Carolina adults and found that PTSD was associated with a 90-fold increase in the likelihood of somatization disorder. Of the 39 individuals with a history of PTSD, 5 (11.7%) were diagnosed with somatization disorder, whereas only 4 of the 2,946 (0.1%) without a history of PTSD had this disorder (5). Other studies have noted somatization disorder in 8 to 15% of veterans with PTSD receiving mental health care (16-19).

The putative relationship of physical symptoms to PTSD has important clinical implications for veterans with persistent or undiagnosed physical symptoms since serving in the Gulf War. Baker et al. (20) found that physical symptoms were strongly related to a diagnosis of PTSD among a group of 188 Gulf War veterans. The 13% of veterans with PTSD were between 4.8 and 16 times more likely to report different physical symptoms. Although the magnitude of these associations is impressive, neither this study of Gulf War veterans nor others studying the relationship of physical symptoms to PTSD have controlled for the possible confounding effect of medical illness and the wide range of environmental exposures that may have caused them. Wolfe et al. (21) examined Gulf War veterans and found that PTSD had a statistically significant but small relationship with increased health symptom reporting. However, almost two-thirds Gulf War veterans with elevations in physical symptoms had no axis I psychiatric diagnosis, suggesting that other explanations for physical symptoms were operative (21).

War veterans with the greatest exposure to traumatic experiences may also be the ones most affected by toxic exposures and related medical illness. For example, Helzer et al. (22) found that among Vietnam veterans wounded in action, about 20% had PTSD, compared with 1% of those who were not wounded. During the Gulf War, troops faced a range of potential toxic exposures, including smoke from burned excrement, burning oil wells, and diesel exhaust; toxic paints and pesticides; sand and other particulates; depleted uranium; infectious agents; chemoprophylactic agents; immunizations; and perhaps even chemical or biological warfare agents (23, 24). Increased toxic exposures and related medical illnesses among those with PTSD may therefore mediate the previously observed relationship between PTSD and physical symptoms. Proctor et al. (25) compared Gulf War veterans with individuals deployed to Germany and found that Gulf veterans reported significantly greater physical health symptoms even after controlling for PTSD.

We wanted to test the relationship of PTSD to physical symptoms after controlling for possible confounding effects of exposures and medical illness. Several questions were of concern to us: 1) Does PTSD have a direct and positive effect on a Gulf veteran's physical symptoms? 2) Is the impact of PTSD on physical symptoms mediated or confounded by coexisting medical illness or toxic war exposures? 3) Is the impact of PTSD on physical symptoms consistent even for symptoms of no apparent neuropsychiatric basis? 4) To what extent might PTSD explain the unexplained illnesses veterans have experienced since their service in the Gulf?

To address these questions we analyzed data from the CCEP, a worldwide US Department of Defense program established to evaluate the health of Gulf War veterans with war-related health concerns. The data generated from CCEP are not representative of all Gulf War veterans but are nonetheless useful for hypothesis screening (26) and can help us to understand the health concerns of care-seeking veterans (27).

Methods

Comprehensive Clinical Evaluation Program

Because the purpose of the CCEP is primarily clinical, participants seek CCEP assistance based on self-assessed need and thus are not recruited by use of a systematic sampling strategy. Written guide-lines help program clinicians decide how to evaluate participants and when to refer them to specialists. The approach to specialty consultations, testing, and clinical assessment is lengthy, inclusive, and thorough. At the time of presentation, the CCEP is fully explained to participants and written consent is obtained to use their data for aggregate examination of illnesses after Gulf War service. Current analyses focus on the first 21,244 Gulf War veterans who completed the CCEP.

Measures

All CCEP participants answered a series of questions about demographics, symptoms, and Gulf War-related environmental exposures. Physical symptoms were determined using a 16-item symptom checklist, including abdominal pain, bleeding gums, depressed mood, diarrhea, difficulty concentrating, fatigue, hair loss, headache, joint pain, memory loss, muscle pain, rash, shortness of breath, sleep disturbance, weight change, and "other symptoms." Analyses consider each symptom (reportedly present/not present) as well as the total symptom count (number of symptoms reported of 16). A second symptom count was also considered that excluded five symptoms potentially overlapping with those of PTSD and other mental disorders (depressed mood, difficulty concentrating, memory loss, sleep disturbance, and fatigue).

On completion of the CCEP clinical evaluation, the provider coordinating evaluations at the medical facility where the evaluation is performed transcribes the diagnoses as ICD-9 codes and rank-orders them according to their estimated clinical importance. Provider diagnoses used were ICD-9 psychological conditions (codes 290-320), PTSD (code 309.81), medical conditions (codes 0-289.99 and 320.01-999.99), and "healthy" (code V65.5). Provider diagnoses were recorded dichotomously (diagnosed/not diagnosed). An environmental exposure count was created using the number of exposures endorsed by the veteran out of 20. Exposures were determined with a checklist like that used for symptoms. Exposures addressed were oil fire smoke, tent heater smoke, chemical agent-resistant paint, other paints, solvents, diesel fuel, other petrochemicals, depleted uranium, nerve gas, mustard gas, microwaves, pyridostigmine bromide pills, insect repellents/flea collars, botulism immunization, anthrax immunization, malaria prophylaxis, food not provided by the military, contaminated food, water not provided by the military, and contaminated water. Each exposure was measured dichotomously (experienced/not experienced).

Four demographic characteristics were used in multivariate analyses: age (in years at the time of evaluation), gender, marital status (two dichotomous variables: currently married/other and currently not married/other), and ethnicity (white/nonwhite). Cigarette smoking (two dichotomous variables: nonsmoker/other and current or past smoker/other) is considered in analyses as a non-Gulf War-related health risk factor. The two coding strategies used for marital status and cigarette smoking lessened the cumulative loss of subjects due to missing values in multivariate analyses. As a result, there are only 12 missing cases in the data analysis.

Statistical Analysis

Bivariate analyses examined the relationship of symptoms to PTSD and psychological conditions besides PTSD. A correlation matrix of all variables used in the analysis was examined (available on request). We used multiple regression to model the symptom counts while adjusting for potentially confounding variables (war-related environmental exposures, medical illness, psychological conditions besides PTSD, and demographic characteristics, including smoking status). A stepdown analytic approach was used to test the putative relationship of PTSD to physical symptoms and then explore whether exposures or medical illness confounded the direct effect of PTSD on physical symptoms. First, a full model including all independent variables was specified, and then medical illness and exposure count were removed sequentially from the model. As these variables were removed, we examined for appreciable changes in the regression coefficient for the PTSD variable. If the magnitude of such changes are small (<10%), then it is reasonable to conclude that the direct impact of PTSD on Gulf veterans' physical symptoms is not significantly confounded by war-related environmental exposures and current medical status.

Results

Table 1 presents the distribution of symptom counts among 21,232 CCEP participants (the effective sample excluding the 12 missing cases). A total of 16.2% of veterans did not report any symptoms, whereas 8.6% reported 10 or more. A majority of veterans reported fewer than four symptoms.

Table 2 shows the proportions of CCEP participants who have checklist symptoms within three mutually exclusive categories: PTSD, psychological condition but not PTSD, and no psychological condition. Veterans with PTSD (5.2%) were more likely to report each of the checklist symptoms. Fatigue, sleep disturbance, joint pain, memory loss, headache, depressed mood, and difficulty concentrating were their most commonly reported symptoms (in order of frequency). Of those diagnosed with a psychological condition but not PTSD, the proportion reporting a symptom was lower for all symptoms than the proportion for the group diagnosed with PTSD. Nonetheless, more than half those with a psychological condition but not PTSD reported fatigue, joint pain, and headache.

Table 1
Percentage Distribution of Number of Physical Symptoms Among CCEP Participants: Effective Sample, 1994-1996

Physical Symptoms (N)	Distribution (%)	Sample Size (N)
0	16.3	3452
1	12.5	2658
2	12.4	2639
3	11.4	2425
4	9.8	2073
5	8.1	1726
6	6.7	1427
7	5.7	1211
8	4.8	1018
9	3.7	789
10	2.9	624
11	2.2	457
12	1.4	305
13	1.0	204
14	0.6	118
15	0.3	70
16	0.2	36
Total	100.00	21,232

The largest proportion of individuals was not diagnosed with any psychological condition, although they still reported important symptomatology. As a group, however, veterans who were not diagnosed with any psychological conditions were the ones least likely to report a symptom compared with the PTSD and non-PTSD psychological condition groups. Not surprisingly, symptom counts were highest for the PTSD group, second highest for the non-PTSD psychological condition group, and lowest for the group without any psychological conditions diagnosed. This relationship was quite similar when using the symptom count excluding neuropsychiatric symptomatology (PTSD group: 3.7, SD = 2.6; psychological condition but not PTSD group: 3.1, SD = 2.3; no psychological condition group: 2.0, SD = 1.9; not shown in Table 2).

In Table 3 the relationship of PTSD to checklist symptoms was examined using 4 overlapping diagnostic groupings: those with a PTSD diagnosis, those with any diagnosed psychological condition (including PTSD), those with any diagnosed medical condition (including those with a coexisting psychological condition), and those diagnosed as healthy. Among those diagnosed with a medical condition, the proportion having each of the checklist symptoms is significantly lower than for the group diagnosed with PTSD or the group diagnosed with any psychological condition. Veterans diagnosed as healthy were the least likely to report various physical symptoms. For each symptom, the proportion of healthy veterans with that symptom is much lower than those diagnosed with medical or psychological conditions. However, symptoms were not infrequent even among those veterans diagnosed as healthy. Here again, symptom counts revealed the same ordering effect even after exclusion of neuropsychiatric symptoms (PTSD: 3.7, SD = 2.6; psychological conditions: 3.2, SD = 2.3; medical conditions: 2.5, SD = 2.1; healthy: 0.9, SD = 1.4; not shown in Table 3).

Multivariate Predictors of Physical Symptom Count

Table 4 displays the results of ordinary least square (OLS) regression models predicting symptom count. Column 1 lists the explanatory variables considered in the present research. Model A is a full model to estimate the effect of PTSD on the number of physical symptoms independent of the potentially confounding influences of demographic status, war-related environmental exposures, and medical conditions. The other two models are reduced forms created by sequentially removing the medical condition variable and the environmental exposure count. This approach allows an estimation of the independent impact of PTSD on physical symptoms as well as the degree of confounding effects present because of medical conditions and war-related environmental exposures (the latter by evaluating the magnitude of the difference in regression coefficients for the PTSD variable).

Table 2
Proportions of CCEP Participants Who Have Specific Physical Symptoms by Psychological Status: Effective Sample, 1994-1996

	Psychological Condition			
Physical Symptom	PTSD (%)	Psychological Condition but not PTSD (%)	No Psychological Condition (%)	Total Sample (%)
Abdominal Pain	26.7	21.1	12.9	16.2
Bleeding gums	14.8	11.2	6.3	8.3
Depressed mood	55.2	37.4	12.0	22.2
Diarrhea	28.3	22.7	14.3	17.7
Trouble concentrating	53.8	39.2	17.6	26.3
Fatigue	68.0	57.7	35.6	44.2
Hair loss	17.2	14.5	9.8	11.7
Headache	58.0	54.4	27.0	37.2
Joint pain	62.9	55.0	40.9	46.4
Memory loss	58.9	46.4	23.5	32.5
Muscle pain	35.5	27.9	16.4	21.0
Rash	37.4	31.0	25.5	27.8
Shortness of breath	28.0	22.6	14.0	17.4
Sleep disturbance	64.4	45.3	23.2	32.3
Weight change	14.3	8.8	4.7	6.5
Other physical symptoms	47.0	38.3	30.7	34.0
Physical symptoms (N)				
Mean	6.7	5.3	3.1	4.0
SD	3.9	3.5	3.0	3.5
Sample Size	1096	6667	13,469	21,232

TABLE 3
Proportions of CCEP Participants Who Have Specific Physical Symptoms by Diagnosis of Illness: Effective Sample, 1994-1996

	Provider ICD-9 Diagnosis			
Physical Symptom	PTSD (%)	Psychological Conditions (%)	Medical Conditions (%)	Healthy (%)
Abdominal Pain	26.7	21.9	17.3	4.0
Bleeding gums	14.8	11.7	8.8	2.9
Depressed mood	55.2	39.9	23.1	6.4
Diarrhea	28.3	23.5	18.8	6.1
Trouble concentrating	53.8	41.3	27.5	7.1
Fatigue	68.0	59.1	46.6	15.0
Hair loss	17.2	14.9	12.3	4.4
Headache	58.0	54.9	39.3	9.7
Joint pain	62.9	56.1	49.7	13.8
Memory loss	58.9	48.1	34.2	9.8
Muscle pain	35.5	29.0	22.4	6.0
Rash	37.4	31.9	29.9	7.7
Shortness of breath	28.0	23.3	18.8	2.9
Sleep disturbance	64.4	48.0	34.0	8.7
Weight change	14.3	9.6	6.8	2.4
Other physical symptoms	47.0	39.5	36.1	11.2
Physical symptoms (N)				
Mean	6.7	5.5	4.3	1.2
SD	3.9	3.6	3.4	2.2
Sample Size[a]	1096	7763	19,059	1605

[a] Total Sample, N = 21,232

Table 4
Three Multiple Regression Models Predicting Symptom Count Among CCEP Participants[a]

Independent Variable[b]	Regression Coefficient	SE	T Score for H_o	p[a]
Model A				
PTSD	3.21**	0.10	32.33	.0001
Other psychological conditions	2.00**	0.05	42.38	.0001
Environmental exposure	0.13**	0.01	20.02	.0001
Medical condition	1.96**	0.07	27.50	.0001
F (11,21220)	413.75**			.001
Model B				
PTSD	3.27**	0.10	32.42	.0001
Other psychological conditions	2.09**	0.05	43.51	.0001
Environmental exposures	0.14**	0.01	21.31	.0001
F (10,21221)	366.47**			.0001
Model C				
PTSD	3.48**	0.10	34.34	.0001
Other psychological conditions	2.13**	0.05	44.02	.0001
F (9,21222)	349.29**			.0001

[a] All models adjust for age, gender, ethnicity, marital status, and smoking (N = 21,232)
[b] Figures in parentheses are the degrees of freedom for the model and error, respectively
[c] Probability > |t|
** p < .01.

Model A estimates the independent effects of the explanatory variables on symptom count, which indicates the strongest impact for PTSD (3.2 more symptoms than those without PTSD, other variables held equal) compared with that for psychological conditions other than PTSD (2.0 more symptoms than those without these conditions, other variables held equal) and medical conditions (diagnosis is 2.0 more symptoms than those without, other variables equal). Note that for simplicity, the regression coefficients of control variables are not presented in Table 4. Because the effects of all three diagnostic variables are positive, those without a medical and a psychological condition diagnosis, including PTSD, have the lowest symptom counts. The PTSD regression coefficient was quite stable irrespective of whether medical conditions and war-related exposures were included in the regression model (< 8% difference from model C to model A). The results essentially confirmed the bivariate relationships noted in Tables 2 and 3.

When we modeled the symptom count that excluded symptoms overlapping with those of PTSD in exactly the same manner, we found very similar results. For example, in model A, the regression coefficient for PTSD was 1.92 (SE = 0.068); for psychological conditions but not PTSD it was 1.29 (0.033); for medical conditions it was 0.55 (0.034); and for war-related environmental exposures it was 0.080 (0.004). The PTSD coefficient was similarly stable across models (10% difference from model C to model A), and model A accounted for only 11.5% of the variance in symptom count.

Discussion

The results shown above provide evidence that care-seeking Gulf War veterans diagnosed with PTSD report significantly more physical symptoms than care-seeking Gulf War veterans who were not diagnosed as having PTSD. The relationship between PTSD and different physical symptoms is remarkably consistent, irrespective of whether a given symptom overlaps with the diagnostic criteria for PTSD. Furthermore, the positive association between physical symptom count and a diagnosis of PTSD remains nearly unchanged even after taking into account the potentially confounding influences of veteran-reported environmental exposures and provider-diagnosed medical illness. These war-related environmental exposures and medical illnesses were, however, important determinants of physical symptoms in their own right.

Veterans diagnosed with PTSD reported the highest symptom

counts, even after adjusting for all important and potentially confounding variables available to us, including the presence of medical conditions and war-related environmental exposures. This effect persisted even when common symptoms that overlap with the diagnostic criteria for many mental disorders, such as depression, difficulty concentrating, sleep changes, and fatigue, are removed from the physical symptom count. Psychological conditions besides PTSD were also related to increased physical symptom counts, although less so than was PTSD. Indeed, PTSD was associated with the highest proportion of symptom reporters for each of the 16 checklist symptoms examined, followed by other psychological conditions and then medical conditions and individuals described as healthy by the examining physician. This ordering of effect was preserved even for symptoms that have little or no apparent relationship to either the phenomenology or neurophysiology of PTSD, such as bleeding gums.

There are several limitations that must be considered when attempting to ascertain the validity and generalizability of our findings. The absence of symptom severity measurements is a drawback. It is not clear whether the symptoms that veterans endorsed are clinically significant. However, it is reasonable to assume that the number of symptoms endorsed is a surrogate measure of overall symptom severity. Veterans participating in CCEP are a selected sample assessed within a unique context, and the degree to which these findings may be extended to all Gulf War veterans is unknown. For instance, compensation is often at stake during CCEP evaluations, and this may distort veterans' symptom reports. Therefore, it may not be appropriate to generalize these findings to all Gulf War veterans. Interpretation of these data is also complicated by the fact that PTSD and psychological condition diagnoses were not uniformly made in specialty mental health care settings, and the validity of diagnoses is not well characterized. The validity of CCEP PTSD diagnoses, however, was supported in previous analyses showing that veteran-reported Gulf War stressors were significantly related to the CCEP diagnosis of PTSD but not to other CCEP psychological conditions (28, 29). Furthermore, the multicenter, clinical, and worldwide nature of CCEP means that the average CCEP assessment is likely to more approximate providers' routine diagnostic practices than an epidemiological study using research diagnostic practices. Random regional variations in diagnostic practices can offset one another in a large worldwide clinical sample such as the one that CCEP offers. Lastly, the cross-sectional nature of the sample weakens the confidence with which causal inferences may be made. For example, because symptoms and distress were assessed simultaneously, one cannot discern whether distress may be causing amplified estimates of physical symptom severity or whether physical symptoms are resulting in distress.

The multivariate models we presented represent a conservative test of the hypothesis that PTSD is linked to physical symptoms among Gulf War veterans. Our backward stepwise approach to modeling the PTSD-physical symptom link assumes that the impact of PTSD on physical symptoms is not mediated by smoking or medical illness. Research on veterans from other wars suggests that PTSD may well antedate and subsequently alter their health habits and illness experience (4). These effects, although possibly occurring among CCEP participants, seem minor and would cause us to err on the side of a falsely negative or underestimated PTSD-physical symptom link. Similarly, the effect previously mentioned of random misclassification of PTSD due to regional variation in diagnostic practices would increase the chance of falsely accepting the null hypothesis. These considerations suggest that the relationship of PTSD to physical symptoms may indeed be even stronger than we have estimated.

Assuming Gulf War veterans with PTSD are more likely to use medical services than are other Gulf War veterans, one would expect the prevalence of PTSD among CCEP participants to be higher than it is in the general Gulf War veteran population. Only 5.2% of CCEP participants were diagnosed with PTSD. Although a great deal of empirical research consistently implicates PTSD as an important cause of physical symptoms, it seems clear that there are other important and potentially Gulf War-related causes of physical symptoms among ill Gulf War veterans. Some illness may be due to other psychological conditions (many of them under-recognized and readily treatable in primary care settings). Other illness may well relate to physical etiologies or important environmental exposures experienced in the Gulf. Longitudinal studies are under way to address the long-term impact of PTSD on Gulf War veterans' health (21, 25) (Table 4).

Note

The views expressed in this article are those of the authors and do not reflect the official policy or position of the Department of the Army, the Department of Defense, or the US Government.

References

1. Health status of Vietnam veterans. II. Physical health. The Centers for Disease Control Vietnam Experience Study. *JAMA* 1988; 259:2708-14.

2. Litz BT, Keane TM, Fisher L, Marx B, Monaco V. Physical health complaints in combat-related post-traumatic stress disorder: a preliminary report. *J Trauma Stress* 1992;5:131-41.

3. Shalev A, Bleich A, Ursano RJ. Posttraumatic stress disorder: somatic comorbidity and effort tolerance. *Psychosomatics* 1990; 31:197-203.

4. Solomon Z, Mikulincer M. Combat stress reactions, post traumatic stress disorder and somatic complaints among Israeli soldiers. *J Psychosom Res* 1987;31:131-7.

5. Davidson JRT, Hughes D, Blazer DG, George LK. Post-traumatic stress disorder in the community: an epidemiological study. *Psychol Med* 1991;21:713-21.

6. Breslau N, Davis GC. Posttraumatic stress disorder in an urban population of young adults: risk factors for chronicity. *Am J Psychiatry* 1992;149:671-5.

7. Golding JM. Sexual assault history and physical health in randomly selected Los Angeles women. *Health Psychol* 1994;13: 130-8.

8. Koss MP, Koss PG, Woodruff WJ. Deleterious effects of criminal victimization on women's health and medical utilization. *Arch Intern Med* 1991;151:342-7.

9. Wolfe J, Schnurr PP, Brown PJ, Furey JA. Posttraumatic stress disorder and war-zone exposure as correlates of perceived health in female Vietnam war veterans. *J Consult Clin Psychol* 1994;62:1235-40.

10. Leserman J, Drossman DA, Li Z, Toomey T, Nachman G, Glogau L. Sexual and physical abuse history in gastroenterology practice: how types of abuse impact health status. *Psychosom Med* 1996;58:4-15.

11. Hovanitz CA. Physical health risks associated with aftermath of disaster: basic paths of influence and their implications for preventative intervention. *J Soc Behav Pers* 1993;8:213-54.

12. Lutgendorf SK, Antoni MH, Fronson G, Fletcher MA, Penedo F, Baum A, Schneiderman N, Klimas N. Physical symptoms of chronic fatigue syndrome are exacerbated by the stress of Hurricane Andrew. *Psychosom Med* 1995;57:310-23.

13. Escobar JI, Canino GJ, Rubio-Stipec M, Bravo M. Somatic symptoms after a natural disaster: a prospective study. *Am J Psychiatry* 1992;149:965-7.

14. Phifer JF. Psychological distress and somatic symptoms after natural disaster: differential vulnerability among older adults. *Psychol Aging* 1990;5:412-20.

15. McFarlane AC, Atchison M, Rafalowicz E, Papay P. Physical symptoms in post-traumatic stress disorder. *J Psychosom Res* 1994;38:715-26.

16. Escobar JI, Randolph ET, Puente G, Spiwak F, Asamen JK, Hill M, Hough RL. Post-traumatic stress disorder in Hispanic Vietnam veterans. *J Nerv Ment Dis* 1983;171:585-96.

17. Roszell DK, McFall ME, Malas KL. Frequency of symptoms and concurrent psychiatric disorder in Vietnam veterans with chronic PTSD. *Hosp Community Psychiatry* 1991;42:293-6.

18. Sierles FS, Chen JJ, Messing ML, Beysner JK, Taylor MA. Concurrent psychiatric illness in non-Hispanic outpatients diagnosed as having posttraumatic stress disorder. *J Nerv Ment Dis* 1986;174:171-3.

19. Sierles FS, Chen JJ, McFarland RE, Taylor MA. Posttraumatic stress disorder and concurrent psychiatric illness: a preliminary report. *Am J Psychiatry* 1983;140:1177-9.

20. Baker DG, Mendenhall CL, Simbartl LA, Magan LK, Steinberg JL. Relationship between posttraumatic stress disorder and self-reported physical symptoms in Persian Gulf War veterans. *Arch Intern Med* 1997;157:2076-8.

21. Wolfe J, Proctor SP, Erickson DJ, Heeren T, Friedman MJ, Huang MT, Sutker PB, Vasterling JJ, White RF. Relationship of psychiatric status to Gulf War veterans' health problems. *Psychosom Med* 1999;61:532-40.

22. Helzer JE, Robins LN, McEvoy L. Post-traumatic stress disorder in the general population. *N Engl J Med* 1987;317:1630-4.

23. Institute of Medicine Committee to Review the Consequences of Service During the Persian Gulf War, Medical Follow-up Agency. *Health consequences of service during the Persian Gulf War: Recommendations for research and information systems*. Washington DC: National Academy Press; 1996.

24. NIH Technology Assessment Workshop Panel. The Persian Gulf experience and health. *JAMA* 1994;272:391-6.

25. Proctor SP, Heeren T, White RF, Wolfe J, Borges MS, Davis JD, Pepper L, Clapp R, Sutker PB, Vasterling JJ, Ozonoff D. Health status of Persian Gulf War veterans: self-reported symptoms, environmental exposures and the effect of stress. *Int J Epidemiol* 1998;27:1000-10.

26. Rothman KJ, Greenland S. Types of epidemiologic studies. In: Rothman KJ, Sanders S, editors. *Modern epidemiology*. Philadelphia: Lippincott-Raven; 1990. p. 67-78.

27. Silver H, Abboud E. Drug abuse in schizophrenia: Comparison of patients who began drug abuse before their first admission with those who began abusing drugs after their first admission. *Schizophr Res* 1994;13:57-63.

28. Engel CC Jr. *Psychological conditions in the CCEP*. Presentation to the Presidential Advisory Committee on Gulf War Veteran's Illnesses; 1996; Cincinnati, Ohio.

29. Engel CC Jr, Ursano R, Magruder C, Tartaglione R, Jing Z, Labbate LA, Debakey S. Psychological conditions diagnosed among veterans seeking Department of Defense care for Gulf War-related health concerns. *J Occup Environ* Med 1999;41: 384-92.

Decontamination Issues for Chemical And Biological Warfare Agents: How Clean Is Clean Enough?

Ellen Raber, Alfred Jin, Kathleen Noonan, Ray McGuire, Robert D. Kirvel

Abstract: *The objective of this assessment is to determine what level of cleanup will be required to meet regulatory and stakeholder needs in the case of a chemical and/or biological incident at a civilian facility. A literature review for selected, potential chemical and biological warfare agents shows that dose information is often lacking or controversial. Environmental regulatory limits or other industrial health guidelines that could be used to help establish cleanup concentration levels for such agents are generally unavailable or not applicable for a public setting. Although dose information, cleanup criteria, and decontamination protocols all present challenges to effective planning, several decontamination approaches are available. Such approaches should be combined with risk-informed decision making to establish reasonable cleanup goals for protecting health, property, and resources. Key issues during a risk assessment are to determine exactly what constitutes a safety hazard and whether decontamination is necessary or not for a particular scenario. An important conclusion is that cleanup criteria are site dependent and stakeholder specific. The results of a modeling exercise for two outdoor scenarios are presented to reinforce this conclusion. Public perception of risk to health, public acceptance of recommendations based on scientific criteria, political support, time constraints, and economic concerns must all be addressed in the context of a specific scenario to yield effective and acceptable decontamination.*

Introduction

This paper attempts to address an interagency need for up-to-date, summary information necessary to evaluate acceptable decontamination levels and protocols. The longer-term issue is to determine what level of cleanup will be required to meet both regulatory objectives and stakeholder (including public) needs in the event of a terrorist attack involving the use of chemical and/or biological warfare (CBW) agents.

Recent use—or the suspected use or development—of CBW agents in various parts of the world reinforces the need to prepare for such threats proactively and to strengthen public and scientific awareness of the problem (Kadlec et al. 1997). Possible threats to health from CBW agents, in the hands of terrorists or otherwise, are receiving increased attention. For example, approximately 100,000 US troops may have been exposed to low levels of chemical warfare agents in Operation Desert Storm (US General Accounting Office 1998). If this finding is substantiated by additional studies, the US military policy toward troops exposed to chemical warfare agents could be affected. In a related study, US civilian and military defense groups are sharing knowledge and expertise to make difficult decisions that will be required to provide protection to all personnel against possible low-level exposures (Tucker 1997).

The need for risk-informed decision making and planning is urgent, yet the obstacles to effective planning are formidable. The problems include limited data, incomplete regulatory standards, problematic definitions of terms and cleanup criteria, inadequately defined sampling and analysis strategies in the context of a broader decontamination protocol, and the site- and population-specific nature of health risks and procedures, to name only a few.

This assessment is an attempt to define the issues relevant to decontamination and cleanup criteria, summarize data that are relevant and available, use existing information and models to define requirements, and bound the nature of uncertainties that remain. The scope of the assessment is necessarily broad because of the range of complex issues that are germane to decontamination. This paper addresses each issue by providing summary tables where data are available. In cases where data are unavailable or controversial, or when the issue is not directly linked to hard data, possible strategies or methods are discussed. Conclusions are summarized and recommendations are made in the final section of the paper.

Limited Data and Health Standards for Potential CBW Agents

Established threshold limit values are not available for many CBW agents because most of the research on them has been associated with production and battlefield use. Limited scientific work has been conducted in establishing safe criteria for public exposure to CBW agents. The health standards that do exist have often been developed for the military or occupational (worker) environments. Toxicological database tools use the structure of molecules to help determine possible toxicological effects; however, such tools have limited use and applicability for conditions relevant to the public sector. Several factors must be incorporated into developing standards for the general public, including the consideration of individuals in the general population who may be at higher risk for illness and injury (e.g., developing fetuses, children, and the immunocompromised). Furthermore, to prevent virtually any health effect, whether acute or chronic, much more strict criteria are typically used. An example of such a standard developed for the public is the accepted risk reduction of cancer to something less than one in a million.

CBW agents can be divided into three categories: biological agents, biological toxins, and chemical agents. It is important to recognize that the three categories of materials and agents within them differ in many ways, including their production, dissemination, incubation period, and effects on health. Although it would be advantageous to identify a single strategy that is effective against any agent, a decontamination decision process must address the specific warfare agent that is used in a particular scenario.

Biological warfare agents that have the potential to cause serious public health catastrophes include those microorganisms (viruses, bacteria, and fungi) identified in Table 1. As defined and reported in the literature, incubation periods and infectious doses are summarized along with associated fatality rates of selected biological warfare agents (Benenson 1990, US Army 1996, Department of the Army 1996a, Office of the Surgeon General 1997, Centers for Disease Control 1999b, Inglesby 1999). In this and subsequent tables, ranges are given where one or multiple sources specify different values.

Table 1
Incubation Period, Infectious Dose, and Fatality Rate for Selected Biological Warfare Agents

Biological Agent	Disease and Likely Route of Acquisition	Incubation Period (Days)	Infectious Dose (particles /m^3)	Fatality Rate (%)
Bacillus anthracis (anthrax)	• Pneumonia by inhalation • Cutaneous anthrax by direct contact or inoculation	•1-60 •1-7	•8,000-10,000 •unknown	• ~ 100 if untreated • 5-20
Brucella (4 species)	• Brucellosis by inhalation • Brucellosis by ingestion	• 5-60 • 5-60	• Unknown • Unknown	• 2-6 • 2-6
Clostridium botulinum	• Wound by tissue infection • Infant by tissue infection • Classic by ingestion of preformed toxin	• 12-36h •Unknown • 12-36 hr	• Unknown • Unknown • Unknown	• Unknown • 2 • 15
Coccidiodes immitis	• Valley fever by inhalation • Desert fever by inhalation	• 7-14 • 7-28	• Unknown • Unknown	• Unknown • Unknown
Coxiella burnetti	• Q fever by inhalation of infected aerosols	• 7-21	• 1-10	• < 1
Ebola (human)	• Viral hemorrhagic fever (VHF) by unknown vector	• 2-21	• Unknown	• 50-90
Ebola (primate)	• Simian hemorrhagic fever (SHF) by unknown vector	• 4-16	• 1-10	• Unknown
Francisella tularensis	• Tularemia by inhalation • Tularemia by ingestion	• 2-10 • 2-10	• 10-50 • 108	• 5-10 • 5
Marburg virus	• Viral hemorrhagic fever (VHF) by exposure to infected blood / tissue	• 3-9	• Unknown	• 25
Variola virus	• Smallpox by exposure to aerosolized virus	• 7-17	• Low	• 15-40
Venezuelan equine encephalitis (VEE) virus	• Adult encephalitis by arthropod vector • Infant / child encephalitis by arthropod vector	• 2-6 • 2-6	• Very Low • Unknown	• < 1 • 20
Yersinia pestis	• Bubonic plague by flea bite • Pneumonic plague by inhalation	• 2-10 • 2-6	• 100 • < 100	• 50 • 100

Incubation periods of biological agents are important to a decontamination decision process because casualties may not be reported for days following exposures. With increasing time, fewer biological agents, or perhaps none, might survive under environmental conditions specific to a given site. Infectious doses are germane because they also can influence decisions about the level of decontamination, if required at all, and when to allow re-entry into contaminated areas or buildings following cleanup to a specified level. Infectious dose is expressed in Table 1 as a function of the type of microorganism: as the number of spores (e.g., inhalation anthrax), organisms (e.g., Q fever-aerosol), or plaque-forming units (e.g., Ebola) acquired through ingestion (e.g., tularemia), inhalation of aerosols (e.g., smallpox, Q fever), or arthropods (e.g., VEE).

Table 2 summarizes the time to onset of symptoms and fatality rates, where known, for biological toxins (or biotoxins) that have the potential to cause serious public health catastrophes (Department of the Army 1990a, 1996, Franz 1996, US Army 1996, Office of the Surgeon General 1997). The lethal dose 50 (LD_{50}) in Table 2 is the dose of a substance that is fatal to 50% of test animals, and lethal dose values are given for mice unless otherwise specified.

Table 2
Origin, Route of Intoxication, Time to Onset of Symptoms, Fatality Rate, and Lethal Dose for Selected Biological Toxins

Biological Toxin	**Origin and Route of Intoxication, Where Specified**	**Time of Onset of Symptoms**	**Fertility Rate**	**LD_{50} (μg/kg)**
Lethal effects (< 5 min)				
• Aatoxin A (VFDF) neurotoxin	• Bluegreen algae; ingestion	• Unknown	• Unknown	• 170-250
• Conotoxin	• Cone snale; inhalation	• Unknown	• Uknown	• 3-6
• Palytoxin	• Marine soft coral; inhalation, ingestion, absorption through skin or eyes	• Unknown	• Unknown	•.08 human 0.15
Lethal effects (5 min to 1 hr)				
• Batrachotoxin	• Arrow poison frog; inhalation	• Unknown	• Unknown	• 0.1-2.0
• Diptheria toxin	• Bacterium; inhalation (droplet and self innoculation via fomite), rarely ingestion	• Unknown	• Unknown	• 0.03-0.10

(continued)

Biological Toxin	Origin and Route of Intoxication, Where Specified	Time of Onset of Symptoms	Fertility Rate	LD_{50} (μg/kg)
• Saxitoxin	• Marine algae in shellfish; inhalation	• 15 min	• Unknown	• 1-2
	• Marine algae in shellfish; oral ingestion	• 10-60 min	• Unknown	• 7 human oral 10
• Tetrodotoxin	• Puffer fish; ingestion	• Unknown	• Unknown	• 30 human
Delayed lethal effects (> 1 h)				
• Botulinum toxins	• Bacterium; ingestion	• 12-72 h	• 50-60 < 5 treated	• 0.001 0.01 human
• Clostridium perfringens toxins	• Bacterium; route unspecified	• Unknown	• Unknown	• 0.1-5
• Ricin (A-D)	• Castor bean plant; oral, dermal, or inhalation	• 18-24 h	• ~ 6	• 3.0 1000 human oral
Staphylococcal enterotoxin B (SEB)	• Bacterium; inhalation	• 3-12 h	• Low	• 0.02-1.7 human 27 monkey
• Trichothecene fusarium (e.g., T-2)	• Fungal mycotoxin; inhalation	• 2-4 h	• Unknown	• 25-50 human respiratory 1210

Public health exposure limits are not clearly established for either biological agents or biotoxins. Worker exposure limits for biological agents are problematic. Usually, a material is evaluated for biological risk on the basis of its biological exposure index, which serves as a reference value. However, biological exposure indexes have only been developed for chemicals, and they do not exist for biological warfare agents.

Table 3 summarizes the lethal dose (Office of the Surgeon General 1997), lethal concentration (Department of the Army 1990, Office of the Surgeon General 1997, USAMRICD 1998), and published maximum permissible concentrations of representative chemical warfare agents in air and water. For chemical agents GA, GB, and GD in ambient air, the general population guidelines [time-weighted-average (TWA) concentrations] and acute exposure guidelines (AEG Level 1) shown in Table 3 are taken from a recent evaluation by the Edgewood Research, Development, and Engineering Center (Mioduszewski et al. 1998). In addition, 8-h AEGL-1 values, which are not available, would be highly useful because such exposure limits could be potentially applied to both workers and the general population. The general population TWA guideline for mustard is from the US Army (1991); that for VX is from the US Army (1990); and that for Lewisite is from the Centers for Disease Control (CDC 1988). The AEG Level 1 value for mustard is from the National Advisory Committee for AEGLs for Hazardous Substances (2000).

The general population values in Table 3 give an acceptable level of risk to the most sensitive members of the population. In contrast, Table *3* also shows occupational TWA short-term exposure limits (STELs; 15 min x 4/day) reported in the literature for GA, GB, and GD (Mioduszewski *et al.* 1998). STELs for cyanogen chloride and chlorine are taken from the American Conference of Governmental Industrial Hygienists (ACGIH 1997).

The occupational threshold limit values (TLVs) in Table *3* are based on a TWA for a normal 8-h workday and a 40-h workweek. The ACGIH (1997) defines TLVs as airborne concentrations of substances, representing conditions under which it is believed that most workers, but not necessarily all, may be exposed day after day without adverse effects (see also Lauwerys 1986). TLVs are based on the best available information from industrial experience and studies in animals and in human volunteers. The TLVs for GA, GB, and GD are taken from Mioduszewski et al. (1998). The TLVs for VX and Lewisite are from the CDC (1988); the TLV for mustard is from the US Army (1991); and TLVs for phosgene, chlorine, and arsenic are from the ACGIH (1997).

The maximum allowable concentrations identified in Table 3 for chemical agents in potable water represent levels used by the Departments of the Army, Navy, and Air Force (1999) for military personnel. Water-quality objectives and the problem of surface/soil cleanup levels for chemical agents are discussed later in this article.

Decontamination Management and Methods

The process of determining an effective decontamination approach depends on the defined objectives to be met within the context of a specific operational scenario. Approaches can range from no action or

Table 3. Lethal dose (LD_{50}), lethal concentration (LCt_{50}), airborne exposure limits, and maximum permissible concentration of selected chemical warfare agents in air and water

Chemical agent	*Lethal dose LD_{50}* (mg/kg)*	*Lethal conc. LCt_{50}† (mg min/m³)*	*General population TWA 24 h × 7 days/week ambient-air concentration (mg/m³)*	*General population Acute Exposure Guideline (AEG Level 1) (mg/m³)*	*Occupational TWA 15 min × 4/day short-term exposure limit (STEL) (mg/m³)*	*Occupational 8-h TLV-TWA ambient-air concentration (mg/m³)*	*Combined US Forces maximum drinking water concentration‡ (mg/m³)*
Tabun (GA)	14.3	400	0.000003	0.0012 (1 hr) 0.0003 (4 hr)	0.002	0.0001	0.012
Sarin (GB)	24.3	100	0.000003	0.0012 (1 hr) 0.0003 (4 hr)	0.002	0.0001	0.012
Soman (GD)	5.0	50	0.000001	0.0006 (1 hr) 0.0001 (4 hr)	0.001	0.00003	0.012
VX	0.14	10	0.000003‡	Unknown	Unknown	0.00001	0.012
Mustard (HD)	100	15,000 (vapor)	0.0001	0.01 (1 hr)	Unknown	0.003	0.14
Phosgene (CG)	Not applicable	3000	Unknown	Unknown	Unknown	0.4	Not applicable
Lewisite (L)	> 30	14,000 respiratory 100,000 percutaneous	0.003‡‡	Unknown	Unknown	0.003	0.8
Cyanogen chloride	Not applicable	~ 11,000	Unknown	Unknown	0.75 (ceiling‡‡‡)	Unknown	6
Chlorine	Not applicable	6000	Unknown	Unknown	2.9	1.5	Unknown
Arsenic	Unknown	NA	Unknown	Unknown	Unknown	0.01	0.3

* LD_{50} is the dose necessary to cause death in 50% of the population with skin exposure.
† LCt_{50} is the vapor or aerosol exposure necessary to cause death in 50% of an exposed population.
National Research Council (1997) proposed values are as follows: GA = 135, GB = 70, GD = 70, VX = 30, and HD = 15,000 mg/l.
†† Maximum allowable concentration in water by the Combined US Forces for consumption at 5 l/day, not to exceed 7 days.
‡ Suggested modification is 0.0000003 (US Army 1999).
‡‡ This concentration may be too large in that it reflects limited sensitivity of the measurement instrument using 1987 technology.
‡‡‡ Threshold limit value ceiling (TLV-c) is the airborne concentration that should not be exceeded during any part of the exposure period.

a simple reduction in concentration of an agent, to total sterilization or destruction of contaminated materials. The two approaches that should be carefully considered are: (1) decontamination by natural attenuation and (2) decontamination by the application of various reagent materials or physical energy sources.

Decontamination Management

The approach to be taken in a domestic, urban setting would be somewhat different than the standard military approach to decontamination. In a battlefield scenario, it is critical to decontaminate to a useful level in a short time so that soldiers can continue their mission. In a domestic, urban scenario, time may be of less consequence, but collateral damage and recertification (public perception and stakeholder acceptance) are of much greater importance. Similarly, the decontamination process may need to be a staged procedure, with cleanup of gross contamination (e.g., puddles) followed by more localized decontamination approaches in hidden areas, such as ductwork or inaccessible cracks. Long-term decontamination or prophylaxis might include the application of paints or coatings to contain small quantities of residual agents.

A recent report by the Centers for Disease Control (1999) on bioterrorist threats of anthrax exposure in four US states is illustrative. All threats, made by telephone or letter during 1998, were hoaxes and are under investigation. Although the authors of this report did not provide any scientific basis for the actions taken, the decontamination approaches used in each case may suggest some interim guidance for responding in an urban scenario. Potentially exposed individuals showered with soap and water plus dilute bleach solution and were sometimes given chemoprophylaxis with ciprofloxacin at local emergency departments. Surfaces were washed with a 5% hypochlorite solution (i.e., standard household bleach), and personal clothing and effects were placed in plastic bags. In each case, direct fluorescent antibody testing and cultures of samples were negative for *Bacillus anthracis*.

The Working Group on Civilian Biodefense (Inglesby et al. 1999) has developed consensus-based recommendations for measures to be taken by medical and public health professionals following use of anthrax as a biological weapon. Given cost, logistics, and current supplies, the authors advise against population-wide vaccination but recommend consideration of post-exposure vaccination of essential service personnel and possibly others. For symptomatic inhalational anthrax infection, early antibiotic administration is recommended (e.g., ciprofloxacin or other efficacious antibiotic), with intravenous antibiotic therapy recommended in a contained casualty setting. Oral fluoroquinolone or tetracycline antibiotics are recommended for treatment of cutaneous anthrax. Special precautions are discussed for children and pregnant women. In terms of decontamination, Inglesby et al. (1999) conclude that secondary aerosolization of anthrax spores appears unlikely. This conclusion is also supported by Department of Defense studies (William Patrick, presentation, Homeland Defense Symposium, Rand Corporation, February 2000). Decontamination of large urban areas or buildings is not indicated; however, persons coming into direct physical contact with anthrax should perform thorough washing of exposed skin and clothing with soap and water.

It is important to recognize that there is a balance between somewhat less effective decontamination methods that can be implemented quickly, and more effective ones that may require a much longer time to complete. Social, political, and regulatory issues must be considered prior to implementing a particular decontamination approach. For example, the decontamination reagent used should not be an environmentally hazardous material, such as a carcinogen, unless it has a very short lifetime so that it will decompose without endangering civilian populations.

We must also work on understanding, and even influencing, the answer to the question: "How clean is clean enough?" Obviously, decontamination methods that work for destroying 90% of a threat may not be effective if the goal is to destroy 99.999999% of the same agent. The level of decontamination required will influence the choice of the systems under consideration. The optimum objective is to use a decontamination approach that is noncorrosive and results in nontoxic byproducts. The overall issue of "How clean is clean enough?" and the methods by which the answer is determined (e.g., sampling and verification) are key to establishing effective and successful decontamination methods. In other words, it is possible to do a poor job of decontamination and to make it look good by doing a poor job of sampling and analysis. In final application, decontamination must be defensible to regulatory agencies and to the public. Therefore, it will be important to anticipate the issues and to educate the relevant parties on both the decontamination methods and the verification methods to be used.

Natural Attenuation Approach

Under some scenarios, the destruction or degradation of CBW agents by natural attenuation over time may be the most effective approach to minimize health risks. Meteorological and environmental factors can have a profound impact on the effectiveness and longevity of many agents. More specifically, the factors include outdoor environmental conditions such as high wind, sunlight, high temperature, high humidity, or rain.

Phosgene and Lewisite agents rapidly decompose at a relative humidity > 70%. Water can cause hydrolysis of Lewisite agents and release of nonvolatile, though toxic, arsenic byproducts. Phosgene hydrolyzes rapidly into hydrochloric acid and carbon dioxide (ACGHI 1997). Sarin and many biological toxins are also water soluble and hydrolyze under neutral to basic conditions. The solubility of many CBW agents is pH dependent, and they only dissolve in a narrow pH range. For example, VX is only soluble under acidic conditions.

Inversion weather conditions cause chemical warfare agents to remain near the ground, reducing the rate of dispersion. Warmer ground-surface temperatures tend to increase the dissipation of liquid chemicals through the evaporation process. McGuire et al. (1993) conducted studies to characterize the degradation of specific chemical warfare agents in soil and on concrete surfaces as a function of time. The tests were conducted at Porton Down, UK, as part of a cooperative study between two laboratories. Various matrices (soils, concrete, and gasket materials) were contaminated outdoors with GD, VX, and HD, then sampled and analyzed as a function of time. Results showed that the chemical warfare agents GD and VX degrade and/or hydrolyze within 3-5 days to nonhazardous levels. The data suggest that in all locations studied, there would be no need for decontamination of GD or VX after *3* days. Harvey et al. (1997) showed that mustard (HD) agents are typically not hydrolyzed as effectively as most other chemical warfare agents. However, the data to date, although inconclusive, suggest that mustard on concrete and in soil will also degrade within *5* days. The consideration of natural attenuation as a decontamination approach is important. Among other advantages, this alternative is cost effective and would cause less potential infrastructure damage.

Biological agents require specific environmental conditions to survive. Environmental factors, such as available sunlight, temperature, relative humidity and/or rain, and the presence of atmospheric pollutants, should be considered. For example, *Yersinia pestis* can survive near-freezing temperatures from months to years, but this agent is killed by several hours of exposure to sunlight. Ultraviolet light will naturally inactivate most biological agents, although shadowing effects must be considered. High-molecular-weight toxins (i.e., proteins) are usually more sensitive to ultraviolet light, heat, and oxidation than are low-molecular-weight nonprotein toxins (Department of the Army 1990).

Decontamination Methods

Decontamination methods are based on the chemical modification of an agent by hydrolysis, catalysis, or oxidation; chemical sorption; or physical removal by absorption, washing, or evaporation. The optimum technology would be a single decontamination system that could be used against any agent and that is nontoxic, noncorrosive, and easily deployable. The reagents should allow for detoxification or degradation to nontoxic and environmentally acceptable components rather than necessitate complete destruction. Currently available military systems, although effective, do not meet environmentally acceptable criteria. Several technologies now under development are aimed at meeting such requirements in a civilian setting.

Factors that may impose constraints in managing decontamination during a crisis situation include time and material limitations, and available detection and diagnostic capabilities. In addition, it is important to distinguish between specific decontamination objectives, namely, prevention of immediate illness or death following exposure to an agent versus prevention of residual effects to the environment.

Scenario-Dependent Nature of Cleanup Levels

In the context of a potential release of CBW agents, three kinds of sites may bound the response and decontamination approach to be taken. They are (1) an outdoor site, such as a stadium or campus; (2) a semi-enclosed site, such as a subway or airplane hangar; and (3) an indoor environment, such as an office building, home, or room. For outdoor sites, weather can be an important consideration in terms of an inability to contain contaminants, and dilution and natural attenuation are among the most effective approaches. In contrast, indoor environments are more likely to be well-controlled or closed systems. Thus, in terms of cleanup, ventilation and physical energy sources, such as ultraviolet light or thermal treatment, might be used to advantage. On the other hand, public perception is a major consideration, and cleanup to acceptable levels may be very difficult. A semi-enclosed site is a hybrid of outdoor and indoor sites. Major considerations are the positive effects of ventilation and the likelihood of short residence times for people.

To help elucidate the site-specific dependence of outdoor, chemical warfare agent decontamination efforts, we performed simple modeling to calculate soil cleanup levels for two specific sites, the 3Com San Francisco sports stadium and the City of Baltimore Municipal stadium. For the purposes of this study, it was necessary to first define the target cleanup levels to be met for selected contaminants.

At the time this study was initiated, there were no standards establishing acceptable soil or surface cleanup levels for chemical warfare agents. Therefore, for purposes of establishing cleanup levels, it is useful to look at compounds that are related to lethal chemical agents. The related compounds listed in Table 4 appear to be the *only* relevant compounds, with respect to chemical warfare agents in soil and water cleanup, for which the US Environmental Protection Agency (EPA) currently has established some regulatory guidelines. For example, arsenic is contained in Lewisite, is one of its degradation products that lingers for extended times, and would be the component of Lewisite most likely to result in a residual threat to the environment. EPA regulatory guidelines identifying acceptable concentrations in drinking water exist for arsenic. Isopropyl methyl phosphonate is a degradation product of nerve agent GB, and EPA guidelines for permissible water concentrations also exist for that compound. The compounds fonofos, malathion, and parathion are included because of their familiarity to the general public and the fact that they are all organophosphates, as are most of the nerve agents. Therefore, their residual effects on the environment should be similar to that of the nerve agents, and the approach to determining a cleanup level would also be similar.

Table 4
Conservative Cleanup Levels for Compounds Related to Chemical Warfare Agents

Related Compound or Pesticide	Maximum Contaminant Level (MCL) in Drinking Water (μg/l)		Suggested No-Adverse Response Level (μg/l)	California State Action Level (μg/l)
	CA DHS*	U.S. EPA	U.S. EPA	RPHLs DHS**
Fonofos	Not specified	Not specified	10	Not specified
Glyphosate	700	700	700	700
Isopropyl methyl phosphonate	Not specified	Not specified	700	Not specified
Malathion	Not specified	Not specified	200	Not specified
Methyl parathion	Not specified	Not specified	2	30
Parathion	Not specified	Not specified	30***	Not specified
Arsenic	50	50	Not specified	Not specified
Cyanide	200	200	Not specified	Not specified

* California Department of Health Services
** Recommended public health level from the California Department of Health Services
*** Value given by the National Academy of Science

Using the information on related compounds in Table 4, we can begin to draw some preliminary conclusions that may help to establish conservative cleanup levels for some of the chemical warfare agents. Cleanup to, for example, 700 parts per billion for isopropyl methyl phosphonate in water may be a useful rule of thumb. This value represents a conservative cleanup level, in the sense that concentrations below this level would probably have no adverse health effects, and decontamination would generally not have to be done to a more stringent criterion for this compound. Other values in Table 4 could be applied similarly.

In the modeling exercise, we used the State and Federal water-quality objectives identified in Table 4 as the basis for establishing conservative soil cleanup levels for selected chemical compounds. Such values are useful for modeling purposes because they represent established and published concentrations that are acceptable to protect human health, and the compounds are identical, or similar, to degradation products of chemical warfare agents. The values could also represent acceptable cleanup levels for decontamination activities involving these compounds.

Our basic question was straightforward. If soil were contaminated in a specific scenario with a specific agent, how much cleanup would be required to avoid groundwater contamination based on standard EPA gas chromatography and mass spectrometry methods (i.e., 8260 and 8270 for volatiles and semi-volatile organic compounds) to detect residual compounds or byproducts? We used a simple water-quality model to determine pollutant transport through the vadose zone into the groundwater. The model is California's Designated Level Methodology (Marshack 1992*)* developed by California's Central Valley Regional Water Quality Control Board. This model is currently used by the Central Valley and the San Francisco Bay Regional Water Quality Control Boards and others to determine necessary cleanup levels for soils.

To model pollutant transport from the base of a contaminated area down to groundwater, the Designated Level Methodology can use generic attenuation factors.

- A factor of 100 is used for most pollutants with at least 30 feet of alluvial materials containing significant clays above the highest groundwater level.
- A factor or 1000 is used for copper, lead, and zinc at sites of the type characterized above.
- A factor of 10 is used for all other sites.

We used the following equation to calculate the soluble designated level [C_{sol}] above which leachate may carry a pollutant to ground or surface water in amounts that could cause water-quality goals to be exceeded:

$$[C_{sol}] = [(\text{water quality goal}) \times (\text{environmental attenuation factor})] \div (\text{dilution factor}),$$

where $[C_{sol}]$ is expressed in mg/l, the water quality goal is expressed in mg/l, the generic attenuation factor is unitless, and the dilution factor is either 10 or 20. Soluble concentrations of constituents in soil or solid waste would be determined by performing the Waste Extraction Test (WET) for metals or the Toxicity Characteristic Leaching Procedure (TCLP). Because the WET extract is expected to be 10 times more dilute than soil (or waste) leachate, and the TCLP extract is expected to be 20 times more dilute, the dilution factor to be used in the equation is either WET = 10, or TCLP = 20.

Our modeled concentrations $[C_{sol}]$, which used a dilution factor of 10, can then be compared with water-quality criteria, such as the drinking water maximum contaminant level (MCL) or other criteria, to determine if a particular pollutant will deleteriously affect groundwater quality and its identified public uses.

The simple model using the generic attenuation factors we applied does not fully consider pollutant characteristics, such as volatility, reactivity, and partitioning coefficients, which would tend to increase the generic attenuation factors. Conversely, the model does not take into account other characteristics that could act to decrease the generic attenuation factors. More detailed site-specific hydrogeological characteristics, along with natural attenuation and degradation, should be used to develop the appropriate site-specific attenuation factors for more complete modeling to further refine cleanup values.

To illustrate the kinds of results that can be obtained with our modeling approach, Table 5 shows calculated soil cleanup levels for two different sites: the San Francisco 3Com Sports Stadium and the City of Baltimore Municipal stadium. We located Superfund sites at or near these two sites to approximate model inputs, such as depth to groundwater and the geological materials present in the vadose zone above groundwater. A literature search was done to further characterize the hydrogeology of these two sites.

Table 5 shows the Combined US Forces maximum allowable concentrations in drinking water for certain agents (Departments of the Army, Navy, and Air Force 1999) at 5 liters/day, not to exceed 7 days. The maximum concentrations shown for GA/GB/GDNX, mustard, and Lewisite (arsenic fraction) were used because they are the only existing values available for consumption of actual chemical warfare agents.

These concentrations should not be construed as acceptable for public consumption.

Table 5
Water-Quality Maximum Contaminant Levels (MCLs) and Model-Calculated Outdoor Soil Cleanup Levels at Two Sites

Constituent	Published Surface Water MCL (μg/l)	Published Groundwater MCL (μg/l)	Model-Calculated Soil Cleanup Level (μg/l)
San Francisco 3 Com sports stadium (water table < 30 ft)			
Arsenic	36*	50**	50
Isopropyl methylphosphonate	700***	700***	700
Malathion	0.1†	160†† Combined US Forces drinking water maximum†††	160
GA/GB/GD/VX	Not available	12	12
Mustard	Not available	140	140
Lewisite (arsenic fraction)	Not available	80	80
Baltimore Municipal stadium (water table > 30 ft)			
Arsenic	36*	50**	500
Isopropyl methylphosphonate	700***	700***	7000
Malathion	0.1†	200*** Combined US Forces drinking water maximum†††	2000
GA/GB/GD/VX	Not available	12	120
Mustard	Not available	140	1400
Lewisite (arsenic fraction)	36*	80	800

* US EPA national ambient water quality criteria for saltwater acquatic life protection, 4-day continuous concentration
** California and Federal drinking water maximum contaminant level (MCL)
*** US EPA suggested no-adverse-response level (SNARL)
† US EPA national ambient water quality criteria for saltwater aquatic life protection, instantaneous maximum
†† California Department of Health Services state action level
††† Maximum allowable concentration by the Combined US Forces for consumption at 5 liters/da, not to exceed 7 days

Results in Table 5 show that for the Baltimore Municipal stadium scenario, where the water table is > 30 ft, the projected soil cleanup level necessary to meet published water-quality objectives is one order of magnitude less stringent than that required at the San Francisco sports stadium, where the water table is < 30 ft. The results for arsenic, isopropyl methylphosphonate, malathion, GA/GB/GD/VX, mustard, and Lewisite all represent an order of magnitude difference at these two scenarios. Such findings show the highly site-dependent nature of decontamination in meeting defined water-quality goals. In the absence of a more detailed health-risk assessment and for the particular constituents and scenarios modeled, we believe that it should not be necessary to clean up soil to more stringent levels than those identified in Table 5.

It is also possible to calculate cleanup levels necessary to protect surface receiving waters when a site is located near water bodies or there is a potential that materials could be discharged into the storm drainage system. Because discharges to surface water bodies do not allow the opportunity for constituents to be attenuated as they move through a soil matrix, the cleanup level is developed directly from the receiving water's water-quality objective. For certain constituents, the water-quality objective for aquatic life protection is more stringent than that for protection of human health. This is best shown in Table 5 for malathion. The surface water quality objective is 0.1 μg/l, whereas the drinking water quality objective is 160-200 μg/l. If a surface water body were threatened by release of an agent similar to malathion, the cleanup level would be much more stringent than if the release were contained to ground.

Further studies need to be initiated to address issues associated with semi-enclosed and indoor scenarios. Such studies would include indoor air-quality models, consideration of the residual airborne concentrations of selected chemical compounds, and the potential associated health risks.

After our modeling work was completed, the US Army (US Army Center for Health Promotion and Preventive Medicine 1999) further refined its health-based environmental screening levels (HBESLs) for chemical warfare agents in residential and industrial soil. The reader is referred to Table 11-2 of that report for HBESLs by individual agent, and the associated detailed methodology that was used. The values reported by the US Army generally fall within the range of values in Table 5 of the present report. However, our ranges are only generic for all nerve agents (GA, GB, GD, and VX) and, therefore, are generally more conservative. In addition, the U.S. Army HBESLs ". . . did not address ecological risk, and may not be sufficiently conservative to protect all ecological receptors at all sites."

Problematic Cleanup Criteria for Biological Agents

A similar modeling approach could be applied for scenarios involving biological agents and toxins. However, a key issue is that it is much more problematic to establish target cleanup levels for biological agents. The difficulty arises, in large part, because of public acceptance and perception issues. That is, biological cleanup criteria are strongly driven by stakeholder concerns. For example, the public may demand zero living organisms after decontamination of enclosed sites, such as offices or public buildings. However, it is important to point out that some potential biological agents, such as *Bacillus anthracis,* are already indigenous to many farming communities, without incident. According to Cox and Wathes (1995), *Bacillus anthracis* in outdoor air may naturally range between 0.5 and 5 endotoxin units (EU per m^3). Unreliable reporting makes it difficult to estimate the true incidence of inhalation anthrax in humans. In recent years in the US, the annual incidence of human anthrax has steadily declined to about one case per year for the past 10 years, and most cases are cutaneous. Under natural conditions, inhalation anthrax is extremely rare, with only 18 cases reported in the US in the twentieth century (Office of the Surgeon General 1997). Therefore, zero concentration of a biological agent, and zero risk, in many cases is clearly not a necessity. It is likely that economic drivers will also influence stakeholders to accept higher risks.

Although the US Department of Defense has considerable experience in the decontamination and handling of biological warfare agents, such methods may not be readily applicable to public settings. Alternative practices and standards might serve as useful guidelines for public acceptance of some risks, including those established for disinfecting biological research facilities, hospitals, and public swimming pools. The published practices or standards that might be adapted for public sector use include:

- *Biosafety Reference Manual,* American Industrial Hygiene Association (1995).
- *Biosafety in Microbiological and Biomedical Laboratories,* Centers for Disease Control (1999b).
- *NASA Standards for Clean Rooms and Work Stations for Microbially Controlled Environments,* National Aeronautics and Space Administration (1967).

Education is also an important consideration in public acceptance of some risks. In general, the public accepts hospital disinfectant methods, although such methods are certainly no guarantee of zero risk. Similarly, public swimming pools must meet defined treatment standards that are accepted by the public, yet there have been instances in which children have died from exposure to and ingestion of *E. coli* from public swimming pools. The current public health standards for swimming pools are:

- 1-2 ppm of free chlorine, and pH from 7.8 to 8.4, as specified by the US Army (1982). (California Code of Regulations, Title 22, Division 4 values are similar, with at least 1.5 ppm free chlorine and pH from 7.2 to 8.0).
- Total bacterial count < 200 colony forming units (CFU) per 100 ml in 85% of samples tested, as specified by the US EPA (1979a).
- Total coliform bacteria < 2.2 MPN per 100 ml (most probable number, or median), as specified by California Code of Regulations, Title 22, Division 4.

Table 6 shows various indoor and outdoor cleanup levels for coliform bacteria, as recommended by various agencies, including NASA (1967), the US EPA (1979a, b, 1981, 1982), the California EPA (California Code of Regulations, Title 22), and Streifel et al. (1989). In terms of decontaminating surfaces, US EPA guidelines (98-9.999% reduction) do not address the original quantity of organisms, which is a relevant consideration. For drinking water, the California Code of Regulations, Title 22, also specifies that a public water system is in violation of the total coliform maximum contaminant level (MCL) when any of the following occurs:

- for a system collecting more than 40 samples per month, more than 5% of the samples collected during any month are total coliform positive; or
- for a public water system that collects fewer than 40 samples per month, more than one sample collected during any month is total coliform positive; or
- any repeat sample is fecal coliform positive or *E. coli* positive; or
- any repeat sample, following a fecal-coliform-positive or E.-coli-positive routine sample, is total coliform positive.

Such guidelines and the values in Table 6 may serve as a starting point for developing public guidance in case of an incident involving biological agents. Any new standards for a particular biological agent would have to address how infectious a specific organism is and possible modes of transmission. In addition to the values in Table 6, the current Combined US Forces drinking water standard (for short-term field use) is identified as 26 µg/l for T-2 toxins (Departments of the Army, Navy, and Air Force 1999).

Risk-Informed Decision Making

In response to requirements for the destruction of bulk chemical agents and chemical agent munitions, comprehensive health risk assessments have been performed as part of the procedure for selecting both the sites and the destruction processes. The studies are not precisely applicable to this paper because they give significant weight to the low probability of a dispersal event, but the post-event methodology could provide relevant models for establishing cleanup criteria. However, such demilitarization assessments are not based on low-level chronic-effects data. To our knowledge, little information is available relating long-term health effects to low-dose exposures for chemical warfare agents. The recent US Army report on derivation of health-based environmental screening levels for chemical warfare agents (US Army Center for Health Promotion and Preventive Medicine 1999) will serve as a useful guideline in establishing regulatory limits. Additional related studies were recently undertaken by the National Academy of Sciences for the Department of Defense (Wartell et al. 1999). The US Army Edgewood Chemical and

Biological Center recently initiated an experimental study to evaluate low-level dose effects of chemical warfare agents. The latter study should be available within the next year or two and will further help to refine exposure limits.

Table 6
Suggested Indoor and Outdoor Cleanup Levels for Biological Agents in Water, Air, and Surfaces

	General Population and Worker Threshold Limit Values		
Description of Medium, Area, or Surface	**Total Coliform Bacteria**	**Heterotrophic Plate Count**	**NASA Laboratory Standards**
Water			
Maximum allowable for potable water	Absent in 95% of samples collected	500 CFU / ml*	Not applicable
Maximum allowable for nonpotable water	< 240 CFU / 100 ml	500,000 CFU / ml	Not applicable
Maximum allowable for swimming pool water	< 2.2 MPN /100 ml (median) < 2.3 MPN/100 ml (total)	<200 CFU/100 ml in 85% of samples tested	Not applicable
Air			
Air-conditioned areas	Not applicable	Unknown	< 18 CFU / m^3
Industrial (non-air-conditioned) areas	Not applicable	Unknown	< 88 CFU / m^3
Hospital	Not applicable	< 15 fungal CFU/ m^3	Not applicable
Surfaces			
Air-conditioned areas	Not applicable	Unknown	< 7 CFU / m^2
Industrial (non-air-conditioned) areas	Not applicable	98% reduction	< 32 CFU / m^2
Hospital	Not applicable	99.999% reduction	Not applicable
Carpets	Not applicable	99.9% reduction	Not applicable

* Current US EPA national primary drinking water standard

Therefore, to evaluate potential residual health effects for a particular chemical or biological agent in a scenario involving infrastructure decontamination, some type of simplified, scenario-specific health risk assessment would be necessary. A risk-based approach means that cleanup guidelines should be based on a defined, "acceptable" level of risk to health. Many factors must be considered in developing standards and realistic cleanup goals to protect health, property, and resources. The following considerations are among the most important.

First, it is necessary to determine whether a risk actually exists or is perceived to exist. An actual risk depends on the presence of three elements: a threat or hazard, a receptor (human or ecological), and a pathway (physical or environmental migration route) that connects the two. If any one of the three elements is absent, then by definition, no actual risk exists. If a risk does exist, a determination of the timing and potential severity of an incident must be made. Interrelated considerations are the release scenario and site descriptions; contaminant migration and longevity; projected land, resource, or property use; and any use restrictions.

Cleanup and decontamination decisions must then be made with input from stakeholders representing both public and regulatory concerns. Relevant risk-informed decision-making considerations include:

- potential acute and long-term chronic health impacts, including health effects on key populations, such as pregnant women or immunocompromised individuals;
- damage to land, water, property, and equipment as a function of cost;
- detectability of agent(s) and long-term fate of contaminants;
- cost of decontamination or restoration options as well as time constraints;
- availability of decontamination methods and methods for the associated sampling, analysis, and verification of decontamination;
- aesthetic considerations;
- other site-specific factors that may be relevant;
- potential over-reaction that may cause more panic or chaos than warranted.

An important factor underlying each risk-based decision is the uncertainty and reliability of available data. Uncertainties in the magnitude and location of residual agents, site-specific features, and prediction of natural attenuation or potential dilution effects all contribute to decisions about whether appropriate decontamination levels have been reached. In most cases, statistically valid "hot spot" sampling (or other appropriate statistical sampling methods) could be used to reduce uncertainty both in site characterization and in the likelihood that an appropriate decision has been made. This type of sampling strategy would take into account the way in which decontaminating agents are applied, as well as the geometry of the contaminated site. In addition, the target or hot spot is well modeled by the circular or elliptical assumption of the hot spot analysis, and the hot spots can be considered primarily a surface characteristic. Hot spot sampling is typically conducted by griding the area to be sampled, and collecting samples from the grid nodes. The model is then applied to the results, and an overall assessment can be made of the site (Gilbert 1987, Singer 1972, 1975).

The recommended, scenario-based health-risk assessment approach begins with a multimedia, multipathway dose assessment. For example, the resuspension, subsequent multimedia transport, and fate of a substance or microorganism must be determined. This means that the ability of the contaminant to move into and off of contaminated materials must be determined or assumed. Consideration must be given to the mobility of a contaminant under both unusual conditions, such as fires, and mundane ones, such as painting a building. The toxicology of the agent must be evaluated, and human morbidity, mortality, and latency of effects must be determined, if known. Integrating multimedia transport and fate with multipathway exposure (e.g., inhalation, secondary ingestion, or dermal absorption) and physiologically based pharmacokinetics (if available) for modeling toxicity should yield an estimate of noncarcinogenic hazard and carcinogenic risk, especially from short-term exposures. If possible, an empirical biomarker or biodosimetric procedure should be identified so that those given permission to reoccupy a building or structure can be monitored.

An alternative and commonly accepted approach is to study contaminated versus uncontaminated environments. Elevated concentrations of an agent can then be used as an index for evaluating relative contamination levels and to determine whether decontamination treatment should be repeated. For example, to evaluate anthrax contamination in a building located in a farming community, where anthrax is indigenous, one would measure the relative anthrax concentration inside versus outside the building to ascertain whether decontamination should be implemented or repeated. Acceptable levels should be somewhere between background and the lowest dose for any kind of infection.

We have published a conceptual decision process for chemical and/or biological decontamination following a terrorist attack (Raber et al. 1999). The details of this decision framework are beyond the scope of this paper. However, an important point is that the major decision areas defined in the framework are derived from risk-based decision making. The steps to follow include evaluation of the timing and severity of impact of an incident; whether specific site conditions pose unacceptable risk to health, ecosystems, or property and thereby warrant decontamination; and a definition of decontamination goals, including cleanup concentration and target time frame to achieve the goals. The framework includes key decision points for regulatory and stakeholder review. Any perceived risk, and potential community outrage associated with the perceived risk related to a CBW incident, will need to be addressed carefully. Stakeholder involvement is critical whether there is an actual or perceived risk.

Conclusions and Recommendations

This review represents a summary of the type of information and evaluations necessary to begin laying a framework for establishing realistic cleanup criteria. Clearly, much remains to be done to ensure acceptable cleanup of contaminated facilities and infrastructure following the release of CBW agents. To help direct future efforts, we summarize several important conclusions and offer some specific recommendations.

Conclusions

1. Literature searches and discussions with key US agencies demonstrate that additional information is needed to establish safe criteria for exposure to CBW agents. Toxicological database tools have limited use and applicability for conditions relevant to the public

sector. Infectious dose levels are not available for many biological agents, and little information is available relating long-term health effects to low-dose exposures for chemical warfare agents. Therefore, to evaluate potential residual health effects for a particular chemical or biological agent in a scenario involving infrastructure decontamination, some type of scenario-based health risk assessment would be necessary.

2. Cleanup criteria are site dependent. In particular, much stricter criteria are necessary for indoor, long-term reuse than for outdoor scenarios where natural attenuation may be effective for the decontamination or destruction of biological agents, biological toxins, or chemical warfare agents.

3. Cleanup criteria are population specific. Standards must consider worker versus public exposures, and individuals who may be at higher risk, such as developing fetuses, children, and the immunocompromised.

4. A review of existing, though incomplete, environmental regulatory limits indicates that conservative cleanup concentrations (i.e., suggested no-action-required levels, or SNARLS) range from about 2 to 700 ppb for some residual byproducts of actual chemical warfare agents or closely related compounds. Such values were used in modeling studies to project soil cleanup levels necessary to meet published water-quality objectives. Results for two outdoor scenarios reinforce the site-dependent nature of cleanup criteria. New health-based environmental screening levels for chemical warfare agents have been recently proposed by the US Army (1999).

5. Cleanup issues for biological agents have added complexity because many organisms are indigenous; risk is a function of effective dispersion, exposure (often by inhalation), and infectivity; and public perceptions of acceptable risk must be addressed. Practices described by the American Industrial Hygiene Association, the Centers of Disease Control, and NASA might be adapted for use in the public sector.

Recommendations

1. A scenario-based risk-assessment approach is needed to understand appropriate cleanup levels and potential residual health effects for both chemical and biological agents. Three elements and the relations

among them in a given scenario must be carefully defined: sources and extent of contamination, applicable receptors, and potential environmental and physical pathways between them.

2. The development of public standards or re-entry criteria must consider not only scientifically based information but also public perceptions about what is safe. Appropriate risk-communication techniques, including an explanation of scientific terminology and methods, should be used to implement recommendations based on scientific criteria. It is important to anticipate the issues and to educate the relevant parties on both the decontamination and verification methods used. Risk-communication techniques have been addressed with regard to demilitarization programs, which may provide a useful framework on which to build.

3. It is necessary to develop and implement a sound, defensible protocol for verification sampling and analysis to demonstrate the effectiveness of decontamination in each of at least three scenarios: indoor, semi-enclosed, and outdoor. Techniques to obtain representative field samples exist, but they will differ for chemical versus biological warfare agents.

Acknowledgements

We express our appreciation to both Karen Folks and Richard Brown, environmental analysts at Lawrence Livermore National Laboratory, for their valuable input and help with the modeling studies reported in this paper. Work was performed under the auspices of the US Department of Energy by Lawrence Livermore National Laboratory under Contract W-7405-ENG-48.

References

American Conference of Governmental Industrial Hygienists (1997) 1997 *TLVs and BEIs. Threshold Limit Values for Chemical Substances and Physical Agents; Biological Exposure Indices.* Cincinnati, OH: ACGHI.

American Industrial Hygiene Association (1995) *Biosafety Reference Manual.* 2nd edn, p. 175. American Industrial Hygiene Association, Publication No. 204-RC-95.

Benenson, A.S. (ed) (1990) *Control of Communicable Disease in Man.* 15th edn. American Public Health Association.

California Code of Regulations. Title 22, Division 4 (Environmental Health), sections 64423-64426.1, 65529-65531, and 60301-60320.

California Code of Regulations, Title 22, Division 4 (Environmental Health), section 65529.

Centers for Disease Control (1988) Recommendations for protecting human health against potential adverse effects of long-term exposure to low doses of chemical warfare agents. *Morbid. Mortal. Weekly Rep. 37(5),* 72-9.

Centers for Disease Control (1999a) Bioterrorism alleging use of anthrax and interim guidelines for management-United States, 1998. *Morbid. Mortal. Weekly Rep. 48(4),* 69-74.

Centers for Disease Control (1999b) *Biosafety in Microbiology and Biomedical Laboratories.* 4th edn, p. 250. HHS Publication 93-8395.

Cox, C.S. and Wathes, C.M. (eds) (1995) *Bioaerosols Handbook.* New York: Lewis Publishers.

Department of the Army (1982) *Occupational and Environmental Health, Swimming Pools and Bathing Facilities.* Washington, DC: US Government Printing Office, Technical Bulletin No. Med 575.

Department of the Army (1990) *Potential Military Chemical/Biological Agents and Compounds. US* Army Field Manual 3-9. Navy publication No. P-467. Air Force manual 355-7.

Department of the Army (1996a) *Handbook on the Medical Aspects of NBC Defense Operations, Part II-Biological. US* Army Field Manual 8-9.

Department of the Army (1996b) *Handbook on the Medical Aspects of NBC Defense Operations, Part III-Chemical. US* Army Field Manual 8-9.

Departments of the Army, Navy, and Air Force (1999) *Sanitary Control and Surveillance of Field Water Supplies.* Department of the Army Technical Bulletin TB MED 577.

Franz, D. (1996) US *Army Defense Against Toxin Weapons.* Fort Detrick, Fredrick, MD: US Army Medical Research Institute of Infectious Diseases, Veterinary Corps., MCMR-UIZ-B.

Gilbert, R.O. (1987) Locating hot spots. In *Statistical Methods for Environmental Pollution Monitoring,* ch. 10, pp. 119-31. New York: Van Nostrand Reinhold.

Harvey *et al.* (1997) *Neutralization and Biodegradation of Sulfur Mustard.* Aberdeen Proving Ground. MD: US Army Armaments Munitions Chemical Command, Edgewood Research Development and Engineering Center, ERDEC-TR-388.

Inglesby, V., Henderson, D.A., Bartlett, J.G. *et al.* (1999), Anthrax as a biological weapon. J. *Am. Med. Assoc. 281(18),* 1735-45.

Kadlec, R. *et al.* (1997) Biological weapons control: prospects and implications for the future. J. *Am. Med. Assoc. 278(5),* 351-6.

Kaufman, A.F., Meltzer, M.I. and Schmid, G.P. (1977) The economic impact of a bioterrorist attack: are prevention and postattack intervention programs justifiable? *Emerging Infect. Dis. 3(2),* 83-94.

Lauwerys, R.R. (1986) Occupational toxicology. In *The Basic Science of Poisons,* 3rd edn. (Casarett and Doull, eds.), New, York, NY: Macmillan.

Marshack, J.B. (1992) *California's Water Quality Standards and Their Applicability to Waste Management and Site Cleanup.* Sacramento, CA: California Environmental Protection Agency, Regional Water Quality Control Board, Central Valley Region.

McGuire, R.R., Haas, J.S. and Eagle, R.J. (1993) *The Decay of Chemical Weapons Agents under Environmental Conditions.* Livermore, CA: Lawrence Livermore National Laboratory, UCRLID-114107.

Meselson M., Guillemin J. and Hugh-Jones M. (1994) *Science 266,* 1202-8.

Mioduszewski, R.J., Reutter, S.A., Miller, L.L., Olajos, E.J. and Thomson, S.A. (1998) *Evaluation of Airborne Exposure Limits for G-Agents: Occupational and General Population Exposure Criteria.* Edgewood Research, Development, and Engineering Center, US Army Chemical and Biological Defense Command, ERDEC-TR-489.

National Advisory Committee for Acute Exposure Guideline Levels (AEGLs) for Hazardous Substances (2000) Proposed AEGL Values. Environmental Protection Agency, *Fed. Reg. 65(51).*

National Aeronautics and Space Administration (1967) NASA *Standards for Clean Rooms and Work Stations for the Microbially Controlled Environments.* Washington, DC: US Government Printing Office, NHB 5340.2.

National Research Council (1997) *Review of Acute Human-Toxicity Estimates for Selected ChemicalWarfare Agents.* Washington, DC: National Academy Press.

Office of the Surgeon General (1997) *Medical Aspects of Chemical and Biological Warfare. Part I. Textbook of Military Medicine.* Department of the Army.

Public Law No. 104-132 (April 24, 1996) Anti-Terrorist and Effective Death Penalty Act of 1996, 42 Code of Federal Regulations Part 72.

Raber, E., Hirabayashi, J., Manciere, S., Jin, A., Folks, K. and Rice, D. (1999) Conceptual biodecontamination decision process following a terrorist attack. Livermore, CA: Lawrence Livermore National Laboratory, UCRL-AR-131181, rev. 1.

Singer, D.A. (1972) ELIPGRID: A Fortran IV program for calculating the probability of success in locating elliptical targets with square, rectangular, and hexagonal grids. *Geocom. Prog. 4,* 1-16.

Singer, D.A. (1975) Relative efficiencies of square and triangular grids in the search for elliptically shaped resource targets. J. *Res. U.S. Geol. Survey 3(20),* 163-7.

Streifel, A.J., Vesley, D., Rhame, F.S. and Murray, B. (1989) Control of airborne fungal spores in a university hospital. *Environ. Int. 15,* 221.

Tucker, J.B. (1997) National health and medical service response to incidents of chemical and biological terrorism. J. *Am. Med. Assoc. 278(6),* 362-368.

US Army (1990) *Occupational Health Guidelines for the Evaluation and Control of Occupational Exposure to Nerve Agents GA, GB, GD, and VX.* Department of the Army Pamphlet 40-8.

US Army (1991) *Occupational Health Guidelines for the Evaluation and Control of Occupational Exposure to Mustard Agents H, HD, HT.* Department of the Army Pamphlet 40-173.

US Army (1996) *Medical Management of Biological Casualties Handbook.* 2nd edn. Fort Detrick, Fredrick, MD: US Army Medical Research, Institute of Infectious Diseases.

US Army Center for Health Promotion and Preventive Medicine (1999) *Derivation of Health-Based Environmental Screening Levels for Chemical Warfare Agents, A Technical Evaluation. US* Army Center for Health Promotion and Preventive Medicine, Aberdeen Proving Ground, MD.

US Army Medical Research Institute of Chemical Defense (1998) *Medical Management of Chemical Casualties Handbook.* 3rd edn. Aberdeen Proving Ground-Edgewood Area, MD: USAMRICD.

US Department of State (1982) *Chemical Warfare in Southeast Asia, Afghanistan; An Update, Report from Secretary of State George P. Shultz.* Special Report No. 104.

US Environmental Protection Agency (1979a) *Antimicrobial DIS-TSS Documents. Efficacy Data Requirements for Swimming Pool Water Disinfectants.* Environmental Protection Agency, DISTSS-12.

US Environmental Protection Agency (1979b) *Antimicrobial DIS-TSS Documents. Efficacy Data Requirements for Sanitizing Rinses.* Environmental Protection Agency, DIS-TSS-4, 1979.

US Environmental Protection Agency (1981) *Antimicrobial DIS-TSS Documents. Efficacy Data Requirements for Carpet Sanitizers.* Environmental Protection Agency, DIS-TSS-8, 1981.

US Environmental Protection Agency (1982) *Antimicrobial DIS-TSS Documents. Efficacy Data Requirements for Disinfectants for Use on Hard Surfaces.* Environmental Protection Agency, DIS-TSS-1.

US General Accounting Office (1998) *Chemical Weapons; DOD Does Not Have a Strategy to Address Low-Level Exposures.* Washington, DC: US General Accounting Office, GAO/NIAD-98-228.

Wartell, M.A., Kleinman, M.T., Huey, B.M. and Duffy, L.M. (eds) (1999) *Strategies to Protect the Health of Deployed U.S. Forces.* Washington, DC: National Academy Press.

Anthrax Threats: A Report of Two Incidents from Salt Lake City[1]

Eric R. Swanson
David E. Fosnocht

Abstract: *The ongoing threat of anthrax as an agent of bioterrorism in the U.S. is very real. The highly visible and potentially devastating effects of these threats require a well-coordinated and well-organized Emergency Medical Services (EMS) and Emergency Department (ED) response to minimize panic and reduce the potential spread of an active and deadly biologic agent. This requires planning and education before the event. We describe the events of two anthrax threats in a major metropolitan area. The appropriate EMS and ED response to these threats is outlined.*

Introduction

Two terrorist threats claiming exposure to inhaled anthrax occurred in a major metropolitan area 8 days apart. These incidents are similar to other bioterrorist threats across the nation that have been occurring with increasing frequency. In 1998, there were 37 incidents involving a threat of anthrax exposure. In the first 2 months of 1999, there were ten such incidents [1]. All of these threats have been determined to be hoaxes. However, it is clear that the potential for terrorism with biologic agents exists in the United States. Emergency physicians are often the front-line providers of care for patients exposed to chemical and biologic agents and are likely to be the medical control for the Emergency Medical Services (EMS) agencies operating at the scene of these incidents. We describe the two incidents and present current guidelines for the prehospital and emergency department (ED) management of patients with a potential exposure to inhaled anthrax.

Incident 1

A 32-year-old female Planned Parenthood employee opened a Christmas card with a return address from Kentucky. The employee was suspicious of the letter because of a recent briefing by the Federal Bureau of Investigation (FBI) prompted by similar threats to Planned Parenthood clinics. The employee opened the letter cautiously and saw a brown residue inside. She immediately closed her office door and called 911. Fire department paramedics were dispatched to the scene and called the emergency department on arrival. The FBI, fire department hazardous materials (HAZMAT) unit, state health department, and police department all responded to the scene. The hospital departments of public affairs, security, and infectious diseases were contacted. The medical directors for poison control and the fire department (both emergency medicine faculty) as well as the federal Centers for Disease Control (CDC) were also contacted. The coordinator of the hospital's emergency management and hazardous materials program responded and assisted with incident management.

Ventilation to the clinic was turned off, and the patient was decontaminated at the scene with soap and water and a dilute hypochlorite solution. Her clothing and personal effects were bagged, and the patient was transported to the ED. The area where the letter was opened was decontaminated with a 0.5% hypochlorite solution. The 20 additional persons in the building at the time of the potential exposure were placed in a bus and interviewed by EMS personnel to determine their risk of exposure. All of them were judged to be at low risk because of their lack of proximity to the suspected agent. After information was collected from these individuals, they were debriefed and released from the scene. The patient transported to the ED was started on prophylactic antibiotic coverage with ciprofloxacin pending culture results. She was debriefed and given contact persons with phone numbers for follow-up before discharge. The state department of health and the FBI evaluated samples from the letter. Cultures and fluorescent antibody testing performed at the Naval Medical Research Institute were negative for *Bacillus anthracis*. Antibiotic coverage was stopped with the return of negative culture results at 48 h.

Incident 2

A 21-year-old female, 44-year-old male, and 44-year-old female were in the mail room of a church office building when a letter was opened that stated, "Congratulations, you have just been exposed to anthrax." The individuals did not note any powder or residue in or on the letter. They called building security and 911. As in the first incident, the EMS response at the scene involved paramedics, HAZMAT team members, local police, FBI, and the state health department. Emergency department and hospital staff response included the departments of public relations and security. The regional poison control center, the hospital's department of infectious diseases, and the CDC were contacted. The three patients were decontaminated at the scene with soap and water. All personal effects and clothing were bagged. The site where the letter was opened was locally decontaminated with dilute hypochlorite solution. The lack of a residue or other material in the letter was judged by officials to place the incident at low risk of being an active threat. No other persons in the building were decontaminated, and the building was not evacuated. The three patients were transferred to the ED, where they were debriefed and given prophylactic ciprofloxacin pending culture results. Cultures and direct fluorescent antibody testing of the letter were performed at the Utah State Health Department Laboratory and were negative for *B. anthracis*. Antibiotic coverage was stopped with the return of negative cultures at 48 h.

Discussion

Presentation and Diagnosis

Anthrax is caused by *B. anthracis*, a ubiquitous spore-forming bacterium found in the soil. Animals may contract the spores while grazing, and humans contract the spores from animals through direct contact, ingestion, or inhalation. Human-to-human transmission of anthrax has not been documented [2 and 3]. The clinical presentations of anthrax in humans are cutaneous, gastrointestinal, and inhalational.

Cutaneous anthrax is primarily a disease of animal and animal product handlers. A break in the skin is required for bacterial spore entry. A raised itchy bump is followed over 1-2 days by a vesicle and then a painless ulcer with a black necrotic center and eschar. The lesions are generally 1-3 cm in diameter. Local and extremity edema with lymph node swelling is common. Oral antimicrobial therapy is effective for all but the more severe cases. Gastrointestinal anthrax follows consumption of contaminated meat and results in acute inflammation of the intestinal tract. Nausea, vomiting, severe diarrhea, and fever with abdominal pain and gastrointestinal bleeding are common. The mortality of intestinal anthrax is reported to be 25-60%.

The inhaled form of anthrax is the most serious infection in humans and can cause a necrotizing hemorrhagic mediastinitis [4]. Aerosol delivery of anthrax spores is the most likely method to be used in an act of biologic warfare or terrorism [3]. As with many biologic agents, the initial presentation of inhalation anthrax resembles a viral syndrome that makes early diagnosis difficult. An incubation period of 1-5 days is generally noted although periods as long as 43 days have been reported [3]. A prodrome of fever, malaise, fatigue, and nonproductive cough are the initial symptoms. A chest radiograph may reveal a widened mediastinum and pleural effusions. There may be symptomatic improvement for several days after the prodrome or immediate progression to respiratory distress, septic shock, and death [5]. Treatment of inhalational anthrax after onset of symptoms is not effective, with a mortality of 90% [3 and 6]. In a large epidemic of inhalational anthrax from an accidental release from a military facility in Sverdlovsk in the former Soviet Union, autopsy findings revealed the frequent occurrence of hematogenously disseminated infection in addition to hemorrhagic mediastinitis. Out of 42 patients autopsied, there were 21 cases of hemorrhagic meningitis and 39 cases of multiple gastrointestinal submucosal hemorrhagic lesions [4]. *B. anthracis* may be visualized by a Gram's stain of peripheral blood or isolated by blood cultures, but this may occur late in the disease process. ELISA may be used to detect toxin in the blood. Gram's stain, cultures, or direct fluorescent antibody testing may be performed on the source of an alleged anthrax threat to exclude or confirm the presence of an active biologic agent.

Prehospital Management

Upon notification of the EMS system, every effort should be made to initiate early control of the scene and prevent further spread of contamination. At a minimum, the person calling must be advised to leave the object of the threat and retreat to a safe location that minimizes potential exposure to others. Isolating the potential area of exposure by closing doors and turning off ventilation systems to the building is ideal. As much information as possible regarding the number of persons exposed and the nature of contamination should be obtained from the person calling to determine the appropriate level and volume of EMS and hospital disaster response.

HAZMAT and law enforcement (local and FBI) officials should respond to the scene. Initial EMS and HAZMAT personnel should use full protective gear and self-contained breathing apparatus until exposure risk and contamination can be assessed by trained personnel. Medical control and public health officials (local, state, and the CDC) should be contacted. EMS and HAZMAT personnel should establish the potential risk of exposure and, with the assistance of law enforcement personnel, control the scene. If decontamination is appropriate, persons should remove their clothing and personal effects, place all items in plastic bags, and be showered using copious quantities of soap and water. The addition of a dilute hypochlorite solution to the soap and water decontamination, as occurred in the first incident, is not required and not part of current decontamination guidelines for anthrax exposure.

After the crime scene investigation, samples of the suspected agent should be collected and the environment in direct contact with the suspected agent should be decontaminated with a 0.5% hypochlorite solution [2]. If a significant exposure has occurred, patients should be transported to an emergency department that is designated for biologic and chemical exposures. Public health officials should collect contact information from potentially exposed persons for notification of laboratory results or other follow-up. EMS triage and discharge of nonsignificantly exposed patients is critical to avoid overwhelming emergency department resources. Persons discharged from the scene should be given information regarding the signs and symptoms of illness associated with the biologic agent, whom to contact, and where to go should they develop symptoms.

Emergency Department Management

For medical control, as much information as possible should be obtained from the scene as early as possible. The hospital disaster plan should be referred to and a response of personnel appropriate to the level and volume of the threat should be initiated. Hospital security and public affairs staff members should be notified, and any additional personnel needed should be called in. If it is suspected that adequate decontamination was not done at the scene, patients should be decontaminated with a soap and water shower before entry into the ED. Quarantine or isolation is not required after decontamination measures, as person to person spread of anthrax has not been documented. Emergency department personnel should use only typical barrier protection equipment for prevention of exposure to blood-borne pathogens.

Post-exposure prophylaxis for *B. anthracis* consists of chemoprophylaxis with antimicrobial agents until exposure has been confirmed or excluded. Chemoprophylaxis is recommended with ciprofloxacin (500 mg by mouth twice a day) or, if contraindicated, doxycycline (100 mg by mouth twice a day) until *B. anthracis* exposure has been excluded by cultures of the suspected agent from the scene. If exposure to *B. anthracis* is confirmed, chemoprophylaxis should be continued for at least 4 weeks and until three doses of vaccine have been administered. Chemoprophylaxis should continue for 8 weeks if vaccine is not available.

Patients who have developed inhalational anthrax should receive ciprofloxacin (400 mg every 8-12 h i.v.) until sensitivity data are known [2 and 6]. The need for ICU care with supportive therapy for shock and airway management should be anticipated for symptomatic individuals. Chemoprophylaxis in children is recommended with ciprofloxacin (20-30 mg/kg per day divided every 12 h) or, if contraindicated, with doxycycline (5 mg/kg per day divided every 12 h). Continued treatment for confirmed exposure may be done with amoxicillin (40 mg/kg per day divided every 8 h) if the organism is penicillin-susceptible. The risks of tetracycline and fluoroquinolone treatment in children must be weighed against the possibility of developing life-threatening disease [2].

The anthrax vaccine is a sterile filtrate of cultures from an avirulent strain that produces protective antigens. Pre-exposure vaccination is recommended for high-risk industries with exposure to imported animal products, and is being carried out for active duty military personnel. The vaccine can be requested through the CDC. Post-exposure vaccination consists of an injection as soon as possible after confirmed exposure and again 2 and 4 weeks later. The vaccine has not been evaluated for safety and efficacy in children under 18 or adults over 60 years of age [2 and 7].

Summary

The appropriate EMS and ED response to a potential anthrax exposure requires knowledge of the disease and its mechanism of spread. Our own experience with these events confirms the importance of a predefined plan and knowledge of the actions to be taken in the event of a potential exposure to anthrax or another biologic agent. These events have highlighted both the strengths and weaknesses of the disaster management systems in place at our facility and allowed a much more highly trained and competent response to be available for future events. This knowledge should be spread among the EMS and Emergency Medicine communities to provide the necessary and appropriate response for future events in other locations.

Notes

[1] Selected Topics: Disaster Medicine is coordinated by *Irving "Jake" Jacoby*, MD, of the University of California San Diego Medical Center, San Diego, California.

References

1. Stern, J. Anthrax Incidents, Hoaxes, and Threats. National Symposium on Medical and Public Response to Bioterrorism. February 16, 1999.

2. Bioterrorism alleging use of anthrax and interim guidelines for management–United States 1998. *MMWR* 1999;48:69-74.

3. M. Meselson, J. Guillemin, M. Hugh-Jones *et al.*, The Sverdlovsk anthrax outbreak of 1979. *Science* 266 (1994), pp. 1202-1208.

4. F.A. Abramova, L.M. Grinberg, O.V. Yampolskaya and D.H. Walker, Pathology of inhalational anthrax in 42 cases from the Sverdlovsk outbreak of 1979. *Proc Natl Acad Sci USA* 90 (1993), pp. 2291-2294.

5. P.S. Brachman, Inhalational anthrax. *Ann NY Acad Sci* 353 (1980), pp. 83-93.

6. D.R. Franz, P.B. Jahrling, A.M. Friedlander *et al.*, Clinical recognition and management of patients exposed to biological warfare agents. *JAMA* 278 (1997), pp. 399-411.

7. Anthrax vaccine. *Med Lett Drugs Ther* 1998;40:52-3.

The Threat of Biological Terrorism In the New Millennium

Steven Kuhr
Jerome M. Hauer

Abstract: *The use of biological weapons in times of war has a long and detailed history in the 20th century. Today analysts, law enforcement, and intelligence experts suggest that biological weapons may be used to cause mass illness and death by terrorists domestically and internationally. Government agencies at the local, state, and federal levels must establish programs to detect natural or intentional epidemics early so as to afford the maximum protection for citizens by way of mass prophylaxis and mass medical care.*

The use of biological weapons by terrorists has the potential to harm and kill thousands of people. With forethought and planning, local government agencies can develop programs that can detect an outbreak early in its progress and implement a response that will reduce morbidity and mortality. This is critical in the new millennium. We now face an ever-growing threat of the use of bacterial and viral agents by terrorist groups, some of which may have ties to rogue nations known to manufacture and have in their arsenals products including agents that can cause diseases such as anthrax and tularemia.

The Threat

Biological weapons are known to have been produced by rogue nations such as Iraq and are believed to be in the possession of other nations such as North Korea. Harmful pathogens can be produced with some very rudimentary skills in biology. The question is whether they can be produced by amateur biologists at or near the military specifications needed to cause mass illness and death. Biological agent development is also relatively inexpensive, making it an attractive choice for today's economy-minded terrorists. However, an individual or group of individuals with some basic laboratory skills and basic knowledge of biology can produce a biological agent in quantities large enough to sicken and even kill a large number of people. This point was clearly illustrated in 1984, when followers of the Rajneesh, the leader of a cult based in Oregon, placed *Salmonella typhimurium* bacteria on open salad bars in a number of restaurants throughout the city of The Dalles. About 750 people became ill, but no deaths are known to have occurred as a result of this incident (Cole, 1996; Torok et al., 1997; WBFF Staff, 1997; Wildavsky, 1999).

Biological agents are generally categorized as either bacterial, viral, or toxin agents. Table 1 briefly displays the agents believed to convey the greatest threat based on the history of their development and ease of production.

Preparing for Biological Terrorism

Early recognition of an event is the frontline defense against biological terrorism. Unlike chemical agents, which act quickly, biological agents take longer to produce effects due to their incubation period as well as other environmental factors present during their release. These include meteorological factors such as wind speed and direction, time of day (sunlight contributes to the decay of biological agents), and temperature, which has an effect on inversion layers, affecting the ability of an agent to remain airborne. A narrow window of opportunity exists during which aggressive medical treatment, including prophylaxis (for bacterial agents), can positively affect the outcome of the disease.

To ensure that an outbreak is recognized early, hospital emergency departments, emergency medical service (EMS) personnel, and primary care physicians—the group most likely to observe an emerging disease incident (either natural or intentional)—must be trained to recognize the signs and symptoms of the diseases considered

Table 1
Most Threatening Biological Agents Based on Development and Ease of Production

Agent	Disease	Class	Incubation Period	Treatment	Early Signs and Symptoms
Baccillus anthracis	Anthrax	Bacteria	1 to 5 days	Ciprofloxacin	Fever, malaise, fatigue, cough, chest discomfort and dyspnea, diaphoresis, stridor, cyanosis
Francisella tularensis	Tularemia	Bacteria	1 to 10 days	Streptomycin, doxycycline	Fever, chills, headache, malaise, substerbal discom-fort, prostration
Coxiella burnetii	Q fever	Bacteria	14 to 26 days	Tetracycline, doxycycline	Fever, cough, pleuritic chest pain
Brucella species	Brucellosis	Bacteria	5 to 21 days	Streptomycin, tetracycline	Fever, headache, weakness, fatigue, chills, diaphoresis, arthralgias, myalgias
Yersinia pestis (contagious)	Plaque (pneumon-ic)	Bacteria	1 to 3 days	Ciprofloaxin, doxycycline	High fever, chills, headache, hemoptysis, dyspnea, stridor, cyanosis
Variola (contagious)	Smallpox	Virus	10 to 12 days	Supportive care	Acute onset with malaise, fever, rigors, vomiting, headache, backache followed by lesions in 2 to 3 days
Venezuelan equine encephalitis virus	Venezuelan equine encephalitis	Virus	1 to 6 days	Supportive care	General malaise, fever, rigors, severe headache, photophobia, myalgias
Staphylo-coccus enterotoxin (b)	Intoxication (aerosol exposure)	Toxin	1 to 6 hours	Supprotive care	Sudden onset of fever, chills, headache, myalgia, nonproductive cough, possible chest pain and dyspnea, nausea, vomiting and diarrhea (if swallowed)

Sources: Slidell, Patrick, and Dashiell (1998), U.S. Army Medical Research Institute of Infectious Diseases (1998)

to be biological terrorism threats. This will hopefully raise their suspicion when considering differential diagnosis surrounding an unusual infectious disease or fever of unknown etiology.

In addition to passive surveillance, whereby trained medical practitioners look for signs of an event through their patients, an active surveillance system is designed to identify an outbreak early by aggressively monitoring and analyzing health and medical indicators. One critical indicator in health data surveillance is EMS demand. EMS serves as a gateway to health care for many Americans, especially in densely populated, urban areas where economic conditions often bring people to public health care by EMS conveyance. Variations in EMS data are often associated with events that affect the population. These include summer and winter weather extremes and certainly unusual disease outbreaks. This makes EMS data an excellent barometer for assessing and analyzing the health of a given populace. Other data include hospital emergency department activity as well as death statistics from medical examiners and coroners. Once a baseline is established for a specified area, perhaps a metropolitan area or region (an analysis of at least 3 previous years is recommended), the daily evaluation of current indicators against the baseline is made simple.

Advanced surveillance can also be conducted by analyzing medical data in more specific terms. Considering that most diseases resulting from biological agents present as influenza-like illnesses, monitoring hospital and EMS data for the signs and symptoms of influenza, influenza-like illnesses, and even respiratory illnesses can aid in early detection.

Reporting

Many local public health departments require physicians and other medical personnel to report unusual infectious and contagious diseases. The eight agents listed in Table 1 should be on every local list as reportable diseases. However, the requirement should also include that notification be made on encountering any unusual or suspicious disease. This will allow public health agencies to acquire information from multiple sources, which will alert them that an unusual outbreak is occurring. This has benefits far beyond monitoring for acts of terrorism: The system is simple yet robust enough to signal even naturally occurring outbreaks. Reporting emerging diseases must become routine; it is the responsibility of public health agencies to ensure that medical practitioners are instructed to make timely notifications. Conversely, public health agencies must notify medical practitioners of emerging disease events as they become aware of them. This will alert medical personnel and hopefully raise their awareness and suspicion.

Responding to Biological Terrorism

Once an incident of biological terrorism is recognized, there is little time to put a response into operation. This is critically important when dealing with bacterial agents, especially anthrax, for which early prophylaxis and treatment can have a profound effect on the outcomes of those infected or possibly infected. Signs and symptoms of anthrax generally appear from 24 to 36 hours after inhalation of anthrax spores. Once clinical effects appear, even aggressive antibiotic therapy may not prevent serious illness and death.

Considering that an aerosolized release of a military-grade product in a populated, confined environment such as a theater or airport can infect hundreds or even thousands of individuals, the medical community and government agencies will find themselves faced with a rapidly evolving incident. As the situation unfolds, strong potential exists for events to become overwhelming very quickly. Two medical strategies will be needed at this point: mass prophylaxis and casualty management.

Mass Prophylaxis

Two basic models exist for the distribution of mass quantities of medication to a large population: Deliver the medication to the people or bring the people to the medication. One caveat exists: There must be a stockpile of antibiotics large enough to provide to the population for at least the first dose regimen. For example, the recommended preliminary dose of ciprofloxacin required to treat anthrax is 500 milligrams taken twice daily for 4 weeks. Multiplied by the size of a given population, one gets an idea of the problem of designing a mass prophylaxis program.

In bringing antibiotics to the people, a large, organized, personnel commitment (perhaps the military or national guard) is needed for door-to-door delivery. When bringing people to antibiotics, less of a human resource commitment is needed. People are simply instructed, through a mass media campaign, to report to medication distribution centers, which can be set up in community-based facilities such as community centers and houses of worship.

Casualty Management

Hospitals and EMS agencies will become overwhelmed very quickly. Strategies to compensate for this should be developed in the planning stages, long before an incident occurs. Mutual aid agreements for the sharing of ambulance resources with surrounding municipalities and the identification, staff and equipping of alternate care facilities to offset the demand on hospitals should be determined well in advance of an incident. The integration of federal and state resources should be a part of the plan as well. The U.S. government has enacted programs to augment and support local medical activities during a disaster. These programs include Disaster Medical Assistance Teams (DMATs), which are essentially mobile hospitals, as well as DMATs specially trained and equipped to treat chemical and biological casualties, called National Medical Response Teams.

Fatality management is another critical undertaking. As the disease evolves, deaths will occur more and more frequently. To avoid an additional public health emergency and to ensure that appropriate dignity is offered to the deceased as well as the living, strategies for mass quantities of fatalities should be developed in advance of an incident. This would include alternate mortuary facilities, alternate means of storage and disposal, and plans to offer dignified, professional services to family and friends of the deceased.

Multijurisdictional Response

Biological terrorism knows no borders. Consider the release of a biological agent in an outbound commuter rail car. Depending on the agent, the disease may not manifest for many hours or even days. Once the disease emerges, cases will be scattered. Even if the disease is not contagious, like smallpox, people who were on the train will seek medical care throughout the region. Planning and preparedness must take a regional approach. This especially includes surveillance programs whereby data such as those mentioned above are monitored throughout a region and reported to a centralized location for analysis and action. Public health and emergency management agencies at the local, state, and federal levels must all be tied in. Mass prophylaxis and mass casualty planning should also be coordinated regionally. The demand for services and resources will not be localized; therefore, federal partnerships including the Federal Bureau of Investigation (the lead agency for crisis management), the Federal Emergency Management Agency (the lead agency for consequence management), and the U.S. Public Health Service (the lead agency for medical emergency management) should be an integral element on the planning team.

Program Agenda

In an effort to bring it all together, a solid biological terrorism program agenda is needed. Table 2 presents a comprehensive agenda designed for local jurisdictions endeavoring to create an effective plan and response protocols to counter biological terrorism.

Preparing for the Future

Improvements in our capabilities and systems will evolve as we learn more and more about recognizing and combating biological terrorism. Technology is needed for devices that can rapidly identify biological agents in the environment as well as in humans. Disease monitoring and information distribution systems using various forms of media and technological outlets must be refined for the rapid sharing of reports of outbreaks, and research and development must continue in the areas of vaccine development and mass production. We must also ensure that our political leadership is well versed in the topic to ensure a steady stream of funding for research and development, planning and preparedness, and major emergency response. Considering the threat

Table 2
Agenda for Local Jurisdictions Endeavoring to Create an Effective Plan and Response Protocols to Counter Biological Terrorism

Planning Issue	Objective(s)	Agencies Needed
Threat / risk assessment	Identify actual threats as well as possible threats based on local politics, population density, economics, etc. Attempt to validate the planning process	FBI, state and local law enforcement, public health, emergency management
Hazard analysis	Identify potential worst-case and other scenarios on which to base planning	FBI, state and local law enforcement, public health, emergency management
Public safety agency capabilities	Assess and enhance local capabilities such as plans and materials for field biological hazmat operations, proper levels of personal protection and training, documentation and recording, testing, sample collection and analysis, and interagency participation	Fire department, hazmat team, EMS, local law enforcement, public health, emergency management
Health surveillance	Assess local public health surveillance to identify whether it is sensitive enough to signal a biological agent release. Develop and establish routine surveillance of local indicators such as EMS demand, hospital activity, and medical examiner volume.	Emergency management, EMS, public health, medical examiner/coroner, hospitals
Laboratory capabilities	Assess state and local public health lab capability to analyze biological samples. Enhance capabilities to rapidly identify biological agents locally.	
EMS capabilities	Assess capacity of local EMS system to manage a surge of calls for service. Develop regional mutual aid agreements. Train EMS personnel to recognize biological agent signs and symptoms. Provide personal protection when confronted with a contagious agent.	Regional EMS agencies, emergency management

(Continued)

Table 2 (continued)

Planning Issue	Objective(s)	Agencies Needed
Mass prophylaxis	Develop a mechanism to distribute medication / antibiotics en masse using community-based distribution centers.	Emergency management, public health, EMS, law enforcement, national guard
Medical system capabilities	Assess the patient capacity at local hospitals. Identify on-hand and just-in-time stocks of antibiotics (ciprofloxacin, doxycycline, penicillin, tetracycline, streptomycin, gentamycin, and others as determined by public health). Identify regional quantities of ventilators (need for many inhaled infectious agents, e.g., anthrax and tularemia). Develop capabilities to rapidly expand hospital internal and external patient care capabilities. Undertake initiatives to fill identified gaps.	EMS, hospitals, public health, emergency management, FEMA, U.S. Public Health Service, NDMS
Medical examiner capabilities	Assess capacity of regional mortuaries. Undertake efforts to expand mortuary processing and storage capabilities. Train medical examiner personnel in personal protection.	Local and regional medical examiner / coroner, U.S. Public Health Service, NDMS
Emergency management capabilities	Assess emergency management agency capability to coordinate the response to a major, region-wide public health emergency. Assess capacity of the local emergency operations center and its technology. Coordinate the biological terrorism planning program.	Local and state emergency management agencies
Field incident (biological hazmat)	Assess and expand on local capability to operate at field biological incidents such as a package suspected to contain a biological agent (e.g., recent anthrax hoaxes).	Fire department, hazmat team, EMS, emergency management, FBI, local law enforcement, public health

NOTE: FBI = Federal Bureau of Investigation, hazmat = hazardous materials, EMS = emergency medical services, FEMA = Federal Emergency Management Agency, NDMS = National Disaster Medical System.

and gravity of the release of a biological agent in a city, now is the time to plan and prepare. Continuous education of medical and health care professionals, private physicians, and EMS personnel and a strengthened public health infrastructure designed to recognize emerging diseases early will hopefully allow us to avert a catastrophe.

References

Cole, L. A. (1996, December). The specter of biological weapons. *Scientific American, 275,* 60-65.

Convention on the prohibition of development, production and stockpiling of bacteriological (biological) and toxin weapons and on their destruction [Online]. (1972). Available: http://fletcher. tufts.edu/multi/texts/BH596.txt

Excerpts: F.B.I. report on domestic terrorism (domestic terrorism shifts to the right) [Online]. (1997, April 17). Available: http://www.usis-israel.org.il /publish/press/justice/archive/1997/april/ jd10418.htm

Harris, S. H. (1994). *Factories of death: Japanese biological warfare, 1932-45, and the American cover-up.* London: Routledge.

Hornsby, M. (1996, July 22). Anthrax outbreak casts shadow over homes site. *The Times* [Online]. Available: http://www.cyber-dyne.com/~tom/anthrax.html

Kristof, N. D. (n.d.). Unlocking a deadly secret. *The New York Times* [Online]. Available: http:// centurychina.com/wiihist/germwar/germwar.htm#killgirl

Patrick, W. (1998, July). *Lecture at Department of Defense biological weapons improved response program* [Online]. Available: http://dp.sbccom.army.mil /bwirp/index.html

Protocol for the prohibition of the use in war of asphyxiating, poisonous or other gases, and of bacteriological methods of warfare [Online]. (1925, June 17). Available: http://www.lib.byu.edu/~rdh/wwi/hague/hague13.html

Roberts, B. (Ed.). (1993). *Biological weapons: Weapons of the future?* Washington, DC: Center for Strategic and International Studies.

Sidell, F. R., Patrick, William C., III, & Dashiell, T R. (1998). *Jane's chem-bio handbook.* Arlington, VA: Jane's Information Group.

Tien-wei, W. (n.d.). *A preliminary review of studies of Japanese biological warfare Unit 731 in the United States* [Online]. Available: http://www-users.cs. umn.edu/~dyue/wiihist/germwar/731rev.htm

Torok, T. J., Tauxe, R. V., Wise, R. P., Livengood, J. R., Sokolow, R., Mauvais, S., Birkness, K. A., Skeels, M. R., Horan, J. M., & Foster, L. R. (1997). A large community outbreak of salmonellosis caused by intentional contamination of restaurant salad bars. *Journal of the American Medical Association, 278,* 389-395.

U.S. Army Medical Research Institute of Infectious Diseases. (1998, July). *Medical management of biological casualties: Handbook* [Online]. Fort Derrick, MD: Author. Available: http://www. vnh.org/BIOCASU/toc.html

WBFF Staff. (1997, August 10). *Food terrorism* [Online]. Baltimore, MD: WBFF Available: http:// www.wbff45.com/news/97/ft.htm

Wildavsky, R. (1999, January). Are we ready for bioterror? *Reader's Digest, 154,* 84-91.

About the Editor

Harvey W. Kushner, Ph.D.

As an internationally recognized authority on the subject of terrorism, Professor Kushner has advised and trained numerous governmental agencies, including the FBI, FAA, and U.S. Customs Service. At present, he serves as a Terrorism Analyst for U.S. Probation Department/Eastern District of New York. Kushner has traveled throughout the world lecturing and sharing his expertise on terrorism with a variety of governmental agencies, corporate entities and university think-tanks, including the FBI Academy's Behavioral Science Unit in Quantico, Virginia; the United Nations Congress in Vienna, Austria; and the Chief of Naval Operation's Strategic Studies Group (SSG), Naval War College, Newport, Rhode Island.

International advocacy groups and government committees, as well as victims of terrorism, also rely on his expertise. In the past, Kushner wrote the expert's report in a successful multimillion-dollar civil litigation arising out of the 1993 bombing of the World Trade Center and served as an expert observer on terrorism for the United Nations. He just completed service as an expert in the U.S. Embassy bombing trial and a landmark matrimonial case involving the threat of international terrorism. In addition, he has counseled families of the victims of the Pan Am 103 bombing, the Empire State Building shooting and the September 11th destruction of the World Trade Center. And he most recently testified on terrorism and safety in New York City's public spaces before the Committee of Public Safety of the Council of the City of New York.

Kushner's work on terrorism has been published extensively. His latest books include *Terrorism in America* and *The Future of Terrorism*, and his much-anticipated *Encyclopedia of Terrorism* will be ready for publication later this year. He also edits an annual issue on terrorism for the *American Behavioral Scientist* and serves on the journal's international advisory board.

Kushner's knowledge of terrorism is much sought after by the international media. His commentary appears regularly on CNN, BBC, MSNBC, Fox News Channel, the ABC and CBS national radio networks, and in articles in Reuters, Associated Press, *Washington Post, New York Times,* and other wire services, newspapers and magazines worldwide. As the *New York Times* reported, "Whenever there's a threat or attack or a bomb explodes or an airliner crashes, Dr. Kushner's renown goes up." And most recently, Dr. Kushner was profiled in the *New York Times's* Public Lives section as the media's "go-to" guy for plain talk about the subject of terrorism. As a member of the working press, Kushner writes a monthly column on civil aviation security matters for the *Airport Press.* He is also an occasional guest host on WABC Radio in New York where he provides public information on terrorism and related issues.

Kushner received his Ph.D. degree in political science from New York University. He is currently professor and chair of the Department of Criminal Justice and Security Administration at Long Island University.

Permissions

The articles in the anthology appear with the permission of the authors or publishers of the journals or books in which the articles originally appeared. Original citations are as follows:

Anderson, S. (1998). Warnings Versus Alarms: Terrorist Threat Analysis Applied to the Iranian State-Run Media. *Studies in Conflict and Terrorism, 21(3), 277-305.*

Braungart, R. & Braungart, M. (1992). From Protest to Terrorism: The Case of SDS and the Weathermen. *International Social Movement Research, 4, 45-78.*

Cooper, H. H. A. (2001). Terrorism: The Problem of Definition Revisited. *American Behavioral Scientist, 44(6), 881-893.*

Crenshaw. Martha. (2001). Counterterrorism Policy and the Political Process. *Studies in Conflict and Terrorism, 24(5), 32-40.*

Damphousse, K. & Smith, B. (1998). The Internet: A Terrorist Medium for the 21st Century. In Kushner, H. (Ed.), *The Future of Terrorism* (pp. 208-224). Thousand Oaks, CA: Sage.

Difede, J., Apfeldorf, W., Williams, J., Cloitre, M., Spielman, L., & Perry, S. (1997). Acute Psychiatric Responses to the Explosion at the World Trade Center: A Case Series. *Journal of Nervous and Mental Disease, 185(8), 519-522.*

Engel, C., Liu, X., McCarthy, B., Miller, R., & Ursano, R. (2000). Relationship of Physical Symptoms to Posttraumatic Stress Disorder Among Veterans Seeking Care for Gulf War-Related Health Concerns. *Psychsomatic Medicine, 62(6), 739-745.*

Goldstick, D. (1991). Defining "Terrorism." *Nature, Society and Thought, 4(3), 261-266.*

Hoffman, B. (1999). The Mind of the Terrorist: Perspectives from Social Psychology. *Psychiatric Annals, 29(6), 337-340.*

Koopman, Cheryl. (1997). Political Psychology as a Lens for Viewing Traumatic Events. *Political Psychology, 18(4), 831-847.*

Kuhr, S. & Hauer, J. (2001). The Threat of Biological Terrorism in the New Millennium. *American Behavioral Scientist, 44(6), 1032-41.* Abrdiged for this volume.

Kushner, Harvey. (1996). Suicide Bombers: Business as Usual. *Studies in Conflict and Terrorism, 19(4), 329-337.*

Langman, Lauren & Morris, Douglas. (2002). Islamic Terrorism: From Retrenchment to Ressentiment and Beyond. (Originally written for the anthology).

Nacos, Brigitte, Fan, David, & Young, John. (1989). Terrorism and the Print Media: The 1985 TWA hostage crisis. *Terrorism, 12(2), 107-115.*

Pattnayak, S. & Arvanites, T. (1992). Structural Determinants of State Involvement in International Terrorism. *Current World Leaders, 35(2), 269-285.*

Post, Jerrold M. (2000). Terrorist on Trial: The Context of Political Crime. *Journal of the American Academy of Psychiatry and the Law, 28(2), 171-178.*

Raber, E., Jin, A., Noonan, K., McGuire, R. & Kirvel, R. (2001). Decontamination Issues for Chemical and Biological Warfare Agents: How Clean is Clean Enough? *International Journal of Environmental Health Research, 11(2), 128-48.*

Schwartz, T. P. (2002). Terror and Terrorism in the Koran. (Originally written for the anthology).

Steiker, Jordan. (2001). Federal Habeas and the Death Penalty: Reflections on the New Habeas Provisions of the Anti-Terrorism and Effective Death Penalty Act, originally published as Did the Oklahoma City Bombers Succeed? *The Annals of the American Academy of Political and Social Science, 574, 185-194.*

Swanson, E. & Fosnocht, D. (2000). Anthrax Threats: A Report of Two Incidents from Salt Lake City. *Journal of Emergency Medicine, 18(2), 229-232.*

Stern, Jessica. (2000). Pakistan's Jihad Culture. *Foreign Affairs, 79(6), 115-126.*

Winkler, C. (1989). Presidents Held Hostage: The Rhetoric of Jimmy Carter and Ronald Reagan. *Terrorism, 12(1), 21-30.*

Zuk, G. & Zuk, C. (2000). Negation Theory as a Cause of Delusion: The Case of the Unabomber. *Contemporary Family Therapy, 22(3), 329-336.*